William Smith gives us the comp[illegible] controversial biography of Joseph Smith's most famous sermon, guiding us through a bramble of textual sources, disavowals, obscurity, and reappraisals. Along the way, Smith gives us a window into the always changing and sometimes unspoken ideas and assumptions that undergird the foundation of Latter-day Saint ideas, doctrine, and practice.

—John Turner
author of *The Mormon Jesus: A Biography*

William V. Smith has produced a monumental biography of Joseph Smith Jr.'s greatest public discourse, the King Follett Sermon. This book seamlessly combines fine-grained textual analysis with wide-ranging intellectual history. Although in one sense a foundation stone of Latter-day Saint thought, Smith demonstrates that the sermon has more often than not proven to be a stumbling block for those wrestling with the Smith Jr.'s variegated theological legacies.

—David W. Grua
The Joseph Smith Papers

In this volume, Smith offers us the most exhaustive and useful textual and reception history of the King Follett Discourse we have. The most important sermon in the broad sweep of the Mormon tradition, the discourse has deserved this treatment for quite some time. The book is worth a read for the careful parsing of the sermon's textual history alone. But Smith's able command of not only the complicated genealogies of the various versions of the sermon, but also of the intellectual history of the LDS church and the religious atmosphere in which it found itself, means that he is able to think through the sermon's rising and falling fortunes in a way that will be useful to scholars of the LDS church but also American religion more generally.

—Matthew Bowman,
President of the Mormon History Association

A wonderful deep dive into Joseph Smith's most powerful, most controversial, and most important sermon. William Victor Smith not only helps us to understand the mysterious text but leads us carefully through the next 200 years of reception. This is a one-of-a-kind book and a must read for students of the Latter-day Saint tradition.

—Christopher Blythe
author of *Terrible Revolution: Latter-day Saints and the American Apocalypse*

THE KING FOLLETT SERMON

By Common Consent Press is a non-profit publisher dedicated to producing affordable, high-quality books that help define and shape the Latter-day Saint experience. BCC Press publishes books that address all aspects of Mormon life. Our mission includes finding manuscripts that will contribute to the lives of thoughtful Latter-day Saints, mentoring authors and nurturing projects to completion, and distributing important books to the Mormon audience at the lowest possible cost.

WILLIAM V. SMITH

THE KING FOLLETT SERMON

A BIOGRAPHY

Essays in Mormon Studies

The King Follett Sermon: A Biography

For information contact
By Common Consent Press
4900 Penrose Dr.
Newburgh, IN 47630

Cover design: D Christian Harrison
Book design: Andrew Heiss

www.bccpress.org
ISBN-13 (paperback): 978-1-948218-85-6

10 9 8 7 6 5 4 3 2 1

Contents

The voices of the past are especially lost to us. The world of unrecorded sounds is irreclaimable, so the disjunctions that separate our ears from what people heard in the past are doubly profound. . . . Almost all of history is eerily silent, and so, to evoke these stilled and faded voices, the historian must act as a kind of necromancer.

—Leigh Eric Schmidt, *Hearing Things*

I saw that there was a way to Hell, even from the Gates of Heaven.

—John Bunyan, *The Pilgrim's Progress*

Do you not see how necessary a World of Pain and troubles is to school an intelligence and make it a soul? A place where the heart must feel and suffer in a thousand diverse ways.

—John Keats, April 21, 1810

Abbreviations

D&C Doctrine and Covenants of the Church of Jesus Christ of Latter-day Saints.

JSP The Joseph Smith Papers (references are made to the various volume series such as, *Documents*, *Journals*, *Histories*, *Revelations & Translations*, *Administrative Records*, etc., for example, Documents series volume 1 page 56 would be *JSP*, D1:56 while Journals volume 2 page 45 would be *JSP*, J2:45, etc. in the notes. These abbreviations are expanded in the references collection at the end of this book). The JSP's digital presence is josephsmithpapers.org.

CHL The Church History Library of the Church of Jesus Christ of Latter-day Saints, Salt Lake City, Utah.

LTPSC L. Tom Perry Special Collections and Manuscripts Library, Harold B. Lee Library, Brigham Young University, Provo, Utah

Parallel Joseph An online compilation of audits of Joseph Smith's sermons. See, http://boap.org/LDS/Parallel

ms history (Manuscript History of the Church.) Church Historian's Office. History of the Church, 1839–circa 1882, CR 100 102, CHL.

Abbreviations

Introduction

December 12, 1848, was an intensely cold Tuesday in Great Salt Lake City. Heavy snow had fallen the previous evening and would continue again that night. In the evening, available members of the Thirtieth Quorum of Seventy met at the home of Joseph Cain.[1] The brief minutes for the meeting read,

> Opened by Singing & Prayer
> A Sermon was read that was preached by the prophet Joseph Smith on the Death of King Follet some good exortations were given by Brethren after which the meeting adjourned[2]

1. The "Seventy" were male church officers generally assigned to proselytizing and were organized into groups—quorums—of seventy men after the New Testament mention of seventy or seventy-two preachers (Luke 10). The number of these quorums ballooned after the death of JS for strategic as well as hopeful growth reasons. The church's apostolic leaders had scriptural mandates to supervise the Seventy (D&C 107:34). The more males ordained into the ranks of the Seventy the greater the apostolic influence. Such missionary preachers were needed to continue the growth required to establish a new church headquarters in the West.

2. Seventies Quorum Records, 1844–1975. The records are found in the Church History Library of The Church of Jesus Christ of Latter-day Saints, Salt Lake City, Utah (hereafter, CHL).

The minutes raise vital questions regarding practice in these early, isolated church venues and, more importantly, the reading of a sermon, the King Follett Sermon. Unfortunately, nothing regarding the "good exortations" is revealed, but questions about the text that they read linger in the air. Where did it come from? Was it manuscript or imprint? Why was it selected? How was it selected? Was it considered "scriptural" by the listeners?[3] Was there some democratic process behind its selection? Some of these questions can be answered, others only guessed at. Two things the episode reveals with certainty: the Seventies meant to fill their meeting time with authoritative instructional material, and they considered the sermon an important statement of church teaching. The need to define authoritative teachings shaped the future role of the Follett sermon in public Mormon literature and preaching over the next century, yet for any number of sometimes opposing reasons, Smith's sermon of April 7, 1844, is widely recognized as his single most important preaching event and perhaps the most important Mormon sermon of all time.

The discussion which follows assumes some familiarity with the outline of the story of early Mormonism, Joseph Smith's biography, as well as some understanding of the churches that originated from his teachings and acts. It is most relevant to the history of the church now known as the Church of Jesus Christ of Latter-day Saints. Other branches of his original founding church almost all eventually

---

3. In the nineteenth century, the term "Standard Work" may have applied. In early Utah Mormon speech, Standard Work encompassed a wider literature than its current reference to the Mormon canon: the King James Bible, the Book of Mormon, the Doctrine and Covenants, and the Pearl of Great Price. In those early years it included familiar titles that defined the faith for the rank-and-file. For example, Parley Parker Pratt's popular *Voice of Warning* was on that list. Terryl L. Givens and Matthew J. Grow, *Parley P. Pratt: The Apostle Paul of Mormonism*, 191–120, 181. Thomas D. Brown, "I gave notice . . . ," 96; John Taylor, "Our Religion is From God," 220; George A. Smith, "Raising Flax and Wool," etc., 363.

rejected the sermon as inauthentic (possibly even naming it as a fraudulent construction made after Smith's death), or an excursion of error (and therefore safely ignored)[4]. The textual sources demonstrate that neither of these claims are viable.[5]

I have argued elsewhere that because Mormonism was largely founded in new revelation, its early preaching events generated few substantial documentary records.[6] The potential for chaos resulting from the ethos of *continuing* revelation led Mormon founder Joseph Smith, Jr. (hereafter, JS) to articulate a revelation formalizing a hierarchy of value in religious expression. In that hierarchy, which was a developing reaction to democratic forces, sermons were marked as ephemeral oral events and were not to be recorded. But cross-pressures arose from a developing methodology of church governance: governance by councils headed by JS.[7]

---

4. Granville Hedrick who joined the church in 1843 remained in Illinois after Brigham Young departed. Hedrick became president of the Church of Christ in 1863 (the name signified a return to the Mormonism of 1830–31). He called the Follett sermon a "high-handed attempt . . . in blasphemy." Hedrick, *Truth Teller* 1, no. 4 (1864): 53.

5. The choice of academic literature for the beginner is broad here. Three suggestions for the curious are the following: on JS, Richard Lyman Bushman, *Joseph Smith: Rough Stone Rolling;* on the religious trajectory, Jan Shipps, *Mormonism: The Story of a New Religious Tradition* and Laurel Thatcher Ulrich, *A House Full of Females: Plural Marriage and Women's Rights in Early Mormonism, 1835–1870*; on present day Latter-day Saints, Emily W. Jensen and Tracy McKay-Lamb, *A Book of Mormons: Latter-day Saints on a Modern-Day Zion*. For a comprehensive contemporary source bank on Joseph Smith, see the Joseph Smith Papers Project, josephsmithpapers.org.

6. William V. Smith, "Joseph Smith's Preaching and the Early Mormon Documentary Record."

7. This prohibition on recording has surfaced from time to time in Latter-day Saint regulations for local visitation events, but it has not been uniform. By "democratic forces" I refer to the precipitating events to D&C 28 and the social dynamic behind them.

The quest for order and consistency led councils to audit decisions on policy, doctrine, and discipline. Councils at first served as witnesses to, and distributors of, JS's prophetic pronouncements in answer to council queries. These practices gave rise to the instructional/regulatory sermon, and gradually such sermons were audited with increasing detail and sometimes published. This instructional preaching, fittingly classed in the genre of the "visitation sermon," took its place as one of the mature forms of JS's revelations.[8] These cross-pressures and others framed the evolving documentary record of JS's preaching. The nature of that record can be most readily analyzed through theoretical work on preaching records and note-taking strategies.

This transition, from the dictation of revelations to answer queries to an instructional sermon with similar but broader purpose, became the design for at least some of JS's public preaching. Public "conferences" of the church were modeled after Protestant praxis, which made them part of church council culture. The documentary record of preaching by JS grew as increasing importance was attached to his sermons.[9] That record—longhand audits by some official clerks and a growing regiment of pew auditors—is most complete in 1843–1844, the final years of JS's life, but it was still nothing like a modern stenographic report or contemporary video recording.[10]

---

8. Visitation sermons were (often extemporaneous) sermons delivered by Anglican bishops to priests and vicars of parishes in Britain, offering instruction and correction to church administration and practice. Robert Ellison, "The Tractarians' Sermons and other Speeches," 24, 47–49.

9. I use "sermon" in preference to the also common "discourse" in Mormon literature, largely because the former is more indicative of the religious character of the subject and it better integrates with the larger world of preaching.

10. For a more detailed account of the evolution in the Mormon sermon value system, see Smith, "Joseph Smith's Sermons." The present work is an expansion of

The surviving audits of JS's sermons fit largely in the category of *content* audits—a *technique de reportage* described by Meredith Neuman in her work on Puritan preaching. A content audit reports a sermon through paraphrase and thus inevitable commentary, a method that blurs the verbal frontier between auditor and preacher. Some important exceptions to this classification are "aural audits"—reports that attempt a verbatim capture of the preacher's words. An aural audit must not be construed as a complete verbatim representation of the archetype, that is, all the words spoken at a given preaching event. Moreover, a given audit may share characteristics of aural audit and content audit at different points in that record. Two such aural audits are important to this book. They are reports of the sermon delivered on the afternoon of Easter Sunday, April 7, 1844, during a special conference of the church and subsequently known as the King Follett Sermon.[11]

The April 7 sermon was advertised weeks before its delivery as a funeral address for one of JS's long-time friends.[12] Fifty-five-year-old King Follett had perished on March 9 from injuries suffered in a construction accident. JS delivered an important address on Sunday, March 10, 1844, the day Follett was buried. That sermon was sometimes labeled as a funeral sermon for Follett.[13] However, Louisa Tanner Follett—King's wife of twenty-eight years—requested that

a part of chapter 7 of my forthcoming book, *Every Word Seasoned with Grace: A Textual Study of the Funeral Sermons of Joseph Smith*.

11. Meredith Marie Neuman, *Jeremiah's Scribes: Creating Sermon Literature in Puritan New England*, ch. 2.

12. King was the surname of a family friendly to Follett's parents. On Follett, see Joann Follett Mortensen, "King Follett: The Man Behind the Discourse," 113–133. On the announcement of the sermon, see *Nauvoo Neighbor*, March 20, 1844, 2.

13. See, for example, "Sermon Book," index, MS 3435, CHL.

JS preach another sermon on Follett's behalf.[14] Typically identified as the King Follett Discourse or King Follett Sermon, it is best known through a redacted version produced in Utah in 1855–56. This book discusses that version, its prehistory, its chronological interpretative evolution, its theological critique, and the social ecosystem that helped furnish that critique.

A study of the sermon's audits fails to reveal important aspects of the original event, such as JS's speed of delivery—in this sermon he preached for nearly two-and-a-half hours in the open air—or his nonverbal methods of communication. However, a close comparison of those audits suggests that the archetype's themes appear with some fidelity in the sum of the surviving audits. I will discuss the work of the "gentlemen historians" of the 1856 Latter-day Saint church and their male and female colleagues and successors as it effected the sermon's textual transmission. I use gentleman historians to describe the work of the people who drew together and constructed the first lengthy narrative of JS's life and work in a devotional and institutionally directed framework. These workers were untrained; they wrote eulogy, not history as it is understood today. That they kept and used significant records is yet astonishingly admirable. This book is a biography of one of the more influential texts of early Mormonism as it was determined, reacted to, rejected, revived, and ultimately submerged in an evolving religious tradition.

It may seem odd to devote an entire book to one example of antebellum extemporaneous preaching. However, as I hope to demonstrate to the reader, this sermon had deep influence on Latter-day Saint thought of the nineteenth and twentieth centuries, often

14. On Tanner Follett, see Joann Follett Mortensen, *The Man Behind the Discourse: A Biography of King Follett*, 457–64. On the request and the announcement that the request would be honored, see *Nauvoo Neighbor*, March 20, 1844, 2; General Church Minutes April 7, 1844, page 7, CHL.

through unconscious textual linkages where the sermon helped redefine scriptural hermeneutics against the theological assumptions of the Protestant North Atlantic World. While this is the diachronic story of a text, it is fraught with human personalities, their interactions, and the history of ideas, which also require analysis. Hence, this work is not merely the story of a text's origin and evolution, it is the story of human beings who sought (and sometimes failed) to rationalize its contested meanings within their religious and broader cultural worlds.

The sermon's hermeneutical history is a plain illustration of the fact that sufficiently robust religions (those that survive their creators)—form overdetermined systems—and therefore fail to exhibit completely consistent narratives. It is only by constructing—and reconstructing—meaning that a theology or a body of religious teaching becomes a consistent arc of thought in any given moment. Mormonism's success at this reconstructive attempt is a part of its story.

The Follett sermon embodied JS's view of eternity's engine. In so many ways it was a product of American antebellum thought, not just religious thought, but the culture of the western edges of America, with a deep need to remold the past into a coherent picture of the present. It was thought that was filtered through a mind heaped with an inspired, recombinant vision of the canon, a vision that brought with it buried hints of the many existential, epistemological, intellectual, and behavioral issues inherited from a wide selection of mostly Protestant and folk representations of modern upheavals of the religion, science, and philosophy of the North Atlantic World.

Mormonism shares the conflicted ancestry of the rest of the modern religious world as it was caught between two poles: the Enlightenment and the deposed queen of the sciences, theology. The Follett sermon represents a complex and vital explanation of how and why the Latter-day Saints responded to modernism, particularly after Latter-day Saint literature and thought encountered the work of

Charles Darwin in the first decades of the twentieth century. Many Saints watched and supported the anti-evolution rhetoric of William Jennings Bryan in the 1925 Scopes "Monkey" Trial, and while Bryan mostly feared the consequences of a growing popularity of *social* Darwinism (the poor were poor because they were defective and it was the fittest—the richest—who should flourish), evolution was a proxy for how many Mormons and other religious believers interfaced with the continuing growth of scientific knowledge, and Follett was in some respects a proxy for Genesis as things played out in the conservative Christian wars with Darwin seeing the biologist's work as proxy for a dreaded materialism.[15]

This work is divided chronologically into four chapter-periods with occasional contextual overlaps: 1830–1844, 1845–1890, 1891–1926, and 1927–1996 with a few notes on later developments. Appendix A contains a "transparent" critical edition of the Follett sermon with some notes regarding various audits. Appendix B contains reference material for chapter 3.

The first period (the focus of chapter 1) is the JS epoch in terms of textual influences in the sermon with a few forward-looking exercises.

---

15. Bryan was a popular figure in Utah (see chapter 3 below). On the Mormon view of the Scopes evolution trial, see Editors' Table, "William Jennings Bryan." For Scopes' effect on the teaching of evolution in Utah and other K–12 schools, see Judith V. Grabiner and Peter D. Miller, "Effects of the Scopes Trial," 832–837. The 2019 Utah State School Board was still having heated debates over science in the schools (religious conflicts with evolution and climate change). See Courtney Tanner, "Utah's science standards will be updated–despite concerns over what students will learn about evolution, climate change and humans being 'like pigs'," https://www.sltrib.com/news/environment/2019/06/07/utahs-science-standards/ (accessed December 27, 2020). On Bryan's deep social liberalism—wealth redistribution, pacifism, the silver standard—combined with a likewise deeply bigoted fundamentalism, see Michael Kazin, *A Godly Hero: The Life of William Jennings Bryan*. On various claims that were labeled materialism in the nineteenth and twentieth century, see Matthew Bowman, *Christian: The Politics of a Word in America*, 6–12.

Bringing to bear some of the theoretical tools of sermon and textual studies provides a framework for discussing audits of the sermon and tracing their relation to Follett itself. In addition, I briefly look at the historical-ideological context of the sermon's expressions. Illustrating the space-time tracings of the entire theological tapestry of the sermon is too large a task. Instead, I mainly focus on a few crucial elements of the discourse, first beginning with a fairly detailed summary of the sermon through the extant sermon reports and then a discussion of the major points that appear in the later portions of its acceptance history—its biography—such as the nature of the human soul, the resurrection of the body, the history of God, and JS's studied version of the inhabitants of Hell—while describing the topology of ideologies that influenced the redaction and interpretation of the sermon's manuscript sources and following imprints.

The second period (which I call Middle Mormonism) is the focus of chapter 2, which considers the origin and early influence of the 1856 pivotal text of the sermon up to 1890. That 1856 text was largely fashioned by persons who were not present at the delivery of the archetype and have hitherto remained in the historical shadows. I use "archetype" in a special sense here and throughout this work. Archetype for this work refers merely to the original and largely inaccessible oral text of the sermon, rather than the literary or philosophical sense of the term. This meaning of archetype still shapes any received text like a literary archetype in the meaning of "origin."

Figures like Eliza R. Snow and William W. Phelps played important background roles in the elaboration of belief that in some ways was set against the Follett sermon. Their influence on the sermon's reception was important but external and environmental. Here I must introduce the enigmatic Jonathan Grimshaw, who was assigned to gather JS's sermon materials and create coherent texts from scattered archetypal remnants. In the post-1844 period, the new social predicament of a transitioning wilderness church helped emphasize parts of the sermon and reread others. I am referring to, among other issues, a now-public polygamy (1852) and the scribing of theologies to contain that thorny subject—along with an effective identification of church and state and the resulting troubled interface between Utah and its parent government in Washington. Such emerging—and sometimes competing—theologies and their necessarily associated ideologies exhibited *strain* in the evolving redaction/understanding of the Follett sermon text.

I occasionally use the term strain as it appears in Clifford Geertz's classical sociological-anthropological work on ideology. As a particular and relevant example, religion may not remove the effects of personal crisis or even explain it, but it may offer the hope of an overall ordering of reality in which suffering and loss have meaning. The way in which religion or theology adapts to perform such functions I call *strain*.[16] In effect, the Follett sermon was *translated* by the attractors of 1. plural marriage, 2. the interacting politics of a nation vectoring toward civil war, and 3. a Utah territory desperately wanting to act the part of an antebellum American state.[17] That translation continued through succeeding periods to the present day, generated by different attractors (the explanatory structures built around polygamy are still there) such as explaining Mormonism's uniqueness, adaptation to modernist theological cross-pressures from science (physics, biology, mathematics), and philosophy, etc. And here Follett displayed more and more of its textual "abundance" as it paradoxically slid beneath the advertised surface of church belief, leaving behind bits and pieces like Eternal Progression and Exaltation.

16. Clifford Geertz, "Ideology as a Cultural System," 47–76.

17. For a view of Follett's radical theology as a reaction to early persecution of Mormons (something I assign more directly to the failure of Zion), see Adam J. Powell, *Irenaeus, Joseph Smith, and God-Making Heresy*, 189–223.

Chapter 3 considers the sermon's cultural story in the three decades after 1890. LDS historiography was changing by the turn of the twentieth century as various competing persons and interests hoped to write the story of the church, and the publishing of early texts in official histories displayed some discontinuities with accepted traditions in a number of ways, including theological ways. Criticizing JS's ideas directly (as they appeared in church imprints) was never lightly undertaken. At the same time, post-Nauvoo interpretative structures tried to trace various contemporary teachings to JS, such as the exclusion of Black persons from temple ritual and the inclusion and then subsequent exclusion of all women from healing ritual.[18] When practice changed, JS was seen as being on the right side of that history. This view of history was not confined to Mormon historiography; it was and is very typical of religions in general. Allusion to JS and others might simply be avoided in case early texts conflicted with then-current elaborations of doctrine.[19]

Instead, the undercurrent of critique, for Follett in particular, finally found expression in the only culturally available culprit: the builders of the texts (scribes and secretaries). Two manifestations of strain appeared: annotation of the text to explain its place in Utah theological tradition and, contrariwise, rejection of the text as a whole as being unreliable. In the latter case, by 1912, a number of church

18. On Black persons and priesthood/temple logic, see W. Paul Reeve, *Religion of a Different Color: Race and the Mormon Struggle for Whiteness* and Martha Ertman, "Race Treason: The Untold Story of America's Ban on Polygamy." On women and Mormon ritual, see Jonathan A. Stapley, *The Power of Godliness: Mormon Liturgy and Cosmology*.

19. For an important example, see Stephen C. Taysom, "A Uniform and Common Recollection: Joseph Smith's Legacy, Polygamy, and the Creation of Mormon Public Memory," 121–52. On editing Smith's Relief Society sermons, see Ulrich, *A House Full of Females*, 311; also, The Parallel Joseph, April 28, 1842, and chapter 2, below.

leaders (including the First Presidency of the Church of Jesus Christ of Latter-day Saints) wished to erase the Follett sermon from Latter-day Saint publication and memory, attributing troubling passages to the blunders of clerks who rendered mistaken reports. The desired effect was to shade the received 1856 sermon text as a whole for decades.

Some of those critiques began to suggest that JS disavowed reports of the sermon prior to his death. Others saw the Follett text as a valid extension of Mormon scripture and the ideologies of early Utah that could help harmonize puzzling scripture passages with the sociology of heavenly polygamy and its progeny, post-Manifesto public Mormonism and its re-rationalized domestic heaven. Like Nauvoo and early Utah-era redactions and interpretations of the Follett sermon, the drama of the early twentieth-century expositions and denials requires us to consider the personalities and personal histories of the protagonists and their cultural milieu. This is a story of cross-currents rising out of the transitioning political, hierarchical, and social landscapes of Utah and America and this means politics and church leader responses to modernity become a necessary part of the story. The contested views of the sermon in the early twentieth century continued in subdued ways into later decades as advocates representing various theological strains rose in the pews as well as the church's hierarchy.[20]

The narrative of chapter 3 is somewhat more complex than that of the rest of the book. To understand the influence and counter influence of and on the sermon's received text (the 1856 text) I need to examine politics, personalities, both public and behind the scenes, and this sometimes prevents a straight-forward chronological progression. The public personalities were largely men but women had roles. People like Brigham H. Roberts, a church leader and brilliant

20. See, for example, Charles W. Penrose, "Earth Life a Definite Part of the Divine Plan for the Salvation of Mankind. Address Delivered in the Eighteenth Ward Chapel, Salt Lake City, March 2, 1924," 42.

autodidact, Joseph F. Smith who became the head of the church during this period (and subsequently banned the sermon from church imprints) and his fellow leaders like Lorenzo Snow, George Q. Cannon, Bathsheba W. Smith, Charles Penrose, Reed Smoot and Anthon H. Lund play various roles, as well as geologist and future apostle James E. Talmage.[21] Politics, the end of polygamy, and the attempts at resolution of public and private theological tensions feature importantly in the story of the Latter-day Saints that wanted to ignore or reinterpret Nauvoo's ontological and cultural adventures.

There are remarkable influences from people otherwise unknown in the historical record like Arthur MacDermott who merits a whole appendix in this work (Appendix B). The challenge to integrate church belief and practice into mainstream America while struggling with the changes in church marital teachings brought personalities such as John A. Widtsoe and Orson F. Whitney into the story of the sermon. Science, especially astronomy, biology, and physics, interweave in the narrative, tied mostly to the church's perceived need to educate its youth. One of those threads involves genetics (both in its more primitive meaning and the vision afforded by DNA) and biological evolution as prefigured above.

In chapter 4, I look at Follett as a part of the modern *unthought* of Mormonism—its place in a background of unarticulated assumptions—a framework that limits and helps define the theoretical value system of recent Utah Mormonism. This system is perhaps most succinctly expressed in the 1995 statement by the church's leadership, *The Family: A Proclamation to the World*. I am borrowing unthought from Foucault, in the sense of an unacknowledged genesis of certain cate-

21. Roberts was not completely self-taught. He attended Utah schools and excelled there but his opportunities were more limited than his fellow intellects like Talmage and Widtsoe.

gorical structuring within church belief and practice.[22] The Follett sermon's historical superstructures and networks of thought still surface in the general conferences of the church (though Follett itself is usually not mentioned) and those thought networks and traditions still influence contemporary issues: the role of women within the church, the church's positions on LGBTQ+ persons, the eschatological and social partitioning of adults and children outside the circle of "sealed" relationships, the ultimate meanings of church liturgy, and the very visible critiques by conservative Protestant literary engines ranging from deep theology to that of popular critiques from the worlds of film and social media (for example, *The God Makers* enterprise) largely directed to JS's work around theosis.

Another question lurks in the background at this point and remains through most of this biography: were many Latter-day Saints acquainted with any of the textual sources and the internal pot boiling that surrounded them and the sermon's imprints? Oral communications like preaching have little lasting and broad effect unless they are translated to print or endlessly repeated from mouth to ear and then, finally, written anyway.[23] Before the last fifty years, most Latter-day Saint print circulation was troubled since it was expensive to create and generally required purchase or subscription—the Utah Saints were quite poor. Even fundamental texts like the Bible and Book of Mormon might not be present in the typical Utah household. Take, for example, the first edition of the *Pearl of Great Price*. First published in 1851 in Liverpool, England, it had only one print run (not counting a Welsh translation) of roughly 12,000 copies. It consisted mostly of lesser known but foundational texts from

22. An example of what I'm trying to get at is found in William J. Ramp, "Durkheim and the Unthought: Some Dilemmas of Modernity."

23. Smith, "Joseph Smith's Sermons and the Early Mormon Documentary Record."

Joseph Smith (a similar but somewhat different lineup from the present-day version). Those 12,000 copies had not sold out before Orson Pratt's second imprint in 1878 (Pratt's version became part of the Latter-day Saint canon in 1880). At the 1851 first printing there were between 50,000 and 60,000 Latter-day Saints in the world. By 1878, there were about 125,000 names on church records and Utah church leaders complained that members did not have canonical texts in their homes.[24] Partly that may have reflected the persistence of a barter economy and a fairly significant rate of illiteracy in the Pioneer Corridor.[25] Texts like the Follett sermon were quite likely to be thinly spread. Therefore, the Follett-related doctrinal evolutions of Middle Mormonism represented to some degree the thought circulation at the visible iceberg-edge of the church where a richer print world lived. Print scarcity would change somewhat in the twentieth century with broader circulation of church related materials, but those materials were still subject to things like subscription drives or the presence of a bookstore with church literature and, of course, available cash.[26]

---

24. See George A. Smith, "Home Manufactures, etc.," 364.

25. On illiteracy conditions in the mountain states (Utah was a positive exception by 1916 but it still had challenges), see "Current Population Reports," February 12, 1963, Series P-23, No. 6, No. 8, US Census Bureau; Winthrop Talbot, "Adult Illiteracy," Bulletin, 196, No. 35, Bureau of Education, Department of the Interior, 8–13.

26. Offsetting this general rarity was the church's missionary force. These (mostly male) emissaries developed some familiarity with the biblical arguments pioneers like Parley Pratt had constructed to widen the cracks in the denominational barriers. Some found time and resources to dig a bit deeper with Latter-day Saint mission support literature like Pratt's many times reprinted *Voice of Warning* and such mission newspapers like *Liahona The Elders' Journal* as the twentieth century unfolded or *Latter-day Saints' Millennial Star*, in Europe in earlier decades, etc. Missionaries returned with a better-than-average knowledge of the Bible and other materials, like the popular 1884 Richards and Little *Compendium* or B. H. Roberts's many instruction manuals (see the epigraph of chapter one).

Practice and tradition among Latter-day Saints were more important than literature until nearly the twenty-first century. Even the Latter-day Saint temple ritual was often a single-instance experience for Saints in outlying congregations until the last quarter of the twentieth century. In 1865, what *may* have been heard *repeatedly* from the pulpit or by rumor was far more likely to be top-of-mind than anything about what Joseph Smith *really* said on such and such a day.[27] This tendency is still true today among the actively participating rank-and-file Saints. Perhaps this tempers what comes next, yet I still want to know about this fascinating family of documents and their retinue of influences and influencers.

27. Hearing from the pulpit was often infrequent. A very large fraction of early Utah Saints might be stalwart believers but rare attenders on Sundays. Church-generated statistics for pioneer Utah, copy in possession of the author.

CHAPTER I

History and Prehistory: Early Mormonism

The 1830–1844 Textual Foundations of 1856

We consider the Bible, Book of Mormon, Book of Doctrine and Covenants, Pearl of Great Price and sayings of Joseph, the Seer, our guides in faith and doctrine.

—*A Compendium of the Doctrines of the Gospel* (1884)

He who can go to the fountain, does not go to the water jar.

—Leonardo da Vinci

Man can do nothing without the make-believe of a beginning. Even Science, the strict measurer, is obliged to start with a make-believe unit, and must fix on a point in the stars' unceasing journey when his sidereal clock shall pretend time is at Nought. . . . No retrospect will take us to the true beginning, and whether our prologue be in heaven or on earth, it is but a fraction of the all-presupposing fact with which our story sets out.

—George Elliot, *Daniel Deronda*

§1.1 A Source Summary of the King Follett Sermon

Conferences of the Church of Jesus Christ of Latter Day Saints, as Mormonism was known by 1844, [1] were gatherings that typically carried out regulation of church government, heard reports of satellite congregations, decided cases of church discipline, or heard appeals of local discipline. They were also informed by sermons, usually from church leaders including JS when the conference was at church headquarters. The April 1844 conference promised to be a dramatic one, as dissenters planned to bring public charges against JS over various issues, including polygamy.[2] JS short-circuited that plan by declaring in the opening moments on April 5 that the conference would hear no cases of that sort. This was unusual, and it frustrated JS's opponents. This was positive for JS on more than one front, as the dissenters saw the teachings of April 7 as blasphemous.[3] Large crowds gathered to participate in the proceedings, far more than could conveniently hear what was said from the wooden, outdoor platform-pulpit on an unfortunately windy afternoon.[4] JS complained of illness the first

1. For an example of the name use, see the title page for volume 4 of the Nauvoo *Times and Seasons*. The name was accretive: Mormonism began with the title, "Church of Christ." Then, in the mid-1830s, the Church of the Latter Day Saints. An 1838 revelation combined the two names (Doctrine and Covenants 115:3–4). Literary influences made Day into day, and in Britain by 1842, Latter day became hyphenated: Latter-day Saints.

2. On this dissent and its motivations, see Robert M. Call, "Anatomy of a Rupture: Identity Maintenance in the 1844 Latter-day Saint Reform Sect." By the end of the month, the dissenting church numbered in the hundreds. Benjamin E. Park, *Kingdom of Nauvoo*, 223–228.

3. On JS's adjustment to the proceedings, see the conference minutes, General Church Minutes, 1839–1877, April 5, 1844, William Clayton audit, page 1, CHL.

4. Estimates of attendance varied. Wilford Woodruff wrote that 20,000 persons were present. Woodruff's journal was later redacted to read 10,000. Wilford Woodruff journal, April 7, 1844, MS 1352, CHL. Scott G. Kenney, *Wilford Woodruff's Journal, 1834–1898*, 2:382.

two days of meetings and did not preach until the afternoon of the third day, April 7, 1844. It was then that he fulfilled the wish of Louisa Tanner Follett.

What follows is a summary of the sermon taken from some of the reports of JS's remarks. As noted above, this book attempts to map the influence of, and reaction to, certain topics in the reports of the sermon through time: the nature of the human soul, the resurrection of the body, the history of God, and the nature and inhabitants of Hell. I will mark out those portions of the sermon summary below with headings.

Two official clerks, Thomas Bullock and William Clayton, had been appointed to keep longhand notes of the conference. Both were experienced notetakers. JS's private secretary and historian, Willard Richards, kept brief notes. Other unofficial notetakers, pew auditors, kept records of varying character. To provide some context and mark out parts of the sermon that form important themes in the rest of the book, I will add occasional comments. I will not provide source citations for the quotations and summaries I give below; that will come later and then in full detail in Appendix A. The purpose here is to acquaint, or re-acquaint, the reader with the bones of the sermon, give some flavor of its view of salvation, and provide a reference point for the work in the rest of the book. I take some liberties here with source documents by expanding abbreviations and occasionally changing some spelling, hopefully without doing damage to meaning. I will usually quote directly from sources, and these appear within quotation marks. Some comments on these quotations appear between [brackets]. Other comments and summations appear simply as unquoted text.

After the opening of the afternoon conference session of April 7, 1844, JS stood and began his open air sermon. JS noted that there was a wind, and this likely impeded his thousands of listeners, especially those at some distance from the wooden preaching platform.

His preaching was directed to Louisa Follett but also to others in the audience who mourned the loss of family and friends; yet JS's extemporaneous remarks were not a eulogy, and they cannot be said to be unrehearsed. He had stated all his points before in various settings. JS offered short praise of Follett's life, but he gave few details or memories of his friend.[5]

Instead, JS offered a kind of cosmological overview of the purpose of life, summarizing various aspects of his own preaching largely taken from the period of 1839 to 1844, parts of which had textual roots in his earlier revelations and teaching. Put another way, he laid out his "theological anthropology"—the ontology and cosmology of the nature of human beings—and thus, as he argues, God's nature. Paraphrasing from one audit, "If we comprehend our own nature, then we comprehend God's nature."[6] Sounding like a startlingly humanist claim, it had quite a different meaning within the thought-world of the sermon.

The History of God

Speaking as loudly as possible, JS requested his listeners to think back to the beginning, the "beginning of creation." Then, "for us to take up beginning at the creation [it is] necessary to understand something of God" in the beginning. One clerk reported, "I want to go back to the beginning and so get you into a more lofty sphere than what the human being generally understands: I want to ask this congregation, every man woman and child "what kind of a being is God[?]" He wanted them to understand two things: what was in God's mind at the beginning of creation and the nature of God at the same point. He saw the latter as a prerequisite to the former, and he hoped his present

5. On April 8, 1843, JS spoke nearly identical words about the wind. *JSP*, D12:186.

6. JS's secretary (Willard Richards) wrote the (equivalent) contrapositive: "If men do not comprehend the character of God they do not comprehend themselves."

teaching would occupy their minds for the rest of their lives. Quoting from Jn 17, JS said in one report, "The apostle says this is eternal life to know God and Jesus Christ who he has sent—if any man enquire what kind of a being is God if he will search diligently his own heart that unless he knows God he has no eternal life." JS made this his first point, and he wished to be able to make this point clearly enough that his audience would have his teaching sealed in their hearts by the Holy Spirit. If he failed at this, he promised to renounce his claims to prophethood. There is some high drama around these potential consequences. There was an underground movement to remove him in part because of the teachings he will (re)introduce here—he had preached them all before in various and often much smaller venues, but his then-present audience may have been largely new to such preaching for reasons of recent immigration or those limited former audiences.[7]

"God himself who sits enthroned in yonder Heavens is a man like unto one of yourselves who holds this world" "in its sphere or its orbit–[and] the planets" "& upholds all things by his power, if you were to see him today you would see him" "in all the person image, very form of man, For Adam was created in the very fashion of God. Adam received instruction, walked [and] talked as one man with another."

"In order to understand the subject of the dead for the consolation of those who mourn for the loss of their friends it is necessary to understand the character and being of God for I am going to tell you how God came to be God." "God himself the father of us all dwelt on an Earth the same as Jesus Christ did and I will show it from the Bible." Here JS appealed to Jn 5 where in the KJV text Jesus tells his

7. For a consideration of JS's earlier texts that suggest human deification, see Jordan T. Watkins and Christopher James Blythe, "Christology and Theosis in the Revelations and Teachings of Joseph Smith."

audience that he only does what he has *seen* his father do [Jn 5:19]. In other words, God the Father had been a mortal at some point. Moreover, JS reads Jn 5:26 to imply that God's mortal body died at some point in his existence and that he took it up again just as Jesus would do. [How did listeners respond to this? One content auditor summarized his experience of this part of the sermon as an expansion of the Pauline theology: "Jesus Christ spoke in this manner; I do as my Father before me did. Well what did the Father do? Why he went and took a body and went to redeem a world in the flesh and had power to lay down his life and to take it up again and this is the way we become *heirs with God and joint heirs with Jesus Christ*."[8]]

The sermon goes on in one report, "You have got to learn how to be a god yourself in order to save yourself—to be priests and kings as all Gods has done—by going from a small degree to another—from exaltation to exaltation—till they are able to sit in glory as with those who sit enthroned." [This was perhaps a nod to insiders who had experienced the temple rituals before the temple itself was completed.] Another audit says, "sit in everlasting power as they who have gone before & God in the L. D. while certain individuals are proclaiming his name is not trifling with us—." [L. D. probably means "last days". Certain individuals may refer to a group of dissenters who had organized a competing church or perhaps a reformed branch of the main church.]

"[These are the] 1st principles of consolation: how consoling to the mourner when called to part with husband father wife child to know that those being[s] shall rise in immortal glory to sorrow die nor suffer any more. & not only that to contemplate the saying they shall be heirs of God &c.—[&c meant "and so forth" and was probably a time/space saving move by the auditor since the reference was likely well known to the audience—Rom. 8:17 again.] "What is it—to

8. George Laub report, emphasis added. See §1.6 below and the following section, §1.2.

inherit the same glory power & exaltation with those who are gone before. What did Jesus do? Why, I do the things that I saw the father do when worlds came into existence." [Once again, Jn 5:19.] In one audit JS interprets the Johannine passages more bluntly: "I saw my Father work out his Kingdom with fear & trembling & I must do the same" "And when I get my kingdom w[orked] [out] I will present [it] to the father & it will exalt his glory and Jesus steps into his [tracks] to inherit what God did before." [One auditor reported his impressions of this part of the sermon this way: "we are to go from glory to glory and as one is raised to a higher, so the next under him may take his degree . . . When we get to where Jesus is, he will be just as far ahead of us again in exaltation." There is a kind of conveyor belt or stair step theology at play here, and as we will see, it was thought by some such as Brigham Young to be infinite in both directions, meaning that there was never some "first" god, nor would the process ever end.[9]] "This is some of the first principle[s] of the gospel . . . You have got to find the beginning of this history & go on till you [have] learned the last—for it is a great thing to learn salvation beyond the grave & it is not all to be comprehended in this world" [here JS stated that he would use the Bible as his proof text to blunt the claims of critics—meaning that everyone accepted this source. Note that JS made no mention of his own visions of God as proof texts for his assertions about the form of God; this was a public sermon, and the Bible was the appropriate source in an audience of skeptics, the faithful, and curious visitors.]

"I shall go to the first Hebrew word in the Bible the 1st sentence: In the beginning [the Hebrew word is] Berosheat [pronounced *bray-sheeth.*]—[begins with] Bara, I want to analyze the word—*ba*—[means] in, by, through & everything else [JS was making reference to his Hebrew grammar purchased in 1836 from his Hebrew teacher in

9. George Laub report. On the Utah theological picture, see chapter 2.

Kirtland, Ohio][10]—*rosh*—the head [JS was breaking the word down as ba-rosh-sheit]—when the inspired man wrote he did not put the Ba there–But a jew put it there. It read in the first—the head one of the Gods brought forth the Gods—[this] is the true meaning—*rosheet* signifies to bring forth the Elohim. if you do not believe it you do not believe the learned man of God–no man can tell you more than I do: thus the Head God brought forth the Gods in the Head [or Grand] council." JS interprets his translation as "The Head God called together the Gods & set in Grand Council, the grand councilors set in yonder heavens and contemplate the creation of the worlds that was created at that time." JS noted that his interpretation was his own and that "Some learned doctor might say the scriptures say thus & so and we must believe the scriptures" and that they are not to be altered, "I am going to show you an error" [in the KJV Bible—his point was that it is not inerrant in the strictest sense—and therefore it requires interpretation—or retranslation in his terms] "I have an old book in the Latin, Greek Hebrew & German" [JS had a polyglot (literally, "many tongued") New Testament, the 1602 compilation by Elias Hutter, *Novum Testamentum harmonicum ebraice, graece, latine et germanice.* Hutter's German translation text was Martin Luther',s and JS stated in the sermon that he believed it was the most correct, meaning that it corresponded most closely to his own views.[11] Prussian-born British convert Alexander Neibaur (1808–1883) was

10. While JS was a beginner at Hebrew, his auditors were even less skilled, which made this portion of the sermon very difficult for them to report without confusing readers. When Thomas Bullock merged his own and William Clayton's audits for the *Times and Seasons,* he removed all the attempts at ancient languages pronunciations. On JS's work with Genesis 1:1, see Kevin L. Barney, "Joseph Smith's Emendation of Hebrew Genesis 1:1." On JS's clerks struggling with Hebrew, see Ronald V. Huggins, "Joseph Smith and the First Verse of the Bible."

11. For JS's use of Luther, and Luther's translation, see the summary in Kevin L. Barney, " 'Faith Alone,' in Romans 3:28 JST," 10–16.

apparently JS's German tutor and perhaps the source of the polyglot New Testament.[12]]

There were three aspects to JS's introduction of the Hutter New Testament. First, to show that the King James Bible—accepted as a primary authority by his critics—had important errors. The second was to bolster his claims of skill in dealing with his primary text: Genesis 1:1. The last was to show that if the Bible, at least in its authorized version, was capable of error and preachers and ministers quoted or taught such errors without fear of life and limb, then he should enjoy the same privilege, whether what he was teaching was true or not. He noted according to one report, "I have been reading the German: I find it to be the most correct that I have found & it corresponds the nearest to the revelations that I have given the last 14 years." "It talks about Yachaubon the son of Zebedee–this means Jacob. The New Testament says James–now if Jacob had the keys you might talk about James and never get the keys.[13] The Hebrew says–means–Jacob–Greek says Jacob, German says Jacob. Thank God I have got this book & I thank him more for the gift of the Holy Ghost. I should not have brought up this word" "were it not to back up [my ability to explain] the [Hebrew] word *rosh*–the head father of the Gods" "Now I ask all the learned men who hear me [why] the learned men who are preaching salvation say that God created the Heavens & the Earth out of nothing &" "they account it blasphemy

12. Polyglot Bibles had the text in various languages placed in parallel columns. That JS's polyglot was Hutter's 1601–2 New Testament is suggested by the fact that it is the only known polyglot with the languages noted by JS. Polyglot Bibles were mentioned in purchase invoices from JS's brother in Kirtland, Ohio, in 1836. It is unknown if any of these Kirtland polyglots was the same one JS used here, though the relative rarity of the Hutter makes this unlikely. "Invoices, H. Smith & Co. to William Smith and Jared Carter, November 1836," *JSP*.

13. JS used "keys" in several different ways. Here it may mean knowledge, which was the context of the sermon.

to contradict the idea—They will call you a fool–You ask them why they say don't the Bible say he created the world & they infer that it must be out of nothing." "the reason is that they are unlearned & I know more than all the world put together, & if the Holy Ghost in me comprehends more than all the world I will associate with it" "The word create came from the Barau–don't mean so–it means to organize–same as man would use to build a ship–hence we infer that God had materials to organize from–chaos–chaotic matter.–element had an existence from the time he had. The pure pure principles of element are principles that never can be destroyed–they may be organized and reorganized-but not destroyed"[14] "they coexist eternally–" This portion of the sermon, like all the polyglot–based discussion, was troublesome for auditors. JS repeated much of this translation argument in a sermon of June 16, 1844, defending himself against the critics of the "new church." Only one auditor left a report of the June 16 sermon, so the clerks of a decade later merely copied reports of this portion of Follett into the June 16 sermon record.

The Human Soul

The first major point of the sermon was that God was not always God but went through a similar pathway as Jesus. God was once, in effect, a human being and saved a world as Jesus had done, again, not the first time JS had stated this (see subsequent sections of this chapter). This idea was a key teaching in the nineteenth-century Utah church. In the twentieth century, it would fade from public church teaching (chapters 3 and 4 below). Why did JS begin his project with this idea? It gave a *near* universalist tinge to the future: there is much to do,

14. It is unlikely that William Clayton, who reported this sentence, meant to write "pure" rather than "pure pure." The latter seems to be an emphasis on the most basic constituents of "element," perhaps meaning the Aristolelian basics, earth, air, fire, water. JS referred to these as the "elements" elsewhere.

great things, infinite progress, awaiting both the living and the dead with one important and central exception—a stark warning to and about dissenters that surfaced later in the sermon.

JS set the stage for the second major point of his sermon: the human soul has no beginning and no end. This figures into his project of comfort by assuring Louisa Follett and other grieving people in his audience that the person they knew, their loved one, was not lost in death. Those persons, their souls, or spirits, or minds, cannot die, since they have individually always existed. They are, in a word, uncreated beings, individual permanent fixtures in an eternal cosmos of gods, humans, and devils. This astonishing assertion, a violation of a founding principle of science and philosophy for centuries, had been a part of JS's preaching for years; indeed, it was one of his most repeated themes over the last five years of his life, perhaps because it played strongly into conceptions of freedom and independence and his desire to push back against the political, religious machines of the United States. Eventually the idea was dimmed by two forces, as I argue below. One of these was a more-enduring part of his legacy: polygamy; the second was the transition from the theological freedom of Nauvoo and the time of Brigham Young to an increasingly text-based religion, ending with a tiered authority with Mormon Scripture at the top as a true canon—everything was to be measured by the Standard Works (whose interpretation rested with the hierarchy). The logics of that dimming faded somewhat with the fading of polygamy, but even so, they helped make the sermon *persona non grata* seven decades later (chapter 3).

"I have another [subject] to dwell on & it is impossible for me to say much" "It is associated with the subject in question, the resurrection of the dead" "the soul–the mind of man–they say God created it in the beginning. The idea lessens man in my estimation." "I don't believe the doctrine I know better: hear it all ye Ends of the World for God has told me so I am going to tell of things more noble" "[I will] make a man appear a fool before he gets through if he don't believe it" "we say God himself is a self-existing[15] God, who told you so, how did it get into your head? Who told you that man did not exist in like manner?[16]" "[It] Dont say so in the old Hebrew–God made man out of the earth and put into him his spirit [JS is reading *breathed into his nostrils the breath of life* as inserting the spirit for breath—something he believed his Hebrew lessons allowed] and then it became a living body" "the mind of man—the mind of man is as immortal as God himself–" "I know that my testimony is true hence when I talk to these mourners what have they lost? They [the dead] are only separated from their bodies for a short season but their spirits existed coequal with God" "& now converse one [with] another [the] same as we do–does not this give you satisfaction?" [This implied physicality is displayed in JS's earlier preaching.]

"I want to reason more on the Spirit of Man for I [am] dwelling on the body of man, on the subject of the dead" "Is it logic to say that a spirit is immortal and yet have a beginning? Because if a spirit have a beginning it will have an end–good logic–" "It does not have a beginning or end" "I take my ring[17] from my finger and liken it unto the mind of man, the immortal spirit because it has no beginning.[18]

15. Self-existent, that is, not contingent, but a necessary part of reality as brute fact, i.e., a being whose existence is not caused by something else. Another option is a being whose non-existence yields a logical contradiction, a *logical* necessity, these may be different types of necessity. The popular use of the term in English language imprints reached its height in the mid-1820s.

16. This is a rhetorical question. People in the day knew that JS's "doctors of religion" was the antecedent.

17. Mormon collector Buddy Youngreen suggested that the ring used in the sermon was one handed down by Emma Smith to her son Alexander Hale Smith and thence to Glaud Leslie Smith, a great-grandson of JS. Youngreen, a JS descendant, purchased the ring from Glaud Smith prior to his death in 1986. *Ensign* 13, no. 1 (1984): 32.

18. JS had used the ring illustration in at least one prior sermon (January 5, 1841).

Suppose you cut it in two but as the Devil lives there would be an end. All the fools & wise men from the beginning of creation who say that man had a beginning" "prove that he must have an end and if that doctrine is true then the doctrine of annihilation is true."[19] One listener summarized the thought this way: "How came the spirits? Why they are and were self existing as all eternity & our spirits are as eternal as the very God is himself." "God never had the power to create the spirit of man at all" "All the spirits that God ever sent into this world are susceptible of enlargement" [This is a link back to the first point of the sermon.]

"God himself finds himself in the midst of spirits and glory, because he was greater, saw proper to institute laws" "to instruct the weaker intelligences" "for those who were in lesser intelligence that they might have one glory upon another in all that knowledge power

---

19. A considerable debate raged in JS's time on whether the soul was or could be annihilated, either for a time between death and resurrection or permanently perhaps sometime after consignment to Hell for the wicked. The idea that either personal existence came to an end with death until resurrection (an extreme version of Luther's "soul-sleep") or those consigned to hell had their souls annihilated while the body remained forever burning in hellfire were some extreme variations on a theme. Philo was an early proponent of soul death. Irenaeus suggested a literal interpretation of "second death" biblical passages. (Edward Beecher, *History of Opinions on the Scriptural Doctrine of Future Retribution*, 29–33). While annihilation was a point of disagreement for centuries, by the time of this discourse, a controversy was brewing over the idea among various faiths in the United States. Brigham Young applied the idea to "sons of perdition," the only truly damned in Mormonism—they would be snuffed out of existence *as individuals* (for example, *Journal of Discourses* 1:275–6; 2:124; 3:203; 6:346; 7:57; 8:29; 9:149–50). These and other variations show that the succeeding Mormon generation was at least mildly flummoxed by JS's claims. JS was probably acquainted with Charles Buck's *Theological Dictionary* (1802 and various later editions). Buck's long article on "Destructionists" echoes a number of sentiments that JS reflects on in this sermon. On Buck and JS, see Matthew Bowman and Samuel Brown, "The Reverend Buck's Theological Dictionary and the Struggle to Define American Evangelicalism, 1802–1851."

& glory & so took in hand to save the world of spirits. You say honey is sweet & so do I. I can also taste the spirit of Eternal life I know it is good & when I tell you of these things that were given me by Inspiration of the Holy Spirit you are bound to receive it as sweet & I rejoice more & more." [The *sweetness* may be an allusion to Psalm 119:103.]

JS then moves into the part of the sermon that was often remembered in Utah as temples were constructed. JS's own temple in Nauvoo was working its way up from the ground, and beyond baptisms for the dead, it functioned as a sacred space for church meetings and the endowment and sealing rites for Latter-day Saints in the Nauvoo region after JS's death. JS had spoken of performing proxy versions of these rituals for the dead the previous year, but those sermons were generally to smaller audiences and not widely circulated.

"Man's relationship to God: I will open your eyes in relation to your dead. All things which God in his infinite reason has seen fit to reveal to us in our mortal state in regard to our mortal bodies are revealed to us as if we had no bodies. And those revelations which will save our dead will save our bodies" "save our spirits with them" "God reveals them to us in the view of no eternal dissolution of the body—hence the awful responsibility that rests upon us for our dead—for all the Spirits must either obey the gospel or be damned. Solemn thought, dreadful thought. Is there nothing to be done for those who have gone before us without obeying the decrees of God" "no salvation for our fathers & friends who have died and not obeyed the decrees of the son of man—would to God I had 40 days & nights I would let you know that I am not a fallen prophet—what kind of beings can be saved although their bodies are moldering in the dust? When his commandments teach us it is in view of eternity."

"the greatest responsibility that God has laid upon us is to look after our dead–the apostle says [This is a reference to Hebrews 11:15 and to his own letter to the Latter-day Saints written September 6,

1842. See D&C 128:15, 18] they without us cant be Perfect–now I am speaking of them I say to you Paul, you cant be perfect without us.– those that are gone before & those who come after must be made perfect–& God has made it obligatory to man" "God said he shall send Elijah &c [Mal.4:5] I have a declaration to make as to the provision which God made from before the foundation of the world [D&C 128:8].

The Damned and Their Hell

What has Jesus said? All sins & all blasphemies, every transgression that man may be guilty of there is a salvation for him" [Matt 12:31] "either in this world or in the world of spirits" "every spirit in the eternal world can be ferreted out & saved unless he has committed that sin which cant be remitted to him" "neither in this world or in the world of spirits" "Every man who has a friend in the eternal world who hath not committed the unpardonable sin you can save him. A man cannot commit the unpardonable sin after the dissolution of the body" "there is a way for his escape" "Knowledge saves a man and in the world of spirits a man can't be exalted but by knowledge.[20] So long as a man will not give heed to the commandments he must abide without salvation." [JS's fundamental *anti*-universalist argument.]

This idea that there is a class of persons who *cannot* be saved was not new to Christian thought of the time (Calvin's double predestination for example). JS's position draws a firm line between Universalism and his own teaching. He now spends some effort to explain this irredeemable class who commit an unpardonable sin, commonly called the *sons of Perdition* in Mormon parlance, and the concept's deep influence over salvation in general. These ideas formed another class of frequent themes in JS's preaching. They are

20. This idea appeared in a number of JS's sermons prior to this one. Sermons of April 2, 1843; May 14, 1843; May 17, 1843; and August 27, 1843 share the same idea.

also starkly represented in several of his longer and more fundamental revelation texts, including D&C 76, 88, and 132 (2013 LDS edition).

"I have no fear of hell fire, that dont exist" "A sinner has his own mind" "A man is his own torment hence the saying they shall go into the lake that burns with fire" "as exquisite as a lake burning with fire & brimstone" "I know the scriptures I understand them–no man can commit the unpardonable sin after the dissolution of the body but they must do it in this world–" "hence the salvation that the saviour wrought out for the salvation of a man if it did not catch him in one place it would another [living or afterlife]" "The contention in heaven [before the world, Rev. 12, D&C 29, etc.] was Jesus said there were certain" "souls that would be condemned [who] would not be saved, the devil said he could save them" "–as the grand council gave in for Jesus Christ so the devil fell & all who put up their heads for him." "All sin shall be forgiven except the sin against the Holy Ghost [to sin against the Holy Ghost] he has got to say that the Sun does not shine while he sees it he has got to deny Jesus Christ when the heavens are open to him"[21] "After a man has sinned the sin against the Holy

21. The "War in Heaven" is an enduring teaching in Latter-day Saint thought and sermons. Indeed, earth-life's conflicts between good and evil are often styled as a continuation of this War, with cast down, failed human souls (the Devil as their king) tempting humanity on one side and Jesus and his servants inspiring goodness on the other. The War's dimensions and meanings vary somewhat over time, but the participants in JS's vision are God, Christ, and the premortal souls of humanity (of which the Devil is one and leader of the opposition). JS's teaching here is rather different than is common in current LDS literature, where it is stated that the genesis of the War was the Devil's assertion that he would *force* all souls on the then-future earth back to heaven. For JS, this was not the issue. In his view, there were a few souls in the pre-existent world who would (in the foreknowledge of God) choose not to be saved after they became embodied on earth. The Devil would push them away from the choice of Hell instead of heaven. The issue was not the freedom of the general mass of humanity. For a primer on the evolved standard Mormon picture here, see Terryl L. Givens, *Wrestling the Angel*, ch 17.

Spirit there is no repentance for him. Hence like many of the apostates of the Church of Jesus Christ of Latter day Saints they go too far, the spirit leaves them, hence they seek to kill me, they thirst for my blood–they never cease–[they have] got the same spirit that crucified Jesus. You can't renew them to repentance–awful is the consequence [Matt 12:33]" "the same Spirit that sins against the Holy Ghost." [This identification of Mormon dissenters among the unforgivable was a frequent theme in JS's preaching in the first years after his escape from Missouri authorities (1839–1841). There it was advertised as a principle equal to the most important and foundational tenets alongside baptism, for example. The principle was called *Eternal Judgment*, borrowed from Heb 6:1–8.[22] Now that dissenters were, in his mind, once again a deep threat to JS and his program, the idea of eternal judgment resurfaced. JS returned to the topic of the irredeemably damned in the final segment of the sermon below.]

"I can enter into the mysteries. I can enter largely into the eternal worlds–for Jesus said, in my Father's mansion there are many mansions &c. There is one glory of the moon, sun, & stars &c we have the reason to have the greatest hope & consolation for our dead–for we have aided them in the 1st principles for we have seen them walk in the midst & sink asleep in the arms of Jesus & hence is the glory of the Sun—you mourners have occasion to rejoice for your husband has gone to wait unto the resurrection & your expectation & hope are far above what man can conceive–for why God has revealed to us & I am authorized to say" "to you my friends in the name of the Lord" "by the authority of the Holy Ghost that you have no occasion to fear for he is gone to the home of the just–don't mourn don't weep–I know it by the testimony of the Holy Ghost that is within me–rejoice O Israel–your friends shall triumph gloriously–while their murder-

22. For example, see JS sermons of June 27, 1839; August 8, 1839; January 12, 1841; May 16, 1841; October 3, 1841; May 12, 1844. (*Parallel Joseph*)

ers shall welter" "in torment until they pay the utmost farthing." "I say for the benefit of strangers I have a" "father, brother, children," "friends who are gone to the world of spirits–they are absent for the moment–then shall we hail our mothers fathers friends & no fear of mobs–&c but all one Eternity of felicity–"

The Resurrection of Children

The last point of the sermon that has a major role in its reception history is its unusual claim about the resurrection of children. It would help anathamize the received text (designated RC, below) for decades in the twentieth century and contribute to its continued marginalization.

"Mothers you shall have your Children for they shall have it–for their debt is paid there is no damnation awaits them for they are in the [world of] spirits–as a Child dies so shall it rise from the dead & be living in the burnings of God, it shall be the child as it was before it died out of your arms. Children dwell & exercise power in the same form as they laid them down" "It will never grow, it will be in its precise form as it fell in its mothers arms. Eternity is full of thrones upon which dwell thousands of children reigning on thrones of glory not one cubit added to their stature." "[They will have] Dominion upon dominion just as you [will]." [The last portion of this segment of the sermon on the resurrection of children gradually became a festering controversy (as we will see in later chapters), but just as with other topics of the sermon, it was not the first time JS had expressed the idea. The discussion of JS's cultural work on this issue along with his Utah successors is mostly postponed to §3.2, where the chronological thread of interpretation reaches its apex.]

The next and final part of the sermon concerned the doctrine of baptism and returned momentarily to the idea of damnation. Possibly JS had spied someone in the audience that made an object lesson.

"I will leave this subject here and make a few remarks upon baptism" "bless those who have lost friends" "The baptism of water without the baptism of fire and the Holy Ghost attending it are necessary" "inseparably connected." "He must be born of water & spirit in order to get into the kingdom of God [Jn 3] & in the German text bears me out same as the revelations which I have given for the 14 years [previous]–I have the testimony to put in their teeth that my testimony has been true all the time. You will find it in the Declaration of John the Baptist (reads from the German) John says I baptize you with water but when Jesus comes who has the power he shall administer the baptism of fire & the Holy Ghost. Great God, now where is all the sectarian world? & if this testimony is true they are all damned as clearly as any Anathema ever was–but those who sin against the Holy Ghost cannot be forgiven in this world or in the world to come but they shall die the 2nd. death–but as they concoct scenes of bloodshed in this world so they shall rise to that resurrection which is as the lake of fire & brimstone–some shall rise to the everlast burning of God [Isa 33] and some shall rise to the damnation of their own filthiness–same as the lake of fire & brimstone–" "There has also been remarks made concerning all men being redeemed from Hell, but I say that any man who commits the unpardonable sin must dwell in hell worlds without end."

"I have intended my remarks to all–to all rich & poor bond & free great & small I have no enmity against any man. I love you all–I am their best friend & if persons miss their mark it is their own fault–if I reprove a man & he hate me he is a fool–for I love all men especially these my brethren & sisters–I rejoice in hearing the testimony of my aged friend"

"You never knew my heart. No man knows my history–I can not do it. I shall never undertake [it]–if I had not experienced what I have I should not have known it myself–I never did harm any man since I have been born in the world–my voice is always for peace–I cannot lie down until my work is finished–I never think evil nor think any thing to the harm of my fellow man–& when I am called at the trump &

weighed in the balance you will know me then—I add no more God bless you. Amen."

"Aged friend" was a reference to JS's fellow church leader Sidney Rigdon who had, during previous sessions of the conference, given long speeches about his experiences in the early church and its history. The wording would be changed in 1856 to avoid the reference to Rigdon who had parted ways with Brigham Young and the apostolic leadership in 1844. JS's following remark about history was probably directed to Rigdon's remarks and secondarily to Rigdon himself. Sidney Rigdon had been part of the early days of JS's work, first meeting JS in December 1830. Rigdon's conference preaching had related his early history of the church and his presence in the background of the current church work, even an oblique suggestion of his membership in the secret Council of Fifty: JS's response was that no one knew *his* history. The point was that though Rigdon had been a partner in the work, JS's truth in a sense encircled Rigdon's. This remark and subsequent elaborations helped to create what historian Christopher Blythe has called a "Josephology," in part a circulating battery of mysteries that only insiders could understand. In death, JS assumed a medieval, saint-like stature as in the 1844 William W. Phelps hymn "Joseph Smith," subsequently known as "Praise to the Man."[23] JS was now, after death, "mingling with gods" or later that he was even, or had become, the third member of the Godhead.

JS's remark was a response to Rigdon's long speeches, suggesting a more complex story that Rigdon had rejected (polygamy, many gods, and so forth). With time, the remark became divorced from its context. And in full circle, Rigdon rejected the Follett sermon's theology.[24]

23. The text first appeared in *Times and Seasons* 5 (August 1, 1844): 604. See Michael Hicks, "Poetic Borrowing in Early Mormonism," 139–140.

24. On the change of wording, see Appendix A or a text such as *Teachings of the Prophet Joseph Smith* (later in this chapter, see the descendants of "RC"). On Rigdon's speeches, see General Church Minutes file, April 5, 6, 1844, CR 100 318,

JS may have concluded his remarks, but he had more to say on the subjects of the sermon. He continued some of the themes in a short sermon the following day, then in a sermon on May 12, 1844. A few days before his death, he returned again to the idea of many Gods, God's father, his father, etc. in a sermon delivered on June 16, 1844.[25]

§1.2 The Documentary Sources of JS's Theological Anthropology

> Beloved, now are we the sons of God, and it doth not yet appear what we shall be: but we know that, when he shall appear, **we shall be like him**; for we shall see him as he is.
>
> — 1 Jn 3:2

There are a number of textual precursors to JS's declarations about God and the human potential to become like God. To eyes used to JS's 1840s preaching, it may seem clear that passages from his early revelations—like Moses 1 (Moses is of the category of Christ—1830), D&C 76:51–70 (the saved and exalted in the Celestial World are like God—1832) and D&C 93:1–29 (the passage of mankind is in many respects the image of Christ's—1833)—were the foundations of the Follett sermon's idea that humans are potential gods.[26] The Mormon version of the ontological distance between the human and divine was nothing like that of Calvin's translation of Augustine: creator God

CHL. On Blythe's "Josephology," see Christopher James Blythe, "'Would to God, Brethren, I Could Tell You Who I Am!': Nineteenth-Century Mormonisms and the Apotheosis of Joseph Smith." JS had already proposed a general theology of progress that allowed for something similar (§1.2). On Nancy Rigdon, see Todd Compton, *In Sacred Loneliness: The Plural Wives of Joseph Smith*, 239–240, 634.

25. See *Parallel Joseph* under these dates (boap.org/LDS/Parallel), also *JSP*.

26. Watkins and Blythe, "Christology and Theosis in the Revelations and Teachings of Joseph Smith," 125–131.

vs. creature man—two categories that could *never* intersect for the typical American Protestant preacher. However, it is not at all clear that the average Saint of the 1830s read such passages as those above as in any way signaling the open declarations of Follett and its precursor sermons of the 1840s.[27] Many of those earlier episodes occurred in small venues; their distribution, individual interpretation, and immediate theological influence is unclear.

While early Mormon preaching went largely unrecorded, JS's revelatory pronouncements were often reported in some detail, the Book of Mormon being an ideal example, followed by the initial collation of early revelations in Revelation Book 1, a text containing some of the earliest available manuscripts of many of JS's revelations.[28] The Book of Mormon may have hinted at the preexistence of human souls, but it was JS's revision of the Bible that told of God creating—a loaded term in church discourse as JS grew to disfavor *creatio ex nihilo* —or manufacturing the spirits or souls of human beings prior to their inhabiting the physical world (as that revision was later understood by many Latter-day Saints).[29]

In 1835, JS and his scribal assistants embarked on a new translation project. Some Egyptian funerary papyri had come into JS's possession, purchased from a traveling showman who passed through Mormon headquarters at Kirtland, Ohio. The publication of this translation in 1842 announced that human spirits not only preexisted embodiment but were without beginning or end, an advancement

27. For example, sermons of January 5, 1841; January 30, 1842; June 11, 1843; June 16, 1844. All can be found at *Parallel Joseph* (boap.org/LDS/Parallel) and at *JSP*.

28. For an excellent transparent display of this collection, see *JSP*, MRB. I borrow some of the material in this section from my previous work. See, for example, Smith, "Joseph Smith's Sermons and the Early Mormon Documentary Record."

29. See Moses 6:36 in the Pearl of Great Price.

of the theology of the early Bible revision work.[30] JS's translation of the papyri, titled the Book of Abraham, provides reflections of JS's interaction with other literature in his environment. In the first two chapters of the new expansion of the biblical account in Genesis chapters 11 and 12, JS echoes the works of Josephus naming for example, the mysterious Iscah of Gen. 11:29. The first printing of the Book of Abraham replaces Iscah with Sarah and identifies her as the daughter of Haran, one echo among several of Josephus's text. The third chapter of the new book demonstrates frequent echoes of Scottish teacher, Presbyterian minister, and scientist, Thomas Dick, through his work, *Philosophy of a Future State*, a text known among Latter-day Saints of the mid-1830s. The word *intelligences* is a frequent referent to human beings, souls, or spirits in Dick's work, and the Book of Abraham introduced the same word to its audience. Dick argued that *immaterial* was not an essential descriptor of soul and even that it may have a finer material structure, finding another echo in JS's theology of the same period as the Book of Abraham.[31] Dick compared the structure of the cosmos with that of intelligences and deploys the term *organized intelligences* in his work. All these ideas find echoes in the Book of Abraham (as "intelligencies"—a synonym for "intelligences"—intelligencies appeared in the first imprint of the Book of Abraham). Dick—a believer in *ex nihilo* creation—argued that souls are contingent but would almost surely not be annihilated in the future and that salvation might entail not God-status but yet a kind of asymptotic approach to God-like elevation. JS's logic in Follett is carefully different on such points (and seems to parallel his Book of Abraham work). Dick's work was influential in the continuing evolution of JS's thought—Dick's speculations, arguments, and language

30. See JS, "Book of Abraham," *Times and Seasons* 3 (March 15, 1842): 720; Book of Abraham 3:16–18, the Pearl of Great Price. *JSP*, R&T4.

31. Thomas Dick, *The Philosophy of a Future State*, 121.

served as point and counterpoint for JS—and perhaps sharpened his response to the Christian world of his youth.[32] The woodcut facsimiles of Egyptian vignettes and the final chapters of the Book of Abraham demonstrate clear relation to JS's 1836 Hebrew studies in usage and spelling, JS's encounter with Freemasonry in Nauvoo, and the new order of plural marriage started by JS in 1841. These forces, set against a background of Jacksonian-era civil violence toward marginalized movements like Mormonism, are reflected in the thought of JS's post-Missouri–period sermons. Nearly all these influences are present in the Follett sermon.[33] Chapter 3 of the Book of Abraham was linked to Follett in the early twentieth century by exegetes of the sermon (see chapter 3). This is one more marker that JS's translation work and his preaching work were coherent (at least at their later stages), their processes were largely parallel, and as I remarked in the Introduction, became almost a substitute for his revelatory dictations; in the case of Follett, JS declared his words to be given by the Holy Spirit.[34]

Aside from Follett, other JS sermons reveal similar links. After the expulsion of the Mormons from Missouri in 1838–1839, JS took the thousand-mile journey to Washington, DC, to appeal for redress to congress and the president. The mission faced a reluctant state rights Democratic congress and a president, Martin Van Buren, whose patronage lay partly in the hands of influential Missouri senator Thomas Hart Benton.[35] The mission was doomed for many reasons,

---

32. On the general historiography of Dick's influence in Mormonism, see Benjamin E. Park, "'Reasonings Sufficient': Joseph Smith, Thomas Dick, and the Context(s) of Early Mormonism."

33. On Hebrew, see the sermon summary in §1.1.

34. On JS using Hebrew, see Matthew J. Grey, "Approaching Egyptian Papyri through Biblical Language: Joseph Smith's Use of Hebrew in His Translation of the Book of Abraham."

35. On the effort to recover losses incurred in Missouri by vigilante and state approved acts of robbery, murder, and rape, see *JSP*, D7:xxiv–xxviii. Benjamin E.

but JS preached in the Washington area on a number of occasions. Journalist Matthew L. Davis wrote to his wife Mary with a content audit of one of these sermons,

> I believe, said [JS], that a man is a moral, responsible, free agent, that although it was foreordained he should fall, and be redeemed, yet after the redemption it was not fore ordained that he should again sin. In the Bible a rule of conduct is laid down for him, In the old and new Testaments the law by which he is to be governed may be found. If he violates that law, he is to be punished for the deeds done in the body. I believe that God is eternal. That He had no beginning, and can have no end. *Eternity means that which is without beginning or End I believe that the Soul is Eternal. It had no beginning; it can have no end.* Here he entered into some explanations, which were so brief that I could not perfectly comprehend him. But the idea seemed to be that the soul of man, the Spirit, had existed from Eternity in the bosom of Divinity; and so far as he was intelligible to me, must ultimately return from whence it came—He said very little of rewards and punishments. but one conclusion, from what he did say was irresistible. *He contended throughout, that every thing which had a beginning must have an ending*; and consequently if the punishment of man commenced in the next world, it must, according to his logic and belief have an end.[36]

JS likely subscribed to a universal clock for the cosmos,[37] but he spoke of a God *within* that cosmos as it was then understood. Hence

---

Park, *Kingdom of Nauvoo*, 36–45.

36. Matthew L. Davis, Letter, Washington, DC, to Mrs. Matthew L. Davis, New York City. Italics added. The letter was recently verified as the production of Davis by historian Richard L. Jensen. The temporary nature of Hell recalls one of Smith's revelations from 1829 (Doctrine and Covenants 19). See Michael Hubbard MacKay, et al., *Documents: Vol. 1: July 1828–June 1831*, 85–95. A digital facsimile of the Davis letter may be found here: https://dcms.lds.org/delivery/DeliveryManagerServlet?dps_pid=IE3258769. On the Davis letter, see *JSP*, D7:175–179.

37. For example, see Doctrine and Covenants 130:4–5. William Clayton journal, April 2, 1843, as found in *JSP*, J2:Appendix 2. On the use of Cosmos as opposed to

he might preach that the divine realm was not timeless within itself. In JS's work on revising the Bible, he added text to the effect of an Augustinian concept of God's time as a gathering of all other times into one, but that notion was modified in later years.[38] Eternity was not platonic timelessness for JS. God has a clock.[39] This and other sermons suggested JS's critique of popular theological works like that of the legendary Methodist preacher at the end of the long eighteenth century, Lorenzo Dow.[40] Dow published tales of his itinerant work in the Second Great Awakening, including his own rather eclectic theology and some of Dow's language seems entrenched in JS's speech. It is reasonable to believe that JS had access to Dow's widely distributed works, and JS's developed protological (what came before mortal life) picture of human beings used one of Dow's ideas in reverse. Dow wrote,

> If every thing which had a beginning must have an end; then that which had no beginning can have no end . . . if Nature *exists* by emanation, from the will of its *Author*; by the same rule it must continue to exist, or go out of Being; but when agreeable to His pleasure.[41]

---

the modern *universe*, see comments below and in chapter 3.

38. See Moses 1:6–7; D&C 130:7; Abr. 3:2.

39. Abr 3:4. On time, see Taylor, *A Secular Age*, 69, 107, 210.

40. Dow and JS had a number of things in common, early visions and visits with an angel, encounters with Methodism and a dislike for the Methodist Discipline. On Dow, see, for example, Lorenzo and Peggy Dow, *The Dealings of God, Man, and the Devil*, iv, 10.

41. Emphasis in the original. Lorenzo Dow, *History of a Cosmopolite, or the Four Volumes of Lorenzo's Journal, Concentrated in One: Containing His Experience & Travels, From Childhood to 1814, Being Upwards of Thirty-Six Years*, 247. Dow's words find echoes in the thought of Thomas Dick. Dick's work was extensively quoted in the church's Kirtland serial, *Latter Day Saints' Messenger and Advocate*, December 1836, 423–25. Dow remains an enigmatic figure in American religion.

Other Dow sayings appear as expressions in the Follett sermon. Dow was one of the many stones from which JS would leap.[42] JS eventually rejected *creatio ex nihilo* in a number of different ways. The "elements" as in the Aristotelian fundamentals of nature, earth, air, fire, water or the celestial bodies visible in the night sky, and human souls (minds) were not emanations from God—they coexisted with God. And it was this rejection of creation from nothing that materializes in JS's theological explorations—not plagiarism but creation as organization.[43] The argument used by Dow and later by JS wasn't invented by either of them. Versions were in the air at the time, so to speak. Indeed, JS demonstrated in many ways a practice of plucking out ideas and practices from many sources and molding them to his own revelatory purposes. He announced this as a rule of the faith: embrace truth, whatever its source.[44] Examples included church governance, biblical interpretation, terminology, economic innovation, and the introduction of new religious rites.[45]

See Douglas M. Strong, "The Eccentric Cosmopolite: Lorenzo Dow and Early Nineteenth-Century Methodism," 78–90.

42. Follett wasn't the only JS sermon to echo Dow. Of the several examples, one is JS's sermon of April 7, 1843, on resurrection. It seems clearly related to Dow's teaching. Compare Dow, *History of a Cosmopolite*, 291–292.

43. Philip L. Barlow, *Mormons and the Bible*, xxxii.

44. Joseph Smith, Letter to Isaac Galland, March 22, 1839, 53. "Articles of Faith," 13. Joseph Smith, discourse, July 23, 1843. http://www.boap.org/LDS/Parallel/1843/23Jul43.html

45. An early nineteenth-century translation of Plato's works argued "that which has no temporal beginning . . . cannot have an end" "and those things that are without ending must be without beginning." The argument was one about contingency and had laid roots and branches in early Christian controversies over Christology. The platonic logic was not necessarily one about permanence as JS eventually interpreted it. The matter hinged on how one saw "eternity." The neoplatonic eternal was simply a timeless zone, one where nothing altered or changed. Time in that sense was a moving image of eternity, a necessarily impermanent reflection, shadow, of the truly real. In the platonic sense, the only truly eternal *things* were those that

For JS, souls were not contingent: they were *sempiternal*, that is, by some universal clock, souls had no beginning or end. JS's idea of time was not technically sophisticated, either in terms of modern physics or the arguments of the Christian Church Fathers, but in the Follett sermon and earlier as in his Washington sermon, he positioned the sempiternal soul as an article of deep belief. This article of his faith would play a central role in the subsequent reception history of the Follett sermon.

These and other parts of the 1840 Washington, DC, speech carried through JS's preaching intermittently and then finally into the 1844 Follett sermon. Church writer and leader Eliza R. Snow used "co-existent with the eternal God" in her 1841 poem, "Integrity," demonstrating an intertextual relationship with the 1840 sermon; "Integrity" surely alludes to common threads from the 1840 sermon or one of its successors.[46]

For the mature JS, then, each person is eternal in some *personal* sense, and the Follett sermon elaborated this ontological pluralism as emotional security in its message to Louisa Follett that her husband could never be "gone." JS's claim that "if the soul has a beginning, it will have an end" is an instance of a rigorous mathematical argument from the twentieth century based on the Copernican Principle. The scandal of Copernicus was to posit that the earth is nothing special, at least in terms of its location in the cosmos; it is not the center of that cosmos, but merely one of many billions of planets orbiting one

were lodged in the eternal, outside, transcendent to, time. See Floyer Sydenham and Thomas Taylor, trans., *The Works of Plato, vol. 1*, lxiii, 26. On JS borrowing from civic, religious, and folk traditions, see, for example, Bushman, *Rough Stone Rolling*; Smith, "Early Mormon Priesthood Revelations"; Park, *Kingdom of Nauvoo*, 95–97; Jones, "'We Latter-day Saints are Methodists'"; ch 4, Wayment and Lemmon, "A Recovered Resource"; Barlow, *Mormons and the Bible*, xxxiii–xxxiv.

46. Eliza R. Snow, "Integrity," *Quincy Whig* (March 6, 1841), as in Jill Mulvay Derr and Karen Lynn Davidson, eds., *Eliza R. Snow: The Complete Poetry*, item 75.

of many billions of stars housed in the Milky Way. If one admits that the same is true in regards to time, that is, that our present time as a group of conscious beings in the stream of human existence is not at the beginning or the end of that period of existence, it is possible to estimate our (humanity's) future longevity. In any case, an argument based on this temporal Copernican Principle can serve up a kind of proof for JS's claim about "good logic" in his no beginning, no end reasoning. For some basic details, see §4.4.

The uniqueness of the Follett event in terms of the sempiternal soul consists partly in that use of this radical protology mentioned above to provide hope to the bereaved: if a loved one's individual personhood never began, that person or conscious individual could never cease to exist. One aural audit of the Follett sermon reads,

> The soul the mind of man, where did it come from? The learned says God made it in the beginning, but it is not so, I know better God has told me so. If you dont believe it, it wont make the truth without effect, God was a self exhisting being, man exists upon the same principle. God made a tabernacle & put a spirit in it and it became a Human soul, man exhisted in spirit & mind coequal with God himself, you who mourn the loss of friends are ownly seperated for a moment, the spirit is separated for a little time, they are now conversant with each other as we are on the earth. I am dwelling on the immutability of the spirit of man, is it logic to say the spirit of man had a beginning & yet had no end? It does not have a beginning or end[47]

---

47. See William Clayton audit for April 7, 1844, General Church Minutes file, CHL. Digital image and transcription at http://www.josephsmithpapers.org/paper-summary/discourse-7-april-1844-as-reported-by-william-clayton/6. See also *Parallel Joseph*, April 7, 1844. For JS's consistent use of the notion, see these examples in the *JSP* Documents series volumes. "Discourse," between circa 26 June and circa 4 August 1839–A, as Reported by Willard Richards, *JSP*, D6, 543, and "Discourse," February 5, 1840, *JSP*, D7, 178. See also "Account of Meeting and Discourse," 5 January 1841, as Reported by William Clayton, *JSP*, D7, 494–495; "Discourse," circa 28 March 1841, as Reported by William P. McIntire, *JSP*, D8, 86–87; Book of

The Cartesian dualism (flesh/spirit or body/mind) in this speech shades the struggle for meaning inherent in *sub specie aeternitatis*.[48] It was complicated elsewhere by a distinct Aristotelian thread of materialism with form guiding flesh, spirit form impressing body form, body growing to adopt the spirit's form, but Aristotle argued that this meant, after death, individuality vanished. However, JS's materialism was more like substance dualism than strict materialism.[49]

Framing the divine by the human was a natural step from JS's revelations and the Nauvoo ideas of deification.[50] It was both natural and community inspiring to suggest a heavenly backdrop or paradigm for the earthly. But how was that family ideal to play out in a heavenly context? "Spirit" was already, if obscurely, defined as material by JS.[51] That obscurity existed or would exist in three senses: first, JS's statements on materiality were narrowly circulated at first (though later canonized in 1876); second, the idea of the invisible world having some substance of a finer quality was in no way a novel concept; and the eventual third sense, the relationship of materiality to physicality became an imprecise idea in light of twentieth-century physics (chapter 3).[52]

Abraham Excerpt, 15 March, 1842, *JSP*, D9, 257 [Book of Abraham 3:18]; April 11, 1844, *JSP*, Council of Fifty Minutes, 94.

48. "In the context of eternity" was the common phrase to envision the meaningless predicament of mankind. See, for example, Iddo Landau, "The Meaning of Life *Sub Specie Aeterenitatis*."

49. The Book of Mormon, Ether 3. Christ's spirit seems to impress the form of Christ's body. The theme runs through Orson Pratt's picture of body/spirit.

50. Brown, *In Heaven*. Also, Samuel M. Brown and Jonathan A. Stapley, "Mormonism's Adoption Theology: An Introductory Statement."

51. The assertion became canonical with Orson Pratt's 1876 edition of Doctrine and Covenants 130:1–2. Pratt's source text was the ms history. William Clayton's diary entry for the event is the preferred version and is found in *JSP*, J2:403–406.

52. "All spirit is matter." Doctrine and Covenants 131:7. The source is a diary entry by William Clayton, forming content audits of sermons by JS on May 16

JS's idea is perhaps best thought of as an objection to the contradictory world of immaterialism. It staked out a position that the spiritual was, in a common sense way, "real." The classical divide in the Great Chain of Being, the earthy world of flesh and stone where humans lived vs. the immaterial world of God and angels, formed a ranking from the least of existence (rocks) up to man, the highest rung below the great divide between the material and the immaterial. This didn't mark a fundamental divide of existences for JS. It marked the divide between being and nonbeing. The non-material was nothing.[53] Jettisoning the immaterial created some unexamined logical problems that the latter had served to resolve.[54] Questions about the soul (or spirit) such as: does the soul have parts, or can it be divided, or can the soul be destroyed?—these questions were embedded in Latter-day Saint thought from the early post-Nauvoo era. Materiality implies such questions and other, more difficult ones. One of the effects created by JS's erasure of immaterial beings hinged on a flattened cosmos: God was now a being within the world of humans. This flattening had interesting consequences such as a twentieth-century collision with a universe that is not eternal. Could God's home in the cosmos be that impermanent? JS's claim that "that which is without body or

and 17, 1843. A print sermon probably co-authored by JS and editor John Taylor and published on April 1, 1842, gives a more robust account. "Try the Spirits," 743. That spirit was some sort of *substance* was not unique to JS (Dick had suggested related notions, for example) and was connected to the same ideas that Newton struggled with in understanding gravity. See Hylarie Kochiras, "Gravity and Newton's Substance Counting Problem."

53. JS's counter to the Westminster Confession: "that which is without body, parts, and passions is nothing." William Clayton, *Revelations*, 9. Clayton was quoting JS from a January 5, 1841, speech at the opening of the Nauvoo Lyceum. Clayton's diary reads, "that which is without body or parts is nothing."

54. S. Shoemaker, "Immortality and Dualism."

parts is nothing" is no longer the objection. In the modern world, the objection has moved on (see §4.4).

Even by 1842—two years prior to the Follett sermon—critiques of Mormonism had shown knowledge of JS's ideas, perhaps filtered through the Mormon mission publishing effort or various newsprint mentions. J. B. Turner, an Illinois College professor, wrote, "every Mormon is not only to be a god hereafter; he has, in his own belief, *been a demigod from all eternity*."[55] JS's claim that human souls were uncreated, indivisible, Cartesian minds with no beginning or end played a large role in subsequent twentieth-century *internal* (to Mormonism) skepticism over the Follett sermon sources and their redaction. However, it was JS's preaching on God that marked the 1844 Follett sermon as an *external* (Protestant) flash point, along with the revelation on polygamy and a logic first calibrated in what I call "Middle Mormonism," or roughly 1845 to 1890. It is the latter flash point that dominates most scholarship on Mormonism, probably because the published narrative (devotional or otherwise) of modern Mormonism tends to ignore what the official church ignores: JS's story of the soul.[56] The sermon created an important paradox that surfaced at the turn of the twentieth century, as shown in chapter 3. The God of the sermon would surface once again at the end of the twentieth century in the same way, an object of scorn within missionary tools for some conservative Protestants (see chapter 4).

JS's picture of the divine was intuitively Protestant in terms of atonement anthropology—mankind is fundamentally morally flawed and can be rehabilitated only by God. His biblical and visionary picture of human nature (and God) registered in language from the

---

55. Emphasis added. J. B. Turner, *Mormonism in All Ages*, 241.

56. For example, see literary scholar Peter Coviello's *Make Yourselves Gods: Mormons and the Unfinished Business of American Secularism*, 64–67. Coviello follows the basic story of Utah theological structures, often taken for granted as JS's view even in the academic literature that he appeals to.

Westminster Confession as filtered through the frontier American Methodist and Presbyterian preaching of his youth. In the Book of Mormon and JS's biblical revisions, man is almost wholly lacking in redemptive qualities, with the important anti-Calvinist exception that even fallen beings were still competent to choose salvation. JS's later theological positioning among Protestants is characterized in his sermon of March 10, 1844. Old School Calvinism—typified in Princeton's Charles Hodge—entailed that mankind was incapable of doing or thinking anything unalloyed by evil without divine inspiration and that God not only predestined souls to salvation but also to damnation. In JS's environs, this theology was overtaken by New School Calvinism, which allowed for redemptive choice by the individual.[57] In the Follett sermon, JS displays a stark break with even this modified Calvinism (see Appendix A text):

> The soul—the mind of man the immortal spirit all men say God created it in the beginning. The very idea lessens man in my estimation.

This remarkable expression of Kantian nobility puts JS outside much of earlier Christianity, which found man as wholly in need of rescue. The dimension of human dignity that JS advocates here has no need for God, which was partly the fear that motivated twentieth-century critics of Follett within Mormonism (see chapter 3).[58] Creedal Protestant theology announces faith in an immaterial God, but lay

57. On this spiritual anthropology, see, for example, Kern Robert Trembath, *Evangelical Theories of Biblical Inspiration: A Review and Proposal*, 20–21, 45, 75, 78. Also, Joseph Conforti, *Samuel Hopkins and the New Divinity Movement*; Leo P. Hirrel, *Children of Wrath: New School Calvinism and Antebellum Reform*, 26–40. Compare Lyman Beecher, as in Daniel Walker Howe, *What Hath God Wrought: The Transformation of America, 1815–1848*, 164–170. On the March 10, 1844, sermon, see *Parallel Joseph*. See also Marvin S. Hill, "The First Vision Controversy: A Critique and Reconciliation," 51.

58. Immanuel Kant, *Critique of Practical Reason*, 161.

intuitions in prayer life and Bible reading were more friendly to the markers of an Old Testament God who could be seen by a Moses or an Adam and Eve.[59] JS's witness of his ability to see God, angels, and heaven (an early Mormon definition of the *keys of the kingdom*) emphasized that the divine was optically and aurally accessible, passionate, relatable, and involved.[60] While early Mormon thought carried along some denominational Protestant notions of God, for example, Father as spirit, Son embodied, Holy Ghost as the mind of Father and Son, these were on their way to the discard pile by Latter-day Saints in 1840s Nauvoo.[61]

The great Mormon missionary publishers, Parley and Orson Pratt, took to these notions, describing heaven in terms of houses, lands,

---

59. This is illustrated within the culture of JS's New York youth, full of material religious objects like seer stones and the visions of converts in revivals of the Second Great Awakening, a long thread reaching back to things like Michaelangelo's painting (God reaching out to touch Adam) and the Bible's own narrative of incidents of men-like elohim wrestling with the ancients. Among many possible sources, see Benjamin Brown's (1794–1878) Autobiography in "Testimonies for the Truth," (Liverpool, England, 1853).

60. On the early Mormon ideas of keys of the kingdom, see the narration of Edward Partridge's February 1833 sermon on JS's powers reported in a letter by Salmon Sherwood, *Sangamo Journal*, April 6, 1833, 2. Partly this lies behind other early declarations like D&C 107:19. On other meanings, see William V. Smith, "Early Mormon Priesthood Revelations: Text, Impact, and Evolution," 17.

61. On the official early conception of the Trinity, See *JSP*, R&T2: 362–68. On later conceptions, see John G. Turner, *The Mormon Jesus: A Biography*, 35–7, 153–57, 226–228, 232, 283–84; also Steven C. Harper, *First Vision: Memory and Mormon Origins* observes that some early Mormon concepts of God were consistent with JS's 1838 ideas. Joseph Fielding Smith noted the resulting dissonance between some early ideas and the Follett sermon in a meeting of the apostles on November 5, 1917. Fielding Smith eventually played a key role in the reception history of Follett (see chapter 4, below). See Harvard S. Heath, ed., *In the World: The Diaries of Reed Smoot*, 374. On the developing Protestant logic in denominationalism, see Taylor, *A Secular Age*, 325.

streets, wagons, and kin, all resplendent in the unspoiled, perfect humanness described in terms of the best life images of the era.[62] In the Follett address, JS created what may be described as an archaic cosmology, a cosmopolis, a community within the world of matter that included the divine and the human as physical. This community was archaic, in that God was part of the world and not transcendent in the way required by *ex nihilo* creation or neoplatonic thought. JS's picture of God was not just embodied but enfleshed. By 1841, William McIntire's content audit of a Nauvoo, Illinois, lyceum revealed JS responding to the question, "Did the Lord God make the Earth out of Nothing" and showed that Jn 5:19 was already at hand.[63]

> for his own knowledge the Earth was made out of sumthing for it was impossible for a sumthing to be made out of Nothing fire, air, & watter are Eternal Existant principles which are the Composition of which the Earth–Composed; also this Earth has been organized of other Globes that has ben Disorganized; in tistimoney that this Earth was Not the first of Gods work; he quoted passage from the testament where Jesus said all things that he saw the father Do he had done & that he done Nothing But what he saw the father do John the 5th[64]

62. Parley P. Pratt, *Mormonism Unveiled: Zion's Watchman Unmasked*, 27, 31; Parley P. Pratt, *The Millennium, and other Poems: to which is annexed, A Treatise on the Regeneration and Eternal Duration of Matter*; Parley P. Pratt, *An Answer to Mr. William Hewitt's Tract against the Latter-day Saints*, 5, 9. Parley P. Pratt, "Immortality of the Body," in *An Appeal to the Inhabitants of New York*. Benjamin E. Park, "Salvation through a Tabernacle: Joseph Smith, Parley Pratt, and Early Mormon Theologies of Embodiment."

63. Lyceums were community adult education efforts that generally focused on natural sciences often as construed through a religious lens.

64. William Patterson McIntire, "Journal by Wm P McIntire," page 6.

This version of creation already had the Gospel of John in the service of theology as it appeared later in Follett.[65] William Clayton reported a similar expansion of the Johannine text: "That which is without body or parts is nothing. There is no other God in heaven but that God who had flesh and bones. John 5–26, 'as the father hath life in himself, even so hath he given the son to have life in himself'. God the father took life unto himself precisely as Jesus did."[66] This suggested the inescapable Christian analogy that God was once mortal and then subsequently died and was resurrected—JS's deification thought could be yet more defined but somewhat less public: the Holy Spirit, Jesus, and God represented iconic stepping stones, each one a future status in turn for the ultimately deified man. Wilford Woodruff reported JS saying in January 1842,

> the God & father of our Lord Jesus Christ was once as the Son or Holy Ghost both having redeemed a world became the eternal God of that world he had a son Jesus Christ who redeemed this earth the same as his father had a world which made them equal & the HHoly ghost would do the same in his turn & so would all the Saints who inherited a Celestial Glory so their would be Gods many & Lords many their were many mansions even 12 from the abode of Devils to the Celestial Glory All spirits that

65. The eponymous film adaption (2005) of the Douglas Adams's *Hitchhiker's Guide to the Galaxy* novels shows earth being (re)constructed from raw materials via great machines. This visual seems starkly JS in concept.

66. William Clayton "Private Book." L. John Nuttall, "Extracts of William Clayton's Private Book." On problems with dating the Clayton text, see James B. Allen, "Editing William Clayton," 137. Clayton's "private book" mentioned by Nuttall was an aborted publication compiled from his own and others notes of Joseph Smith's Nauvoo teaching. These words were based on JS's remarks given January 5, 1841. For one of the few surviving imprints of Clayton's book, see William Clayton, *Revelations*, 9. "Private" referred to the fact that public distribution was stopped by Brigham Young. See my forthcoming article, "Public and Private—The Balance of Influence in Early Utah Mormonism: William Clayton's Private Book."

> have bodies have power over those that have not hence men have power over Devils &c.[67]

The process is alluded to in Follett at several points and lies at the back of this enigmatic statement in one report of the sermon:

> when you climb a ladder you must begin at the bottom run[g] until you learn the last prin[ciple] of the gospel for it is a great thing to learn Sal[vatio]n beyond the grave & it is not all to be com[prehended] in this world.

These points sketching an anti–*creatio ex nihilo* theology and deification were gathered into the Follett sermon.

The language in all these episodes was distinctly male gendered. The question of how these exalted propositions appealed or applied to women didn't appear explicitly in the Follett sermon and much of JS's preaching; exceptions included his teaching to the women of the Female Relief Society of Nauvoo in 1842 and, somewhat paradoxically, the July 1843 revelation on plural marriage where marital partners who successfully negotiated the sealing ritual eventually become "Gods."[68] The rather rare glimpses in the minutes of those Relief Society sermons were quoted at meetings of the society when it redeveloped in nineteenth-century Utah but hardly anywhere else.[69] I will return to this "god-cycle" theme in the next section.

The idea illustrated by reading Jesus's life as a reflection of God's history became even more concrete after JS's death, with a Mormon version of the domestic heaven being overlaid on God as in Eliza Snow's poem. In some sense, God's divine life per JS was reflected in the ideal nuclear family relationship of antebellum America. The wider movement—of which this was a part—toward a less transcen-

---

67. Wilford Woodruff, "Book of Revelations," 3, MS 23152, CHL.

68. Doctrine and Covenants 132:19–26.

69. See Jennifer Reeder, "The Textual Culture of the Nauvoo Female Relief Society Minute Book."

dent heaven was, according to historian-philosopher Charles Taylor, essential groundwork that led to an exclusive humanism so widespread in the following century.[70] Such was some of the deep irony of the milieu of JS's Nauvoo thought. Since polygamy was a rung on the ladder to the highest Latter-day Saint heaven, it followed that the human-derived God had many wives in heaven. And since Jesus followed in God's footsteps, Jesus must have been a polygamist. The latter was explicitly articulated in Utah preaching.[71] I will argue that the evolving interpretative superstructure of Follett and JS's revelations were deeply affected by the social predicament of Latter-day Saints after JS's lifetime.[72]

All this represented a kind of worship of the *material*—somehow primary in the Mormon cosmology of the era.[73] At this moment, science was moving in the opposite direction. Michael Faraday was just proposing that matter was not in any way "solid" as we intuitively perceive it, as in, you don't fall through the concrete walkway when stepping onto it. Faraday's work led to the claim that "fields"—not matter—constitute the real underlying reality. Everything else, in effect, consists of virtual mathematical consequences. In the next century, physics at the level of the quantum world would posit the same thing. Those pesky electrons, protons, and neutrons are merely mathematical rules prescribed by the Standard Model of microphysics. The Mormon cosmogony has God manipulating matter to create—the preferred term is *organize*—worlds, stars, etc.[74] JS's inspiration to take from his own experience and create a theology that made present life a part of—even the same as—the heavenly world was remarkable, but today the guardians of Mormon doc-

70. See Taylor, *A Secular Age*, 193.

71. Orson Hyde, "The Marriage Relations," October 6, 1854.

72. See below and in Smith, *The Plural Marriage Revelation*, 77, 170–71.

73. The pre-Follett ideas roiled for a time. Givens, *Wrestling the Angel*, 293–297.

74. On the intersection of this materialism with the science revolutions of the twentieth century, see chapters 3 and 4.

trine in the persons of men and women in church leadership are far less adventurous. Indeed, there is a conservative Protestant ethic at work in seeing scripture as absolute boundary, though that emphasis has varied over time.[75]

To understand the context of JS's claims about eternity and what it meant to *be* eternal, it is useful to understand the cultural background of the notion of *time* and how time played into religious, scientific, and everyday thought, all of which were undergoing varying amounts of evolution in JS's era and thereafter. In Christian thought generally, time and eternity were opposing (or at least distinct) realms. Since Augustine, Christian eternity had "God's time," a kind of gathering together of all events, past, present, and future (some Mormon scripture seems friendly here, such as in Moses 6:5–7). God therefore is present and acting every-when.[76] Platonic Greek philosophy saw eternity—including God as the idea or form of the "good"—as a fixed realm of pristine ideas whose material manifestations were but imperfect shadows or "accidents" of their true eternal forms. Mormon thinkers of JS's generation and during the early decades

75. For example, Brigham Young was at the near opposite of this point of view. For him, the current oracle altogether trumped the previous canon. Brigham Young, "Necessity of a Living Testimony," etc., October 7, 1864, *Journal of Discourses* 10:339. Wilford Woodruff, "Necessity of the Living Oracles," April 8, 1862, *Journal of Discourses* 9:324–25. Journal of Wilford Woodruff, minutes of council meeting, January 27, 1860, Kenney, *Wilford Woodruff's Journal*, 5:429–30. Harold B. Lee was more typical of the twentieth century: any *new* teaching had to be confined within the walls of the canon. "If [any church leader] writes something or speaks something . . . that contradicts what is found in the standard works . . . you may know that it is false regardless of who says it." Harold B. Lee, "The Place of the Living Prophet, Seer, and Revelator," July 8, 1964, "Address to Seminary and Institute of Religion Faculty, Brigham Young University." Barlow, *Mormons and the Bible*, 133–135.

76. See Augustine's discussion in *Confessions* XI. Also, Paul in 1 Cor. See Alexandra R. Brown, "*Kairos* Gathered: Time, Tempo, and Typology in 1 Corinthians."

of the twentieth century did not see *eternity* the way that Christian speakers of the first centuries after Christ saw it or the way science would see it in the next century. For the literate, antique, Christian believers, Christ was not contingent, that is, had no beginning or end *in time*, but he was still "begotten." That had to be interpreted by separating "time" from "eternity" in some way so that Christ could be begotten outside of time. In 1840, JS was arguing in a more intuitive way. Things that don't have an origin point can't have an end point, while things that end must have had a beginning. The only way some "thing" can last forever is when it has no beginning (see §4.4). Here JS marked out a dimension midway between the modern, secular notion of time where everything is placed in a linear order,[77] and the platonic, fixed, unmoving eternity. That dimensional middle way was the sempiternal. In JS's late articulation of the cosmos, things never started unless they ended—and therefore that cosmos should—must—have no beginning. This was still the near universal belief in science at the beginning of the twentieth century.[78] For Mormonism to keep JS's sempiternal cosmos in the face of modern science (advances in astronomy and biology), it seemed necessary to some Latter-day Saint

77. Linear order means if event A comes before B and B before C, then A happened before C too: all events can be ordered in this way, at least they could before Einstein, when time was shown to depend on the observer.

78. Einstein was so uncomfortable that his 1915 General Relativity equations could admit of a universe with a beginning (and some sort of end as a consequence) that he added a special term—a tuned *Cosmological Constant*—to guarantee against it. When astronomer Edwin Hubble demonstrated that in fact the universe was changing, and changing drastically in the sense that it had a beginning in what came to be called a "big bang," Einstein relented. On Einstein and also the historical conceptions of the cosmos, see Helge S. Kragh, *Conceptions of Cosmos: From Myths to the Accelerating Universe: A History of Cosmology*, 132–134. On some of the various notions of time and eternity as used here, see Taylor, *A Secular Age*, 46–47, 240–242. For a particularly readable explanation of time in the universe of Einstein, see Jim Holt, *When Einstein Walked with Gödel: Excursions to the Edge of Thought*, 5–7.

leaders (see chapters 3 and 4) to either require some appeal to the transcendent or try to place science at a cautious distance (or even ridicule, as they pointedly did in the case of Darwin). The latter course affected the King Follett Sermon and was affected in turn by it, in the twentieth century, as I will try to show in succeeding chapters.

Finally, it is important to note one more way that JS's claims about matter and cosmos in the Follett sermon interchange with the mundane. JS's notion of time as a linear structure going back forever (no beginning) and on forever (no end), as with his sempiternal souls, assumes outright that there exist completed "infinities," in this case, the life of every soul. These souls are not identified with some Aristotelian form. They are individuals that can engage in reason and experience love, not *eros* perhaps but *agape* seems a part of this scenario—and as for Louisa Follett, JS was hoping to comfort the widow by such hope.[79] Since souls seem to occupy the cosmos as "material" entities, JS had seen darkly a real world populated by examples of what philosopher and mathematician Georg Cantor half a century later said in his profound theory of infinity. At the time, Cantor's work seemed to be an exercise with platonic ideal objects.[80] For JS, everyone is infinite. All humans, by nature, are metaphysicians.

79. The mind/body dualism here is an obvious echo of Descartes. For Descartes, the soul (mind) is a rational being, one that his training in Stoic philosophy saw as blessed with apothea, that is, untroubled by emotion. As later exegetes connected the Follett sermon with passages of scripture like D&C 93:29, the Cartesian view perhaps seemed more attractive.

80. Many thinkers of Cantor's time thought of such mathematical ideas as very real objects. The notion persisted even in the face of the war on metaphysics. For one example, see Rebecca Goldstein, *Incompleteness: The Proof and Paradox of Kurt Gödel*.

§1.3 The Sermon Event, Supporting Texts, and Their Textual Theory

The April 7, 1844, conference had two assigned clerks. Both had experience with longhand reporting, and both delivered aural audits of the proceedings. From the outdoor "pews," several content audits appeared. These pew audits were almost all of second order, meaning that they are reports fleshed out from memory and notes of the event. Some may have been constructed entirely from memory.[81] One first order audit is represented in JS's own journal, written by his secretary, Willard Richards. Richards was not a robust notetaker, but his report often witnesses (and diverges from) the text produced by the two aural audits.

Bullock	**Woodruff**	**Clayton**
I wish to go back to the begin: of creation—it is necessary to know the mind decree & ordinatn. of the great Eloi beging at the creatn. & it is necy. for us to have an understandg.	Go to the morn of creation to understand of the decrees of the Eloheem at the creation. It is necessary for us to have an understanding of God at the beginning, if we get a	First place wish to go back to the beginning of creation. There the starting point in order to fully acquainted with purposes, decrees &c of the Great Eloheim that sits in the hev. for us to

81. First order notes are often made at the event, though they may represent creations of memory. On notetaking, see Ann M. Blair, "Textbooks and Methods of Note-Taking in Early Modern Europe," 39–73.

Bullock	**Woodruff**	**Clayton**
of God in the beging. if we start right it is very easy for us to go right all the time but if we start wrong, it is hard to get right.[82]	good start first we can go right, but if you start wrong you may go wrong.[83]	take up beginning at the creation necessary to understand something of God himself in the beginning. If we start right easy to go right all the time—start wrong hard matter to get right.[84]

Of the higher order audits, one produced by Wilford Woodruff is the longest. Its text seems to represent Woodruff's digest of both his memory and notes of the event. For example, the center column has a part of Woodruff's report, and the left and right columns are the two aural audits, the left column from Thomas Bullock, the right from William Clayton.

The two aural audits have somewhat more verbal agreement than they do with the Woodruff audit. Note that the final thought in the Clayton audit is one of Lorenzo Dow's proverbs, this time about raising children.[85] The two aural audits are likely textually closer to the archetype. The two aural audits are by no means identical here, and this illustrates the reality for—and technique of—longhand reporters. An unfortunate characteristic of nearly any audit, especially one defining a public imprint, is that auditors tend to erase much of orality. Examples that might be spoken with "in other words" might be cut.

---

82. Thomas Bullock report, April 7, 1844, General Church Minutes.

83. Wilford Woodruff journal, April 7, 1844. Note that Woodruff reports the Dow saying (final two phrases) in reverse order from the other audits.

84. William Clayton, April 7, 1844, General Church Minutes.

85. Lorenzo Dow, *Hint to the Public: Thoughts on the Fulfillment of Prophecy in 1811*, as in the compilation, Lorenzo and Peggy Dow, *The Dealings of God, Man, and the Devil*, 114.

Mistakes of pronunciation, pauses filled by non-words ("uhhhh"), colloquialisms, visual cues, and numerous other clues about delivery and meaning are skipped either out of recording difficulties (can't keep up) or discarded by an auditor from prior knowledge ("and so on") or other reasons. All this complicates scholarly work and casts doubt on any "reconstruction." Two more audit comparisons are useful. The first is once again Bullock, then Woodruff, and then Clayton. Each shows important variations from the others; Woodruff is more content audit at this point, while the other two are struggling to repeat the archetype. For example, the following "ladder" illustration was a part of the archetype, though Clayton does not observe it. It gives background to the other texts. Longhand aural auditors didn't (generally) add constructs while attempting to report wording.

W. Richards	**S. Richards**	**Bullock**
It is plain beyond comprehensn. & you thus learn the first prin of the Gospel when you climb a ladder you must begin at the bottom run[g] until you learn the last prin of the gospel for it is a great thing to learn Saln. beyond the grave & it is not all to be com in this world. I sup I am not alld. to go into	Those are the first principles of the gospel. It will take a long time after the grave to understand the whole If I should say anything but what was in the bible the cry of treason would be herd.[86]	This is some of the first principles of the gospel about which so much hath been.— You have got to find the beginning of this history & go on till you have learned the last—will be a great while before you learn the last. It is not all to be comprehended in this world. I suppose that I am not allowed to go into an

86. Wilford Woodruff journal, April 7, 1844. Note that Woodruff reports the Dow saying (final two phrases) in reverse order from the other audits.

W. Richards	S. Richards	Bullock
investign. but what is contd. in the Bible & I think is so many wise men who wod. put me to death for treason I shall turn commentator today.[87]		investigation of anything that is not in the Bible—you would cry treason. So many learned and wise men here—[88]

Consider the following portion of the Follett sermon reports. On the left is Bullock's report, on the right is Clayton's. Bold type indicates the words shared by the two audits.

Bullock	Clayton
know the mind **decree** & ordinatn. **of the great Eloi beging at the creatn**. & it is **necy. for us to** have an **understandg. of God in the beging**.	fully acquainted with purposes, **decrees** &c **of the Great Eloheim** that sits in the hev. **for us to** take up **beginning at the creation necessary to understand** something **of God** himself **in the beginning.**

Bullock wrote, "have an understanding of God" while Clayton penned, "to understand something of God." Bullock wrote, "know the mind" while Clayton has "fully acquainted with purposes." The phrases are materially different and seem to imply a different thought on the part of the speaker. Instead, they likely represent the quick pens of the auditors, struggling to report JS's words in their own fashion and succeeding only in part. "sits in heaven" reappears in several audits and that suggests that JS used the metaphor in his speech.

Theoretically, shorthand notation techniques could have alleviated some of the difficulties here, but examples from the period

87. Thomas Bullock report, April 7, 1844, General Church Minutes.
88. William Clayton, April 7, 1844, General Church Minutes.

show that even the shorthand process could be plagued by similar (though lesser) difficulties of correspondence with their archetypes (see remarks in chapter 2 below).[89]

Richards's audit is quite brief compared to the three noted at the end of the last section. In the example below, the first column contains Willard Richards's notes, the second a report made by Willard's cousin, Samuel Richards, and the third column on the right is Bullock again. The Samuel Richards segment is vital to understanding every longhand speech report. Independently of the other reports, its (probable) compression forfeits precision of thought, opening a wider range of interpretation.

–Is a man like one of yourselves –should you see him to day. you would see a man in fashion and in form. Adam was formed in his likeness.- - -[90]	God: a man like one of us, even like Adam.[91]	God himself who sits enthroned in yonder Heavens is a man like unto one of yourselves who holds this world in its orbit & upholds all things by his power if you were to see him today you wod. see him a man for Adam was a man like in fashion & image like unto him Adam wakd talked & convd. with him as one man talks & com: with anor. in order to speak for the consoln. of

89. See, for example, Rodney O. Davis and Douglas L. Wilson, *The Lincoln–Douglas Debates*, xxix.

90. JS diary, April 7, 1844. Also, *JSP*, J3:217.

91. Samuel W. Richards, "Joseph's Sayings," p. 93.

Bullock	Woodruff	Clayton
		those who mourn for the loss of their friend it is necy. to understand the char. & being of God for I am going to tell you what sort of a being of God.[92]

Bullock's report seems to place JS's thought far from the mechanist Deistic Cosmos of eighteenth-century figures like Washington and Jefferson. God is constantly holding "the world in its orbit," a theology reminiscent of Benjamin's and Alma II's speeches in the Book of Mormon—rather like the seventeenth-century thought of Isaac Newton puzzling over gravity: how did gravity act without some intervening agency? Did God or angels (or devils!) constitute invisible transferers of force between distant masses? JS's revelation, now numbered as section 88 of the LDS Doctrine and Covenants together with the Book of Abraham, seemed to posit something of the sort (see chapter 4 below).[93]

§1.4 The Sermon's Internal Logic and the Beginnings of Its Cultural Place

God's position in JS's theology was progressive. God "came to be God" as a surviving audit put it. Radical as this seemed over against his medieval creationism noted above—and it has sometimes been called the pinnacle of JS's theology—it was less confrontational than it might have been. The *Nauvoo Expositor*, the one-issue critique of

92. "mourn the loss of their friend" is certainly a reference to Louisa.

93. Mosiah 2:21; Alma 30:44. On God's upholding the cosmos, see D&C 88:6–13; Abr. Facsimile No. 2, Explanation 5.

JS's theological, civic, and social practices, hinted at other teaching that went beyond the audits of April 7. One of the claims of the *Expositor*—alongside the more sensational charges of polygamy—was that JS declared a belief in "many Gods" and "that there are innumerable Gods as much above the God that presides over this universe, as he is above us; and if he varies from the law unto which he is subjected, he, with all his creatures, will be cast down as was Lucifer."[94] None of the Follett audits mention innumerable gods above God, nor does the sermon seem to treat the possible fall of God from heaven, together with "all his creatures" though the idea was already present in the Book of Mormon (Alma 42). Perhaps the *Expositor* author was drawing conclusions (some quite reasonable) from the Follett sermon or perhaps he was referencing remarks in other venues. The point is logically related to JS's "anything that has a beginning has an ending" notion. In an April 11, 1844, meeting of the Council of the Kingdom of God, or Council of Fifty, William Clayton reported JS saying, "if God the Father, the Son, and the Holy Ghost were to disagree, the worlds would come clashing together." As it happens, these were relatively modest claims.[95]

JS's teaching in the sermon suggested that human beings could aspire, even *learn* to be as God, centering JS within an Enlightenment picture of Humans as capable in vital ways *within themselves*. Like his teaching about the human soul, his teaching about aspiration and even mechanism to achieve self-divinity did not begin with Follett. Wilford Woodruff's 1842 note demonstrates that JS's thought about God had evolved in parallel to his thinking/inspiration about the

94. The *Expositor*, edited by Nauvoo city council member Sylvester Emmons, was published by former First Presidency member William Law. See *Nauvoo Expositor*, June 7, 1844, 1.

95. *JSP*, Council of Fifty, 93.

soul.[96] The 1842 remarks also suggest that two of JS's apostles, Heber C. Kimball and Brigham Young, were likely influenced by JS's teaching when they elaborated their ideas of multiple probations (a version of reincarnation) and the identity between Adam and God the Father, respectively. Two days before the Follett sermon, JS had given this instruction in a Council of Fifty meeting: "The chairman [JS] explained the meaning of the word 'Ahman' which signifies the first man or first God, and 'Ahman Christ' signifies the first mans son." Such talk was not without ambiguity.[97] As noted above, aside from its deviance from the twentieth-century Latter-day Saint story of God, this cycle of advancement outlines no position whatsoever for women: it was a men-only club, indeed, a white-men-only club.[98] But Mormon women saw deeper links to their gender. Historian Laurel Thatcher Ulrich has written about this carving out a nineteenth-century female space and how women helped write themselves into the story of Latter-day Saint religion, ritual, and politics, gaining voices through their poetry and preaching in safe dialogues among themselves. Those voices achieved broad influence and helped to refocus JS's history of God (see chapter 2 below).[99]

---

96. Woodruff's quotation of JS on "12 mansions" echoes Doctrine and Covenants 88:51–61. It is not evident whether JS meant this as a subdivision of the Three Degrees of Glory canonized in Doctrine and Covenants 76.

97. *JSP*, *Council of Fifty*, 83–84. Also, *JSP*, D2:215, *JSP*, D3:108. On Kimball and successive mortal probations, see Heber C. Kimball, "Condition of the People," etc. and "Journey to the North," etc., *Journal of Discourses*, 1:356, 4:329. On Young teaching that Adam was already resurrected from a previous life, see Wilford Woodruff's journal, January 27, 1860. See also Jonathan A. Stapley, "Brigham Young's Garden Cosmology."

98. On whiteness and salvation, see W. Paul Reeve, *Religion of a Different Color: Race and the Mormon Struggle for Whiteness*.

99. On Mormon women (largely) writing females into the story, see Ulrich, *A House Full of Females*.

That JS did not forget the January 1842 salvific scheme is illustrated by a report of a sermon in August 1843:

> Joseph also said that the Holy Ghost is now in a state of Probation which if he should perform in righteousness he may pass through the same or a similar course of things that the Son has.[100]

In addition to ontological themes that situated God and humans in radical ways, reports of the Follett sermon show it addressed the nature of salvation. Since 1832, and earlier with the Book of Mormon, JS's revelations tinkered in fundamental ways with the foundations of Reformation orthodoxy. The sermon argues that humans are "saved" by at least ritually following in the footsteps of Jesus, who in turn followed the footsteps of God the Father (the 1842 and 1843 teaching include the Holy Ghost as a step in this progressive deification). This treading in the divine path describes a deification scheme largely unique in Christian circles, though it recalls some aspects of Eastern Orthodox traditions, Irenaeus, and perhaps some Unitarianism. JS offered this alternate history of salvation beginning with his narrative of a "Grand Council" in heaven before creation, where God revealed the divine purposes of the earth and a sacramental theology for man. One consequence of this theology for JS was that "Universalism is nothing."[101] People could be damned.

Working out this preexistent council drama, JS appealed to texts like Revelation 12:7–9, "Then war broke out in heaven. Michael and his angels fought against the dragon, and the dragon and his angels fought back. But he was not strong enough, and they lost their place in heaven. The great dragon was hurled down—that ancient serpent called the devil, or Satan, who leads the whole world astray. He was

---

100. Franklin D. Richards, "Scriptural Items."

101. See "Discourse, 3 October 1841, as Reported by Willard Richards," p. 1. Powell, *Ireneaus, Joseph Smith, and the God-Making Heresy.*

hurled to the earth, and his angels with him."[102] This element of the sermon and more generally—the nature of damnation and salvation—share similar textual elements with many other texts from JS: they have both clear and subtle links to the Johannine corpus. In the case of Follett, this is perhaps most evident in its use of the opening of Jn 17: being saved requires that one know God, not simply that "God is love" or that one must be "born of God" but that one must understand the fundamental nature and history of God because salvation in its most profound sense requires one to walk in the path made by God in his *journey* to his Godhood.

In reference to the Revelation passage above, in time, JS rejected the classical angelology. Instead, the preexistent souls of human beings played the role of Michael (the premortal identity of Adam in Latter-day Saint scripture) and his angels. The dragon and his angels were souls who rejected God's plan of mortal testing. JS invoked texts like Hebrews 6, 11, 12 to define the heavenly war as one where the dragon (in later Christian fashion, Satan—Lucifer—the Devil) made war over an implied danger of this testing. A second order audit of the Follett sermon reads,

> no man can commit the unpardonable sin after the dissolution of the body, but they must do it in this world: hence the salvation of Jesus Christ was wrought out for all men in order to triumph over the devil: for if it did not catch him in one place, it would in another, for he stood up as a Savior. The contention in heaven was, Jesus said there would be certain souls that would not be saved, and the devil said he could save them all; the grand council gave in for Jesus Christ: so the devil rebelled against God and fell, and all who put up their heads for him. All sins shall be forgiven except the sin against the Holy Ghost: after a man has sinned against the Holy Ghost there is no repentance for him, he has got

102. Compare JS's early revelation now found in Doctrine and Covenants 29:36–39.

> to say that the sun does not shine, while he sees it, he has got to deny Jesus Christ when the Heavens were open to him, and from that time they begin to be enemies, like many of the apostates of the church of Jesus Christ of Latter day Saints. When a man begins to be an enemy, he hunts me. They seek to kill me; they thirst for my blood; they never cease.[103]

Crucially, the center of the conflict—as told by Follett sermon reports—was that some souls could be damned forever as "sons of Perdition" should they fail the mortal experiment in the most drastic way—it was this mere *possibility* that was rejected by Satan (Moses 4:3) and a host of preexistent souls in heaven.[104]

JS's logic for the pre-creation war in heaven was just partially preserved in later Mormon theology. Another interpretation became dominant instead: Lucifer–Satan wanted to force *all souls* back to God's presence. JS's own reasoning displays an irony that the other rationale does not: by protesting the possible existence of sons of Perdition, Lucifer and his followers brought that fate upon themselves. One higher order content audit of Follett elaborated,

> But Satan, or Lucifer, being the next heir [i.e., after Jesus] and had allotted to him great power and authority even prince of power of the air.[105] He spake immediately and boasted of himself saying send me I can save all and [he] sinned against the Holy Ghost because he accused his brethren and was hurled from the counsel for striving to break the law immediately. There was a warfare with Satan and the gods and they hurled Satan out of his place and all them that would not keep the sayings of the council. But he himself being one of the councilors would not

103. Bullock combined elements of his own aural audit and Clayton's to produce this report found in *Times and Seasons* 5 (August 15, 1844): 612.

104. Some of JS's earliest dictation referenced the ultimate damned. See Alma 39:5–6, for example.

105. Eph 2:2.

> keep the first estate for he was one of the sons of perdition and consequently all the sons of perdition become devils.[106]

Sons of Perdition were first rationalized by JS in an 1832 vision/revelation on salvific rewards (Doctrine and Covenants 76). The irredeemably damned received an important portion of the text, a complex taxonomy of rewards in the afterlife where only the lowest, Perdition, and the highest echelons (Celestial) received exposition, one that JS gradually refined in later years as described above.[107] The Follett sermon rescues humanity from the insecurities of a theology primarily about *restitution* (fix that borrowed plow, return that stolen horse) to one of *reform* based partly on securities of mechanism (performing ritual), and this worked even for the unredeemed dead: it was a theology of intercession on behalf of the dead. Baptism for the dead as expanded by JS performed the same emotional service (but with a Protestant flavor) that Gregory the Great's purgatory did where one could pray for a deceased father or grandmother, a dead child, and so on, and it could speed their way to heaven. One Follett auditor wrote, "it is a great thing to learn salvation beyond the grave." For JS, a part of this meant proxy sacraments for the dead, performing the same function of binding the living to the dead but also the living to each other.

A part of the sermon's background is the early Mormon take on Justification and Sanctification (the latter probably meant as a Finney-like perfectionism) and a widely distributed (male) priesthood.[108] These

106. George Laub reminiscences and journal, 1845 January–1857 April, MS 9628, CHL, entry labeled April 6, 1843. Laub's second order content audit was written from notes/memory in 1845 and may contain elements from other Mormon teaching as well as Laub's interpretation.

107. See Doctrine and Covenants 76:25–49, 50–70; also 29:36–39.

108. Doctrine and Covenants 20:30–31. But also verses 19–29. See "The Mormon Creed." https://www.josephsmithpapers.org/paper-summary/articles-and-covenants-circa-april-1830-dc-20/1#source-note

were *a priori* correct in the earliest Mormon catechistic belief.[109] A developing departure from Protestant fears of prelate tyranny, the Mormon conception of priesthood was partly democratic in nature, at least in its beginnings. "Priesthood" evolved to a strictly top-down system by the twentieth century, though it continued the inherent Protestant struggle between the priesthood of believers found in the Mormon post-baptism laying on of hands for the "gift of the Holy Ghost" and the priesthood of ordination.[110] These matters lay behind the Follett sermon's insistence on knowledge and order as the bases of salvation.

JS reasoned that soteriological provisions were required for the unevangelized dead, a theme supported by the last topic of the Follett sermon (baptism). JS's inspiration dictated that a preexisting heavenly plan legislated certain rites, demonstrating submission to God's will and acting as gateways that conferred salvific power, through Jesus, on mankind. Mormon proxy baptism for the dead, introduced in 1840, represented the fixed position of God. All must abide by the rites and ordinances, or at least decide whether to accept them, a somewhat different view of the afterlife than the one JS announced in an 1836 vision of his brother Alvin. JS was shocked by a vision of Alvin in heaven. The heavenly voice declared that anyone of the dead *who* would *have accepted authoritative baptism if they had the chance* would be saved in Celestial glory.[111] JS delivered the pronouncement

---

109. See Doctrine and Covenants, section 20. Also *JSP*, D1:113–21, 368–77. On Finney, a contemporary of JS, perfectionism–holiness, and Arminianism, see Charles Hambrick-Stowe, *Charles G. Finney and the Spirit of American Evangelicalism*, 1–35, 165–98.

110. While today's Latter-day Saints routinely ordain every male, there was nothing in JS's early revelations that mandated this. Indeed, a large fraction of early Mormon men *were* ordained but by no means all. Articles of Faith 4, 5, Pearl of Great Price. Stapley, *The Power of Godliness*, ch. 4.

111. Perhaps to soften any *this life* only narrative that may be inferred from JS's 1843 revelation on polygamy and JS's sermon of April 8, 1844 (the day after Follett),

that baptism would still be necessary, only that the all-seeing eye of God could determine the outcome of a counterfactual. If a person *would* have received baptism, then they would merit passage through the heavenly gates. The logic of JS's proxy ordinances for the dead replaced the all-seeing eye with the knife edge of in-the-moment personal choice after death—no Calvinist judgement was involved. From a second order content audit of the Follett sermon,

> those who die without the obedience of the gospel here will have to obey it in the world of spirits for so long as they do not obey they will be miserable and as if they were in torment of fire and brimstone. Thus is the signification of torment[112]

The end of the Follett sermon was devoted to the Protestant battle over baptism (was it salvific—or just a denominational preference?) and the Mormon thought around it, as necessary to salvation—a foundation pointing to other statements in the address. Clayton left the entire segment out of his audit.[113] Wilard Richards noted that the Follett sermon began at 3:15 pm and ended at 5:30 pm, and the discussion of baptism was not an insignificant part.[114] Baptism was a major

---

and passages like D&C 76:73–74, LDS leaders added this January 1836 vision to the 1981 Doctrine and Covenants as section 137. On Alvin and some of the theological reasoning in the developing background, see Grant Underwood, "Baptism for the Dead: Comparing RLDS and LDS Perspectives," 102–103.

112. GL1. The logic of mental torment was present in the Book of Mormon, Mosiah 3:25–27.

113. On baptism, see Turner, *The Mormon Jesus*, 210–11. Matthew Bowman, *The Mormon People: The Making of an American Faith*, 231.

114. Lengthy addresses were common in antebellum preaching. Published sermons could reach many pages in length. A typical New England Sunday service was divided into two sessions, morning and afternoon. Each session involved the church minister preaching for an hour. Methodist camp meetings might have hours of preaching and then more exhortation—and last for days. The length made it worthwhile for rural people who had to travel most of a day to attend. Famed British Baptist preacher Charles Haddon Spurgeon preached two-hour sermons.

feature of church from its outset; it defined the parameters of authority, the power of rites and rituals, and later, the institutional purpose of the church—that is, as a shell in which the temple theology could flourish.[115] JS's argument with the popular denominations of the American Protestant spectrum originated in part from what he saw as a misapprehension of ordinances or sacred rites. Baptism could only be performed by a "legal" actor—a priest who was ordained by angels or their agents, not conferred by the congregation, except in a passive sense, but traceable much like a compressed version of Catholic papal lines to ancient ordination. Salvation was impossible without baptism. Crucially, in JS's revelations, even Old Testament elites had undergone Christian baptism.[116] Without it, heavenly acceptance was ultimately impossible. Since JS rejected Calvinist ideas of predestined salvation and damnation, the fundamental place of human freedom was to receive or reject the Gospel. Justice required a provision for the ignorance of past generations and hence came a joining of past and present through the proxy baptism of one's ancestors.

Baptism for the dead reinforced the Mormon logic of baptism as a salvific necessity and at the same time rationalized JS's 1836 vision of his brother Alvin, noted above. The dead could be evangelized by knowledgeable souls in the afterlife, and upon acceptance of the Gospel and their proxy baptism, this would make the dead equal to

---

William Ellery Channing's famous 1819 Baltimore address on Unitarianism went for an hour and a half. On Spurgeon, see Lewis Drummond, *Spurgeon: Prince of Preachers*, 250. Beth Barton Schweiger, *The Gospel Working Up: Progress and the Pulpit in Nineteenth-Century Virginia*, 36. On Camp meetings and Channing, see Howe, *What Hath God Wrought*, 177, 613. On New England, see Peter Benes, *Meetinghouses of Early New England*, 31–33.

115. See JS's sermon of June 11, 1843. *Parallel Joseph. JSP*, D12:379–396.

116. For example, Pearl of Great Price, Moses 6.

living believers.[117] Salvation was thus on the line in two ways for the living and dead in Mormonism. JS saw that baptism performed by proxy for one's dead ancestors linked that ancestor to the living proxy. He invoked Old Testament Malachi's words, God would send "Elijah the Prophet. . . . And he shall turn the heart of the fathers to the children, and the heart of the children to their fathers, lest I come and smite the earth with a curse." JS placed baptism in this connecting role.[118]

At the beginning of his sermon, JS told his audience that he was aiming toward a discussion of the "resurrection of the dead" but the audits only briefly approached that topic. Instead, the audits speak of preparing for resurrection and lay emphasis on the age-old problem of identity. Do the resurrected preserve their identity? If you get a new body, is it really you again? JS approached the problem more directly once by claiming that the bodies of the dead are "tagged" material. Every "particle" of one's body never becomes part of another body. So in its resurrection, the body is rebuilt from precisely the same material it had (at death?).[119] JS solves the identity dilemma another way—at least in part—by denying the contingency of the self; the soul has continuity. This brought the sermon into conversation with a vigorously contested philosophical and, eventually, scientific world.[120]

---

117. Biblical authority was cited in Paul's first letter to the Corinthians (15:29) joined with 1 Peter 3:18–22, 4:5–6.

118. See, for example, one of JS's canonized (written) discourses in Doctrine and Covenants 128:18. Also, Appendix A and notes there. JS would retranslate the passage on a number of occasions, in this case substituting "seal" for "turn."

119. Sometimes called "extreme resurrection." JS sermon of April 7, 1843. *JSP*, D12:174–180.

120. JS deliberately continued the Follett sermon on three other occasions. Most important are the Sunday sermons of May 12, 1844, and June 16, 1844. For transcriptions, see *Parallel Joseph*. His sermon on April 8 may also be seen as a continuation of the April 7 sermon, pressing for a new but less vulnerable concept of Zion, one more capable of encoding social, theological, and political change. On the problem of resurrection, see, for example, Raymond Martin and John Barresi, *The Rise and*

Gottfried Wilhelm Leibniz (1646–1716) proposed the principle of *Sufficient Reason* to explain the variety of existence. Leibniz would have seen JS's rejection of contingency as a logical error. Uncreated (self-existent) souls made each person a "brute fact" unexplained by argument. Such a multitude of unexplained beings felt *ad hoc*. A long series of philosophers, mathematicians, and ironically the Book of Mormon itself sought to argue from the existence of the world to derive the fact of a single, self-existent being, First Cause, or God.[121] Leibniz argued that Sufficient Reason meant that features of the world *require* explanation.[122] Any contingent fact, such as the color of one's eyes, which might show any number of possibilities, requires us to examine *why is it so*? Logical excursions, filed as Cosmological Arguments that seek to answer such questions, are ubiquitous throughout history. JS's own beliefs supported such an idea. But the asymmetries of his thought-world broke the logical train.[123] There could not be a single foundational being behind the existence of everything. Everyone has a bottomless history—a deep genesis lost in an infinite past within themselves. The Follett sermon and its predecessor teaching not only asserts that *beings-souls-minds* are uncreated, it makes the same assertion about matter. Like person-consciousness, the material world could be shaped but never wink out of existence. This presages the eventual deeper sci-

---

Fall of Soul and Self, 56–57. On persisting questions of identity, see Jacob Berger, "A Dilemma for the Soul Theory of Personal Identity."

121. Parley Pratt made the same argument in his 1839, "The Regeneration and Eternal Duration of Matter."

122. Yitzhak Melamed and Martin Lin, "Principle of Sufficient Reason."

123. The claim that "design" must imply a Designer is precisely the one that was discarded by many post-Deism thinkers. Why does order necessitate something that caused such order? They rightly pointed out that this is not logic, it is analogy from human experience: we see a house and believe a builder existed at some point who built the house. The transfer of improbabilities (the house was always there, a wind storm threw it together, etc.) doesn't scale well to twentieth-century physics.

entific confrontations in the twentieth century with biology, physics, and astronomy where the Follett sermon formed a background for the interface with science (see chapters 3 and 4). For JS, God's existence rested on the same ontological grounds as that of humanity. There is *some* aspect of logical necessity here (§4.4).

Finally, in JS's view, outlined in his February 5, 1840, sermon, for example, God is omniscient. The leap from limited being to all-knowing status is a tall one. Things don't "happen" to an all-knowing being. That is still central to Mormon Christology (Jesus *allowed* himself to be taken and put to death). If something else brought about such a God, it could only be that God allowed it to do so. There is a strange reverse discontinuity here. One can see Anselm's desire for an ontological proof for God's existence. Again, there is just one (internal) explanation: JS's cosmopolis of Gods and humans is a brute fact. For JS, the world was in many respects irreducible and, thus, deeply miraculous in a sense that is quite alien to the usual "religious" meaning of miracle. The world is irrational in the sense that human souls/spirits/minds are not the products of any creative act nor are they explainable; they simply exist as permanent metaphysical points. Twentieth-century critics of the Follett sermon saw this clearly and found it deeply troubling (chapter 3).[124]

When the Follett sermon audits finally and briefly approach the mechanics of resurrection, they make a fateful claim. JS had long held

124. JS was familiar with Clarke's *Commentary* and certainly Clarke's introduction to Genesis, where Clarke announced a Cosmological Argument, and that the source of all explanations must be the one and only self-existent being in evidence: God. Adam Clarke, *The Holy Bible, Containing the Old and New Testaments: The Text with a Commentary and Critical Notes, Volume 1*, 27. That JS ran around Clarke is reminiscent of his apparent treatment of Lorenzo Dow and Thomas Dick. On Clarke's possible influence and connection to JS, see, for example, Thomas A. Wayment and Haley Wilson-Lemmon, "The Use of Adam Clarke's Bible Commentary in Joseph Smith's Bible Translation."

that children who died before the age of responsible choice were not only not subject to the proxy ritual provisions of the Grand Council, they would be resurrected and inhabit heaven. Moreover, the audits repeat another of JS's themes, that their body-age at their resurrection would be the same at the moment of their death. *And they would continue in that state, reigning on heavenly thrones forever.* Internal to Mormon thought, the notion is problematic on several counts—an 1843 revelation (section 132 of the Doctrine and Covenants) had defined the sacrament of marriage extending into the infinite future (called sealing in parallel parlance) as one fixed requirement for the ultimate salvific fate. The Follett statement and its antecedents wrought a mental picture of tiny infants with godlike capacity and power—but were they banned forever from what was (at that point, still undercover in the narrowly circulated 1843 revelation) the ideal heavenly state? Evidently, JS's picture of the hereafter was more complex than that implied by the 1843 polygamy revelation. The post-mortal status of resurrected children made them odd participants in a glorious domestic drama, one that eventually centered in ever-expanding patriarchal dynasties that populated new worlds in a never-ending work. A powerful theological strain developed over time in response to such theological stresses.[125]

First in the pulpit, and then in the pews, this idea of restoration-resurrection was extended to include every age cohort. The elderly would be resurrected in their death age-form, etc. JS discussed resurrection mechanics, as an explicit continuation of Follett, in a May 12, 1844, sermon and, echoing Book of Mormon texts, auditor Thomas Bullock wrote,

> in order for you to receive your children to yourself, you must have a promise, some ordinance, some blessing in order to ascend above principalities or else it [the child] may be an

125. See Doctrine and Covenants 132:16–17.

> angel—they must rise just as they died—we can't here hail our lovely infants with the same glory, the same loveliness in the celestial glory where they all enjoy alike—they differ in stature, in size—the same glorious spirit gives them the likeness of glory and bloom—the old man with his silvery hairs will glory in bloom & beauty[126]

All these ideas in the Follett sermon made it a fulcrum that balanced ontic intermediaries like the nature of something vs. nothing (captured in JS's theology of minds/spirits), and his construction/revelation of new divine histories, over against the questions, policies, and controversies in Mormonism in the following century. These and other points of the sermon played a role in a plan by the 1850s church historians (see chapter 2) to reconstruct JS's oral expression into somewhat acontextual word pictures to define the early Mormon world for future generations. The forthcoming history (really annals) provided little in the way of understanding the influences, texts, dimensions, and wider external events and cultural climates that may have led JS to say and do much of what the history recounted (and what it failed to report). The Follett sermon made a controversial return when the 1850s history of JS was printed in book form during the opening decade of the twentieth century (chapter 3).

§1.5 The *Times and Seasons* Text Tradition

The proceedings of the Special Conference of April 5–9, 1844, were intended for the press from the outset.[127] It was common practice to

126. For the May 12 sermon as a continuation of Follett, see Smith, *Every Word Seasoned With Grace*, ch. 9. The Bullock audit survives within a higher order text found in Joseph Smith Collection, 1827–1844, MS 155, Reel 3, Box 4, fd. 6. CHL.

127. In an effort to encourage support for the two major church building projects, the temple and a corporate hotel to be called the Nauvoo House, JS canceled future regular "general" conferences of the church until they could be held within

publish conference minutes in the Nauvoo church paper. One of the conference clerks, Bullock, was assigned by church apostles to take his own audits of the conference and use them with William Clayton's report to create a single record, to appear in the biweekly Nauvoo *Times and Seasons*. *Times* editor John Taylor spent a day before the sermon practicing German and Hebrew, possibly with advance notice from JS. After the sermon, Taylor again met with Bullock, probably advising him how to compose his manuscript for printing.[128] In the Follett sermon, JS appealed to an argument based on his rudimentary knowledge of Hebrew; rendering a coherent version of this was a challenge for auditors.[129] Short segments of Bullock's commissioned conference minutes began to appear serially with the May 1, 1844, issue of the paper.[130] Through August, other issues of the paper were occupied either with campaign literature for JS's candidacy for president of the United States or the turmoil generated by his death. Moreover,

---

the walls of the temple. Conferences continued on their now-regular April and October timetables, but they were now called "special" conferences. On JS's declaration, see the end of his speech of October 3, 1841, as redacted in *Times and Season* 2, no. 24 (October 15, 1841): 578. Also see *Parallel Joseph*.

128. On April 6, 1844, Bullock was practicing German and Hebrew with John Taylor. Bullock attended the conference meetings as an official reporter, April 6, 7, 8, 9, 1844. He was assigned by the apostles to arrange minutes for printing, April 10, 1844. April 23, 24, 25 Bullock is writing minutes. Bullock continued composing the minutes on April 26, 28, 1844. Later, he carried 30 pages of fair copy minutes to John Taylor, editor of the *Times and Seasons*. See Historical Department office journal 1844–2012, CHL, under those dates. When the 1856 clerks were instructed to flesh out JS's June 16, 1844, remarks, they simply copied Follett's language discussion that had been constructed in 1855 from VOT, which came from TS. See Smith, *Every Word Seasoned With Grace*, ch. 10.

129. For a discussion of the elements of this argument as it appears in the edited version of Follett ca.1856, see Kevin L. Barney, "Joseph Smith's Emendation of Hebrew Genesis 1:1," 103–135.

130. "Conference Minutes," *Times and Seasons*, May 1, 1844.

editor Taylor had been severely wounded in the Carthage attack that killed JS and his brother Hyrum.

The Bullock-redacted Follett sermon finally appeared in print in the August 15, 1844, issue of the *Times and Seasons* (not printed until September). His work, executed by combining his and William Clayton's audits of the sermon, initiated the earliest among three eventual imprint traditions. Some of the daughter texts spawned by the August imprint are summarized in the stemma found in Figure 1. Bullock's manuscript of the fusion text for the conference is not extant.[131] In the table below, the left column is an excerpt from Bullock's original audit, the center column is from Clayton's audit of the same portion of the sermon. On the right is Bullock's fusion text.

Bullock	**Clayton**	**Fusion text**
it is of the greatest importance & the most solemn of any that cod. occupy our attentn. & that is the subj of the dead on the dece of our bror. Follit who was crushed to death in a well—	Subject of the greatest importance and most solemn that could occupy our attention. the subject of the dead been requested to speak on the subject on the decease of bro Follet who was crushed to death &c—	It is of the greatest importance, and the most solemn of any that can occupy our attention, and that is, the subject of the dead; on the decease of our brother Follett, who was crushed to death in a well,

131. Printer's manuscripts were often destroyed during or after typesetting, a practice dating from the earliest presswork. Ann M. Blair, *Too Much to Know: Managing Scholarly Information Before the Modern Age*, ch. 4. Sermons provide an interesting window to authorial care and redactive jealousies for preachers who published their own sermons. JS's picture of prophetic work mirrored the Jeremiah/Jesus model. His work was separate from the scribal pen.

Bullock	**Clayton**	**Fusion text**
	I have been requested to speak by his friends	I have been requested to speak by his friends
& inasmuch as there are a great many in this congre who live in this city & who have lost friend	& relatives & inasmuch as great many here in con-- who live in this City as well as elsewhere who have	and relatives, and inasmuch as there are a great many in this congregation who live in this city, as well as
	deceased friends feel disposed to speak on	elsewhere, and who have lost friends, I feel
I shall speak in genl. & offer you my ideas so far as I have ability & so far as I shall be inspd. by the H S. to dwell on his subjt. I want your prayer faith the inspn. of Alm God	the subject in general and offer my ideas as far as ability & as far as inspired by H. S. Want your prayers faith the inspiration of Almighty God the Gift of H. S. that I may set	disposed to speak on the subject in general, and offer you my ideas so far as I have ability, and so far as I shall be inspired by the Holy Spirit to dwell on this subject. I want your
to say things that are true & shall	forth truth things that can easily be comprehended	prayers and faith, the instruction of Almighty
	and will carry	God and the
carry the testimony to your hearts	the testimony to your hearts.	gift of the Holy Ghost, that I may set forth things that are true, that can easily be comprehended, and shall carry the testimony to your hearts;[132]

Bullock's editorial work as shown in this section is typical. Where his audit differed slightly from Clayton, he used his own text for the report. Where Clayton had more detail, Bullock usually deferred to him. Significant portions of the two aural audits are nearly identical. Textual witnesses of the Follett sermon suggest that Bullock's fused

132. "Conference Minutes," *Times and Seasons* (August 15, 1844): 613.

text in the *Times* was a reasonable representation of the sermon in two ways. It displayed apparently archetypal words from JS and it was relatively complete in terms of the subjects of the sermon. Little was left in the air, so to speak, though none of the audits come close to relaying every word. The sermon was over two hours in length, but even a "dictation speed" reading of the longest aural audit does not approach two hours (see Appendix A below). A careful comparison of the reports shows that neither clerk could keep up with JS. The Clayton and Bullock audits are more robust in some portions than in others. A comparison of the two suggests how they left out or summarized material on the fly. Gaps in coverage were often indicated by a dash.[133] Unfortunately, imprints of the sermon generally erased such clues.

After the August (September) 1844 printing of Bullock's fusion text, an edition of that *Times* text appeared in the church's British Mission print organ/serial, the *Latter-day Saints' Millennial Star* (MS1). The following year, William W. Phelps and John Taylor printed a version of the *Times* text as part of a collection of political documents called the *Voice of Truth* (VOT). Intended as campaign literature for JS's presidential run, thousands of copies of the VOT were printed for distribution in population centers. With JS's death in June 1844, a redacted version of the *Times* Follett sermon (the redactions make the VOT version easily identifiable as a source text in later editions) was added to the VOT to salvage the material for distribution to the church with the hope of recouping costs and memorializing JS's life and thought. The VOT was largely a compilation of ghostwritten or collaborative material for JS's presidential campaign. When it became a memorial, its audience became internal, with a few important excep-

133. See Appendix C which can be explored online at http://boap.org/LDS/KFS-Appendices/Appendix-C and a new construction of the sermon in §5 of that chapter which I have taken as a basis for the text of the sermon found in Appendix A at the end of this book. For the source for Appendix A, see http://boap.org/LDS/KFS-Appendices/Appendix-F.

tions noted in chapter 3, below. A wrapper was printed with a table of contents to note the added presence of the sermon, which was labeled as JS's "last sermon." It was not his last sermon, but the title stuck.[134] Thirty years later, Isaiah Combs wrote,

> At 4 o'clock this P. M. preached the funeral sermon of Bro. McCall's babe. Myself and wife took supper at Bro. Hardy's after which sister Hardy and her sister who is visiting her, Sister Commings came to our house and we have been enjoying a good time reading the last sermon of the Prophet Joseph Smith and some of his correspondence also in conversing on some principles of the gospel.[135]

It was almost surely the VOT version of Follett that Isaiah Combs read in 1875, just as it was almost surely VOT that was read to the Thirtieth Quorum of Seventy on that cold January evening of 1848. As Combs had read the sermon in 1875, church missionaries copied VOT into their journals.[136]

In the end, the Follett sermon's contents (only portions are considered in any detail in this book) may best be thought of more as a kind of fractal version of spiritual reality than some avatar of a perfect text from a higher realm. Such a visual hermeneutic appeals in many of JS's productions, such as the Book of Mormon and his later and longer revelations encoded in church canon: the January 19, 1841, revelation now known as Doctrine and Covenants Section 124 is perhaps

---

134. Peter L. Crawley, *A Descriptive Bibliography of the Mormon Church, vol. 1*, item 271.

135. Isaiah M. Combs, diary, Monday September 27, 1875. For a missionary copy of VOT, see Walter E. Hanks notebook, 1888, 1–17.

136. The *Times and Seasons* text had small circulation. MS1, DN, may have existed in isolated Utah, though their circulation at the time was small as well—the more likely text was VOT with more than ten thousand copies available. *Voice of Truth* contained some JS correspondence. Combs apparently never went to England, so a British imprint seems unlikely. Crawley, *Descriptive Bibliography*, 1:271.

a prime example. This fractalization becomes more apparent in the critical text found in Appendix A below, where I present an edition of the sermon represented both by the agreement and the disagreement of its source audits.

§1.6 King Follett Sermon Sources, Editions, Abbreviations, and a Timeline.

Since I will refer to many of the manuscripts and imprints of Follett below, I will summarize their bibliographic data here and give a graphical representation of many of these texts in a stemma. I then give a brief timeline for the sermon. These tools will be useful in situating the content of later chapters.

An Abbreviated Enumerative Bibliography: Manuscripts and Selected Editions of the Sermon Text.

The context for many of the entries below will be described in succeeding chapters. See the timeline below for some additional imprints.

1. King Follett Sermon, JS's funeral (memorial) address for King Follett, delivered on the afternoon of Sunday April 7, 1844, at a Special Conference of the church.
2. TB. Thomas Bullock's conference minutes of the sermon. TB was docketed by Bullock probably near or at the time of the report. Cataloged as CR 100 318, Box 1, fd. 19, CHL. Custody of the minutes seems to have been shared by Bullock and Willard Richards initially and the minutes then formed part of the corpus of church records, packed and transported to Utah, beginning in 1846 (see remarks at entry 4).

3. WC. William Clayton's conference minutes of the sermon. CR 100 318, Box 1, fd. 19, CHL. On custody, see TB.
4. WR. Willard Richards' report of the sermon as entered in the JS diary for April 7, 1844. MS 155, Box 1, fd. 8, CHL. The JS diaries for the period of Follett were in Richards's possession. They likely remained in his custody until they were packed in boxes of materials that were then transported from Nauvoo in 1846. The JS diaries were filed at the new church historian's office in Salt Lake City, November 6, 1855. The diary entry for WR may have been penned at the time of the sermon's delivery, April 7, 1844. Richards had reserved six pages of the diary for his report prior to the sermon. He did not intend a detailed audit.[137]
5. WW. Wilford Woodruff's second order audit, expanded from his notes of Follett. That expansion appears in his journal under the date of April 7, 1844, and which is presently filed as MS 1352, Box 2, fd. 1, CHL. Woodruff's journal largely remained in his custody until his death in 1898. The clerks of the church historian's office in Utah borrowed the early diaries on occasion to copy historical material from them, in particular Woodruff's audits of JS's sermons, including WW.
6. SR. Samuel W. Richards's notes of the sermon. Samuel W. Richards notebook. Box 1, fd. 1, MS 1841, CHL. Richards copied SR from another source, his own notes possibly, thus it is at least a second order

137. For more information on the JS diaries, see *JSP*, J1: xliii–lvii; *JSP*, J2: xiii-xxxii.

manuscript. Richards's notebooks were donated to CHL in 1959 by a descendant. Prior to that time the notebooks were evidently in the custody of the Richards family.

7. GL1–2. Two higher order content audits of the sermon by George Laub. Laub made two manuscripts, one submitted to church historians ca. 1855, one kept in his possession and later donated to church archives. Both content audits are now preserved in CHL as portions of MS 9628 (GL1, here), "George Laub reminiscences and journal. 1845" and MS 1983 (GL2 here), "George Laub reminiscences and journal, 1845–1846." The early provenance of the notebooks is not clear, though both claim composition in 1845. MS 9628 appears to be the earlier of the two compositions with respect to Follett. GL2 is likely an edition of GL1. MS 9628 was probably composed of various individual manuscripts supplemented by memory. MS 9628 was donated to CHL by Laub descendants in 1988.
8. TS. Thomas Bullock's April 1844 conflation of his own conference minutes (TB) with those of William Clayton (WC) for the sermon. TS appeared in the *Times and Seasons* (Nauvoo, Ill.) 5, no. 15 (August 15, 1844): 612–17, hence the designation (actually the August issue did not appear until September—the print shop personnel were all ill with Nauvoo's summer complaint). Editor of record, John Taylor.
9. MS1. A mildly edited reprint of TS appearing in the church's Liverpool, England, publication, *Latter-day Saints' Millennial Star* 5, no. 6 (November 1844): 87–93. Editor of record, Thomas Ward.

10. VOT. W. W. Phelps/John Taylor redaction of TS for the memorial pamphlet *The Voice of Truth*, distributed in 1845, Nauvoo, Illinois.
11. ZW. A reprint of VOT in the Sydney, Australia, Mormon serial, *Zion's Watchman* 1, no. 32–33 (April 12, 1855): 249–56. Edited by Augustus Farnham.
12. GM0. Jonathan Grimshaw's fusion of VOT with WW and WR, carried out during the first weeks of October 1855. MS 155, Box 4, fd. 6, CHL
13. GM1. Descended from GM0 as edited by George A. Smith, Brigham Young, Thomas Bullock, Grimshaw, and perhaps by others, November 1855. MS 155, Box 4, fd. 6, CHL.
14. RC. The version of GM1 entered into the Manuscript History of the Church (hereafter, ms history) by Robert Lang Campbell, April 1856. CR 100 102, 6:1968–79, CHL.
15. DN. The first imprint of RC appeared in *The Deseret News* (Salt Lake City, Utah) 7, no. 18 (July 8, 1857): 1, edited by the church historian's staff.
16. MS2. Reprint of DN in *Latter-day Saints' Millennial Star* (Liverpool, England) 23, no. 17 (April 20, 1861): 245–48; 23, no. 18 (April 27, 1861): 262–64; 23, no. 19 (May 4, 1861): 279–80. Editor of record George Q. Cannon.
17. CON. Reprint of MS2 in the church's magazine for male youth, *The Contributor* (Salt Lake City) 5, no. 7 (April 1883): 252–61, Editor of record, Junius F. Wells.
18. R1. *The Improvement Era* (Salt Lake City), the church's magazine for men and male youth of the period, printed a B. H. Roberts edited version of MS2 in its January 1909 issue (12, no. 3): 169–91.

Roberts took some liberties with the text, omitting material and changing a few words, which he may have regarded as archaic or incorrect. He also added footnotes, many of which survived in later printings as well as other texts. R1 began a new text tradition of Follett.

19. R2. *Liahona The Elders' Journal* (Independence, Missouri) 9, no. 24 (December 5, 1911): 369–79, 382–83. An edition of R1. Editor of record, Joseph A. McRae. The Journal planned to distribute 12,000 copies of the issue because of a large demand from subscribers.[138]
20. R3. An edition of the R1 printed by Magazine Printing Co. (Salt Lake City), 1913(?), edited by B. H. Roberts (10,000 copies, reprinted 1926, and subsequently (see the timeline below).
21. R4. A version of R1 which appeared in *Teachings of the Prophet Joseph Smith* (Salt Lake City: Deseret News Press, 1938), 342–62, edited by Joseph Fielding Smith.
22. R5. An edition of R1 appeared in the second revised edition of *History of the Church* (Salt Lake City: Deseret Book Co., 1952), 6:302–17. Titular editor, Joseph Fielding Smith.
23. R6. An edition of R5 appeared in the *Ensign* (Salt Lake City), a then-new monthly magazine of The Church of Jesus Christ of Latter-day Saints, April and May, 1971 issues. Editor of record, Doyle L. Green.

---

138. The First Presidency intervened to prevent distribution but were too late to stop the distribution of several thousand copies. In the following issue, December 12, 1911, the *Liahona* printed a sermon by Charles Penrose that set out a counter-theology.

Timeline

1844

April 7. The Follett sermon is delivered at 3:15 pm west of the temple construction site, Nauvoo, Illinois.

April 7. TB, WC, WR composed during the address.

April 10. Thomas Bullock receives the assignment to ready minutes of the conference for publication in the Nauvoo *Times and Seasons*.

April 23–26. Thomas Bullock composes minutes of the April 5–9 conference, fusing TB and WC for the Follett sermon report.

April 25. Thomas Bullock meets with *Times and Seasons* editor John Taylor, possibly to flesh out JS's Hebrew discussion in the sermon.

June 27. JS is assassinated at Carthage, Illinois.

August 15. TS publishing date in the *Times and Seasons,* and it was not printed until September due to illness among the printing staff.

November. TS is reprinted in Liverpool, England, in *Latter-day Saints' Millennial Star* (this is MS1).

1845

The bulk of the *Voice of Truth* was printed in 1844, but an edited version of TS (VOT) is added, creating a revised version of *Voice of Truth* in 1845. The booklet's original purpose had to do with JS's campaign for the US presidency.

January. William W. Phelps publishes a hymn, *A Voice From the Prophet: Come to Me*. (Speaks of a Mother in heaven).

May. William W. Phelps publishes a story, *Paracletes*. (Speaks of spirits born in heaven).

October. Eliza R. Snow publishes a poem, *My Father in Heaven*. (Speaks of a Mother in heaven).

1846

February 3–5. Thomas Bullock and Willard Richards packs church minutes including TB and WC for the journey west beyond the United States.

[*9 years*]

1855

April 12. VOT appears in the church mission periodical *Zion's Watchman* (ZW) in Sydney, Australia (this was the final "church" printing of TS, but see 1903 and 1974 below).

October 3–10. Jonathan Grimshaw uses VOT together with TB, WC, WW, and WR to compile GM0.

October–November. George A. Smith and Thomas Bullock and perhaps others review and redact GM0 creating GM1.

November 18. GM1 is reviewed and revised by Brigham Young with the assistance of Bullock.

1856

April. Robert Campbell cancels a copy of TS in the ms history and after the cancelled text, he inserts a copy of GM1, creating RC.

August 9. Brigham Young, Jedediah M. Grant, Wilford Woodruff, and Leo Hawkins review RC. Hawkins adds a notation to the head of RC regarding sources used in its creation but makes no mention of its most significant source, VOT.

1857

July 8. RC is printed in *The Deseret News* (DN) as part of the continuing publication series of the ms history under the earlier *Times and Seasons* rubric, "History of Joseph Smith."

Franklin D. Richards publishes a book for mission work, *A Compendium of the Faith and Doctrines of the Church of Jesus Christ of Latter-day Saints*. Richards quotes from the Matthew Davis letter, "I believe that the soul is eternal, it had no beginning, it can have no end." (p. 145) See 1882.

[*2 years*]

1859

DN is reprinted in Liverpool, England, in George D. Watt's *Journal of Discourses* 6:1–11.

[*2 years*]

1861

April 20. DN is reprinted in Liverpool, England, as part of the *Latter-day Saints' Millennial Star*'s run of the "History of Joseph Smith" from the July 8, 1857, *Deseret News* instance above.

[*17 years*]

1878

July 26. MS2 is reprinted in the St. George, Utah, *Union* newspaper (page 2) and continued in its successive biweekly issues.

[*4 years*]

1882

Excerpts of TS appear in Franklin D. Richards and James A. Little, *A Compendium of the Doctrines of the Gospel*. It is somewhat remarkable that TS is used and not MS2, since the former was not the approved construction (RC) and TS had a small circulation in its day. More remarkable still is the selection of one of the most controversial portions, the pericope on the resurrection of children.

1883

April. An edition of MS2 is printed in *The Contributor* magazine (pp. 252–61). This is CON in the bibliography above.

[*5 years*]

1888

Short excerpts of MS2 are reprinted in Andrew Jenson's *Historical Record*. Curiously, Jenson's longest selection is from the section on the unpardonable sin and Hell.

[*7 years*]

1895

Nels Lars Nelson uses MS2 as a basis for his deduction that man's core being is not contingent. *The Contributor* 16, no. 12 (October 1895): 737–38.[139]

[*8 years*]

1903

February. John R. Winder, a counselor to church president Joseph F. Smith, quotes from Follett in the service of proxy work for the dead. *Young Woman's Journal* 14, no. 2 (February 1903): 52.

August. An edition of VOT is printed by the Presbyterian Teachers Association of Utah. The front page for the little pamphlet (16.5 × 9.5cm)

139. The language echoes that of an 1895 address by B. H. Roberts. Roberts gave an address on January 27, 1895, in which he said, "The commandment which God gave to man in the Garden of Eden, 'Multiply and replenish the earth,' was just as pure a commandment as 'Repent and be baptized.' It is upon this principle of procreation that intelligences are begotten as spirits in the pre-existent worlds." B. H. Roberts, "What is Man?" *Deseret Weekly* 50 (March 16, 1895): 385–88 (reprinted in *Millennial Star* 57 [July 4, 1895]: 417–21; 433–37).

stated: "Joseph Smith's Last Sermon, As issued by Elder John Taylor, Nauvoo, Ill., June, 1844: Now republished according to resolution of the Presbyterian Teachers' Association, August, 1903; Salt Lake City, Utah."

1904

April. B. H. Roberts outlines some of his forthcoming YMMIA manual in an April 3 general conference address.

1905

B. H. Roberts's YMMIA Manual is released. This manual of instruction for the church's young men organization was a part of Roberts's three volume work, *New Witnesses for God* (volume one appeared in 1903).

1906

A private reprint of MS2 by C. C. Anderson. The volume contained other material in support of plural marriage and thus is one of the initial efforts to go back to the original Mormonism rather than the shockingly (for some) deflated post-manifesto version.

1907

B. H. Roberts–F. M. Lyman report answering questions from readers of Roberts's 1905 manual (see above). The report is published as the lead article in the January issue of the *Improvement Era*. See chapter 3 below.

[*2 years*]

1909

January. MS2 is reprinted by B. H. Roberts in the *Improvement Era* with his own annotation. (This is R1.)

[*2 years*]

1911

December. R1 is reprinted (R2) in *Liahona The Elders' Journal*, including Roberts's annotation (12,000 copies). There are many minor variations from the 1909 imprint. Church leaders had by then determined Follett was a misleading text and wished to extract the sermon from current and future LDS literature and sought to halt distribution. See chapter 3.

1912

January 23. *Liahona The Elders' Journal* prints a notice that no more orders for the Follett issue would be filled: "The edition of the King Follett Discourse is exhausted. No more orders can be filled after this date."

RC (actually, MS2) is excluded from *History of the Church of Jesus Christ of Latter-day Saints, Period I*. See chapter 3. The First Presidency essentially anathomizes the sermon, and it does not appear in the *History* until a revised volume is issued in 1952.

The date is uncertain, but the church's New Zealand Mission publishes what appears to be a version of R2.

1913 (1912?)

Summer. Historian T. Edgar Lyon suggests that R1 was reprinted by Magazine Printing and Publishing (Salt Lake City) at the insistence of B. H. Roberts.

[*6 years*]

1919

June. LeRoi C. Snow, "Devotion to a Divine Inspiration." Snow's article is a tribute to his father's (former church president Lorenzo Snow) contributions. Snow notes the several editions of the Follett sermon and some of their problems. (See chapter 3.)

[*7 years*]

1926

Summer. Magazine Printing reprints R1. They reprint several more times.

[*12 years*]

1938

Joseph Fielding Smith, Jr., LDS Church Historian, reprints R1 in his *Teachings of the Prophet Joseph Smith*. This brings RC back into the official favor from which it had fallen in the second decade of the twentieth century. The book is used as a church instruction manual.

[*5 years*]

1943

A version of Follett is published in German at Basel, Switzerland, at the height of World War II. *Die King Follett-Ansprache: Personenlichkeit und wesen gottes: unsterblichkeit der Intelligenz Menschen* (The King Follett Address: Personality and Essence of God: Immortality of the Intelligence of Man). Translation of R4 by the Swiss Mission of the LDS Church. Roberts's notes were translated by Max Zimmer (1889–1957?).[140]

[*9 years*]

140. Zimmer was born in Colmar, Alsace-Lorraine, and was probably living in Basel (about 50 miles south of Colmar) by 1904. The text includes biographical information on Richards, Woodruff, Bullock, and Clayton together with other annotations taken from R2.

1952
History of the Church vol. 6 is issued in a revised edition. Under the direction of Joseph Fielding Smith an edition of R1 is included with streamlined notes. Smith felt the sermon was too advanced for rank-and-file Saints and the public, though he now accepted it himself.

[*4 years*]

1956
Alma P. Burton's *Discourses of the Prophet Joseph Smith* contained short excerpts of the sermon. See 1977.

[*9 years*]

1965
James R. Clark included R5 in his multi-volume compilation, *Messages of the First Presidency* 1:209–25.

[*6 years*]

1971
April–May. The LDS Church's *Ensign* magazine printed R4, but did not include the notes of B. H. Roberts—aside from short quotations this appears to be the most recent "official" printing of RC.

[*3 years*]

1974
Anthologies became a popular form for Mormon publishing houses at this period. One series contains an edition of TS. Richard H. Cracroft, ed., *Believing People: Literature of the Latter-day Saints*, 167–72 (and later reprints). The editor mistakenly ascribes the text to four sources, confusing TS with RC.

[*3 years*]

1977
Alma P. Burton's *Discourses of the Prophet Joseph Smith*, 2nd ed. reprinted R5 as "Appendix A."

1978
The journal *Brigham Young University Studies* vol. 18, no. 2 (Winter 1978): 179–226, publishes several articles on the Follett sermon, including a new edition of the text.

[*2 years*]

1980
Editions of TB, WC, GL2, WW, SR, WR are published in Andrew F. Ehat and Lyndon W. Cook, eds., *The Words of Joseph Smith.*

[*9 years*]

1989
An edition of RC is published in Robert L. Millett, ed., *Joseph Smith: Selected Sermons and Writings*. Millett supplied notes reflecting some modern interpretations of Follett (via Elder Bruce McConkie's writings).

[*5 years*]

1994
June 26. Gordon B. Hinckley, a counselor in the First Presidency of the Church, refers to Follett as a "doctrinal document."[141]

[*5 years*]

141. Gordon B. Hinckley, "Nauvoo's Holy Temple," 59–62.

1999
An edition of Follett appeared in the Michael Warner produced anthology, *American Sermons: The Pilgrims to Martin Luther King Jr.* (New York: Putnam, 1999). The 1989 Millett text above was advertised as the basis for this edition of Follett.

[*14 years*]

2013
The Follett sermon appears as background in an apologetic text published by the LDS Church as one of a series of essays called Gospel Topics. Titled "Becoming Like God," the intent was to situate the deification ideas of Follett and other JS texts within a biblical view of the world.[142]

§1.7 Archetype, Text, and Intertextual Issues

An Imprint Stemma

There is no one text to identify as the *base text* for the Follett sermon.[143] Instead, there are multiple audits, some of which were eventually used by church clerks and authorities to construct a string of texts (TS→VOT→GM0→GM1) funneling into one standard text or what I have called elsewhere the pivot text: RC (see figure 1). *Intertextuality* is a way of speaking about how texts may exist in one another. Words like *allude*, *echo*, *quote* are often used to describe the presence of one text within another. For example, the Follett archetype, the actual oral event of the Follett sermon, seems to quote parts

142. See https://www.churchofjesuschrist.org/study/manual/gospel-topics/becoming-like-god. For an account of the genesis of the Gospel Topics essays, see Matthew L. Harris and Newell G. Bringhurst, Introduction: Why the Gospel Topics Essays," in *The LDS Gospel Topics Series: A Scholarly Engagement*.

143. See G. Thomas Tanselle, "Editing without a Copy-Text," 1–6.

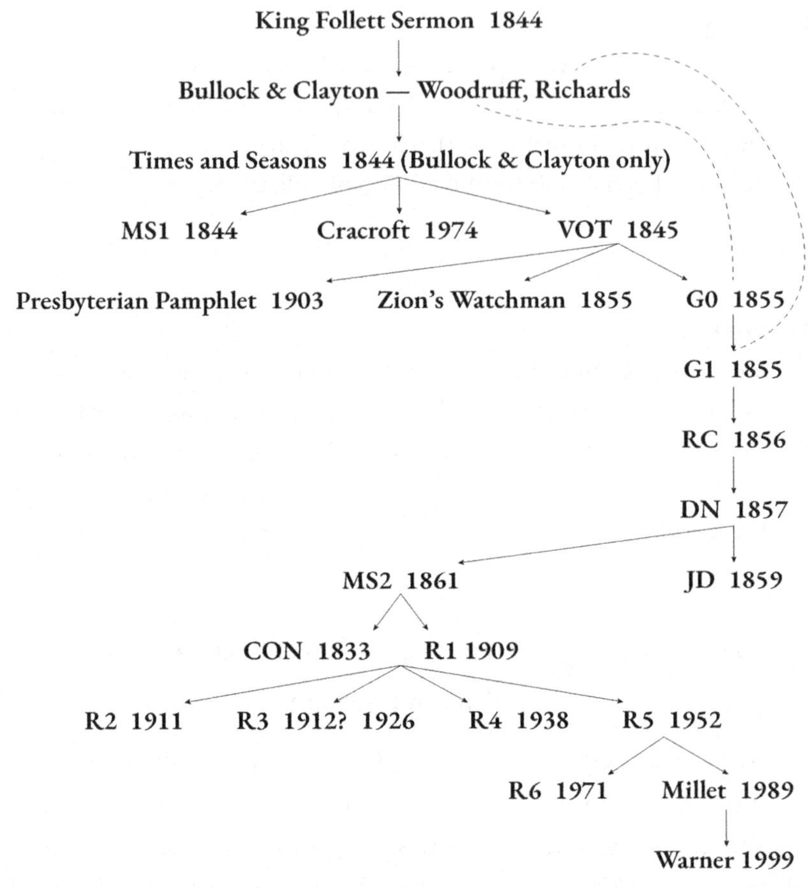

Figure 1: A Partial Imprint Stemma for the King Follett sermon

of Jn 5 and Jn 17, meaning that the sermon repeated words or phrases from those chapters of the Gospel of John. The sermon alludes to those texts as well, meaning that it refers to them, they are referenced within the archetype, not necessarily *quoted*, but nevertheless referenced explicitly. I note several parts of source texts for Follett that *echo* the words of Lorenzo Dow's works, for example. "Echo" is a weaker reference than allusion or quotation, where the text in question (a Follett source text in this case) appears to relate to another text

(Dow's). Dow's text appears to be weaved into Follett in the sense already mentioned.[144] JS seems to have borrowed and modified sayings from Dow to give another layer of meaning in his sermon. Concepts or ideologies from other texts may be merged, perhaps very subtly, into the target text. The Dow texts and Follett fit this notion as well as the redactions of VOT that appeared in RC. These senses of intertextuality are starting points for understanding the process at play here. A text is present within itself for instance: once we reread a text, the previous reading becomes present within the text, perhaps in bits and pieces since human memory is fraught. JS may have generated some intertextuality unconsciously, foregrounding texts of other speeches he had given, texts he had read or heard within the extemporaneous milieu—this undoubtedly takes place in several instances that I have already mentioned above and more below. Any text is in this sense a kind of *palimpsest*, a collection of preceding texts that lie underneath that text. It is impossible to trace all these intertextual threads or to do much justice to the concept here, but I bring it up to note that my work with the Follett text by no means exhausts what might be done in the future. The notion of intertexuality and the examples in this chapter along with many others of the same ilk illustrate one of the difficulties with the phrase: *Joseph Smith said*.[145]

144. Dow's words are near quotations in some Follett texts noted above, illustrating the complex nature of intertexuality.

145. JS's occasional written sermons are valuable in that context. On the other hand, some meager records were—somewhat puzzlingly—elevated to canon, creating some difficulties in interpretation. Important examples appear in Doctrine and Covenants 130. For more on these issues, see Smith, "Documentary Record." Intertextuality is bound to several schools of thought. See for example, chapters 1 and 3 of Boris Gasparov, *Speech, Memory, and Meaning: Intertextuality in Everyday Language*.

CHAPTER 2

Follett and the Ideological Landscape of Middle Mormonism, 1845–1890

Scribality, Re-Creation, and Polygamy

§2.1 Developing Ontological and Cosmological Counter Themes to Follett—

Some Possible Religious and Social Origins

The Follett sermon publicized JS's long-developing conceptions of ontological/cosmological reality. It was reproduced with perhaps better fidelity than any other extemporaneous Mormon sermon, prior to the gradual acceptance of thorough shorthand auditing techniques that began the following year in Nauvoo. It is not clear why JS did not encourage shorthand reporting of his sermons by experts like George Watt, who was in Nauvoo at the time of Follett. Some hints exist along several different lines. First and perhaps most important, JS did not trust his preaching to convey all that he meant to give or more precisely, to *match his intention* pre- or post-sermon. His work with secretary Willard Richards and clerk William Clayton from the April 1843 church conference at Nauvoo may illustrate this best. Two aural audits of JS's remarks at that conference exist, neither of which match any imprint. JS went back and dictated a whole new version of that sermon that was then redacted once again.[1] Second, JS had little confidence in the reporter to make JS his best verbal self: smoothing his verbiage and *matching the record with insider knowledge* perhaps as Wilford Woodruff may have done in his audit of the Follett sermon.[2] A third reason may have been a lack of trust in the methodology of shorthand. Who would check such reports? The symbology may have seemed all too familiar with JS's own experience of attempting to decipher Egyptian.[3]

Despite its relative textual authenticity, Follett would become the most contested of all JS's preaching records, where other sayings with far less textual support became standards of belief. These later threads of conflict stemmed from two sources: JS's introduction of polygamy and biblical language describing God's relation (Father) to humans interpreted in a way that gradually diverged from Protestant theologies where rebirth through Christ was the one and only way to be a child of God as in Jn 3:5, etc.[4] JS's early revelations had already

1. The evolution of this conference address is discussed in volume 12 of the Documents series of the Joseph Smith Papers. I thank historian David Grua for insights into JS's 1843 preaching audits.

2. JS anointed Willard Richards "a man after his own heart, in all things, that he could trust with his business." Willard Richards, Letter to Jennetta Richards, Feb. 26, 1842. See Alex D. Smith and Andrew H. Hedges, "Joseph Smith's Nauvoo Journals," in *Foundational Texts of Mormonism: Examining Major Early Sources*, 234.

3. See Smith, "Documentary Record." Also "Historian's Office Reports of Speeches, 1845–1885." Ronald O. Barney, "Joseph Smith and the Conspicuous Scarcity of Early Mormon Documentation," 397–98.

4. The Reformation reinforced the theological differences between "child" and "creature" (meaning created). God became Father as Christ made the child and created human one and the same by the creature's faith, being born again. The theological rift between creature and child is prominent in Augustinian teaching and is echoed in Book of Mormon sermons (2 Nephi 9, etc.). The hermeneutical waters

endorsed a God who *created* human spirits/souls in one or another sense. The picture here is complicated by early interpretations of such passages, but by 1844 the meaning had largely stabilized in ways Mormons would recognize today, and some fellow believers had written a scenario that took God's fatherhood of the Bible and saw a Mormon version: the Father of human souls in a creation/construction that echoed the biblical account of the making of Adam and Eve from the dust.

The preexistence of humanity was not a universal element in Mormon teaching prior to 1839. Passages in the Bible, Book of Mormon, and JS's early revelations that were later used to support the preexistence of the soul were interpreted in other ways in the beginnings of Mormonism.[5] The first parents were made from the dust of the earth, and human souls were made from the dust of a spiritual realm. That impulse, a classical one with broad genealogy, which made all individuals contingent on God's necessity, impressed itself on the early efforts of Mormon literary minds like Orson Pratt, Parley Pratt, and Lorenzo Snow.[6] Precisely *when* the soul was created and

---

are deep, and I won't go further into them here. A useful summary of Latter-day Saint views and Christian history is Turner, *The Mormon Jesus*, ch. 6.

5. For example, see Alexander, "Reconstruction," note 23. Harrell, "Development of the Doctrine of Preexistence."

6. On Parley Pratt, see his pamphlet, and *An Appeal to the Inhabitants of the State of New York, etc.*, 36–40, his 1845 "Mormon Proverbs," also his 1853 sermon "Spiritual Communication." On Lorenzo Snow, see his speculative 1842 work in "Letter to Elder Walker." Also, his 1872 speech in Snow, "Progression—The Fatherhood of God," 302. On Orson Pratt, see his *Prophetic Almanac for 1845*, 4–5, and more creatively, his 1849 *The Absurdities of Immaterialism*, 26–29 and, *The Seer* (Washington, D.C.) 1 (1853): 103. Also see *Millennial Star* 11, no. 11 (June 1, 1849): 161–66, 11, no. 17, (September 1, 1849): 257–60, 11, no. 18 (September 15, 1849): 273–74. Crawley, *Descriptive Bibliography*, 2:90–92. For one Mormon view in 1835 see Warren A. Cowdery's letter to the editor of the church's *Messenger and Advocate* (May 1835): 113, "we have proven to the satisfaction of every intelligent being, that

what it was might be argued, but JS's early revelations saw human souls existing prior to mortal humanity in some sense.[7]

The Pratts, Snow, and others expounded this contingency of the soul before and after JS's time. That contingency became more refined after JS's death. However, JS himself took a more controversial stance: the human soul was a self-existent being, a necessary being, an uncreated being, without beginning or end, and thus, there exist infinitely many "first" causes, not at all the logic of classical belief. Even though he preached that stance frequently, it was largely discarded within a few years of his death and would not return in strength for more than five decades. The reasons for that are partly social (see below), partly physical. The physical issue was circulation. Many of JS's teachings did not circulate widely while he lived because they either weren't publicly preserved or they weren't widely distributed. After his death, selections from his letters and the journal entries of listeners describing his teaching became enshrined in the canon—but the selection of those items was made within a different set of parameters than the ones existing when they were uttered.

The refinement of the claim of a *contingent* soul in Mormon teaching was best illustrated by two new post martyrdom poems/hymns for Latter-day Saints. Eliza R. Snow, the Mormon thought leader, theologian, and poet, took the notion of a contingent soul and combined it with JS's July 12, 1843, revelation on polygamy. The

---

there is a *great first cause, prime mover*, self-existent, independent and all wise being whom we call God." Emphasis added. Parley still saw spirit as immaterial in 1839 (though uncreated substance) when he penned, "A Treatise on the Regeneration and Eternal Duration of Matter" in a Missouri jail.

7. I use *created* broadly to mean either created from nothing, or formed, or made, though JS came to emphasize that *creatio ex nihilo* was impossible. See, for example, Book of Abraham 3:17–25. See also Orson Pratt, sermon, August 29, 1852, MS 4534 Box 1, fd. 7, transcription by Lajean Carruth, October 18, 2013. Cp. Doctrine and Covenants 29:30–32; Doctrine and Covenants 49:17; Moses 3:5.

revelation had been produced to lay out the theological justification of polygamy to JS's first wife, Emma Hale. Passages in the revelation either seen by Snow or communicated by speech about the exalting power of polygamy—its cosmology founded on a ritual "sealing," a marriage to extend into the afterlife—led Snow to interpret these revelatory words to mean that exalted humans would propagate their species in heaven and that this process was a reflection of God's own life.[8] The July revelation read

> it shall be done unto them in all things whatsoever my servant hath put upon them, in time and through all Eternity and Shall be of full force when they are out of the world and they shall pass by the angels and the Gods which are Set there, to their exaltation and glory in all things as hath been Sealed upon their heads which glory Shall be a fullness and a continuation of the Seeds for ever and ever. Then Shall they be Gods, because they have no End. Therefore Shall they be from everlasting to everlasting because they continue Then Shall they be above all because all things are subject unto them. Then Shall they be Gods because they have all power and the angels are Subject unto them.[9]

Alternatively, TB suggests that JS's vision of God's work was not some kind of divine sexuality or a forming of spiritual clay but an adoptive gift. Bullock's audit reads

> God himself finds himself in the midst of Sp[irits] & bec[ause] he saw proper to institute laws for those who were in less intelligence that they mit [might]. have one glory upon another in all that knowledge power & glory & so took in hand to save the world of Sp[irits][10]

---

8. On the revelation, see Smith, *The Plural Marriage Revelation*.

9. Doctrine and Covenants 132:19–20. This text is extracted from the earliest surviving manuscript of the revelation, copied from the original by Joseph C. Kingsbury. Smith, *Plural Marriage Revelation*, addendum. *JSP*, D12:457–478.

10. Appendix A.

George Laub's content audit of Follett (GL1) put it this way: "How came the spirits? Why they are and were self existing as all eternity." If JS's sermon took his 1843 revelation text into account, the revelation's passage suggests that "continuation of the seeds" meant carrying on God's work by adopting souls into the divine family and JS's revelations may be thought of as writing "seeds" for "posterity" in any number of senses.[11] Others who knew the (at the time) secret revelation on polygamy saw the clear implications that would fully flower in Utah: peopling new worlds by creating Adams and Eves. Eliza Snow's poem revised JS: the Gods propagated the Seeds by sex in heaven, with divine females birthing spirits, not adopting them. As a metaphysical justification of polygamy, this reinterpretation would surpass a variety of competing stories.[12]

Eliza Snow's text was eventually used to marginalize any figurative interpretation of the 1843 revelation on polygamy. She wrote a year after JS's death in "My Father in Heaven,"

> O my Father, thou that dwellest
> In the high and glorious place;
> When shall I regain thy presence,
> And again behold thy face?

11. For an elaboration of this adoption, see Samuel M. Brown, "Believing Adoption."

12. The text of RC was modified to add the germ of this idea. See Appendix A. Perhaps Heber C. Kimball's 1843 reverent wish for forgiveness and salvation may be read this way: "O that I was such a man as I would desire to be, and Thou O God knowest I wish [to] be pure in hart, that all of my sins may be bloted out. . . . [and] [n]ever sepperate me from my dear Vilate or anny of those that are con[ne]cted to me by the ties of Na[t]ure Thou knowest I Love my dear family, and may it increase more and more, that [no] power can sepperate us from Each other, that we may dwell to gether through out all Eternity, and thare be [enthroned] on worlds, to propragate that thare may be no end to us or our Seeds." Stanley B. Kimball, ed., *On the Potter's Wheel: The Diaries of Heber C. Kimball*, 52. Stapley, "Brigham Young's Garden Theology."

In thy holy habitation
Did my spirit once reside?
In my *first* primeval childhood
Was I nurtur'd near thy side?

For a wise a glorious purpose
Thou hast plac'd me here on earth,
And witheld the recollection
Of my former friends and *birth*
. . .
I had learn'd to call thee father
Through thy spirit from on high;
But until the key of knowledge
Was restor'd, I knew not why.
In the heav'ns are parents single?
No, the thought makes reason stare;
Truth is reason-truth eternal
Tells me I've a mother there.[13]
. . .

City of Joseph, Oct. 1845.

Snow's text made popular a reading of God's domesticity that fellow poet William W. Phelps had already engaged in two steps: first, (January 1845) in a hymn titled, "A Voice from the Prophet: Come to me," Phelps wrote, "Here's our Father in heaven, and Mother, the Queen," and second, in a short piece of fiction, *Paracletes*. In the latter, spirits are begotten in female wombs in a heavenly place.[14] In

---

13. Eliza R. Snow, "My Father in Heaven," emphasis in second stanza added. See also Edward William Tullidge, *The Women of Mormondom*, ch. 19. As a continuing measure of the poem's influence, see the *Millennial Star*'s outline for 1909 Church lessons in "Sunday School Lesson for Theological Department," 623.

14. Phelps's work, the Follett sermon, and the teachings of James Strang may have influenced Charles Thompson, a dissenter from Young and the apostolic leadership. Thompson produced an inspired translation of the Book of Enoch in 1852, which spoke of God creating "many wombs; and . . . impregnated" them "with the seed of intelligence." The wombs brought forth "many Intelligences" clothed

Paracletes, Adam and Eve play a role that might be seen as forerunner to Brigham Young's ideas about Adam and Eve. Phelps continued the theme in a hymn, "Father Adam and Mother Eve."[15]

Eliza Snow's work was not likely meant to be fiction like Phelps's work, and it helped confirm a public reading of the July 1843 revelation as a mirror of the divine after the revelation became public in 1852. By 1855, the *Deseret News* noted that "O My Father" was Brigham Young's favorite *hymn*.[16] Snow's text was used to support the idea that human souls were "born" in heaven to God the Father and Mother.[17] The poem speaks of spirits born in a preexisting state to Heavenly Parents and those "spirit" children enjoy a "primeval childhood," a theme of *imitatio parenti* that developed in succeeding decades to make Mormon marriage praxis an earthly duty that imi-

with refined matter. Charles Thompson, "Inspired Enoch," 73. On Thompson, see Christopher James Blythe, "Recreating Religion: The Response to Joseph Smith's Innovation in the Second Prophetic Generation of Mormonism."

15. W. W. Phelps, "A Voice From the Prophet: Come to Me." Michael Hicks, "Poetic Borrowing in Early Mormonism," 140–41. Phelps's fanciful *Paracletes* fiction did not precisely refer to a Mother in the more developed theology of Utah but it functions as a literary precursor to Snow. See "Paracletes," *Times and Seasons* 6, no. 8 (May 1, 1845): 8919–2 and "The Paracletes, Continued," *Times and Seasons* 6, no. 10 (June 1, 1845): 917–18. On the theological place of the work, see Samuel Brown, "William Phelps's Paracletes, an Early Witness to Joseph Smith's Divine Anthropology."

16. *Deseret News* (June 20, 1855): 120. The poem appeared set to music soon after JS's plural marriage revelation was published (1852). It was a popular text with many musical settings. Brigham Young's favorite setting was the Stephen Foster tune, *Gentle Annie*. See Michael Hicks, "'O My Father': The Musical Settings."

17. Literature on the Mother includes Linda Wilcox, "The Mormon Concept of a Mother in Heaven." John Heeren, Donald Lindsey, and Marylee Mason, "The Mormon Concept of Mother in Heaven: A Sociological Account of Its Origins and Development." See chapter 3 below. See also Mattie Horne Tingey, "The School of Experience," 387, and Stapley, "Brigham Young's Garden Theology."

tated and engaged the heavenly world in a very literal way.[18] A part of Follett was a backstop for this theological development, requiring humans to tread in the paths of the Gods if they were to achieve the ultimate in salvation.

The logic of sexuality in heaven had little relationship to JS's teaching in Nauvoo, but the expansion/rewriting of that teaching seemed inevitable. Eliza Snow, William Phelps, Brigham Young, Orson and Parley Pratt, and others of JS's followers would struggle to construct and rationalize the concepts of a material afterlife, sex, and polygamy, after JS's death. To Nauvoo insiders familiar with polygamy, JS's call in the Follett sermon that "you have got to learn how to be gods yourselves" may have seemed an obvious allusion to the July 1843 polygamy revelation and its relative incarnation in proto-temple rituals that JS introduced between the spring of 1842 and the fall of 1843. This opened the door to theological developments in future generations: Mormons had the key of knowledge, showing them that their families made bodies for the souls procreated by the Parents in Heaven and that human biology and heavenly biology were one. By the lights of such post-Nauvoo extrapolation, the marital culture of the rest of the world was an ignorant and imperfect imitation of divinity because the world lacked this knowledge and perspective on the divine.

§2.2 Polygamy and Diaspora—
The Post-Nauvoo World in a Follett Cosmos—
Providing a Metaphysics for Polygamy

Brigham Young led an initial company of Saints from Nauvoo in February 1846. It was a strung-out exodus, hurried out of a planned move partly for fear of attacks on church leaders by mobs from the

18. I'm borrowing from Thomas à Kempis, *De Imitatione Christi* from the fifteenth century.

surrounding county. As the Saints gradually left the city, there came missionaries from already developing competitors to the apostolic leaders. James Strang recruited membership from the remaining residents of the city. Sidney Rigdon had already made his case that the church should be under the former first counselor's guidance. The only surviving brother of JS, William had laid claim to leadership. While the dissenting church led by William Law had wilted, Law himself was initially attracted to Strang's claims, which echoed an early JS: translation of more plates, angelic conferral of authority. Strang had joined the Mormons in January 1844, had little connection to insider Nauvoo, and was not involved in polygamy (though he later changed his mind on that), the city government, high church office, or the secrect Council of Fifty. Yet for some midwestern Saints, Strang's old time Mormonism held attraction. Neither Strang, nor Rigdon, nor William Smith held out any hope of backing the Follett theology.

William Law had already rejected the sermon as one more sign that JS was a fallen prophet. George J. Adams gained some following in his Church of the Messiah after an association with Strang. Adams in particular was closer to JS than many in Nauvoo. Adams was sponsored by JS as a member of the Council of Fifty and preached at the April 1844 conference. His later trajectory gave no sign that Follett made a lasting impression.[19]

JS's expanding sacred rites included the "endowment," the ritual meant for the temple then being built in Nauvoo. Such rites represented the provisions of the grand council of heaven. In some Follett sermon audits, JS claimed that securing these rituals (by proxy) for the dead was the most sacred of all duties. An earlier revelation described

---

19. Newell G. Bringhurst and John C. Hamer, eds., *Scattering of the Saints: Schism Within Mormonism*. Vickie Cleverley Speek, *God has Made us a Kingdom: James Strang and the Midwest Mormons*. Robin Scott Jensen and Benjamin E. Park, "Debating Succession, March 1846: John E. Page, Orson Hyde, and the Trajectories of Joseph Smith's Legacy."

any failure to build the new temple where those proxy ordinances would be delivered as a Rubicon. It would result in God's rejection of the church "with their dead"—a frightening prospect. Midwestern Mormons who chose not to follow church apostles to Utah sometimes used the "rejection" motif as a foundation for a reorganization of the church with JS's oldest son as its head.[20] The Follett sermon reordered Mormon priorities by registering proxy rituals for the dead as the most important duty of Latter-day Saints.[21] The remark was remembered nearly forty years later by one auditor who was present as a young adult: "Some of you may remember the sermon that the Prophet Joseph preached at the time King Follett was killed in a well—one of the last sermons he delivered. He told us in that sermon that 'The greatest responsibility in this world that God had laid upon us was to seek after our dead.' "[22] At the same time when Utah Saints were defining proxy ordinances for the dead as a main feature of their faith—encouraged by completion of the landmark Salt Lake Temple—in an 1899 letter, JS's son and Reorganized Church President Joseph Smith III expressed that "whatever the [Nauvoo]

---

20. See JS's revelation that ratified a decision to build a temple in Nauvoo: Doctrine and Covenants 124:32 [*JSP*, D7:xxxi, 510]. On the continuing reaction, see Nauvoo Female Relief Society Minute Book, July 15, 1843, page 98, CHL. Jill Mulvay Derr, et al., eds., *The First Fifty Years of Relief Society: Key Documents in Latter-day Saint Women's History*, 106–8. On the RLDS logic, see Roger D. Launius, "An Ambivalent Rejection: Baptism for the Dead and the Reorganized Church Experience." Also Mark A. Scherer, "Answering Questions No Longer Asked: Nauvoo, Its Meaning and Interpretation in the RLDS Church/Community of Christ," 29–30. Alma R. Blair, "Reorganized Church of Jesus Christ of Latter Day Saints: Moderate Mormonism," 228. On ordinances set by ancient earthly and heavenly councils, see Jordan T. Watkins, "Early Mormonism and the Re-Enchantment of Antebellum Historical Thought," 199–200.

21. See TB and WC for "the greatest responsibility . . . is to seek after our dead." It was an "awful responsibility." Also see Appendix A.

22. Franklin D. Richards, "Discourse by Elder Franklin D. Richards."

belief in a plurality of Gods may have been; in the Gospel economy we see but one, and his son a duality only."[23] Years earlier in 1865, Smith had advised the RLDS Quorum of Twelve Apostles to simply let the Follett sermon die of neglect. In the 1899 letter, Smith opined that the Follett sermon was a lesser document, not equal to JS's published revelations,

> The Church so far as I have been able to learn never formulated a stated belief based on the King Follett sermon. Personally I have no testimony concerning the correctness of the fragment as we have it. . . . . What my private opinion of [it] may be, may not concern the Church, as we allow much latitude of private opinion. Much of his teaching is excellent, and I try to profit by it. I cannot regard everything my father did, or said, as the utterance or action of the Spirit, hence, whether any specific item be thought good, or bad, I do not care to enter into a discussion of it, for or against; as I cannot see how it may affect his work recognized as by direct inspiration.[24]

In some ways, a portion of present-day Latter-day Saints seem to share exactly this opinion. Decades later, Smith's hierarchical descendant, Israel A. Smith, would be more insistent that JS never actually preached Follett. Israel believed it was a fictional production of Utah (see chapter 4). The heritage of the sermon after JS's death seemed to be in Utah where JS's public and *secret* Nauvoo history was of paramount importance.

Out of early Mormon theological thought in the few years surrounding the death of JS, competing human protologies (theories of

23. By duality, Smith was undoubtedly referring to the theology lectures that had been published with JS's revelations since 1835, later called the "lectures on faith." One of the lectures identified the Godhead as two persons; the lecture called their shared mind the Holy Ghost.

24. Joseph Smith III, Letter to Joseph Davis, October 13, 1899, Francis M. Lyman letterpress copybooks, Box 1, MS 2497, CHL.

beginnings) in the Brigham Young–led church emerged. As noted, JS rejected *ex nihilo* creation, so these protologies had to work with that constraint in the way they treated consciousness. Was the soul—as a conscious individual being—a creative act of God, or was the individual soul uncaused, or was it the result of some spontaneous action?[25] Wilford Woodruff's 1847 pioneer trail diary noted the crucial boundary between the developing rationalization of polygamy with its eventual and particular sacralization of sex, and JS's claims exemplified in the Follett sermon.

> During our travels today I walked most of the way with Professors [Orson] Pratt, & Carrington and our conversation turned upon the subject of the original formation of God, Angels, man & Devils the begetting of Spirits in the eternal worlds, & who by, the begetting of children on the earth, the death of man & children & the resurrection of All. . . . One of the most important items if true was presented by Professor Pratt. . . . It was upon the subject of the original formation of the first God; we all admitted in the first place that which we believed to be an important truth ie the eternal duration of matter spirit, intelligence in some form or other we also agreed in the opinion that neither God nor man always had from all eternity the same formation that they now have but did exhist in some form. . . . then the question arose how did God recieve his present formation the answer given by Professor Pratt was something in the following language. . . . An eternity was filled as it were with particules of intelligences who had their agency, two of these particles in the process of time might have joined their interest together exchanged ideas & found by persueing this course that they gained double strength to what one particle of intelligence would have & afterwards were joined by other par-

25. Here I use this monadic language since it matched some early Mormon thought on human spirits as "pre-images" of flesh humans (for example, D&C 77). Orson Pratt would subdivide the soul. Consciousness is a loaded term for modern audiences, but it seems to describe JS's meaning with respect to a human soul.

> ticles & continued untill they organized a combination or body though through a long process & as they had power over other intelligences in consequence of their combination, organization & strength and in process of time this being—or God seeing the advantage of such an organization desired company or a companion and having some experience got to work & organized other beings by prevailing on intelligences to come together & may form something better than at the first and after trials of this kind & the most perfect way sought . . . it was found to be the most expeditious & best way to recieve there formations or bodies either spiritual or temporal [was] *through the womb*.[26]

Woodruff acknowledged the issues and Pratt's ideas suggest that the men felt somewhat conflicted over JS's protology. The difficult shadow of human self-existence plagued most interpreters of the Follett sermon: was there really no first cause of spirits? JS had wrenched the logic of the Cosmological Argument: there had to be a first cause for everything. Pratt's theological structure was one of the earlier attempts to correlate JS's protology, post-mortal kingdom theology, Snow's Mother theology, and Pratt's logic in connecting them via an *emergent* material soul. For Pratt, human souls were a kind of material, a material formed from intelligent agent-atoms coalescing via the mechanics of a divine woman's uterus and subsequently born as a "spiritual" infant.

Pratt conjured and modified many of the threads of early Mormon thought in his western trail speculation, and he did it in a starkly literal way: God as father of spirits, spirits constructed or *built up* out of eternal agent-beings, Father God and Mother God as sexual beings in which the 1843 polygamy revelation's "continuation of the of the Seeds" is loosed from any allegorical or adoptive interpretation. Pratt probably saw Greek atomism as the appropriate metaphor for what

26. Emphasis added. Journal of Wilford Woodruff, June 26, 1847. Kenney, *Wilford Woodruff's Journal*, 3:217.

always exists and is always in flux, though the intended biological role of God the Father is less clear in this theological tour de force. Was God's semen a spiritual fluid of agent atoms? And did those atoms form a kind of colony that somehow drew other agents to it? The questions are real for Pratt's picture of heaven.

In Pratt's thought, the *original* God, long before the Father of Jesus, in some unimaginably distant past, was the result of the agent atoms perceiving some symbiotic advantage in cohesion to form a spirit *in human form*. The form vector is the reverse of evolutionary biology. The body-form is original, not developed out of some inchoate spiritual logic. This is fundamentally Aristotelian via St. Thomas Aquinas. For Aquinas, the soul was the "form" around which the body was organized. The idea seems to appear in Mormon thought around the soul as the organizer of the body and the body is the image of the soul (spirit), perhaps an interpretation of a vision found in the Book of Mormon.[27] The soul occupies all portions of the body, not just the head (or later, the brain). One feels that Pratt, if not a reader of, at least echoed Voltaire's character from his novel *Micromegas*, where a giant interstellar traveler from somewhere near the dog-star, Sirius, who, upon observing the microscopic humans is astonished to see that the invisibly small folks possessed souls. Voltaire had his character call the humans, "intelligent atoms." Pratt interpreted JS's spiritual matter as flexible, a kind of substance with form memory. It could somehow occupy an infant body by "compression" and yet be a pattern that led the infant body toward the form of the occupying soul-spirit.[28]

Despite Woodruff's portrayal of Pratt as paralyzed in speculation with a take-it-or-leave-it attitude, Pratt had already published on the subject and went on to formalize the ideas during a polygamy pub-

---

27. Ether 3.

28. Orson Pratt, *The Absurdities of Immaterialism*, 23–24. James E. Talmage, "Man's Eternal Progression—Infinite Possibilities of His Estate."

licity missionary tour in the eastern United States in the wake of the 1852 public reveal of the July 12, 1843, revelation.[29] His 1853 work in his short-lived Washington, DC, paper *The Seer* didn't meet with complete approval by Brigham Young, but on the point of spirits born in heaven, they agreed. The logic was an important theological pillar for polygamy among the Mormons, who came to believe that their eternal marriages were not only proof against death but forever fecund.[30] Heavenly gestational mechanics—Pratt noted that it took time to grow a baby, even in Celestial Wombs—provided the real reason for polygamy, its metaphysics as it were. The project of expanding God's kingdom (and one's own at the same time) meant the need for more wives, thus more children, thus more glory and that provided the metaphysical justification for polygamy—a powerful motive that buried JS's protological assertions. Church Apostle Orson Hyde's 1845 sermon claimed that "children will be born in the likeness of parents there [heaven] as here. . . . and multiply eternaly as Abraham and Sarah. They are even now enjoying the blessing . . ." [31] The point of JS's materiality was avoiding paradox: how could an immaterial thing be real? Orson Pratt's own scientific world made him posit that "everything that existed was composed of parts, that there could not exist anything as a whole unless it existed as parts." And his version of the soul shared in that dictum. These assertions floated in the belief systems of the long eighteenth century, and the Follett sermon was

29. See Pratt's article in *The Seer*, Orson Pratt, "The Pre-Existence of Man," 102–3. For Pratt's earlier work, see Jordan Watkins, "The Great God, the Divine Mind, and the Ideal Absolute: Orson Pratt's Intelligent-Matter Theory and the Gods of Emerson and James."

30. Samuel W. Richards, "Samuel W. Richards notebook, circa 1844–1845," 88–89.

31. See, for example, Martha Sonntag Bradley and Mary Brown Firmage Woodward, "Plurality, Patriarchy, and the Priestess: Zina D. H. Young's Nauvoo Marriages," 98. Smith, *The Plural Marriage Revelation*, ch. 6.

one among them, drawing, enfolding, redesigning, and at times, discarding parts of them to make a worldview out of them.[32]

JS's denial of a contingent soul was left behind in Pratt's formulation, where the soul has a beginning, not materially *ex nihilo*, since it is somehow material, but as a potential being in the Mother's uterus. JS's claims were rethought as statements about the category of human beings and the process of generation and redemption rather than in terms of individual persons (see the following section). Woodruff shows that the Snow doctrine and the backroom discussion around it had worked a transformation on the Follett sermon protology with "the begetting of Spirits in the eternal worlds, & who by, the begetting of children on the earth, the death of man & children & the resurrection of All." Woodruff hints at more than one of the controversies (the death of . . . children) that followed the Follett sermon over the century after its delivery.

§2.3 Three Parallels

Institutional Boundary Construction, the Inroads of Deism and Rational Theism and Atheism in American Protestantism, and Follett's Hermeneutical Trajectory After Nauvoo

Here we should at least begin to consider a process that profoundly affected a theological turn in Mormonism between Nauvoo and Utah—one that drove through the heart of the Follett sermon. The process itself was not unique to the Mormon social/religious interface but appears in any number of stories of cultural change. I'll give

32. Orson Pratt, "Salvation Tangible," etc., November 12, 1876, *Journal of Discourses* 18:288. Pratt's atomic agents are replicated in "cellular automata," abstract computational systems capable of a finite number of "mental" states. Cellular automata have been used to formulate metaphysics through theories on the reduction and emergence of, among other things, mind.

two examples: one from pre-twentieth-century Mormonism and one from what has been called a disenchanted worldview.[33]

Early Latter-day Saints had experienced the theology of disappointment, and in some measure, the disappointment of theology in the failure of the Missouri Zion project. The Mormon legacy of persecution defined their interface with the federal government for the seventy years after Follett, parallel to the lesser-known theological definition I mentioned above (and will discuss more carefully later). New Mormon converts were schooled in the narrative fires of persecution by preaching and their own troubled gatherings to Zion—both the Missouri Zion and its less-well-defined counterpart in Illinois—and finally for those that followed Brigham Young, in Utah. Mormonism's transition from the communal experiments with roots in New York to the fleeting capitalism of Nauvoo is something like a microcosm of the American Protestant transition—there is a similar sense of discontinuity, catastrophe, and disappointment in both.[34]

---

33. The disenchantment I speak of began with the Protestant Reformation through to the rise of American religious democracy and the public acceptance of irreligious lifestyles. Here I follow Charles Taylor's division of secularism into three magisteria: separation of church and state, the diminished participation in religious practice, and finally, the reorienting of common opinion from one where belief in God is universal, to one which sees such a belief as one possibility among many real and practiced options. It is the last that I refer to here. Taylor, *A Secular Age*, 9–11, 22. For a complication of this narrative, see David A. Hollinger, "Christianity and Its American Fate: Where History Interrogates Secularization Theory." For a broader critique of the claim of disenchantment, see Jason A. Josephson Storm, *The Myth of Disenchantment*.

34. David F. Holland, "Anne Hutchinson to Horace Bushnell: A New Take on the New England Sequence," 163–201. Joanna Brooks, "From Edwards to Baldwin: Heterodoxy, Discontinuity, and New Narratives of American Religious-Literary History," 425–40. Richard A. Hughes, "A Civic Theology for the South: The Case of Benjamin M. Palmer," 447–67.

The Mormon version saw institutional reflection constructing a congratulatory persecution/failure narrative to unify Latter-day Saints who could "make the cut." That narrative served an *us versus them* story that fueled an isolated devotion. The rereading (and rewriting as noted above) of Follett in post-Nauvoo teaching refracted JS's ontic/cosmic framework, a rationalization of polygamy, the associated idea of sealing couples in marriage for eternity, and their effect on community and culture. The retread changed JS's uncreated spirits into the sexual offspring of God-Mothers and a God-Father. Polygamy was then a critical social/spiritual duty in two ways. First, it made elite males (who usually had many wives) into analogues of God by their fecundity, providing more ideal space on earth among the righteous for the spirits born in heaven. Second, by these acts and others, men emulated the same processes in heaven, their heavenly spouses continuing from mortality into the afterlife, and those heavenly sexual partners would then gestate spirit beings.[35] The program implied some infinitely receding succession of Gods. Orson Pratt felt uncomfortable with the risky ontic foundation of that infinite stack of divinity and proposed the alternative of the original agent atoms who formed a first God.

Brigham Young and the other apostles were not merely passive leaves floating down the outflowing stream of Nauvoo Mormonism. Neither were they the authors or translators of the most fundamental Mormon texts; but their own inspirations and influence entered into the metaphysical and practical worlds of Mormonism by preaching,

---

35. The concept of a gestation of spirits was normative enough so that by 1876, Orson Pratt could insert it as a footnote to verse 63 of section 132 of his new edition of the Doctrine and Covenants. The footnote was removed in the 1921 edition. See also Smith, *Plural Marriage Revelation*, ch. 6. On Young's communitarian movements and the relation to polygamy, see Lawrence Foster, *Women, Family, and Utopia: Communal Experiments of the Shakers, the Oneida Community, and the Mormons*. Also Leonard J. Arrington, Feramorz Y. Fox, and Dean L. May, *Building the City of God: Community and Cooperation Among the Mormons*.

extending, modifying—and occasionally reversing—those outlined by JS. Indeed, the effect of sealing a man and woman who would engage in a future sociality patterned on their mortal state in some sense made sexual activity a conceivable thing for the resurrected bodies of man and woman. A wholesale incorporation of domesticity into the future heavenly life seemed necessary and normative on those several fronts: a comforting future in the face of an isolated frontier life, a rational basis for polygamy, an explanation of eternal marriage as a cosmic duty rather than just the forever continuation of a (hopefully) wonderful companionate relationship.[36]

Sociologist Max Weber's axiom of routinization applies to JS and his apostolic successors in several interesting ways. I refer to Weber's often-quoted phrase "routinization of charisma" as it is applied to new religious traditions. In part, Weber's theory posits that a movement begins with a charismatic figure but that to survive it must move to a bureaucratic priesthood where charisma becomes embedded in ritual.[37] It drew a new line that defined tradition from JS's work within the cross currents of settling a frontier (dispersal), binding up and rationalizing a new and fragile religious tradition (gathering), addressing the social fireworks of the revelation on polygamy (near violent/chaotic emotion), and resisting the United States government's breach of the polity of Deseret (fight or flight: Washington's territorial appointees, Johnston's army, etc.). The process began to

36. On rereading founders, see Malcolm D. Lambert, *Franciscan Poverty*, 70–75, Victor Turner, *The Ritual Process: Structure and Anti-Structure*, 134–37. On a similar change in the remapping of body and soul by American Puritans, see Martha L. Finch, *Dissenting Bodies: Corporealities in Early New England*, xii, 4–9, 17. J. Gordon Melton, "When Prophets Die: The Succession Crisis in New Religions," 1–12. And Taysom, "A Uniform and Common Recollection," 121–52.

37. See Jonathan H. Turner, et al., *The Emergence of Sociological Theory*, 212. Max Weber, *The Sociology of Religion*. Also Matthew Bowman, "Matthew Philip Gill and Joseph Smith: the Dynamics of Mormon Schism."

support a retelling of Nauvoo Mormonism for which Follett was an important, if partial, proxy. Like Ann Lee's followers, who after her death began to gather memories of her words to form a founding text, the Latter-day Saint apostolic leadership sought out recollections and then focused the early tradition to match Utah realities.[38]

All of this was part of the historical struggle to bring meaning to ordinary life through a belief in something more transcendent. While JS seemed to make abstract war with classical transcendence (*everything* is material), the movement also needed something higher, a testament of a better afterlife with meaning not in abstraction but in transcendent ordinariness.[39]

§2.4 More on the Ontological Rereadings of King Follett

Competing Theologies, Polygamy, Analogical Strains.

Religion helps give meaning to the world and rationalize issues of ultimate concern. It offers correspondence between the cosmos and our

---

38. Thomas F. O'Dea, *The Mormons*, 54–55; Jan Shipps, *Mormonism: The Story of a New Religious Tradition*, 24. On the analogue to ancient Christianity, see Powell, *Irenaeus, Joseph Smith, and God-Making Heresy*. On social forces at work in the transition from Nauvoo to Utah, see Kathleen Flake, "Re-placing Memory: Latter-day Saint Use of Historical Monuments and Narrative in the Early Twentieth Century," 73–76. See also Smith, *The Plural Marriage Revelation*, 93–98. On Ann Lee, Mormonism, and analogous redefinitions, see Stephen C. Taysom, *Shakers, Mormons, and Religious Worlds*. On the forces behind theological strain, see Benjamin E. Park, "(Re)Interpreting Early Mormon Thought: Synthesizing Joseph Smith's Theology and the Process of Religious Formation." Taysom, "A Uniform and Common Recollection."

39. As in JS's reported saying, "that same sociality that exists among us here [on earth], will exist among us there, [in heaven] only it will be coupled with eternal [transcendent?] glory." Doctrine and Covenants 130:2.

limited—in space and time—existence on earth.[40] To borrow from strain theory, after Geertz, theological innovation is a facet of social, religious, and cultural stress. A loss of orientation in life direction, a challenge to personal assumptions (say, the death of a loved one or some broader cultural or physical change) and the need to explain such things gives rise to theological activity. Change or innovation from science, technology or the environment, the surfacing of humanity's capacity for moral ugliness, the tragedy of loss and separation, the failure of expectation, the dissonance between event and hope, the desire to give hope—these can all manifest in religious/theological/interpretive strain.[41] For example, when the Cliff Dwellers of Mesa Verde faced the stress of a deadly thirty year drought, they left no readable texts to help divine their cosmological struggle—but archeology revealed the continued expansion of kiva sacred space, part of the strain that derived from intense famine.[42]

In Geertz's work, strain can be thought of as deformation. JS's April 7 sermon and its antecedents were a part of the strain constructed out of the failure of the Missouri Zion. The struggles in the Nauvoo temple building project, the illness and death that plagued the inhabitants of Nauvoo, the rising tide of internal and external criticism of JS partly over his introduction of polygamy and the Mormon interaction with the politics of Hancock County, Illinois and the state itself.[43] The Follett sermon wrought a salvific context for the Mormon masses, one where God was less a sovereign than supreme exemplar, declaring that God was one with Jesus in a new way, a way that included them.

40. Thomas A. Tweed, *Crossing and Dwelling: A Theory of Religion*, ch. 5.

41. Geertz, "Ideology as a Cultural System," 64.

42. From a 2016 conversation between the author and site archeologists.

43. On the failure of Zion, see Stephen C. Taysom, "'There is Always a Way of Escape': Continuity and Reconstitution in Nineteenth-Century Mormon Boundary Maintenance Strategies," 184–90. On Nauvoo Politics, see Park, *Kingdom of Nauvoo*.

By quoting or alluding to the Gospel of John in the Follett sermon, JS's interpretation marked God's life as already the great example and prior to and a mirror of Jesus's life. Chapter 5 of Jn was invoked in Follett: "I do nothing but what I have seen my Father do" is the essential takeaway. Human beings can follow in the footsteps of Jesus—not through a repeated Passion (at the moment at least) but through sacramental/ritual grace—a Jesus who had already followed in the footsteps of God. The sermon brought *imitatio dei* to public Mormon literature as it already existed in private: "they shall be gods, because they have all power."[44]

JS appreciated the shock value of his preaching.[45] Perhaps he meant to reduce attention to rumors of Nauvoo's underground polygamy by this innovative teaching. Instead, it added fuel to the dissenting fires, though it did provide him with the opportunity to publicly defend some part of his theological, soteriological, and ontological exploits. JS continued and defended the Follett sermon up to the end of his life in June 1844; for example, he did so in sermons delivered on May 12, 1844, and June 16, 1844.

JS's public preaching never really confronted the specter of polygamy, beyond deploring scattered copycat attempts at recruiting spiritual wives by those outside his circle of (authorized) insiders. His sermon of May 26, 1844, did address the polygamy issue—but not in a way that any insider saw as a denial. They saw it as preaching against *unauthorized* polygamy.[46] It was JS's apostolic successors who

44. Doctrine and Covenants 132:20, a text first made public eight years after JS's death.

45. "It has always been my province to dig up hidden mysteries, new things, for my hearers," from a May 12, 1844, sermon audit (*Parallel Joseph*).

46. Young women who were part of polygamy in Nauvoo may have referred to themselves as "spirituals." According to one witness, the practice made for a kind of dating roulette among young unattached men. See "Orange L. Wight Reminiscences, 1903 May-December." On the May 12, May 26, and June 16, 1844,

demonstrated a small part of the strain polygamy enacted in the 1855–56 reconstruction of the Follett sermon.

Another example of such strain within the church historians' 1850s sermon project was the redaction of Eliza R. Snow's reports of JS speaking to the Nauvoo Female Relief Society. Snow originally reported JS delivering keys to the society, working to make them a kingdom of priests, "as in Enoch's day." Church historian George A. Smith rewrote Snow's account with JS "delivering the keys of the Priesthood to the church and that the faithful members of the Relief Society should receive them in connection with their husbands." In Snow's report, JS asked that the Society place confidence in their chosen presidency (Emma Smith, Sarah Cleveland, Elizabeth Whitney). In the revision, the women were enjoined to faith in their husbands and church leaders. The reasoning for these and other changes was founded in apostolic succession and the situating of Emma Hale Smith as dissenter and enemy of the church. Brigham Young distrusted the Relief Society for those reasons and the suggestion that it had some parity of ecclesiastical standing with male dominated institutions.[47]

In JS's founding documents—including Follett—his successors found an afterlife that was made joyful and glorious by remaining eternally connected to an expanded family and their earthly descendants. This cosmology required little reassignment of terms to *come to, and believe in*, a God who sired those spirits, just as human parents

---

sermons see *Parallel Joseph*. Also Smith, *Every Word Seasoned With Grace*, chs. 9, 10. On dissent and JS's denials, see Richard Lyman Bushman, *Joseph Smith: Rough Stone Rolling*, 533–38.

47. Snow's original text for April 28, 1842, may be read online at *JSP*. George Smith's revised text, approved by Brigham Young, is found in Church Historian's Office. History of the Church, 1839–circa 1882, vol. 3, pp. 1302, 1326, vol. 4 addenda pp. 26–27, 38–43, CR 100 102, CHL. See also Church Historian's Office Journal, vol. 17, pp. 361–62, CR 100 1, CHL. For the two texts in parallel, see *Parallel Joseph* (April 28, 1842).

propagated their species. Yet the linking of God and sex was as repugnant to Illinois Mormons in Nauvoo times as it was to Protestants.[48]

Brigham Young saw a new vision of his own in his reformatting of the Godhead, with Adam and Eve as birth parents of all human souls *and* the first human bodies after Eden, an idea beginning to settle by the time of the westward Mormon migration in 1847.[49] Young saw this same Adam returning to earth to sire Jesus. Eve was Mother on earth and Mother in heaven—indeed, the very mother of all. In many ways, this constellation of ideas marked the apex of Mormon alterity, yet in its focus on a domestic or later, a nuclear family, heaven represented a feature of the age. In the medieval and early modern epochs of the Christian era, it was not the preservation of earthly loving that preoccupied believers but the dread of facing the Last Judgment after death, something that the Reformers of the sixteenth century encouraged.[50]

Orson Pratt rejected the theological turn of Adamic godhood; he wished to keep the fatherhood of Jesus within the classical Christian package.[51] But even his system required a God-Wife, a Heavenly Mother, who was once a mortal woman; in turn, this pressed Mormonism into more than the three-story religion of Protestant Christendom.

---

48. See Blair Dee Hodges, "'My Principality on Earth Began': Millennialism and the Celestial Kingdom in the Development of Mormon Doctrine," 44.

49. On the transition, see Brigham Young, December 6, 1847, Council Minutes, Leonard J. Arrington papers. Stapley, "Brigham Young's Garden Cosmology."

50. On Adam, see for example, Kenney, *Wilford Woodruff's Journal*, 3:295, 6:508. Eliza Snow's vision of God the Father and Mother became one with Adam and Eve. She made Young's assertions explicit in her own theological declarations. See, for example, her poem, "To Mrs.—," lines 75–84, item 252, in Derr and Davidson, *Eliza R. Snow: The Complete Poetry*. On earlier times and the evolution of afterlife concerns, see Philippe Ariès, *The Hour of Our Death*.

51. For example, Pratt, *The Seer*, 103. Gary James Bergera, "The Orson Pratt-Brigham Young Controversies: Conflict Within the Quorums, 1853–1868," 7–49; David John Buerger, "The Adam-God Doctrine," 14–58. Turner, *Brigham Young*, 231–36.

Mormonism became a religion not just of Heaven, Earth, and Hell, but the religion of one long, connected, and self-replicating cosmos.

Nineteenth-century Mormon leaders like Young announced that Mormonism was simply a description of the way everything worked, by axiomatizing a heaven in the image of earth and positing an infinite regression of Gods mentioned above. Follett offered support here: God was once a man who owed allegiance to his own Father-God. In the end, twentieth-century Mormonism rejected and adopted different elements of both Orson Pratt and Young, cutting away the portions reciting Pratt's atomic-agent–first-cause and Young's vision of Adam and Eve in service of polygamy, while leaving behind a somewhat incoherent package of statements disconnected from their logical antecedents.[52]

Aside from any parallel or post-Nauvoo apostolic interpretation, JS's Nauvoo system established a new calculus of reward in the afterlife: a man's earthly acquisition of (polygamous) wives and both natural and ritually *adopted* children—as in children in a family born prior to their parents being sealed together—meant an advantage in the world to come. That advantage came by virtue of descendants creating and populating worlds, in a sense, expanding a patriarch's *estate*, on a superb scale. Brigham Young and other church leaders extended their families not just by birth but also by sealing other unrelated adults to them. This practice was also termed adoption.[53]

The King James Bible was full of language useful in shaping the contours of a belief in Mother-birthed spirits.[54] The technical details

52. The fundamental mechanism of heaven is found in Doctrine and Covenants 130:1–2. Smith, *Plural Marriage Revelation*, ch. 6.

53. On the beginnings and evolution of adoption theology in Mormonism, see Samuel Brown, "Early Mormon Adoption Theology and the Mechanics of Salvation." Jonathan A. Stapley, "Adoptive Sealing Ritual in Mormonism."

54. Various passages served the purpose such as those found in Gn 1, Mal 2, Mt 23, Jn 1, 5, 9, Eph 1, Col 1, Heb 12 all with an admittedly unique (and anti-Protestant)

of the heavenly family were never fully agreed on in any official way; Brigham Young's rejection of much of Orson Pratt's cosmology, the reticence of the Latter-day Saints to fully embrace Young's own Adamic theology, and the coming assimilation of the Saints into twentieth-century American culture led to a decline in public speech on the issue. Frederick Kesler reported Young's 1869 version of his system:

> He [Young] said adam had previous to being placed in the Garden, had received his exaltation he came here & assisted in Organizing this earth & then him self & Eve eat of Fruits of this earth until thare Sistems were Charged with the same then they Could & did make tabernacles, for the Spirits which he had previously made: thus Commencets [commenced] man upon this earth [55]

The analogy of heaven on earth strengthened the earthy roots and reasons for sealings in Mormonism, though it did take time for this perspective to become normative in the discursive world of Utah. The Middle Mormonism theological exchange of self-existent human souls for a logic of procreated/gestated spirits helped to root the theology of polygamy in a post-mortal picture of life, and provided reasons for communal coherence in a fraught pioneer isolation and deep rationality for polygamy: it persisted in heaven and accelerated the work of God there by allowing many more spirits to be born.[56] Self-

---

Mormon turn. The history of the interpretation of D&C 93 shows how such interpretive work developed over time. See Charles R. Harrell, "The Development of the Doctrine of Preexistence, 1830–1844," 82–84.

55. Sealing was JS's term for ritually binding persons together with the power delivered by Christ to his ancient apostles: "whatsoever thou shalt bind on earth shall be bound in heaven" (Matt 16:19) compare Doctrine and Covenants 132. Frederick Kesler (December 11, 1869) Journal 3, page 210. Compare Wilford Woodruff's journal, December 11, 1869, Kenney, *Wilford Woodruff's Journal*, 6:508.

56. The underlying principle was that not many men would be eligible for exaltation. All the worthy women had to have a consort to perform their divine purpose. This idea persisted up to the end of Mormon polygamy. Elite Mormon men

existent souls did nothing in that scheme. Follett was on that front inconsistent with the ubiquitous analogical arguments of Utah theology that justified so much of church practice on the frontier. The desert West was new and challenging for a burst of recent converts from British centers of Mormon missionary activities, and the picture of heaven on earth provided some basis for believing that the men and women of the church had it in them to win out all the time and make an enduring Zion.[57]

Spirits as offspring was, in an important way, an anti-Christian message: not a lack of belief in a historical and atoning Christ but a limitation on the power of that Christ. The correct raw material had to be there *prior* to Christian belief. This was perhaps partly a disgust for Protestant anthropologies (mostly original sin but other claims as well, especially predestination). Lorenzo Snow's 1872 reasoning shows the importance of human spirits being birthed in heaven (an anticipation of the more explicit biological arguments of the twentieth century). Humans *couldn't* become godlike unless they had the fundamental makings of a god already present within them. And Snow argued that the only way this was possible was through God transmitting his own divine properties by physical inheritance, what in the twentieth century would be thought of as genetics:

> Our spirit birth gave us godlike capabilities . . . in our spiritual birth our Father transmitted to us the capabilities, powers and faculties which he himself possessed.[58]

---

who had many wives would maintain that status in heaven by virtue of their accelerated propagation. Eliza Snow advised young women to marry such men rather than younger men in order to ensure their own status. Smith, *Plural Marriage Revelation*, 194–95.

57. Bowman, *Mormon People*, 126–30.

58. Lorenzo Snow, "Progression—The Fatherhood of God," 302. It was the story of "seed" once again. See chapters 3 and 4 below.

Confidence in the claims for heavenly exaltation was an issue, and the logic gained repeated emphasis in twentieth-century Mormon encounters with biology, philosophy, sociology, psychology, secularity, and science in general. In those encounters, Follett brought strengths and liabilities. The latter would eventually win out in matters of public perception.

While JS's Nauvoo cosmology/ontology in the Follett sermon might comfort the bereaved,[59] the notions of a heaven achievable on earth and the promise of renewing physical love and propagation in the hereafter were potent motivations for enduring the Western frontier. It gave concepts of Zion different and deeper dimension, and folded polygamy (and its natural companion and then successor—sealing/adoption) into a vision of patriarchal progress.[60] It is not difficult to see that this constructive salvation tread with one foot parallel to Unitarianism and earlier some fundamental principles of the Deism of Founding Fathers like Jefferson or the Rational Theism of others like Washington: God had created a benevolent system, but Mankind was required to climb the created ladder laid out in that system. As Follett had it, "you have got to *learn* how to be gods yourselves." Of course, JS rejected the eighteenth-century logic that such

---

59. Here I believe it is as important to read JS's preaching with emphasis on the crafting of discourse (his discourse in general perhaps) rather than what is often attempted: morphing meanings to achieve propositional consistency with Mormon teachings of the next two centuries. The era-dependent theological implications are illustrated by the example of one woman who had recently lost a young daughter in an accident and—having learned of JS's remarks in Follett—expressed it this way: "which comforts more: someone telling you that your daughter's "spirit dust" is eternal or that her soul, her personality, is self-existent? I can tell you my answer." The answer was the Nauvoo theology of JS. (Personal communication to the author.)

60. In terms of his preaching, Smith's Zion experiment is discussed in chapters 8 and 9 of Smith, *Every Word Seasoned With Grace*. For one attempt at systematic development of Smith's ontology/cosmology, see Blake T. Ostler, *Exploring Mormon Thought*. See also Brown, *In Heaven*, ch. 9.

systems entailed a Deity who took no present active role in the world. Petitionary prayer, for example, had no part in the belief of Deists. The God of JS was clearly active within history.[61]

Another consequence of JS's spirit theology was interpreting Mormon adoption as an important *modus operandi* of postmortal family largesse. In JS's world, one's kingdom in the hereafter was extended by adoption of spirits to one's burgeoning heavenly family, a process in the image of the Follett sermon's God. Subsequently, those souls would become embodied mortals acquiring their own descendant kingdoms, expanding the parental heavenly kingdom. The earthly head start on those promised heavenly kingdoms centered on (possibly polygamy-aided) reproduction and for a short time at least, "spiritual" adoption where one man might adopt non-biologically related men and their families into his future heavenly family via a sealing ritual. A limiting factor in this scenario in the post-JS period was Brigham Young's prescription that no earthly eternal adoptions were available without a temple—and Latter-day Saints in the Salt Lake deserts had left their Nauvoo temple behind. JS's *adoptive* vision of heaven (spirits adopted, not born) lacked important pioneer gravitas in the face of a reproductive mythos like that of William Phelps, Eliza and Lorenzo Snow, Orson and Parley Pratt, and Brigham Young.

Perhaps the reason for Young's postponement of earthly adoptive ritual after Nauvoo rested in part on the rather confusing nature of such earthly adoptive "families" and the diverse reactions from Saints who learned of them.[62] As a practical solution to communal binding, it

61. On the founders, see David L. Holmes, *The Faiths of the Founding Fathers*. Taylor, *A Secular Age*, 302, 551. On the modern version of the conflict, see Robert Q. Lewis, "Petitionary Prayer—Caught in the Chaos of Strange Attractors: A Study of Divine Action in the Writings of John Polkinghorne."

62. Turner, *Brigham Young*, 160–61. Stapley, "Adoptive Sealing Ritual in Mormonism." See also, George Laub's (first) journal, pages 102, 106, 182, 194. MS 9628, CHL.

lacked wide application. The idea of a (cosmologically distant) promise of family expansion and linkage by an immediate and temporarily available extra-temple liturgy—*some* sealings, including polygamous ones, could be performed outside temples—filled a gap in the narrative of belonging and patriarchal "kingdom building." Indeed, over time, the hierarchy of the Utah church tended to be strongly interrelated.[63] At the same time, it reflected immediate concerns of cohesiveness and unity—even JS's Abrahamic texts seemed to hint that biological descent was superior to adoption as in the phrase "born in the covenant" and Book of Mormon figures who joyed in their genealogical relation to the first Nephi and similarly in New Testament class society.[64] Since Young specified that sealing of biological children to parents born prior to a marriage sealing (in fact, any sort of parent-child sealing, all were referred to as adoptions) could only be carried out within the walls of a Latter-day Saint temple, the policy was perhaps an encouragement to temple-building. If one lacked biological connection to the elite, loyalty to such important figures might jump over biology by adoption. More broadly, biological heritage had negative as well as positive consequences within Mormonism. For example, Black people as "Seed of Cain" was a common societal ratio-

---

63. See, for example, D. Michael Quinn, "Organizational Development and Social Origins of the Mormon Hierarchy, 1832–1932," together with D. Michael Quinn, *The Mormon Hierarchy: Origins of Power*. See, more generally, David J. Whittaker, "Mormon Administrative and Organizational History: A Source Essay," 611–95.

64. For example, the Gospel of Matthew rests largely on the ancestry of David; alternatively, John emphasizes the Mosaic heritage while Jesus's brother runs the Jerusalem church. On JS and birth vs. adoption, see, for example, his discussion of Election in a sermon of June 27, 1839, and later a sermon given on March 10, 1844. JS felt his first child to be "born in the covenant" (born after JS's death and named David) was to be a successor to him of sorts, a type of Christ. Valeen Tippetts Avery, *From Mission to Madness: Last Son of the Mormon Prophet*, 21–23, 108. Quinn, *Origins of Power*, 230–31. Smith, *Plural Marriage Revelation*, 102–3.

nale for slavery for Latter-day Saints and Americans in general. In this case, the temple could not intervene as Young decided it: Black people did not share in Zion. That doctrine gained its own metaphysics in the image of polygamy: the spirits of Black people were deemed defective, not just their inherited bodies in the stories of Noah and Cain.[65]

An attractive and unifying aspect of the reproductive over the adoptive version of the postmortal family was the male-female aspect of the divine. God was the Father of human souls or spirits, but He required a Mother for that role and that involved—as in Pratt's ideal and William Phelps's fiction—pregnancy and birth. Immortal and mortal biology were reproductively the same. This was the ultimate reason, the metaphysics, for polygamy on earth: it would continue in heaven for reproductive efficiency. Young and other church leaders did not blanch at such notions, but the cultural boundaries of the time made the public *worship* of such a Mother-being far outside institutional norms, as it still remains despite the persistence of polygamy's metaphysics. In Mormonism, as in general society, women were not in the broadest sense externally authoritative persons, and nineteenth-century concepts of the Mormon family left the divine feminine undeveloped. Young saw the divine Mother in the Genesis Eve:

---

65. On Young, see, for example, L. John Nuttall diary, August 24, 1877. On JS's belief that Black persons were the "seed of Cain," see *JSP*, J2:30. On religious rationalizations of American slavery, see Howe, *What Hath God Wrought*, 56, 479. Benjamin Braude, "The Sons of Noah and the Construction of Ethnic and Geographical Identities in Medieval and Early Modern Periods." See also Noel Rae, *The Great Stain: Witnessing American Slavery*. Latter-day Saints pointed to passages in the Pearl of Great Price, Moses 7:22, Abr 1. On the Mormon metaphysical rationale (defective spirits), see B. H. Roberts, *Seventy's Course in Theology* 5 vols., 1:164–166. The trope continued into modern Mormonism. See Ezra Taft Benson, "Trust Not the Arm of Flesh," 55. Max Perry Mueller, *Race and the Making of the Mormon People*. Reeve, *Religion of a Different Color*.

> B. Young Said Our Father in the Heavens is the father of all Spirits—When Adam with one of his wives came into the Garden of Eden he had his Celestial Body—they Eat of that Fruit till it Produced the mortal Body Can you understand that? Who was Jesus' Father? The Holy Ghost was not—For the holy ghost is a Spirit a personage without Tabernacle. The father & lord of this world was Adam[66]

> Some have thought it strange what I have said Concerning Adam But the period will Come when this people of faithful will be willing to adopt Joseph Smith as their Prophet Seer Revelator & God But not the *father of their spirits* for that was our Father Adam.[67]

Perhaps some biological understanding contributed here. In the centuries leading up to JS's era—and during his lifetime—widely accepted notions of conception placed women in the role of mere receptacles: receptacles for male seed.[68] Anatomists had known for centuries that female sex organs were in some ways the mirror image of those of a male. But the notion of female egg combining with male sperm was only speculation and not broadly accepted. Instead, the King James Version of the Bible guided the theology of conception.

---

66. John Pulsipher journal, April 9, 1852.

67. Brigham Young, December 1869, Kenney, *Wilford Woodruff's Journal*, 6:508. See also Brigham Young address, October 8, 1854, Fred Collier, ed., *The Teachings of President Brigham Young*, 3 vols., 3:343–46. "When Brigham Young proclaimed to the nations that Adam was our Father and God, and Eve, his partner, the Mother of a world—both in a mortal and a Celestial sense—he made the most important revelation ever oracled to the race since the days of Adam, himself," Tullidge, *The Women of Mormondom*, 196–97. On Mormon Heavenly Mother theology in print, see David L. Paulsen and Martin Pulido, "'A Mother There': A Survey of Historical Teachings about Mother in Heaven." See also Susanna Morrill, *White Roses on the Floor of Heaven: Mormon Women's Popular Theology, 1880–1920*. An examination of new sources is found in Stapley, "Garden Theology."

68. Aristotle (*Generation of Animals*, 736) and St. Thomas (*Summa Contra Gentiles*, II.89.11) illustrate.

"Seed" was all there was in the way of generation. *Abraham's seed* was a male concept. A male's seed only needed the right garden to flourish and its fruit was the male's property, being a part of him. That garden was woman, and her womb might be closed or open to seed and its flourishing, depending on God's curse or blessing.

The idea was important to polygamy and in a subtle way to the Follett sermon. A man was the source of Life. There was no Christian mystery as to why God could be Father without any Mother, an idea that was, in a way, a reverse Mormonism. Eliza Snow's poem was about far more than JS's revelation of polygamy and the theology of inclusion (divine characters could be women) than about any cultural/theological necessity of Divine partners, in spite of the statement she marked as "reason"—*that* was all about sex. Whether human generation required only male seed (always in evidence) or male and female seed combined was in controversy from Aristotle's time, without a widely understood and accepted evidence for a female component to generation until after JS's day.[69] In the next chapters, I will explore among other things Mormonism's flirtation with Protestant fundamentalism in the twentieth century as a reason for the lack of modern biology's infiltration of its god-talk and its role in the quieting of that talk altogether; these and other issues would help create a ban on church use of RC for close to thirty years and a cautionary note about its public use thereafter.

---

69. For an account of "sperm and egg," see Jill Lapore, *The Mansion of Happiness: A History of Life and Death*, ch. 1; for Rabbinic grappling with the biblical idea, see Edward Reichmann, "The Rabbinic Conception of Conception: An Exercise in Fertility," 35–44. On the science, see Dean Clift and Melina Schuh, "Restarting Life: Fertilization and the Transition from Meiosis to Mitosis."

§2.5 The 1856 Sermon Project

History Making

One of JS's projects was the publication of his own public history. The history project had roots in the beginnings of Mormonism, but gained continuing productive traction in JS's short Missouri residence (1838). The stated purpose of this history was to counter the rumors and unfounded claims that put JS and his followers in a bad light. When JS gained Willard Richards as secretary, confidant, and supervising historian in 1841, the project finally began in earnest. JS dictated his own early history, but as other preserved records like his intermittent scribe-composed diaries and correspondence could be used, JS's role became progressively smaller and ultimately almost non-existent. Richards used past and present Church imprints as source material along with his own work as JS's diarist-ghostwriter.[70] One of Richards's goals was a significant collection of JS's sermons. Unfortunately, as noted above, matters of early Church polity made careful audits of those sermons rare.[71]

With the Mormon diaspora of 1844–1846, the migration to Utah in 1847, and then Richards's long illness ending in death in 1854, the history effort was in stasis until a successor historian, George A. Smith (1817–1875), came on board. George Smith was dedicated to the project and continued Richards's work from its 1838 stopping point to an 1844 completion and then beyond. In 1855, George Smith assigned relatively new clerk Jonathan Grimshaw (1818–1889) to the sermon project.

The Follett sermon is known most broadly through the text (re) constructed by Jonathan Grimshaw in 1855–1856. Grimshaw was a

---

70. Part of Richards's plan for the history is recorded in the manuscript "Church Historian's Office. History of the Church, 1839-circa 1882," vol. 4, first pages of the unpaginated volume, (ms history). See also "Draft Notes," various dates, *JSP*. Also Historian's Office History of the Church (draft) 1845–1867.

71. See Smith, "Joseph Smith's Sermons."

clerk in the church historian's office from 1853 to 1856, when he left Utah.[72] Grimshaw's technique is an illustration of methods used by ancient compilers of teachings and speeches of various great historical figures of the past. Grimshaw took some of the confirmed/blessed sources, using VOT as a base text, and fused them together to form a longer, though not in general more informative or authentic, text. Grimshaw completed his text during the three days ending on October 15, 1855. Both handwriting evidence and contemporary records show this first draft was modified by George A. Smith with the assistance of Thomas Bullock. The pair used manuscript sources, but Smith modified the text sometimes without any manuscript authority (for an example, see below and Appendix A). Following these modifications, the text was again revised by Brigham Young on November 15, 1855. A final approval was given by Young, Jedediah M. Grant, Young's associate in the church presidency, assistant historian Wilford Woodruff, and another copyist/clerk, Leo Hawkins, on August 9, 1856. Prior to that approval, it was copied into volume 6 of "Church Historian's Office History of the Church" (hereafter, ms history). The ms history copy was made by Robert Lang Campbell, yet another clerk in the historian's office, in April 1856. This is RC. RC was published with only slight changes in the Salt Lake City newspaper *The Deseret News* (DN) on July 8, 1857 as a part of JS's history. Stenographer-publisher George D. Watt used DN as a base text for an entry in volume 6 of his Liverpool, England, Mormon sermon serial, *The Journal of Discourses* in 1859. DN was also reprinted in an 1861 issue of the Liverpool *Latter-day Saints' Millennial Star* (MS2) as it reprinted JS's history annals, based on the *News*. As a complete text, RC dropped from print for

72. Some material on Grimshaw is taken from William V. Smith (WVS), "Jonathan Grimshaw and Honorable Doubts." Ardis E. Parshall, "Leaving Mormonism: Jonathan Grimshaw Crosses the Plains from West to East, 1856." See also Will Bagley, "Perilous Journey: The Grimshaw Family's Narrow Escape, 1856."

more than twenty years until the April 1883 issue of the church's magazine for young men, *The Contributor* (CON) (see fig. 1). A new text tradition began in 1909 (see chapter 3).[73]

§2.6 Jonathan Grimshaw: The Disappearing Scribe

Grimshaw was a British convert to Mormonism who had tried more than one religion prior to his contact with the Latter-day Saints. A seeker, he moved from the Particular Baptists of his parents' persuasion to the Miller Adventists in 1844. Born in 1818, Grimshaw experienced Dickensian England at the height of the industrial revolution. The boy left formal education at age eleven but continued self-education after his cobbler apprentice hours. When the master decided to move from town, Grimshaw begged his leave and found work, first in freight transport and then the new railroad between Leeds and Derby. Grimshaw's reputation for honesty and careful work brought him good fortune. In 1844, Grimshaw was in Nottingham when Mormon missionaries arrived. At first he joined in the general skepticism over JS, but eventually he went to hear the Mormon preachers and found he could not "overturn their doctrine or principles." When Grimshaw heard that the elders could bless the sick, he asked them to bless his wife. She was healed. Both he and his wife joined Mormonism in 1849, and by 1850 he was an elder in the Church. The gathering to Utah was an overriding principle of Mormonism of the time, and in December 1850 the family emigrated. The *Nottingham Review* of January 3, 1851, wrote of Grimshaw's departure:

> On Monday last a complimentary dinner as given by the clerks and other employees at the goods station, to Mr. Grimshaw, late manager of the Goods Department of the Railway Station in

73. Further documentary details are found in Smith, *Every Word Seasoned with Grace*, ch. 7.

> this town, who is about leaving this country for the Great Salt Lake City, Deseret, California, at Mr. Starkey's, the Victoria Hotel, Station Street Queen's Road, on which occasion a beautifully embroidered purse containing 15 pounds with the inscription 'J. Grimshaw, Nottingham, 1850' on each side, was presented to him. J.G. left Nottingham by the 10:30 A.M. train for Liverpool on Wednesday accompanied by about thirty friends who are bound for the same destination, Deseret, the Mormon settlement in North America. Along with him went Mr. Abraham Taylor, book-vendor, of this town, Mr. Kirk, and Mr. Hazzledine of Basford, and some others.

The Grimshaws sailed on January 8, 1855, aboard the "Ellen" with another 450 Latter-day Saints. After Grimshaw arrived in New Orleans he noted an incident in his travel journal that reveals something of his character:

> It was a very tiresome job having to handle all the luggage twice over, and many of the boxes got broken, but upon the whole I think we managed pretty well. I went out the last thing to buy a few provisions, being thirsty and weary with the fatiguing business of the day, I took a little brandy which was offered me at Mr. Fisher's store, and it flew into my head and set my tongue a-going like the clapper of a bell. I was as merry as a lark. To speak the truth right out I was regularly fuddled. I have recorded my fault and think now I have a right to record. something in my praise. I remembered in going back to the steamer that I was bringing a dollar's worth of sugar away unpaid for, and I ran back to Mr. Fisher's as fast as my legs would carry me and made the matter right.

Grimshaw came from England with £133, a considerable sum (the transatlantic voyage—always cheap by overland standards—cost less than £3). When the family was in St. Louis, they purchased six oxen, four cows, two wagons, took on a boarder, and departed Winter Quarters, Nebraska, June 22, 1851. They made good time to Salt Lake City, coming in around the end of August that same year. Grimshaw tried to fit into the prevailing barter economy, but he was no farmer. He began clerking for Church and civic interests in the infant county and territorial governments and court systems. While Grimshaw and his wife, Eliza, worked hard at Mormonism, some facets of the faith, including polygamy, the beginnings of the Mormon Reformation, and the difficult near-famine conditions of early Utah proved too much for them. Jonathan and Eliza left Utah in August 1856 on friendly terms with church leaders, but full of doubt about the Mormon enterprise.[74]

74. Grimshaw's early life and later activities are found in his journals, Jonathan Grimshaw Journal, 1850–December 1851, and Jonathan Grimshaw Journal, June 1853–April 1854. Grimshaw's frank admittance to Wilford Woodruff that he could no longer tell if Mormonism's claims were true made the journey from Utah a necessity. Grimshaw saw Utah Mormonism as very different from his first expectations of a modern Israel. The Grimshaws had no debts and left without recrimination with the help of a loan from England. Their wagon train had a near miss with Indian attacks but arrived in St. Louis that fall where he returned to his railroad roots. Grimshaw's report of his journey showed his now skeptical view of Utah's system. The family moved to Jefferson City in 1858 and spent the Civil War years there. Grimshaw had found the town to his liking when coming to Utah, and both he and a son served as mayor after the war. Grimshaw kept quiet about his Latter-day Saint past in the heart of anti-Mormon country and joined the Episcopal Church. Despite his confession of doubt, Woodruff and other leaders found Grimshaw to be an honorable man. George A. Smith, Letter to Brigham Young, Nov. 12, 1856, St. Louis, Missouri. Wilford Woodruff Journal, August 4, 1856, Kenny, *Wilford Woodruff's Journal* 4:433. John Y. Simon, ed., The Papers of Ulysses S. Grant Volume 19: July 1, 1868–October 31, 1869, 343. M. L. Van Nada, ed., *The Book of Missourians*, 455–56. *Portrait and Biographical Record of Johnson and Pettis Counties Missouri*, 162. Philemon C. Merrill journal, August 12, 1856 (typescript). Michael Hicks, *The Mormon Tabernacle Choir: A Biography*, 20; Michael Hicks, *Mormonism and Music: A History*, 46. J. Linforth, "Foreign Correspondence," 27–8. "Adventures of a Mormon Settler."

§2.7 Grimshaw's Editorial Work on Follett and Utah Theological Roots

In June 1853, when Willard Richards hired Grimshaw to work in the historian's office of the church,[75] the crew at the historian's office often did double duty, serving the territorial legislature in mid-winter, keeping records of church ordinances like endowments and sealings/marriages, working at the church newspaper, *The Deseret News*, the post office, and auditing Sunday sermons and church councils among other things.[76]

Richards was editor and proprietor of the Salt Lake City newspaper, *The Deseret News,* from 1850, and it absorbed much of his time and energy until 1853. A chronic illness prevented his restarting JS's history until his death in 1854. One of Grimshaw's contributions to the historian's effort was copying the church's history into some of the large, blank manuscript books, numbered A-1, B-1, C-1, D-1, E-1, and F-1 (particularly the last). The effort, as with Willard Richards, involved copying and connecting already existing reports, journal entries, and other records into a first person narrative in the voice of JS. Eventually, George Smith had Grimshaw focus on JS's sermons. Willard Richards and George Smith had made efforts to accumulate reports of the sermons, but these audits were generally brief and sometimes too idiosyncratic or complicated by distance to be useful.[77]

---

75. Grimshaw wrote to Brigham Young on September 6, 1852, asking for a clerk position. See Jonathan Grimshaw, Letter to Brigham Young.

76. "Deseret" was the Book of Mormon word for honey bee and the name for the huge territory Latter-day Saint leadership initially staked out in the western United States, nearly coincidental with James K. Polk's war for the acquisition of Upper Mexico. That war created the U.S. military district named Utah. See Brent M. Rogers, *Unpopular Sovereignty: Mormons and the Federal Management of Early Utah Territory*. David M. Potter, *The Impending Crisis, 1848–1861*.

77. An example of complication is JS's sermon of October 9, 1843, a funeral address for close friend and father figure James Adams. In 1855, William C. Staines

Grimshaw—never a witness to JS's preaching—was asked to take reports of the sermons of JS (sometimes several reports from different auditors of the same sermon were available to the historians) and fuse those different audits of a given sermon into a single text with logical or church leader mediated expansions. Grimshaw worked on a number of these sermons and some early drafts of his work are preserved, sometimes edited by Thomas Bullock and/or George Smith. Grimshaw's longest effort was the King Follett Sermon. Grimshaw fused the reports of Wilford Woodruff, Willard Richards, and VOT in his first draft (GM0). As noted above, that draft was redacted by George Smith, Bullock, and finally Young (GM1). While Grimshaw used VOT as a base text, a few independent instances of VOT's source texts (TB, WC) appear in GM1.[78] Mostly, the use of the Woodruff and Richards audits resulted in redundant text, since the Woodruff and Richards selections usually echoed the aural audits. But the process increased the length of the text, one of Smith's goals.[79] A short example illustrates Grimshaw's technique. Below on the left is *The Voice of Truth* version of the sermon, on the right is GM1. Italic text originated with Grimshaw and his editors, not the manuscripts, while bold text is from WW, inserted into VOT by Grimshaw.

came to the historian's office and repeated a narrative of a sermon thought to be the Adams sermon. Staines inserted elements in the report that seemed to reflect preaching of a later era. See Smith, *Every Word Seasoned With Grace*, ch. 5, Appendix.

78. VOT differed from any of the manuscript audits beginning right from its opening sentence: "Beloved Saints." The Follett sermon stemma shows the influence of VOT. See also Appendix A. For a more detailed discussion, see Smith, *Every Word Seasoned With Grace*, ch. 7, §3. Also see Appendix D.

79. See chapter 1 above. Also see the source critical analysis of the sermon in chapter 7 §2 of Smith, *Every Word Seasoned With Grace* and Appendix A below.

The Voice of Truth	**GM1**
You have got to learn how to be Gods yourselves; to be kings and priests to God, the same as all Gods have done; by going from a small degree to another,	*and* you have got to learn how to be Gods yourselves, and to be Kings and Priests to God, the same as all Gods have done *before you, namely,* by going from *one* small degree to another, *and* **from a small capacity to a great** *one*;
from grace to grace, from exaltation to exaltation, until you are able	from grace to grace, from exaltation to exaltation, until you *attain* **to the resurrection of the dead,** *and* are able to dwell in everlasting **burnings**, and
to sit in glory as doth those who sit enthroned in everlasting power; and I want you to know that God in the last days, while certain individuals are proclaiming his name, is not trifling with you or me;	to sit in glory as *do* those who sit enthroned in everlasting power; and I want you to know that God in the last days, while certain individuals are proclaiming his name, is not trifling with you or me.[80]

Grimshaw was not the only editor of the 1855 proto ms history text of the sermon. One can see the social and theological influences of the intervening years on the text. Below, for example, on the left is TS, on the right is Grimshaw's final version.

TS	**Grimshaw's final version**
The mind of man is **as immortal** as God himself. I know that my testimony is true, hence when I talk to these mourners; what have they lost, **they** are only separated from their bodies for a short season; their spirits existed **co-equal** with God, and they now exist in a place where they converse	The mind *or the intelligence which man possesses* is coequal with God himself. I know that my testimony is true; hence when I talk to these mourners, what have they lost? *their relatives and* friends are only separated from their bodies for a short season; their spirits *which* existed with

80. For a complete source-redaction criticism of Grimshaw's text, see Appendix C pericope 14. (http://boap.org/LDS/KFS-Appendices/Appendix-C).

TS	Grimshaw's final version
together, the same as we do on the earth. Is it logic to say that **a spirit** is immortal, and yet **have** a beginning? **Because if a spirit have a beginning** it will have an end; good logic. I want to reason more on the spirit of man, for I am dwelling on the body of man, on the subject of the dead.	God *have left the tabernacle of clay only for a little moment as it were,* and they now exist in a place where they converse together the same as we do on the earth. I am dwelling on the *immortality* of the spirit of man—Is it logic*al* to say *that the intelligence of spirits* is immortal, and yet *that it had* a beginning? *The intelligence of Spirits had no beginning neither will it have an end; that is* good logic. *That which has a beginning may have an end. Their never was a time when there were not Spirits, for they are co-equal with our Father in heaven.* I want to reason more on the spirit of man; for I am dwelling on the body and *spirit* of man—on the subject of the dead.

The italic text in the second column was added by the 1855–1856 editors, and it partially reflects the rereading of JS's ideas on the soul. The bold text in the first column was omitted in the second. The "intelligence" of a soul is eternal because it comes from God (in the redacted text).[81] The new Utah cosmology, which would be further elaborated by Young and others, meant a constant flow of new beings into the cycle of life and spiritual government ("there never was a time

81. For example, Brigham Young, sermon, June 3, 1855; Brigham Young, "Nature of Man, etc.," July 3, 1859. An 1833 revelation (Doctrine and Covenants 93) was read this way in early exegesis as reference to a kind of world soul or God's wisdom. It was a common feature of Christian belief that man had no original thought; all important progress—scientific, intellectual, agricultural or technical—was inspired progress. The latter idea was prevalent in Mormon speech in the twentieth century.

when there were not spirits"), not withdrawals from a presumably infinite bank of sempiternal spirits.[82]

Parley Pratt wrote in 1855 that spirits are "begotten by the heavenly Father, in His own likeness and image, and by the laws of procreation."[83] Since they were born, they might (according to JS) also be split, cut up, dispersed, destroyed, and Young and his counselor Heber Kimball made this idea explicit. One wonders if they knew that they were undoing JS's twist of Lorenzo Dow in the process.[84] Young, the Pratts, Kimball, and others leaned into versions of panpsychism where "intelligence" or mind or life was everywhere present either potentially (emergent in spiritual matter as souls are built from it) or in fact in the substance of all creation.[85] Molding (via the biology of sexual congress in heaven) chunks of spirit matter into individual beings was the opportunity of the Gods—this eventually became so exclusivist that some asserted that all others in the heavens had no sex organs or gendered identity. That particular position had to be reversed in the era of gay marriage, when a church proclamation declared gender to be an eternally fixed facet of human beings, before birth and after death.[86]

---

82. See, for example, Brigham Young, July 31, 1859, "Human and Divine Government," etc. Brigham Young, June 3, 1868, "Opposition Essential to Happiness." Brigham Young, February 20, 1870, "The Saints are Strange People Because They Practice What They Profess."

83. Parley P. Pratt, *Key to the Science of Theology*, 50.

84. See, for example, Brigham Young, January 22, 1854, Arrington papers, series 12, Box 55, fd. 7; Brigham Young, February 27, 1853, "Duties and Privileges," etc. Heber C. Kimball, September 27, 1857, "Spiritual Dissolution—Ignorance of the World." Also, Brigham Young, June 22, 1856, "The Gifts of Prophecy," etc. Brigham Young, June 27, 1858, "Peculiarity of 'Mormons'," etc. For more instances, see Stapley, "Garden Theology," 75n24.

85. Brigham Young, *Journal of Discourses* 7:286–87.

86. Taylor G. Petrey, *Tabernacles of Clay: Sexuality and Gender in Modern Mormonism*, 43–46. Joseph Fielding Smith, *Doctrines of Salvation* (Salt Lake City:

The Pratts weren't alone in their claims; Leibniz and Spinoza argued for a distributed mind stuff throughout creation, and during the nineteenth-century this panpsychism was a basis for philosophy of mind. The idea fell out of favor, pressured perhaps by what Charles Taylor has called the "buffered" identity powered by the Enlightenment and more specifically through the rise of the therapeutic in formal disciplines of psychology and psychiatry in Europe. The mind or soul became insulated from the magical/spiritual forces to which it was porous in the premodern world. JS seemed to advocate for some mixture of these ideas, with "God would not exert any compulsory means and the Devil could not; and such ideas as were entertained by many were absurd."[87] Twenty-first-century studies of consciousness have sometimes claimed panpsychism. One argument for the idea runs like this: our brains consist of physical material, and that material may be arranged to produce subjective thoughts and feelings. The properties of such a complex system as the brain cannot come into existence from nowhere as some advocates of "emergence" claim. Those properties must therefore be present in the protons, neutrons, and electrons that make up our brains (and thus all matter that we can detect) and in the right combinations produce the collective conscious experience of each of us. In essence, this was very much like the arguments of Orson and Parley Pratt, Brigham Young, and their Latter-day Saint successors in the twentieth century like Charles Penrose (see chapter 3 below).

Bookcraft, 1954), 2:396. *The Family: A Proclamation by the First Presidency and the Quorum of the Twelve Apostles.*

87. Taylor, *A Secular Age*, ch. 2. One can see at least theoretical examples of the porous in still common Mormon rhetoric about the Devil or God implanting ideas or motivations or temptations in the mind. JS quote from *Times and Seasons* 2 (1 June 1841): 429–30; Clayton, *Revelations*; JS collection, MS 155, sermon item in unidentified handwriting, 2 pages, dated May 16, 1841, CHL.

Brigham Young and the other apostles in Utah found in the King Follett sermon the background foundation of the cosmos. They adopted it with gusto and not a little freedom of interpretation and adaptation. In Middle Mormonism, JS's ideas, sermons, and revelations became schematized—molded and ruled—by the social and environmental realities of a wilderness-settler's world. Those schemata were the applied spiritual science of the times.

CHAPTER 3

King Follett Collides with History, 1890–1926

Joseph F. Smith, B. H. Roberts, and Charles W. Penrose. Follett's Third Textual Tradition. The 1912 Turn.

§3.1 The Sermon's Third Textual Tradition—

A Preview of Follett in the Twentieth Century

In 1909, MS2 reappeared in the church's Utah-based magazine, *The Improvement Era* (R1), annotated by Brigham H. Roberts, an LDS general authority and an assistant church historian. This imprint began a new textual tradition with the attachment of explanatory notes from Roberts and the deletion and modification of some portions of the text. This reprinting of MS2 in the *Era* carried extensive annotation to establish an interpretive context for RC, one that continued through nearly all subsequent church and independent imprints. The new imprint and its cultural and theological reception require the examination of a number of seemingly unrelated persons and events.

Together with his announcement of the end of polygamy in 1890, Wilford Woodruff's 1894 announcement signaling the end of generalized ritual adoption was firmly connected to the idea of begotten spirit children. The deprecation of temple adoptions meant that here-and-now kingdom building for heaven was limited essentially to biological children or legal adoption, as Latter-day Saint plural marriage was in its officially tolerated/promoted two-decade death-throes. A heavenly biology of spirit children (elaborated in Middle Mormonism and alluded to in the previous chapter) afforded expansive hope, a concrete assurance of the eternally expanding kingdoms of the exalted, and the promise of conception to the unmarried or childless on earth. Polygamy and adoption were banned, and to some degree their culture of "participate now or be damned" dimmed.[1] A vision of the (earthly and heavenly) nuclear family gradually took the place of those deprecated visions. The (non-adoptive) spirit "child of God" motif gained strength and authority from the Saints' hymning and preaching, refocusing a here-and-now theology in different ways. For those of the faithful who could have no marriage or children on earth, it offered the promise of Abrahamic posterity, with all the experience of pregnancy and birth, without the sacrifices and oddities of polygamy or extra-familial sealings. An unrealized experience of pregnancy and birth on earth could be recaptured in heaven. But the contradictions between the notions of souls born in heaven and souls with no beginning was not lost on internal critics of the Follett sermon, and even late nineteenth-century non-Mormon observers saw

1. The heavenly biology of early Utah was at least indirectly confirmed in a twentieth-century proclamation by LDS church leaders. *The Family: A Proclamation to the World* identified spirits/souls as having male or female identities as "literal" children of the Heavenly Parents.

the problem. It was not quite so peripheral as a post-Jesus renaissance (1980 and following) Latter-day Saint might think (see chapter 4).[2]

One important transition from post-1890 theology was a move from a heavy Old Testament theme to more of a New Testament basis. Polygamy and the temple were the Pentateuch. JS was very much out of the prophetic tradition: Zion was the centerpiece of Mormonism. A relevant example is his 1832 revelation found in Doctrine and Covenants 84. Modern Mormonism moved toward a distinct reliance on the Jesus of the Gospels. While Follett was partly rolled out of a reinterpreted Genesis 1, it relied heavily on John's Gospel for most of its assertions. In that sense, it was an ideal tool for a monogamous church. It failed to take part in the transition for reasons this chapter will consider.[3]

Scattered through this chapter, various Follett-related events have the year 1912 in common. That year saw various schools of thought and Mormon personalities collide with the effect of the formal dismantling of Follett as an authoritative text. The church's First Presidency began a campaign to expunge references to the sermon from future church publications, including what became, for a time at least, the final volume of *History of the Church*. It also marked the eclipse of B. H. Roberts. As one historian has noted, Roberts's contributions to Mormon discourse did not end in 1912, but it seems his spirit was muted in the direction of history by the events of 1912 and his work in church serials dropped

2. For internal critics of the sermon, see below. For an example of external observation of the problem for the soul, see John M'Clintock and James Strong, *Cyclopedia of Biblical, Theological, and Ecclesiastical Literature*, 637. By post-Jesus-renaissance I mean the re-emphasis by LDS church leaders of the centrality of Jesus after 1985. See Turner, *The Mormon Jesus*, 205–94, 43–45. Barlow, *Mormons and the Bible*, xxxviii.

3. On the change of emphasis, see Bowman, "The Crisis of Mormon Christology."

off.[4] Initially, the *History of the Church* project was conceived as not just a JS-centered work—hence the forward-looking *Period I* title in the six volumes published between 1902 and 1912. The role that Follett played in the termination of that project is a part of this chapter and hopefully excuses some of the peripatetic nature of what appears in the historical and biographical explorations in the sections below. Utah politics formed a background to the tempering of Roberts's voice, in particular his advocacy of the Follett sermon as a key to JS's teachings. The background of the central figures of Utah's religious and political environments in the evolving story is one key to understanding the cultural trajectory of the Follett sermon in the twentieth century.

§3.2 Joseph F. Smith and the Fate of Deceased Children—

Reason and History

The Brigham Young-led branch of Mormonism (the Church of Jesus Christ of Latter-day Saints) may have embraced JS's deification cosmology and extended it, but questions about the Follett sermon surfaced early on in the Utah period. Some of these questions involved short paragraphs in WW and TB. WW contained this statement:

> A question will Mothers have their children in Eternity? yes, yes, you will have the children, But as it falls so it will rise, It will never grow, It will be in its precise form as it fell in its mothers arms. Eternity is full of thrones upon which dwell thousands of children reigning on thrones of glory not one cubit added to their stature[5]

4. Lyon, "Church Historians I have Known," 15. Roberts's commitment to his *Americana* articles continued as did his political, community, and church youth work, and he remained a vigorous missionary for the church. But the combative style of one of the faith's most prolific defenders was moving to the margins.

5. Wilford Woodruff journal, April 7, 1844, Kenney, *Wilford Woodruff's Journal*, 2:387.

While the Latter-day Saints readily accepted the claim that children would be resurrected *as children*, and even the Book of Mormon supported the ideas of both redemption of innocents and rising up as laid down, the static nature of stature was both objectionable to some Saints and supported by others.[6] One of JS's earlier sermons (March 20, 1842) argued that the bodies of resurrected children remain as children forever.[7]

One of JS's confidants, William Clayton, confirmed this in an interview with JS on May 18, 1843.

> I asked the Prest. wether children who die in infancy will grow. He answered No, we shall receive them precisely in the same state as they died in no larger. They will have as much intelligence as we shall but shall *always remain separate and single.* Children who are born dead will have full grown bodies being made up by the resurrection.[8]

A July 12, 1843, revelation (D&C 132) made the phrase "separate and single" a kind of damnation.[9] TB suggests that children remain in their childlike stature forever: "their debt is paid, there is no damnation awaits them, for they are in the spirit.—As the child dies, so shall it rise from the dead and be forever living in the learning of God, it shall be

6. The Book of Mormon, Moroni 8, Alma 11, 40. On divided opinions, see below.

7. Wilford Woodruff journal, March 20, 1842, Kenney, *Wilford Woodruff's Journal*, 2:163.

8. Emphasis added. Andrew F. Ehat and Lyndon W. Cook, *The Words of Joseph Smith*, 136. Compare Brigham Young's thought: "There used to be giants on the earth. . . . if they obtain a resurrection will they not come up as they were laid down? Yes. . . . It may be asked if a child of a premature [still] birth will be resurrected?" Young answered that it may somehow retain that body, or it may take another in another birth. Arrington papers, series 12, Box 55, fd. 7 (Feb. 19, 1854). With regard to temple ritual, Young later ruled that stillborn children need no sealing to parents or any other sacramental rite. See Scott G. Kenney, ed., First Presidency Letterpress Copybooks, January 8, 1894.

9. The image of *separate and single* was a strong one in Mormon rank-and-file thought. See, for example, Wm C. Staines, report, April 24, 1855.

the child, the same as it was before it died out of your arms. Children dwell and exercise power in the same form as they laid them down."[10]

This passage from the Follett sermon, along with other claims of JS about children in the Christian resurrection, left long controversy in its wake.

Joseph F. Smith, a nephew of JS, led a crusade against the sermon's claim that resurrected infants would remain infant-sized forever. Others felt uncomfortable too, and in printings of RC during and after his era (Joseph F. Smith was the sixth president of the Church of Jesus Christ of Latter-day Saints between 1901 and 1918) this segment of the sermon was redacted in various ways. In R1–R6, the paragraph was either deleted, modified, and/or notified with claims that the sermon was imperfectly recorded. This was not correct, but it was the only obvious way to announce a new teaching on the subject.

When preaching at the funeral of William C. Staines, August 4, 1881, Joseph F. Smith claimed JS "said that Children would rise the same stature as they laid themselves down but in the due time of the Lord would attain to the full stature of their spirits whatever that might be."[11] At the 1909 funeral of Rachel Grant, after arguing that resurrected bodies would reappear in exactly the form they had at death, Smith said,

> We not only have the written word, we have it in the testimony of the Spirit of God in the heart of every soul. . . . Would we be satisfied to remain for ever and ever in the form of infirmity incident to age? No! Would we be satisfied to see the children we bury in their infancy remain as children only, throughout

10. Brigham Young repeated the idea as a kind of paean to eternal variety. See Brigham Young sermon, February 19, 1854, Leonard J. Arrington papers, series 12, Box 55, fd. 7, p. 3. Brigham Young, sermon, January 31, 1861, Kenney, *Wilford Woodruff's Journal*, 5:544.

11. A. Karl Larson and Katherine Miles Larson, eds., *Diary of Charles Lowell Walker, 2 vols.*, 2:561.

> the countless ages of eternity? No!. . . . for it was revealed from God, . . . through Joseph Smith the prophet, that in the resurrection, the body will develop until it reaches the full measure of the stature of its spirit, whether it be male or female.[12]

Smith was careful to avoid any of the logic of his Follett-inspired sermons three decades before. His "developing body" claim was partly a work of reason, partly a support of Orson Pratt's "form follows form" (that the spirit's shape and size is impressed on the body in its growth), and the unfolding of the body for resurrected children was vital to his own piece of mind. Well before his statement at Grant's funeral, Joseph F. Smith hoped to find former Nauvoo residents who could claim JS had expressed the idea of children experiencing growth after their death and resurrection as children. He found no contemporary evidence for this, but finally encountered people willing to satisfy his hope. Smith evidently felt this justified his remarks at Grant's funeral.

In a 1918 piece for the *Improvement Era*, he revealed a portion of his journey in certifying his hope as official doctrine. One can see a part of the reasoning that led him to try eliminating Follett from the 1911 *Liahona* and then doing so in the 1912 church history imprint.[13] Smith recounted a part of his skepticism,

> I have read Joseph's discourse at the death of King Follett, as at first published, and I did not believe, never did believe that he was correctly reported or that those who died in infancy would remain as little children after the resurrection. Never had it entered my soul as a possibility that such could be the case; yet, I did not have the courage to say so . . . I really did not care to mention it, because I knew the strong opinions that some people had in regard to little children being resurrected and everlastingly and forever after to remain as little children.[14]

12. Joseph F. Smith, "Our Indestructible, Immortal Identity," 593–94.
13. See Joseph F. Smith, "Status of Children in the Resurrection."
14. Ibid., 571.

After encountering a brother-in-law, an aunt (JS had married the aunt—the widow of his brother Don Carlos, Agnes Coolbrith Smith, in January 1842), and two others who related a story of JS teaching that resurrected children would grow to adult stature—all four named the same occasion, the death of Agnes's five-year-old daughter Sophronia—he had affidavits prepared from the latter two.[15] Whether JS made such statements or not, he apparently taught the contrary both before and after October 1843, in public and in private.

Long after JS's death, Brigham Young claimed to have heard him teach no growth after resurrection, and on a different occasion, growth. He suggested JS did not know the correct position with certainty. That Young announced such a belief may help explain his own freedom to diverge from JS's earlier picture of man and God.[16]

The discomfort with the child resurrection doctrine of RC helped open the door to further speculation about the accuracy of RC and by extension all versions and reports of the sermon (and the records of early Mormonism as whole in some ways). By 1873, the text of RC was challenged by Orson Pratt:

> But I doubt very much in my own mind if those who reported that sermon got the full idea on this subject; and if they did, I very much doubt whether the Prophet Joseph, at the time he preached that sermon, had been fully instructed by revelation on that point, for the Lord has revealed a great many things to Prophets and revelators, and among them Joseph Smith, the fullness of which is not at first given. . . . [deceased infants will]

---

15. Ibid., 573. The funeral would have to be that of Sophronia C. Smith, age 5, d. October 3, 1843. Records of JS's activities around this date suggest that he gave no sermon then. It is possible that JS made informal remarks to his plural wife Agnes, which were heard by others.

16. Brigham Young, sermon, February 19, 1854, Brigham Young, funeral sermon, January 31, 1861.

> grow up to the full stature of manhood or womanhood, after the resurrection.[17]

A year later, Mormon diarist Frederick Kesler reported that Pratt preached at a child's funeral that

> it was his opinion that we would receive our children as we laid them down no Difference what age or Size they ware when they Died But after they ware resurected they tabernacles or Bodies would grow until the arrived unto the Full Size & stature of there spirits. . . . all of which looks reasonable & consistant.[18]

Four years later, Kesler wrote that Joseph F. Smith, a doctrinal protégé of Pratt, remarked

> that it was his opinion that after the resurection the Bodies of infants would grow until they attained unto the full Size of thare Spirits or as large as they would have been had they lived on the earth to maturity.[19]

Perhaps Smith's opinion grew to certainty partly out of his own personal loss of children. By the end of his life, thirteen children had preceded him in death, the last and perhaps greatest shock being his favored son, Hyrum M. Smith, in January 1918, the year of his own death. Joseph F. Smith's confrontation with death always seemed to be before his mind, as evidenced by his frequent recollections of the 1844 murder of his father.[20]

---

17. Orson Pratt, "Revelation on the Judgments," etc.

18. Frederick Kesler, diary, April 23, 1874.

19. Kesler, diary, April 11, 1878. Smith didn't date his encounters with all his witnesses, but he indicates that he did not preach the idea of growth after resurrection until at least then.

20. For Joseph F. Smith's intellectual life, see Taysom, *Like a Firey Meteor*, ch. 5. Taysom notes Smith's admiration of Pratt's systematic teaching based on scripture and JS's sayings rather than Young's idea that the living authority owed little to the previous Word beyond a kind of structural foundation.

The idea that children resurrected in a child's body would grow to adult size (however that might be determined and by whatever mechanism) wasn't precisely new. One of the early Mormon apostles, Orson Hyde, offered that resurrection occurred through *birth*. Departed souls would achieve new bodies by simply being born over again as babies. Those babies would, of course, grow into adults. The details of the idea are not clear but apparently the process might be repeated and even more than one infant might have JS's soul, *at the same time*. Some Latter-day Saints felt that their own children had the souls of JS, or even Hyrum Smith. This "baby resurrection" idea suggests a rather fluid understanding of spirit and the relation of spirit and body but it also highlights the very deep penetration of human analogies some leaders saw in the afterlife.[21]

Suspicion over the 1856 text of the Follett sermon (RC) gradually extended to the sermon in general. Church apostle George Albert Smith wrote to Central States Mission leader Samuel Bennion January 30, 1912:

> Sometime ago I received an invitation, mailed from the Liahona office, to contribute to a fund for the purpose of *mailing* copies of the King Follet's funeral sermon. At the time I was somewhat surprised, because I have thought that the report of that sermon might not be authentic and I have feared that it contained some things that might be contrary to the truth when I knew just what it was . . .[22]

21. Brigham Young, sermon, February 19, 1854.

22. Emphasis added. George Albert Smith, Letter to Samuel O. Bennion, January 30, 1912, George Albert Smith papers. As it turned out, George Albert was far too late in expressing his skepticism. Bennion was president of the LDS Central States Mission, headquartered in Independence, Missouri, the home of the *Liahona*.

Liahona The Elders' Journal (the odd name was the result of combining two other Mormon midwestern serials in 1907)[23] was a church mission publication based in Independence, Missouri. George Albert's reticence about the circulation of RC was connected to earlier discussion about the sermon and its subsequent trajectory and critique as an authoritative text (see §3.6 below). That discussion accelerated in 1905 with the release of the church's Young Men's Mutual Improvement Association's (hereafter, YMMIA) instruction manual for 1905–1906, written by Brigham Henry Roberts (who insisted on compressing his given names by the initials B. H.), a church general authority—a member of the First Council of Seventy—and one of the leaders of the association.[24] Roberts's Manual lit several fires of controversy including the discussion of the Follett sermon. One of those was Roberts's theory of Book of Mormon translation. Roberts laid aside the late narratives of David Whitmer and Martin Harris to

23. https://history.churchofjesuschrist.org/content/library/featured-collection-liahona-the-elders-journal

24. See Roberts's address in the April 1904 general conference of the church which previews one of the manual items and appeals to the Follett sermon (no beginning, no end axiom). B. H. Roberts, "Christ a Revelation of God to Man—Pre-Existence and Immortality of Man." Brigham Young Academy teacher Nels Lars Nelson was probably influenced by Roberts (see B. H. Roberts, "What is Man"). Lay Mormon critics of Roberts occasionally mentioned Nelson in the same breath. See Nels Nelson, "Theosophy and Mormonism," and Nelson's 1904 book, *Scientific Aspects of Mormonism or Religion in Terms of Life*, 78–82. The 1905 period was a hotbed for Follett-sermon-related protology in Mormon writing. Compare Salt Lake Temple recorder Lycurgus Arnold Wilson's *Outlines of Mormon Philosophy or The Answers Given by the Gospel, as Revealed Through the Prophet Joseph Smith, to the Questions of Life*, 35, 39–41, 45–46. Wilson's work was vetted by a First Presidency reading committee, but in light of the developing controversy over the Follett sermon, no doubt the committee would have stopped publication if it had come a few years later. See also John Henry Evans, *One Hundred Years of Mormonism: A History of the Church of Jesus Christ of Latter-day Saints from 1805 to 1905*, 307. Evans's book was also endorsed by a reading committee appointed by Joseph F. Smith.

the effect that JS merely read off English text from his seeing stones; instead, Roberts inserted JS into the translation process, the stones serving as conduits of thought perhaps, but JS expressing that inspiration in his own language and dialect. The response was striking. Many people wrote to the *Era* and church leaders in dismay. Others expressed positive feedback. Fortunately, Roberts had wisely cleared his translation ideas with the First Presidency and the apostles in advance. He apparently did not anticipate a deep response to his Follett-inspired words in the Manual and made no such preparation. That would have important implications.[25]

§3.3 The Roots of 1912

Religion and Politics—George Q. Cannon and Writing of the History of the Church—The Smoot Controversy and VOT

Roberts was a strong personality, whose reputation was somewhat marred by his 1890s political adventures. He was a dedicated Democrat and was elected to the US House of Representatives, but the body declined to seat him as a polygamist. At the same time, church leaders were trying to ensure that church members divided somewhat evenly along major party lines. Since Democrats were largely favored by the Saints, a number of apostles and the first presidency campaigned for and lauded Republicans. Roberts could be an outspoken and ruthless

25. For years, Roberts's manual created significant and continuing negative feedback about its take on the translation of the Book of Mormon—along with a little personal insult (see the April and May 1906 issues of the *Era*). Roberts repeated the assertions in his *Defense of the Faith and of the Saints*, and opponents of the translation theory inside and outside the church took out many newspaper ads charging heresy (in the latter case usually with cynical humor). For example, *Salt Lake Tribune* (February 19, 1909): 2. Roberts's gaining approval of the authorities shielded him from church backlash.

political critic, earning the frustration and disappointment of several apostles, including Joseph F. Smith, and Roberts only narrowly avoided expulsion from his church position. In some ways he is the father of the present church stance on general church leaders: they must not take public positions in politics. After Roberts's political losses and his rejuvenation as a church leader—his appointment as assistant church historian in charge of publishing JS's history may have been partly an attempt to use his interests to keep him out of the political public eye—in 1901 President Lorenzo Snow asked Roberts to put all other activities away while the *History* was being written. That appointment came after a series of false starts. Follett would play an important role in the *History* in two ways: Roberts came to see Follett as representing the peak of JS's revelation, while his colleagues in the Joseph F. Smith First Presidency gradually came to see RC as significantly heretical.

The history of the church was at first an 1895 project of newspaper editor Charles Penrose. Some five decades before the history discussion, a young Charles William Penrose (1832–1925) had recently (1850) been baptized a Latter-day Saint in London, England. Penrose performed long Mormon missionary service in his homeland and became, like Roberts and Talmage, a well-known and rather prolific interpreter of Mormonism. Penrose was already a norming influence among the Mormons of the British countryside, damping extremes of enthusiasm and aligning populist frameworks with the official word from Salt Lake City. Penrose eventually settled in Utah and became editor of the church-owned newspaper, *The Deseret News*.[26] Penrose was later ordained an apostle on July 7, 1904, and still later elevated to the church's leading body, the First Presidency, on December 7, 1911.

---

26. Penrose worked at a number of Utah newspapers. His eventual firing from the *News* by George Q. Cannon helped solidify one of the strange triangles of loyalties that intersected in Follett as fleshed out below.

While Penrose was an experienced writer and missionary, he was not a favorite of First Presidency counselor George Q. Cannon.[27] Cannon had a vision for the *History* that would cover not just JS's life and times but also the intervening years up to and including the period when he (Cannon) was an important figure in Utah politics and religion. Cannon had access to many historical sources for the Utah period that others did not. When Penrose was diverted to other tasks, church leaders seemed divided over who should be the*History*'s writer. Roberts was finally proposed but Cannon carefully guided the discussion of the project so that it would largely be an editorial reprinting of the previously serially published "History of Joseph Smith." In Cannon's mind, Roberts would be merely an interim figure in the *History*'s publication.[28] That Cannon still held on to the idea of writing much of the *History* is apparent from discussions over the still-dormant project in 1900. It was Roberts's apostolic friend, Francis M. Lyman, who put him forward once again for the *History* assignment. Cannon and Church Historian Anthon H. Lund remained less supportive and when Roberts asked for a yearly stipend of $2,500 for the project, Cannon objected—he still saw Roberts as a mere collator and minor editor of the JS period material already published in church serials like the *Millennial Star* (and in fact, Roberts did employ the *Star* imprint as a base text). In the ensuing discussion, James E. Talmage, Joseph M. Tanner, and then Cannon himself came

27. Cannon had Penrose fired from the church newspaper, *The Deseret News*, so as to (in Penrose's opinion) put his sons in the organization. Francis M. Lyman diary, March 28, 1893.

28. On Penrose's appointment, and then Cannon's own disappointment at losing the assignment and his reworking of its purpose for Roberts, see Journal History Jan. 10, 1896, Feb. 4, 1896, Penrose diary, Dec. 17, 1895, Jan. 10, 1896, Franklin D. Richards diary Nov. 14, 1895, Dec. 12, 1895.

up as possible replacements for Roberts, and Cannon accepted the responsibility to produce a sweeping ten-volume work.[29]

When George Cannon subsequently died before making much progress on the project, Lorenzo Snow (church president since 1898) asked Roberts to edit the *History*. Lund was held responsible for the "correctness."[30] On June 4, 1901, (First Council of Seventy minutes) Roberts informed his council that Lorenzo Snow had asked him to devote his attention to the *History* above anything else and that it should be "pushed as fast as possible." As noted, Snow asked Roberts not to delay but give the history his exclusive attention.[31] Apparently, the longer history was still on the table, as Roberts titled his first six

29. On Lyman's suggestion of Roberts to write the history and Cannon's reservations, see Journal History, May 10, 1900. On Lund's report of Roberts's financial request and Cannon's reappointment to write the history, see First Presidency office journal, May 16, 1900. Lund noted that Roberts already received a yearly compensation of $1,200 (about $35,000 in 2021 dollars). Church librarian Andrew Jenson was somewhat disappointed that Roberts was taking on the *History* project, and his contempt toward Jenson's library security. This became moot once Roberts was made an assistant church historian (see Andrew Jenson journal, August 3, 1901 and Brigham Young Jr diary, April 6, 1902).

30. Cannon began working on the history with his son John Q. Cannon and John Henry Evans about typefaces and paper and by comparing the *Times and Seasons* "History of Joseph Smith" with the history published in the *Millennial Star*. On Cannon's history work, see *Journal of George Q. Cannon*, May 21, October 24, 26, 30, 1900, November 1, 3, 6, 7, 1900. On November 8, 1900, Cannon notes that his work on published sources forced a reappraisal of the project and he started comparing manuscript sources with published versions of JS's history. Cannon seems to have worked on the history until mid-November 1900, when his church duties interrupted the history work. He suffered increasing bouts of fatigue over the next months and died on April 12, 1901.

31. On Snow's appointment of Roberts, see First Presidency office journal, May 23, 1901. On Snow's order not to delay, see Roberts's report to his fellow seventies in the First Council of Seventy minutes, June 4, 1901. It is not clear whether Roberts received the stipend increase requested the previous year.

volumes of history (JS's lifetime) "Period I." Roberts spent considerable time with liminal text (footnotes, introductions, etc.) in the volumes, and his influence on the volumes there was strong, though he did not do much with the sources behind the ms history. He seems to have accepted at face value that the first person narrative of the ms history meant that JS himself had dictated/written the history. This was far from the truth, but the methodology of Willard Richards and his successors in the ms history work had become lost in imprint authority. The project would last more than ten years, and in the end, while eventually scheduled for the final volume of Period I, the Follett sermon did not appear. The story of how and why the sermon was removed from the *History* has a number of different dimensions and consequences that I will consider below.

The removal of Follett from the *History* and the ongoing conflict over the sermon in general contributed to the termination of the *History* project in 1912 with volume six. Historian T. Edgar Lyon noted Roberts's discouragement over the removal of Follett as a factor in his putting aside further work on the *History* until the year before his death. Roberts had already begun to feel intellectually isolated from his fellow church leaders and his interests in church administration and his ecclesiastical goals had waned as a number of the apostles saw him as a liability.[32]

In 1928, apostle George Albert Smith, tasked with helping to organize a centennial celebration, asked Roberts to take some of his history work previously published in the American Historical Society's *Americana* magazine, expand it, and produce a centennial history of the church, to be published in 1930 on the hundred year anniversary of the organization of the church. An apostolic committee oversaw the work. The result was *A Comprehensive History of the*

32. Lyon, "Church Historian's I have Known," 15–16; B. H. Roberts, Letter to Isaac Russell, February 10, 1910.

Church, something that at least approximately matched the chronological dimensions of the original project as Cannon had conceived it.[33] In 1932, Roberts produced a final volume in his earlier *History of the Church* that covered the interval between JS's death and Brigham Young's appointment as church president in 1847. Perhaps if he had lived, Roberts may have produced more volumes in that series. As it was, the series ended with his death in 1933.[34]

Roberts's political ambitions would lean into his credibility on other fronts and included his advocacy of the Follett sermon as a critical source of church thought. At the time, it was nearly impossible to separate the church and its leaders' influence from the politics of Utah.[35] After his own political losses in the 1890s, Roberts, a dedicated Democrat, had the potential to be difficult in the church's sensitive dealings with Republican leaders and lobbyists over the election and then the seating battle of church apostle Reed Smoot. Senate critics of Smoot maneuvered to have Roberts called as a witness in the

33. Roberts had asked the church to print the *Americana* history in book form in 1921. The church presidency (Grant, Penrose, Ivins) declined to do so as they felt it would be too expensive. Roberts had been excluded from writing a one volume history at the same time, which troubled him greatly. The apostles had instead appointed two of their own number, Joseph Fielding Smith and John A. Widtsoe, to do that one-volume history. The result was the book *Essentials in Church History* (1922). See Heber J. Grant diary, May 3, 1921. On the *Comprehensive History* work, see George Albert Smith, Letter to John A. Widtsoe, February 26, 1929.

34. One of Roberts's motivations for the final volume, *History of the Church of Jesus Christ of Latter-day Saints: Apostolic Interregnum,* was the inclusion of a speech by Brigham Young to the effect that Seventies were apostles and therefore could organize stakes, ordain bishops, etc. The Grant presidency decided that would confuse church members and rejected including the speech. Heber J. Grant diary, April 30, 1931, March 10, 1932, March 24, 1932. For the typeset pages of this sermon, see B. H. Roberts Collection, MS 1278, CHL.

35. For example, Joseph F. Smith's pamphlet, *Another Plain Talk: Reasons why the People of Utah Should be Republicans.*

Senate hearings over Smoot's seat. Roberts behaved himself, much to the disappointment of a hopeful investigator. However, at home Roberts was a vocal and personal critic of Smoot, labeling him as disloyal and willing to sacrifice his church's beliefs for his political ambitions.[36] Roberts continued to confront other church leaders through the 1920s over philosophical, theological, and political issues, and his time as an official historian did not really dampen his political ardor and voice despite Lorenzo Snow's wish. In January 1909, Roberts was reprimanded by the apostles for his criticism of Smoot and what Roberts saw as Joseph F. Smith's double dealing with Republicans and Democrats.[37]

Tensions seemed to relax at mid-year when Roberts reported a trip east for church business to Smith but became difficult again over political issues. The controversy continued at the October 1909 general conference, when what may have been seen as Roberts's thinly veiled criticisms of Joseph F. Smith in an hour-long address evoked

---

36. In return, Smoot continually lobbied his fellow apostles to have post-Manifesto polygamist men excommunicated or if not that, at least barred from any church leadership. His close friend, Ben E. Rich, was not immune. Smoot vetoed Rich's selection as a church general authority. Roberts may also have been a target, since he probably married his last wife, Margaret Shipp, well after the 1890 manifesto. On Rich, see George F. Richards, "Record of Matters of Special Importance," 31–32; Heath, *In the World*, 34. On Shipp, it should be noted that Roberts was skeptical of the manifesto and deeply troubled by its 1890 announcement. At the October 6, 1890, general conference, Roberts did not vote in favor of it. Eventually he told his friend Francis M. Lyman that he was in harmony with it. Six months later, Lyman discovered Roberts and Shipp were married. See Francis M. Lyman diary, March 31, 1893, October 9, 1893. On Roberts and the conference vote on the Manifesto, see *The Journal of George Q. Cannon*, July 20, 23, 1891.

37. Anderson, *Cowboy Apostle*, 430. David O. McKay diary, January 5, 1909. B. H. Roberts, Address to President Francis M. Lyman and Council of Twelve Apostles 21 January 1909, Box 4, fd 13, Scott G. Kenney Collection. Smoot was re-elected in February 1909.

the wrath of Smith in his own closing remarks—and again in an angry after-conference exchange at the Salt Lake Tabernacle pulpit. Both Smith and Roberts were prone to outbursts of temper and had difficulty forgiving perceived slights (or threats) from others.[38]

This facet of both men may have been a response to their separate perceptions of social and personal ostracism and the difficult circumstances of their youth. Those rationalizations and their concurrent internal social value systems often placed the two devoted men on orthogonal axes of opinion and action. In one tender moment in 1896, both men apologized and forgave each other over their past conflicts.[39] Nevertheless, Roberts's reputation and his conflict with other leaders factored into the interplay between the Follett sermon, Joseph F. Smith, Reed Smoot, and the immediate distribution of the sermon's text. Few people felt comfortable in public disagreement with Roberts.[40] Everyone knew a public challenge over religion or

38. Roberts had been to New York to deal with his publishers and then to visit church historical sites in Ohio and Missouri. B. H. Roberts, Letter to Isaac Russell, July 1, 1909. On the conference tiff, etc., see Moyer, "Dancing with the Devil," 568–73. On Roberts and Smoot, see Jonathan H. Moyer, "Dancing with the Devil: The Making of the Mormon-Republican Pact." On Roberts and Joseph F. Smith, see "Smith Belabors Roberts," *Salt Lake Tribune* (October 18, 1909): 4; "Joseph's Dishonest Spleen," *Salt Lake Tribune* (October 10, 1909): 6; B. H. Roberts, October 6, 1909, *Conference Report*, 101–8; Joseph F. Smith, October 1909, *Conference Report*, 123–25. B. H. Roberts, Letter to Isaac Russell, October 25, 1909. On Smoot's reaction, see Heath, *In the World*, 35. Roberts long felt betrayed by fellow Democrats and churchmen in his fight to be seated in congress. See, for example, B. H. Roberts, Letter to Mr. Moyle, October 29, 1910. On Smith's anger issues, see Stephen C. Taysom, *Like a Firey Meteor: The Life of Joseph F. Smith.*

39. Journal History, March 26, 1896.

40. Apostle David O. McKay's candid ranking of mental ability and expressive power among such luminaries as James Talmage, Orson Whitney, Joseph Fielding Smith, himself, and Roberts, placed Roberts well ahead of the others. David O. McKay diary, February 25, 1907.

politics might draw out dragon fire from the man, and even Smith saw Roberts leaving the leadership as a net loss.[41]

Roberts's early support of Follett may have helped generate another interesting consequence for Smoot. Many American Protestant leaders objected to Reed Smoot's 1903 election to the US Senate on the grounds that he represented a church that still practiced and believed in polygamy, though it was doing so under cover, and that the Saints were still fundamentaly un-American, which at the time was essentially defined as un-Christian. In August 1903, the Presbyterian Teachers' Association of Utah reprinted VOT as a tract to prove that Smoot was a danger to the United States. The front page for the little pamphlet (16.5x9.5cm) stated: "Joseph Smith's Last Sermon, As issued by Elder John Taylor, Nauvoo, Ill., June, 1844: Now republished according to resolution of the Presbyterian Teachers' Association, August, 1903; Salt Lake City, Utah." Inside the pamphlet is a Forward, which is no doubt relevant to how Protestants who knew of it saw Follett. The Association's editor(s) effectively picked out the points that some 1844 Nauvoo Saints found equally troubling:

> Students of Mormonism find that it has published no 'Systematic Theology.' The four so-called church works are voluminous, yet neither of them sets forth *the system*. The card statement, Articles of Faith, does not uncover essential Mormonism. As a brief answer to the inquiry 'Wherein does Mormonism essentially differ from Christianity?' the following sermon is reprinted; it was

41. Roberts, J. Golden Kimball, Joseph F. Smith, Penrose, and even Talmage used the October 1912 church conference as another platform for political disagreement. Heath, *In the World*, 164–66. Roberts argued that in "civil government, one man's opinion is as good as another's." He was called out by nearly all the other speakers. *Conference Report* (October 1912), 30–34. Roberts was back in politics in 1926. Talmage wrote to Widtsoe, "You may have seen . . . that Brother B. H. Roberts has ascended the stump . . . and . . . that his action is causing the Presidency and Twelve great concern." James E. Talmage, Letter to John A. Widtsoe, 29 October 1928, James E. Talmage collection, MS 1232, Box 4, fd. 18, CHL.

> delivered by Joseph Smith at Conference, Nauvoo, Illinois, April 6, 1844 [sic]. The following points may be noted among others:
> As to Godhead: It asserts polytheism instead of monotheism.
> As to Creation: It asserts it to be limited instead of absolute; matter, and all spirits being represented as eternal.
> As to Revelation: It sets up the speakers' so-called revelations as the test of Scripture.
> As to Men Being Saviors: It asserts a ferreting out and saving of spirits gone into the eternal world.
> As to Men in the Future State: It asserts progressive deification—men becoming gods by development.
>
> These teachings, astounding though they be to Bible readers, are the heart of Temple-working Mormonism today, as shown by frequent and extended quotation by ministering elders, by writers in church papers, and by the approved work, 'New Witness for God,' by Elder B. H. Roberts.[42] Out of at least six issues of the sermon from Mormon presses, in the first seventeen years, the very first is chosen, that issued by John Taylor, Nauvoo, June, 1844, and entitled 'Joseph Smith's Last Sermon;' it is given verbatim. THE COMMITTEE.[43]

While the pamphlet didn't offer a specific reason for publication, it was clearly related to religious protests over Smoot.[44] The complaint of the Association that the church had no systematic theology is important to understanding the external impact of the Follett archetype and its resulting texts. The itemized list of heresies is also important. In particular, they do not simply stop at deification or Godhead, usually advertised as the most shocking deviation from a Calvinist ethos. What is perhaps the more interesting departure was the denial

---

42. The editorial voice refers to Roberts's 1895 book, *A New Witness for God*, 465–66. Roberts had quoted several passages from MS2 on God's progression to Godhood.

43. Systematic Theology was the practice, singled out in English literature by the seventeenth century, of attempting a coherent, rational order of "accepted" doctrine.

44. On the protests, see Moyer, "Dancing with the Devil," 323–28; Flake, *The Politics of American Religious Identity*.

of God's singular self-existence. Their point that church missionaries did not teach "advanced doctrine" to church investigators was a long-known practice.[45] There are a few minor errors in the Forward that can be noted here. The broad brushstroke of Christianity is meant to exclude the Saints and lump together disruptive denominational/sectional fault lines. The date of June 1844 is in error, as is the title "Last Sermon," but both derive from VOT itself, not the pamphlet editors. The date of April 6 for the sermon is also incorrect as well as the claim that VOT was the first imprint of Follett. Typographically, the text of the pamphlet differs in some ways from VOT, but these are confined to line length, punctuation, and spelling. Apparently, the Association thought JS's instructions were of such a fabulous and offensive character that they required no comment, emphasis, or internal fudging beyond their Forward.

The Association's reprinting of VOT was intentional. The committee chose VOT because they thought the text was the most authentic available. Moreover, VOT still existed in the attics of some Saints and on at least some of their bookshelves. The association saw it as being endorsed by church president John Taylor; his name appeared as publisher in VOT. When the 1903 pamphlet was printed, Rev. Samuel E. Wishard, president of (Presbyterian) Westminster College in Salt Lake City, Utah, went to Washington to protest the seating of Smoot. Wishard was on record as a doubter of the sincerity of the Woodruff Manifesto calling it "another Mormon trick . . . for the purpose of securing power" in statehood. The Association's purposes didn't die; they carried on in religious and historical circles and resurfaced in the conservative, evangelical activism of the last half of the twentieth cen-

45. For example, Missionaries were forbidden to mention polygamy until its public reveal in 1852, and in 1832, missionaries were advised not to mention the vision recited in Doctrine and Covenants 76. In 1839, new missionaries were told to avoid discussing anything but the "first principles." See "To the Elders of the Church."

tury when Follett became a primary evangelical talking point once again in the presidential campaigns of Mitt Romney (see chapter 4).[46]

The mental and historical calculus demonstrated by Roberts, Smith, and other key figures in the Mormon world highlighted fundamental differences in their negotiations with the Utah church's documentary past and their interpersonal dynamics. That past and those opinions played into the ideological role and status of Follett in their present as I will explore along several axes below.[47]

§3.4 More on the Roots of 1912

B. H. Roberts's 1905 YMMIA Manual, Arthur MacDermott, James E. Talmage and a Mother in Heaven. A Pivotal 1907 Article.

> *I take my ring from my finger and liken it unto the mind of man, the immortal spirit because it has no beginning Suppose you cut it into but as the Devil lives there would be an end all the fools and wise men from the beginning of creation who say that man had a beginning prove that he must have an end*
>
> —TB

46. *The New York Evangelist* (December 4, 1890). Rudger Clawson diary, March 5, 1903, Larson, *A Ministry of Meetings*, 522. On Protestant participation in the Smoot protest, see Flake, *The Politics of American Religious Identity*, ch 1. Earlier, in 1898, when B. H. Roberts had been elected to congress, it was pastor Wiley Paden of Salt Lake City's First Presbyterian Church who led religious opposition to Roberts in Utah. Presbyterians were very active in Utah, hoping to convert the lost souls there. The mission effort spent considerable funds to establish schools for Utah children. R. Douglass Brackenridge, "Hostile Mormons and Persecuted Presbyterians in Utah, 1870–1900: A Reappraisal."

47. Roberts visited Joseph F. Smith on October 15, 1909 and offered to pull his speech from the conference record. Smith asked him to have his counselor Anthon H. Lund go over it with him and he (Smith) would accept whatever they decided. White, *Church, State, and Politics*, 405.

The lead-up to the new (1909) Follett text tradition brought the project within the orbit of several personalities, some public, others nearly historically anonymous. Roberts's YMMIA manual, mentioned above, was part of an episodic printing of a work that grew over time, titled *New Witnesses for God*.[48] In the 1905 manual, Roberts extracted elements of Follett to amplify his interpretations of the Book of Mormon text. He wrote that each person was eternal, without beginning or end, referencing the notion by inference to JS and the Follett sermon. Roberts's manual read:

> Still another fact must be brought into view before we can treat these two great truths—the fall of man and the purpose for his existence—in relation to each other. This fact is the immortality of the "spirit" of man, by which I mean not only a never ending existence for the "soul" of man in the future, through the resurrection, but a proper immortality that means the eternal existence of the "ego"—interchangeably called "mind," "spirit," "soul," "intelligence". . . . There is in man an eternal, uncreated, self existing entity, call it "intelligence," "mind," "spirit," "soul"—what you will, so long as you recognize it, and regard its nature as eternal.

Adult reader questions didn't just focus on Roberts's translation theory. Church members wrote to ask about the passage above. This feedback process, often highly influential in shaping church policy and emphasis at the time, made the period remarkable—as seen, for example, with R1 itself, Roberts's 1909 *Improvement Era* publication of an annotated MS2. In an untitled question-answer series in a 1909

48. Roberts's bibliography for the work is tedious to unravel. *New Witnesses* started as *A New Witness for God* that appeared in 1895. This two-volume work later became volume one of *New Witnesses for God*. Between 1903 and 1906, Roberts's essays became manuals 7, 8 and 9 of the Young Men's Mutual Improvement Association. In 1909 these manuals became volumes two and three of *New Witnesses for God*. Volume 1 was republished in 1911, and volumes two and three were combined and published again as a single volume in 1920, 1926, and 1927.

issue of *Liahona The Elders' Journal* a questioner wrote to the editors and asked,

> In the Pearl of Great Price we read that God created all things spiritually before they were made naturally (Moses 3:5). In the King Follet discourse as published in the *Improvement Era* for January 1909 (p. 183) we read: 'God never had the power to create the spirit of man at all, and there is no creation about it,' etc. Please explain this seeming contradiction. C.W.B., Kirtland, N.M.

The editors wrote in response,

> If we assume that the phrase 'all things' as used in the Pearl of Great Price means all things that ever were created, but that it does not mean things that never were created or made but always existed, the seeming contradiction disappears.[49]

Such church manual exchanges prompted a number of important rulings, statements, and policies from church leaders. One of these exchanges started with a fifty-two-year-old mining company clerk and Scottish immigrant Latter-day Saint, Arthur Louis Fitzgerald MacDermott (1854–1921) of St. Thomas, Nevada. MacDermott helped snowball a whole new era of public critique for the Follett sermon.[50] MacDermott wrote about Roberts's Manual to the Wesleyan

49. *Liahona The Elders' Journal* 6, no. 35 (1909): 848. The YMMIA manuals continued to break somewhat controversial ground. For example, see the 1909 *Era* article, "Age of the Earth."

50. St. Thomas now rests under the surface of Lake Mead. MacDermott, a lifelong bachelor, came to America in 1873. St. Thomas, at one time a Mormon settlement, was abandoned by the Saints in 1871. MacDermott came to St. Thomas through his experience in mining administration after the Mormons returned to the hamlet in 1880. Farming and salt mining were early local economies. MacDermott performed LDS missionary service from 1900 to 1902 as secretary of the European Mission. See Missionary Department Missionary Register, 1860–1959, book C, page 127. United States Census, 1910, National Archives and Records Administration,

University (PhD) trained geologist and prominent public voice of Mormonism, James Edward Talmage, and to church president Joseph F. Smith in December 1905.[51] Joseph F. Smith handed the letter off to Roberts for an answer, but Roberts was delayed by other commitments until early 1907.[52] Consulting geologist Talmage made a professional visit to the small Nevada town in July 1906 and was queried again by MacDermott while there. Talmage wrote to Joseph F. Smith after receiving another letter from MacDermott late in 1906.

MacDermott repeated some of his challenges to Roberts's cosmology (see Appendix §B1):

> If you will examine the new Manual . . . you will see that the pre-existence of the spirits of men is now extended back beyond the "beginning" . . . and the doctrine that we are co-eternal with the Father is specifically taught . . . I think it must lead to the idea that the number of intelligences that could eventually become . . . human beings, must be limited . . . all that can ever come into existence as human beings, already exist and have always existed and there will be an end to creation . . . If the solution of [these] questions of the eternity of the lives of the human family is as we reasoned it out in our discussion in St. Thomas, that the life of the parent is imparted to the offspring, and that while it is still a part of the same life or spirit of the parent, yet as

roll 858 (digital facsimile at https://familysearch.org/ark:/61903/3:1:33S7-9RJ6-6WP?mode=g&i=1&cc=1727033).

51. Gold and copper mines were opened near St. Thomas in 1905. Talmage made a personal connection with MacDermott and the town the following year as a consulting geologist. Talmage had composed his book *Articles of Faith* six years before, and Joseph F. Smith began to trust him as the direction of Mormonism. On *Articles*, see James E. Talmage collection 1879–1933. On MacDermott's letters, see B. H. Roberts collection, MS 1278, CHL, and §B.1 in Appendix B.

52. B. H. Roberts collection, MS 1278, CHL. In early 1907 Roberts was still busy with a large number of projects, including a First Presidency assignment to help write a rebuttal to the accumulated critique of the church during the Smoot Senate committee hearings. James E. Talmage diary, January 4, 1907.

> a separate individual it did have a beginning at the time of birth, is the correct one, we have solution both reasonable and more in accordance with apparent plain meaning of many passages of both ancient and modern Scriptures.

MacDermott referenced Eliza Snow's hymn as proof that individual life begins in heaven.

Talmage requested Smith to write something, or have something authoritative written to squelch various public speculations, something he intensely disliked (Appendix §B2).[53] Talmage went on,

> I inferred from your remarks to me that the letter from Brother MacDermott had been referred to Elder B.H. Roberts with the request that he reply to same.... I venture to say that amoung our young people many discussions have arisen on the point raised by Bro. MacDermott. He quoted to me, as indeed many others have cited, the statements made in the little book issued by L. A. Wilson, which book by the way, is accepted by many as authoritative because it bears the inscription "Salt Lake Temple" at the close of the preface and as it sets forth virtual endorsement by the Church Authorities.... Allow me to suggest that there appears to be a danger both real and great in the seeming certainty of profitless debate on questions such as that brought forward by Bro. MacDermott. Would it be agreeable to you, President Smith, to publish something in the form of a short article on the subject referred to? If so, please command me for any assistance I can render ... in the hope of suppressing injurious debate

L. A. Wilson's book, *Outlines of Mormon Philosophy,* was a small tome that shared some of the same assertions Roberts had made in the 1905 Manual (and various addresses from 1895 on). Talmage disliked uncertainty. Talmage himself reasoned that like a child derives

53. James E. Talmage, Letters to Joseph F. Smith, January 5, 1907, February 13, 1907, Joseph F. Smith papers. On the visit to St. Thomas, see James E. Talmage diary, July 22, 1906.

its fundamental inheritance from its parents, so souls derived their fundamental properties from their heavenly birth parents—what he evidently called the *parent-derived* theory of the soul, a distinct echo of Lorenzo Snow.[54]

Talmage's desire for a systematic Mormonism, or perhaps a desire to discern a systematic, authentic Mormonism from basic texts is apparent from his earliest writing—especially in his *Articles of Faith*, originally a sequence of lessons for a religion course at the University of Utah. Talmage had submitted his lessons to the church apostles for criticism with the result that markedly fuzzy notions about the Trinity (or Godhead) were clarified.[55]

Never a polygamist, Talmage was politically quiet and the questions and answers arising from his apostolic consultation over *Articles* helped move Talmage toward membership in Joseph F. Smith's Kitchen Cabinet (a group populated by the likes of wealthy timber magnate and former British mission friend Charles Nibley). Smith eventually selected Talmage (1911) to fill the vacancy among the apostles caused by the death of his cousin and First Presidency counselor, John Henry Smith, and the elevation of Charles Penrose from apostle to second counselor in the presidency.[56]

A relevant example of Talmage's religious methodology is given by his response to Mary B. Parker. Parker had been a Jehovah's Witness for many years but converted to Mormonism at age 75. She wrote to Talmage after hearing the shocking idea that Latter-day Saints thought there was a Mother in Heaven. Talmage's reply shows the logic that worked in earlier generations, abstracted somewhat from its former patriarchal social power:

---

54. Roberts, "Immortality of Man," 419. A. L. F. MacDermott, Letter to Dr. James E. Talmage, November 1906. See Appendix B.

55. Alexander, "Reconstruction," 28.

56. See B. H. Roberts, Letter to Isaac Russell, February 10, 1913. C. W. Nibley, *Reminiscences of Charles W. Nibley, 1849–1931.*

> There is no definite statement—that 'we have a Mother in Heaven.' There is no definite statement to this effect in any of the Standard Works of the Church, *but we base our belief in this matter on reason and a rational interpretation of Scriptures.* We are positively told that we had an antemortal or preexistent life before our spirits took bodies upon the earth.[57] Jesus Christ, our Elder Brother, is called the Firstborn of the spirit family of God the Eternal Father. If He was born into the spirit state in which He existed prior to His earthly birth, *it is reasonable to assume that that spiritual birth involved complete parentage, and so with all of us.* We base our conception of a Heavenly Mother as well as a Heavenly Father on the scriptural affirmations that God the Eternal Father is literally the Father of our spirits *and on the analogy of spirit-birth to bodily or earth-life birth.*

The Utah logic of Mother in Heaven rested on a turn of biblical phrase and the analogue of human sex—yet the commonly held belief among Latter-day Saint women was also from a profoundly felt desire for inclusion and identification, something the Follett sermon and much of nineteenth-century preaching lacked.[58]

The Roberts–Penrose–Talmage–MacDermott question was a miniature version of an important (though more one-sided) theological debate of the previous century, centering on Charles and Edward Beecher's advocacy of preexistence in search of theodicy. Mormons, of course, already subscribed to a form of human preexistence. What Roberts wanted was a rehabilitation of JS's ideas of the 1840s for which he saw Follett as an iconic proxy but fused with the analogical literalism that developed in Utah in the decades after JS's death

---

57. By "positively told," Talmage means unmistakable words in the Mormon canon.

58. James E. Talmage, Letter to Mary B. Parker, June 22, 1932. Emphasis added. Morrill, *White Roses on the Floor of Heaven*. Kristine Haglund, "Leapfrogging the Waves: A Nakedly Unacademic Response to 'Rethinking Mormonism's Heavenly Mother.'"

(minus, of course, notions of Adam as God the Father of human spirits).[59] The reaction, if not the final resolution, was nearly identical to the response of the Protestant establishment to the Beechers.[60]

In spite of Talmage's offer to do the job, Joseph F. Smith asked Roberts to reply to MacDermott in print—it was at least the better part of valor and the general principle of avoiding the shading of fellow leader influence (Appendix §B3). The *Improvement Era* promised a reply in its May 1906 issue.[61] Roberts recruited senior apostle Francis M. Lyman as a joint author, though Lyman was probably more of a sounding board. Lyman was a transitional figure in Mormonism, pressing for full engagement in American society. He pursued renegade church leaders and members advocating secret polygamy and was uncomfortable with Mormon leaders who did not see the strictures of the Word of Wisdom as a test of faith (Lyman was a smoker earlier in life, and his triumph over the habit steeled him).[62] Lyman and Roberts felt a special kinship that extended largely from Roberts's conflicts with church leaders over politics in 1895. Roberts was about to be removed from his position as a church General Authority when Lyman and fellow apostle Heber J. Grant made a final plea for Roberts to acquiesce to church leaders over issues in the Utah state constitutional convention. Roberts was touched by the continuing

59. In general, that subtraction was not immediate in Mormon discourse. For example, see the editorial question-answer feature in *Liahona The Elders' Journal* 6, no. 2 (June 27, 1908): 33. Compare Roberts, "What is Man," 387.

60. Edward Beecher, *The Conflict of Ages*. "Trial of Rev. Charles Beecher."

61. *Improvement Era* 9, no.7 (May 1906): 553.

62. On Lyman and the Word of Wisdom, see Francis M. Lyman, Letter to Charles W. Penrose, January 18, 1909. Penrose himself was not strict in his use of alcohol and drank wine until his death in 1925. Moyer, "Dancing with the Devil," 574–76; Thomas G. Alexander, *Mormonism in Transition, A History of the Latter-day Saints, 1890–1930*, 260. Bergera, *Confessions of a Mormon Historian: The Diaries of Leonard J. Arrington, 1971–1997*, 1:757.

concern of Lyman and Grant, and the three men were linked in an occasionally stormy friendship from that time.[63]

Roberts and Lyman delivered the report to the First Presidency and several of the apostles. Roberts read the statement to apostle John Henry

63. On Joseph F. Smith's request of Roberts, see handwritten notation on James E. Talmage, Letter to Joseph F. Smith, February 13, 1907. On Lyman, Roberts, and Grant, see Heber J. Grant journal, March 13, 1896. On Roberts and Lyman, see also A. H. Cannon journal, April 3, 1894, LTPSC; also Edward Leo Lyman, ed., *Candid Insights of a Mormon Apostle: The Diaries of Abraham H. Cannon, 1889–1895*, 484–85. On Roberts and Penrose in political opposition to First Presidency policy, see Francis M. Lyman diary, March 23, 1893. Six months before, Lyman's diary reported that on October 11, 1892, Roberts and Thatcher came to the First Presidency to find out what they should do in politics: it was a "very pleasant meeting." Roberts slowly moved out of harmony with other leaders. Fellow Seventy John M. Whitaker's diary of November 1, 1893, and December 27, 1893, shows Roberts's growing difference with the church presidency (particularly Joseph F. Smith) on whether the Seventy (Roberts) or the High Priests (Cannon and Smith) was greater. Brigham Young Jr's diary of April 1, 1895, reported a conversation with Roberts on a suffrage article in the Utah constitution—Young argued that abandoned plural wives making it on their own deserved a voice—while Roberts disliked the idea of a female vote which he feared would be controlled by a Republican church leadership. The following year, Young's diary reported that he told Roberts to come to a meeting with the First Presidency, the Twelve and Seventy on February 12, 1896: "it is imperative that you come." A sequence of meetings were held. Another Seventy colleague, J. Golden Kimball, wrote on February 13, 1896: "Roberts is a noble spirit, intelligent, brave, valiant, and true but . . . in darkness." On March 5, 1896, Roberts was given three weeks to change his mind. After Grant and Lyman had another two hour conference with him (March 13, 1896), Roberts finally gave in: "Elders Lyman and Grant: My Dear Brethren: —I submit to the authority of God in the brethren. While I cannot for the life of me think of anything in which I have not acted in all good conscience, and with an honest heart, since they think I am in the wrong, I will bow to them, and place myself in their hands as the servants of God. This day thirty-nine years ago I first saw the light, and now after this trouble, I feel lighter. I thank you for your goodness to me, Truly your brother, B. H. Roberts." On March 26, 1896, Roberts met with all the presiding quorums and confessed. Everyone wept. Even Joseph F. Smith and Roberts confessed to each other and apologized (Journal History, J. Golden Kimball journal, March 26, 1896).

Smith on February 1. It was then delivered to the entire church presidency on February 6, 1907. Six of the apostles were also present, Francis M. Lyman, John Henry Smith, George Teasdale, Rudger Clawson, Hyrum M. Smith, and George F. Richards. Charles W. Penrose was in England supervising the European mission of the church—an important absence—while the other five, Heber J. Grant, Reed Smoot, George Albert Smith, Orson F. Whitney, and David O. McKay, were absent on other business or from illness.[64] Not all the apostles were clear about Roberts's thinking. The issues were variously distant from their minds. George F. Richards, who came in late to the gathering, seemed to be utterly confused by what Roberts had written.[65] However, the listeners approved a statement to be published with the article.[66]

Roberts published a version of the report in the April 1907 issue of the church's *Improvement Era* magazine and titled it, "The Immortality of Man."[67] The article contained some explanations of Roberts's position, and it had some form of official status at the time—though that did not last. It was MacDermott's questions that formed the basis of the article, and they were addressed one by one (though MacDermott was not named—see Appendix §B4).

Roberts went through each of MacDermott's questions, answering them out of JS's sermons and revelations as he saw them. Since MacDermott never responded to the article, he must have seen that the discussion was over and perhaps he was satisfied. The questions MacDermott asked represented other responses to the Manual and

64. Penrose had left abruptly for England in 1906 over renewed prosecution over continued polygamous cohabitation, the result of anger about the Smoot election. Joseph F. Smith, Letter to Heber J. Grant, October 19, 1906.

65. See George F. Richards journal, February 6, 1907.

66. See Journal of John Henry Smith, February 6, 1907, also Jean Bickmore White, ed., *Church State and Politics: The Diaries of John Henry Smith*, 579.

67. Roberts, "The Immortality of Man." See Appendix §B4.

to other church literature of the time. Those responses would surface again, some of them among church leaders.

The stage was set for an intense debate over the Follett sermon. The 1907 article is a watershed in the history of the sermon in the twentieth century. Roberts's writing revealed the current abstract mileposts of Mormon thought and how the sermon was taken to influence them. It explains much of the reaction of twentieth-century church leaders and members to Follett.[68] Roberts felt free to press the point and in 1908 published *Joseph Smith, the Prophet-Teacher*. In *Prophet-Teacher*, he repeated his assertions of the 1905 manual and the 1907 report and placed them more explicitly in terms of the Follett sermon.[69] Roberts read widely, and in that reading, he looked for (and found) prominent thinkers that confirmed his own theological interrogations of JS or at least parallel the Follett sermon. In March 1910, and then again the following month, Roberts published a two-part series titled, "Joseph Smith's Doctrines Vindicated." The first article, subtitled, "Men are the Avatars of God," used Follett as a basis for human preexistence, structurally an obvious return to his 1905–1907 series of imprints on the subject. The second article, subtitled, "The Existence of a Plurality of Divine Intelligence," interpreted another excerpt of Follett on "many Gods."[70] These kinds of pieces in Mormon periodicals became

68. Somewhat ironically, the facing page of the article is a portrait of Parley Pratt. For an annotated typographical facsimile of the article, see http://www.boap.org/LDS/Parallel/Immortality-of-Man.html. For a digital facsimile of the original, see https://archive.org/stream/improvementera106unse#page/no.

69. For example, see B. H. Roberts, *Joseph Smith, the Prophet-Teacher*, 22–24, 50–54. The book became another church course of study, this time for the Seventies and the YMMIA. See *Improvement Era*, January 1909, 86. It was reprinted by the church press (Deseret) in 1927.

70. B. H. Roberts, "Joseph Smith's Doctrines Vindicated, I. Men are the Avatars of God." B. H. Roberts, "Joseph Smith's Doctrines Vindicated. II. The Existence of a Plurality of Divine Intelligences."

less frequent as LDS leaders gravitated to points of commonality with American Protestantism, and church printing efforts and operations gradually became less independent and content more centrally controlled. Roberts's 1910 *Era* articles marked the beginning of Follett's official declension and in some respects that of Roberts as well.[71]

§3.5 The Emergence of Charles W. Penrose as Theological Opponent of Roberts

John A. Widtsoe Writes His Own Manual and Creates a Storm: Isaac Newton, Albert Einstein, and Charles Darwin Mark a Mormon Retreat From Science that Finds Follett as a Background Issue of Church Response.

The Lyman-Roberts article demonstrated that Mormon belief of the time included a form of Orson Pratt's idea that the human soul is the gestated and birthed spirit-child of God and a Mother in Heaven. Following the time-honored urge for consistency, Roberts wrote that belief over JS's signature as it were.[72] Roberts fused Utah and

71. Much of church book printing was farmed out to firms in Chicago and New York during the first decades of the twentieth century, though they might bear Utah monikers like "Deseret News Press." The British Mission of the church maintained its own print culture and did not necessarily slavishly follow or even notice that of the Pioneer Corridor operations. Church missions in the US had centralized print operations in Independence, Missouri, and editorial decisions were not often supervised by the leading church priesthood quorums. Church auxiliaries ran their own imprints and budgets. Partly this independence was a result of the Raid of the 1880s where President John Taylor attempted to decentralize ownership of church institutions to prevent or slow confiscation/control by federal authorities.

72. See Thomas G. Alexander, "The Reconstruction of Mormon Doctrine: From Joseph Smith to Progressive Theology," 31–32. Roberts, "What is Man," 387. Kenneth W. Godfrey, "The History of Intelligence in Latter-day Saint Thought," 213–36. On Brigham Young and celestial bodies siring spirit children, see General Church Minutes, 1839–1877, December 6, 1847.

Nauvoo by positing monadic (not Pratt's cooperative groupings of atomic agents), eternal, indestructible, uncreated souls/Cartesian minds or "intelligences" that were birthed into spiritual but human-shaped infant bodies by the Mother. Thus, humans were eternal as in JS's ontology but also material children of Eliza Snow's Father and Mother in Heaven. The article was meant to steam roll the idea of a parent-derived soul. However, the parent-derived soul—previously important in the logic of polygamy—was just as serviceable after the end of polygamy, this time with some modern biological roots.

The rise of biological studies of inherited traits from female egg and male sperm, including the "rediscovery" of Mendelian genetics early in the twentieth century, made a parent-derived soul into the ideal explanation of the Follett notion of treading in the footsteps of God—now with a twentieth-century hint toward gender equality.

God the Father and God the Mother might be seen not just as agents of good will offering a plan of progression/salvation to human beings but as transmitters of divine qualities and potential in the same way human parents delivered hair color, size, and other native properties to their offspring (see Mary B. Parker above). That theme continued to be, and still is, a common one in church discourse. Human souls inherit the potential to become gods through divine sexual transmission of spiritual genes as it were.[73] Roberts's folding in JS's protological scheme probably seemed overly complex and too far from received Utah tradition. It was unneeded for a narrative that already existed and was seen as an artificial construct that only served an increasingly suspect body of reporting in early Mormon discourse. It was gradually seen as a simpler course of action to count Roberts's creative solution to JS's difficult assertions as more painful than merely assigning the basis of those assertions to scribal error.

73. The phrase "gods in embryo" became popular in Mormon literature. Hannah T. King, "Meditations on the Passing Year—1884," 97. The inheritance idea is fully displayed in, for example, Marion G. Romney, "Man—A Child of God."

Penrose and Roberts were allies in the tumult of Utah politics in the 1890s. Penrose, Roberts, and church apostle Moses Thatcher were dedicated supporters of the Democratic Party in Utah and all ran afoul of the church presidency's efforts to support the Republican Party.[74] Over the next decades, Roberts and Penrose would find themselves in opposition over the Follett sermon. Francis M. Lyman, Roberts's partner in the construction of the 1907 report, was his political opponent in the upheavals from 1890 into the twentieth century. There was little love lost between them in that arena, and Lyman was irritated over Roberts's alcohol abuse and his continuing opposition to Joseph F. Smith's support of Reed Smoot in the US Senate.[75]

Though politically opposed to Lyman, Penrose was, like Lyman, a proponent of measured assimilation—even after a stormy journalistic career in opposition to the crushing federal presence imposed on church praxis and property over polygamy and church political control.

In 1884, Penrose gave an address in Salt Lake City rationalizing a cosmology that affected his perception of the Follett sermon nearly thirty years later. He was deeply influenced by the panpsychism of Parley Pratt's, *Key to the Science of Theology*.[76] Penrose reasoned:

---

74. See Alexander, *Mormonism in Transition*, 7–15. Journal of Abraham H. Cannon, April 3, 1893, May 19, 1893, in Lyman, *Candid Insights*, 381–86. Moyer, "Dancing with the Devil," 112, 255–56, 508–11. Anthon H. Lund diary, March 23, 1893, as in John P. Hatch, ed., *Danish Apostle: The Diaries of Anthon H. Lund, 1890–1921*, 11–12.

75. Francis M. Lyman, Letter to Charles W. Penrose, January 18, 1909; Francis M. Lyman, Letter to George Teasdale, July 8, 1904. D. Michael Quinn, *The Mormon Hierarchy: Extensions of Power*, 145–46.

76. Penrose later (1915) redacted Pratt's work for another edition and eliminated Pratt's elaborations of intelligent spiritual fluids and an impersonal Holy Ghost. Penrose's third wife, Esther Romania Salina Bunnell (1839–1932), had previously divorced (1880) Pratt's son, Parley P. Pratt, Jr. See Romania B. Penrose papers, circa 1881–1975. Romania was a physician and was a business partner of B . H. Roberts's third wife, also a physician, Margaret Curtis Shipp (1849–1926).

> But, if God is an individual spirit and dwells in a body, the question will arise, "Is He the Eternal Father?" Yes, He is the Eternal Father. "Is it a fact that He never had a beginning?" In the elementary particles of His organism, He did not. But if He is an organized Being, there must have been a time when that being was organized. This, some one will say, would infer that God had a beginning. This spirit which pervades all things, which is the light and life of all things, by which our heavenly Father operates, by which He is omnipotent, never had a beginning and never will have an end. . . . Now, this Spirit always existed; it always operated, but it is not, understood, and cannot be comprehended except through organisms. If you see a living blade of grass you see a manifestation of that Spirit which is called God. If you see an animal of any kind on the face of the earth having life, there is a manifestation of that Spirit. If you see a man you behold its most perfect earthly manifestation. . . . this eternal, beginningless, endless spirit of intelligence. . . . It is embodied in [God's] spiritual personality or spiritual organism. This spirit cannot be fully comprehended in our finite state. It quickens all things. . . . That spirit exists wherever there is a particle of material substance; that spirit is round about it, and in it, and through it; but that we may comprehend it, it must be manifested through organisms. The perfection of its manifestation is in the personality of a being called God.[77]

Penrose's speech on this spiritual æther modeled several Utah Mormon theologies (embodied in polygamy) that controlled and were partly informed by early Utah public policy and Mormon liturgy and were selectively based in the Deity outlined in the Follett sermon (importantly, without attribution). The cooperative nature of Utah economics energized and was in its turn motivated by the family model (an admittedly non-Victorian one) of human progress

77. Charles W. Penrose, "Who and What God is, etc."

to deification.[78] Penrose could also be justified within the earliest corpus of JS's revelations, a point I will return to below.

After the Lyman-Roberts article appeared in print—though it seems to have satisfied or at least silenced MacDermott—inquiries continued to come to the Salt Lake City church headquarters. As noted above, Roberts felt his critics failed to give the Follett sermon its due, and he published the annotated version of MS2 in the *Improvement Era* in 1909 (R1).[79] While Joseph F. Smith was the titular editor of the *Era*, Roberts was involved with the YMMIA and the Seventy, the sponsoring organizations of the *Era* at that point, and took the opportunity to put his crucial new text of Follett in the church's official magazine.[80] His published 1895–1907 interpretations

78. On policy, see Leonard J. Arrington, *Great Basin Kingdom: An Economic History of the Latter-day Saints, 1830–1900*, 51–62, 94; Donald Worster, *Rivers of Empire: Water, Aridity, and the Growth of the American West*, 76–83. Turner, *Brigham Young*, 248, 397–401; Park, "Paradoxes of Democratic Religiosity."

79. B. H. Roberts, ed., "The King Follett Discourse."

80. An internal political angle helped Roberts in his Follett piece. Church leaders had yielded to Roberts's idea that the *Era* should contribute source material for the Seventy's quorums gospel study. The masthead of the magazine reflected the change from a solely YMMIA-themed serial to a dual role with volume 11 November 1907, pages 63–66. Roberts had at least one piece in every issue from that point for many months and members of the First Council of Seventy occasionally had lead articles. The scope was extended to all local quorums a year later and the presence of the Seventy in the magazine diminished to some extent. See *The Deseret Evening News* (January 16, 1909): 5; also *Improvement Era*, 12, no. 4 (February 1909): 323. Within a decade, the Seventy had lost any special presence in the magazine. The initial push to expand the content of the *Era* came from the YMMIA leadership (which included Roberts). One example is General Board of the YMMIA, Letter to President Lorenzo Snow, January 17, 1901. A docket reads, "Read at Council, Feb. 14, 1901 x action deferred." An early and more radical proposal to condense all church serials into a single magazine (still the *Improvement Era*) was General Board of the YMMIA, Letter to President Wilford Woodruff and Counselors, February 5, 1896. One effect of John Taylor's dispersal of church assets during the "raid" was to

of the sermon were pointedly reflected in his annotation of R1, an annotation that (stripped of some nineteenth-century science footnotes) became part of the sermon in a new imprint tradition. It was a way of giving the stamp of church approval to the sermon and keeping his work on Follett in front of a church audience, backed by the words of its founder. It was a power play in the sense of trying to get the truth, as he saw it, out there among the church-going public.[81] Roberts had the ability to talk over his critics in official print, still the most powerful medium of all, but he couldn't do the same in all church media. Penrose saw to that to some degree.

Roberts's printing of Follett was only one straw in a bale that ostracized him from critical church councils that year. These issues were important since they probably removed him from one of the more important church declarations, a November 1909 statement that might have appealed to the Follett sermon and put to use its dual theologies of God and humans. As it happened, the statement would create distance between the approved (as Roberts perceived it) statement of 1907 and the soon-to-be-announced position of Joseph F. Smith's presidency. The latter supported the Young/Pratt vision of heavenly parenthood while ignoring JS's ontological claims; this created space for Charles Penrose.[82] Through 1909, Roberts refused to apologize for some 1908 pre-election political criticism of Smoot,

keep specialty imprints like the *Woman's Exponent*, the *Young Woman's Journal*, and the various mission printing efforts economically and largely editorially independent. Much of that independence remained until the correlation movement in the 1960s.

81. *Era* editor Edward Stevenson previewed the printing of R1 in the December issue, and Roberts advertised the sermon in his *Era* column in the same issue. "Seventies Council Table," *Improvement Era* 12, no. 3 (December 1908): 157–58.

82. On Roberts's understanding that Smith approved of his work and his disappointment in finding he was wrong, see B. H. Roberts, Letter to Rudger Clawson, November 20, 1914.

much to the disappointment of his fellow church leaders. He was again in a position similar to his resistance against the political muzzle in 1896, and he was ready once again to leave the hierarchy over his right to speak freely in public. In 1907, the First Presidency commissioned a new set of "Articles of Faith," read and sustained as an official church text in the April 1907 general conference. One of the new articles was directed at Roberts and other critics of church support for Smoot and claimed that the church supported a complete separation of church and state and total independence of church members to pursue whatever political paths they might choose. Roberts saw continuing behind the scenes support for Smoot as a violation of the document.[83] The tension kept Roberts out of any contribution to the coming pivotal November 1909 First Presidency response to Darwin, which as it happened was prompted at least in part by another church manual.[84]

Eleven months after the *Era* printing of Follett, Penrose countered in part with an article in the British *Latter-day Saints' Millennial Star*, November 18, 1909, where he repeated his 1884 cosmology, this time in support of the 1909 First Presidency message on evolution,

---

83. While sustained by the conference, the new Articles never replaced JS's version. Perhaps their purpose was temporary for the benefit of Smoot, making it official that the church would never try to influence the senator in his political duties. *Conference Report* (April 1907), *Improvement Era* 10 (May 1907): 481–95. https://boaporg.wordpress.com/2011/03/15/b-h-roberts-and-the-salt-lake-ministerial-association-i/

84. See for example, Anderson, *Cowboy Apostle*, 430, 457; *Conference Report* October 1909, 101–8, 123–25. Heath, *In the World*, 35. Years later, Roberts offered the proverbial compromise: *In essentials absolute union, in non-essentials liberty and charity. Conference Report*, October 5, 1912. Joseph F. Smith quoted it in his diary, but it seems likely that the two men had different definitions of where the boundaries were plotted. Joseph F. Smith diary, October 12, 1911, Box 4, fd. 9 MS 1325, CHL. D. Craig Mikkelsen, "The Politics of B. H. Roberts."

published in the same issue of the *Star.*[85] The Penrose article served to bring his ideas on God and the soul to the Saints in Britain over whatever contact they may have had with Roberts, the *Era*, *Prophet-Teacher*, and the Follett sermon in general.[86] The *Star* often reprinted important *Era* content, but it did not reprint the 1909 version of Follett or the Lyman-Roberts 1907 piece, nor did it notice *Prophet-Teacher*—Penrose was editor of the *Star.* For Penrose, the January 1909 text of Follett would end up being one more piece of evidence that RC was at least partly heresy, and those errors were the responsibility of (innocently!) unreliable clerks. The 1909 presidency message was conspicuous in its avoidance of the 1907 *Era* piece or *Prophet-Teacher* or *New Witnesses for God,* and none of the associated ontology/cosmology appeared in the message. Things might have been quite different had Roberts been a part of the discussion. Yet the 1909 message had important commonalities with Roberts's 1907 article.

The November 1909 presidency message shared in part a nearly identical origin point with the 1907 article: it was connected to a YMMIA teaching manual. Coincidentally, the fiftieth anniversary of *The Origin of Species* occurred in 1909, and it was also the centennial of Darwin's birth. This time, the provoking manual was one written by Widtsoe, titled *Science and the Gospel–Joseph Smith as Scientist.*[87] Widtsoe's writing on creation and evolution, while largely derived from previous *Era* articles, collided with worldviews held by some (perhaps most) adult church members. Readers sent their questions to Widtsoe and others. They ranged from whether spirits were cre-

85. The *Star* reprinted the November 1909 First Presidency message almost immediately on November 18, 1909 (*Latter-day Saints' Millennial Star* 71, no. 46, pp. 721–26). The message silently quoted from Follett with "God himself is an exalted man," but that point was never at issue for Joseph F. Smith (or Charles Penrose).

86. Charles W. Penrose, "Life, Matter, The Creature and The Creator," 728–31.

87. "Manual. Free with the Era," *Improvement Era* 11, no. 12 (October 1908): vii (unnumbered front matter in the issue).

ated or eternal, "like God," how Widtsoe reconciled statements in the Pearl of Great Price with an old earth, whether physical phenomena like sound were "substances," what is the "aether," the substance that "floats about in the heavens," how did Widtsoe reconcile his concept of geology with Doctrine and Covenants 77 ("I always did think that the great students of geology profess too much" said one respondent), how evolution could possibly be the method of creation, and so on.[88]

Widtsoe responded to many of those concerns by personal letter and he wrote followup articles in the *Era*. He was joined by editor Joseph F. Smith and assistant editor Edward Anderson, with the latter noting that "several students have asked to know whether the ideas contained in the seventh Y.M.M.I.A. Manual lesson are in harmony with the teaching of the Prophet Joseph Smith."[89] The First Presidency decided the manual needed clarification and perhaps some correction, and Joseph F. Smith himself smarted under the "new" scholarship. Smith disliked the idea that someone other than Moses was the author of the Pentateuch or that Adam and Eve were not the first parents of all humanity. Smith asked his nephew, one of the apostles, Orson F. Whitney—a relatively frequent ghostwriter for the Smith First Presidency since 1902—to draft a response, as much to respond to complaints over Widtsoe's manual as to address the general question of evolution and church belief. Whitney's work was per-

88. For a number of such letters, see John A. Widtsoe Papers, CR 712 2, Box 16, fd. 23, CHL.

89. For Widtsoe, see for example, John A. Widtsoe, "Ether, Holy Spirit, and Holy Ghost," *Improvement Era* 12, no. 5 (March 1909): 391–93, 491–93. For Joseph F. Smith, "Holy Ghost, Holy Spirit, Comforter," *Improvement Era* 12, no. 5 (March 1909): 389–91. Edward H. Anderson, "Age of the Earth," *Improvement Era* 12, no. 6 (April 1909): 489–90. John A. Widtsoe, Ph.D., "Time Length of Creation," *Improvement Era* 12, no. 6 (April 1909): 491–93. *Era* editors copied articles by Penrose from the *Star* that mirrored Joseph F. Smith's take, (see for example, *Improvement Era*, (May 1909): 505–9).

haps influenced by and was certainly connected in spirit to the most famous anti-evolutionist in America, William Jennings Bryan. A number of LDS apostles found in Bryan's popular *Prince of Peace* lecture an important argument that put Darwin in the category of dangerous social elitism set against a common sense Christianity.[90] By September 1909, the presidency had a draft from Whitney and called a meeting with some of the apostles together with Widtsoe and geologist James Talmage.[91]

As judged by his manual-reading public, Widtsoe had done several troublesome things in his 205-page book. He identified the mysterious (and as it turned out, nonexistent) æther of pre-relativistic physics with

90. For Whitney's draft, see Orson F. Whitney papers, MSS 15 Series 2 Subseries 7 Box 3 fd. 15, pp. 22–30, LTPSC. For more of Whitney's work for the church presidency, see Orson F. Whitney collection, Box 2, fd. 11, MS 1302, CHL. Bryan was well known in Utah. He was the guest of honor at the state's 24th of July Mormon pioneer celebration in 1897. *Improvement Era* 20, no. 8 (August 1957): 582. Bryan's *The Prince of Peace*, a sermon first delivered in 1904 and repeated many times thereafter, seems to have deeply influenced both Whitney and Heber J. Grant. See Kristy Maddux, "Fundamentalist Fool or Populist Paragon? William Jennings Bryan and the Campaign Against Evolutionary Theory." On Whitney, Grant, and Bryan, see Cris Baird, "'One of the Most Valuable Books I Have Ever Read:' The Influence of William Jennings Bryan on 20th Century Mormon Responses to the Theory of Evolution," in the LDS Scripture, Education, and Science session of the Mormon History Association conference, Boise, Idaho, June 8, 2018 (copy in the author's possession). The *Improvement Era* editors republished "Prince of Peace" as the lead article in the March 1913 issue. That Bryan was a Democrat placed him outside candidate endorsement by church leaders even though Utah voted for him in droves as the 1896 Democratic candidate for president.

91. White, *Church, State, and Politics*, 632. Jeffery, "Seers, Savants and Evolution," 59. Gary James Bergera and Ronald Priddis, *Brigham Young University: A House of Faith*, 136. First Presidency Letterpress Copybooks, September 24, 1909, Scott G. Kenney Collection, Box 2, fd. 13, MSS 2022, LTPSC. In 1911, the November 1909 message was republished and some of the anti-Darwinism was removed.

the "intelligence" of JS's revelations[92] and he stated that the earth was far older than typical biblical dogma allowed. Importantly, Widtsoe, without understanding that the source used an 1856 silent emendation, cited the Follett sermon as authority for his æther speculation.[93]

In *Science*, Widtsoe made the crucial observation that Mormon theories about the human soul demonstrated remarkable variation, from JS himself (Widtsoe referenced CON—see §1.6), the Pratt brothers' distinct views, and Brigham Young's ideas about spirit and matter. He did not mention the Roberts-Lyman 1907 report.[94] Widtsoe touched on evolution, using the word in a biological context while trying to cast doubt on natural selection as a main source of adaptation. Yet his statements on the origins of the soul, the body, and creation were enough to generate angst in the minds of some of his Latter-day Saint readers and that brought the letters like those noted above to headquarters. This helped lead to a critique of Follett by Joseph F. Smith and his counselors, a response to the cross-pressures generated by Follett's ideas about the origin of God, and on the other side, the (ultimate) origin of human beings. To understand some of the context of their discomfort, it is helpful to consider some of Widtsoe's scientific/religious milieu. I will return to 1909 below and then again briefly in the following section.

Widtsoe's anthem, typical of Mormon intellectual writing of the day and more broadly among many nineteenth-century Americans,

---

92. Widtsoe, "Ether" etc., *Improvement Era* (March 1909): 391–94. The æther was posited as a mechanical background substance akin to air for sound waves or water for ocean waves through which electromagnetic waves (like visible light or microwaves) could propagate. Its properties had to be outlandish: it had to be frictionless, fluid so it could fill space, rigid to be efficient, invisible to not impede light, and have no drag on moving physical objects.

93. "The intelligence of spirits had no beginning." Widtsoe, *Science and the Gospel*, 18, 155. Among church authorities, Widtsoe was ironically more mainstream.

94. Widtsoe, *Science and the Gospel*, 68–71.

was founded on the maxim that no conflict existed between true science and true religion.[95] Mormonism from its early days subscribed to this rather remarkable idea in a primitive way—in the twentieth century, it was sometimes abused when science became discomfiting. Often linked to a magic worldview, JS's formal scripture seemed to gradually mark out something else altogether. An 1832 revelation that received the name "Olive Leaf plucked from the tree of paradise" (canonized now as Doctrine and Covenants 88)[96] speaks of light, the "light that giveth you light" from the sun as the same light from the presence of God and extends through all space—the key to Penrose's anti-Follett argument. This assertion of extension spoke to gritty discussions at the beginnings of the separation of science and religion.

Seventeenth-century thinkers argued over whether it was God's influence that extended through space or God himself. This literal materialist claim of the Olive Leaf—an identification of God's power and influence in the world with an observable—with a hidden effect on the issue of causality—would, by the time of Einstein's 1905 work on Relativity, seem to fix Mormon cosmology within the realm of science. Ever since Greek thinkers like Democritus, the notion of "action at a distance" was a dividing line between the worlds of science and "magic." So important in the beginnings of modern physics was this line that it gave Isaac Newton (1643–1727) some reluctance about his own theory of gravity, something that seemed to "act at a distance" and do so instantaneously.[97] Tying the divine to the physical as this

95. For the general Mormon attitude, see James E. Talmage, "The Methods and Motives of Science," 256. For the broader issue, see Ronald L. Numbers, ed., *Galileo Goes to Jail and Other Myths about Science and Religion*.

96. *JSP*, D2:334–348. An early manuscript in digital facsimile is found here: http://www.josephsmithpapers.org/paper-summary/revelation-27-28-december-1832-dc-881-126/1#source-note.

97. What tied that falling apple to the earth? Nothing material, apparently. It took long years to understand that gravity, like all else in the universe, was restricted

revelation seems to do on modern reflection draws the Mormon God out of the transcendent and into the mundane, something Follett built upon together with William Clayton's notes of a question-answer session with JS in 1843 (an edited version is found in Doctrine and Covenants 130).[98] Logic then dictates that God must be incapable of instantaneous acts from a distance. God's communication (by light has a speed which is one of two fundamental principles in the physical universe (the other is that, in addition to the speed of light, the laws of physics are the same for all observers—including JS's in-universe God).[99]

Follett was at this crossroads of a human and materialist divine. God was not always God. He lived through *some* time and, once upon a time, *became* God. God was once a male human being or something of the same order. Perhaps I am guilty of some over enthusiasm here, when JS could not have guessed what scientific relativity was all about, but both texts (the 1832 revelation and Einstein's 1905 papers) existed in those early decades of the twentieth century, ready to engage with the language of science in Widtsoe's world. Widtsoe's attempts to link JS's world with his pre-Relativity understandings might tend to make Follett seem less relevant as time went by or perhaps create skepticism among the more educated.

It probably wouldn't have helped the First Presidency's peace of mind if Widtsoe had been up to date, and there are hints of this in the rise of Einstein's physics—in 1914, relativity was still a scientific shock

---

by the speed of light, and like light, it was a manifestation of Michael Faraday's (1791–1867) theory of "fields." On Newton's struggle, see Kochiras, "Gravity," 271n40. On Faraday, see L. Pearce Williams, *Michael Faraday: A Biography*. Einstein would show in 1915 that gravity acted at the speed of light and not instantaneously.

98. For the important transcript of the original Clayton content audit, see *JSP*, J2:403–6.

99. It was known in Newton's time that the speed of light was finite, a fact confirmed by Danish astronomer Ole Römer in 1676.

wave, and even after a 1919 confirmation of Einstein's General Theory of Relativity by British astronomers, noted American physicist A. A. Michelson still misunderstood Einstein's 1905 work. Einstein did not win the Nobel Prize for it, the prize was awarded to him for another of his five earthshaking 1905 physics results, the one on the photoelectric effect. The first mention of Einstein in a general Latter-day Saint setting was not from one of the lauded science minds in the church leadership of the age, who never seemed to engage Relativity's reshaping of the cosmos and physical understanding. Most particularly, this engagement might have tackled *time*. Einstein's work showed that no universal Newtonian clock can exist. Einstein's June 1905 paper showed that time was different for each different observer. There is no universal *now*. The same event may be in the *future* for one observer, in the *past* for another.[100]

Widtsoe's *Science and the Gospel* and the response was at least one contributing factor that led Joseph F. Smith to rein in the uncertainty over the origin of the human soul, other questions of creation, and evolution in particular.[101] Whitney performed part of that service

---

100. See Melvin J. Ballard, [untitled address] *Conference Report*, April 1932, p. 59. For the story of Einstein's Nobel prize, see Abraham Pais, "How Einstein Got the Nobel Prize," *American Scientist* 70, no. 4 (July–August 1982): 358–65. On Michelson, see his Chicago speech delivered at the University of Chicago in December 1919, widely noted in the American press. For example, see the notice in the *Ogden Daily Standard*, "Yardstick Shorter Pointing East Than North and South," December 19, 1919, page 14. Michelson had won the 1917 Nobel prize in physics yet was still confused about Einstein's 1905 work, let alone his *pièce de résistance* of 1915. Partly this may have been due to much of Einstein's work being in German at first. And, as is true everywhere, the old guard found change difficult.

101. Trouble was brewing at the Church's Brigham Young University over evolution and biblical criticism. Richard Sherlock, "Campus in Crisis: BYU's Earliest Conflict Between Secular Knowledge and Religious Belief."

with his second draft of the November 1909 message.[102] That message's outsized influence over Mormon discussions of science carried along elements of a seventeenth-century (and earlier) worldview and in some ways drew back from twentieth-century reflections on the innovations of the Mormon 1830s. That worldview entailed a cosmos because it was created by God, which had more in common with the geocentric conceptions of an earlier age where the creation was effectively one community that reacts to the agents within it according to a moral system. The cosmos is conscious of, and reacts to, good and evil—reactions that might be manifested in storms, earthquakes, famine, and disease. This near premodern reasoning could seem legitimate given the canonical stories from the founding of Mormonism that in many ways reinforced pre-critical interpretations of the book of Genesis, for example.[103] However, it served to drive a wedge between such claims and the principles students learned in science: Leibniz's Sufficient Reason among them—if not in name, in method. Sufficient Reason made it imperative to find out cause from effect, in weather phenomena or seismic events, and ascribing volition to rocks or air would not serve. Widtsoe wanted to help his audience try to see science as a part of Mormonism, which by tradition incorporated truth mined from all sources—indeed, its founder described the idea

102. Whitney's first draft was rejected; his second, delivered October 14, 1909 was accepted. Hatch, *Danish Apostle*, 405.

103. JS's inspired revision of the Bible had the earth groaning because of the sins committed on it. Natural disasters were nature's moves to right the instabilities of moral evil. See, for example, James E. Talmage, "Natural Phenomena Related to Human History," 22, no. 2 *Liahona The Elders' Journal* (July 15, 1924): 23–24. On the early modern heritage reflected in Talmage's claims, see William Bouwsma, *John Calvin*, 34. Talmage was not alone in the way he saw science interfacing with religion. For many examples contemporary with Talmage, see Storm, *The Myth of Disenchantment*.

as a fundamental part of the religion.[104] Follett's picture of God holding up the cosmos, which might fail if he lost focus, required some work at eisegesis, work that was painful at times and slow to develop.

Roberts's 1905 manual didn't require massive amounts of feedback to generate a response from church officials. The same was true for *Science and the Gospel*. Joseph F. Smith shared Talmage's abhorrence of uncertainty and its attending speculation. And in any case, the matter was close to Smith's heart. The parent-child ideology of Eliza Snow's hymn was a fixation for Smith, as is clear from the criticism the 1909 message rendered on Darwin. Man was a special creation, not derived from stochastic paths of niche and selection (the nature and role of mutation was still controversial and remained that way in part until the Watson–Crick–Franklin discovery of DNA). Human beings, as preexistent spirits, were "begotten and born of heavenly parents, and reared to maturity in the eternal mansions of the Father, prior to coming upon the earth in a temporal body." All humans were made in the image of the material man-God.[105] In its fundamental critique of science, this represented much of the antebellum environment of JS himself. There, the interplay between reason and revelation made Genesis into a narrative of fact, far superior to biological theory and practice.[106] This approach would remain inside blessed church narratives for the foreseeable future. At the same time,

---

104. Sermon, July 23, 1843, *JSP*, J3: 66.

105. Joseph F. Smith, et al., "The Origin of Man," 80. The November 1909 message was not the final word on the subject, but it may have helped solidify church opposition to teaching evolution at BYU. Four professors would be disciplined for making evolution a part of their curriculum in 1911. Sherlock, "Campus in Crisis." One LDS apostle, Boyd K. Packer (1924–2015), made it clear that the subject was faith-destroying. Boyd K. Packer, "The Snow-White Birds."

106. For example, polygenesis (multiple origins of humans) theories were largely rejected because of Genesis 2 in JS's time. Howe, *What Hath God Wrought*, 2–3, 482.

its theology was wholly from Middle Mormonism, tied to a narrative bulwark for the logic of polygamy—in spirit if no longer in body.[107]

B. H. Roberts was, in many ways, the opposite of the calm, careful, humble, and (as David O. McKay would note) out-of-his-depth Talmage and therefore less likely to be content in the inner circles of church power.[108] Roberts was Mormonism's Origen. His name would not enjoy the enduring institutional imprimatur of a Talmage or the educational status of a Widtsoe or the romanticism of Whitney's prose. Roberts's works were sometimes hidden and neglected but his intellectual and theological frameworks *a la* Follett still continued in many respects, even if they were passed on without his name attached to them, as I shall observe in the following chapter.[109] An example of Roberts's influence on interpretation via Follett was his exegesis of passages like Doctrine and Covenants 93:29. Roberts saw passages like: "intelligence, or the light of truth, was not created or made, neither indeed can be" through the lens of Follett, making them read as statements of personal immortality rather than their ca. 1833 interpretation as a reference to some world-soul, æther, or an allegory for God's future acts.[110] While Roberts wished to find coherence between such passages and Follett's theology, Penrose saw the passage as an extension

107. Joseph Baker, et al., "Acceptance of Evolution among American Mormons."

108. David O. McKay diary, February 27, 1907.

109. The 1911–12 manual for the YMMIA was another flash point. This time the issue was communalism. Roberts may have been the author. Once again, Joseph F. Smith had the publication stopped and attempted to recall all 2,000 copies already printed and distributed. In the end, the last five lessons were deleted, and YMMIA leaders were asked to provide their own source material. Heath, *In the World*, 114. "The 1911–12 Y.M.M.I.A. Manuals," *Improvement Era* 15, no. 1 (November 1911), v (front matter).

110. See Roberts's 1907 *Era* paper (Appendix §B4 below) and his notes in the third major text tradition of Follett, "The King Follett Discourse," *Improvement Era* 12, no. 3 (January 1909): 183n1. On early impersonal or allegorical interpretations of passages like Doctrine and Covenants 93:29 and Moses 3:5–7, see Alexander,

of the Olive Leaf discourse on light (though certainly not through the lens of modern physics suggested above). Both men wanted a consistent cosmology grounded in JS's texts, though *which* texts and which interpretation was the question. Their contested views gave proof to the assertion that their goal was impossible.[111] A reconstituted (1911) First Presidency would force a temporary resolution in 1912.

Meanwhile, Roberts was pressing forward in two major historical projects for the church connected to his assignment as an Assistant Church Historian. One was a series of historical articles on Mormonism appearing in the American Historical Society's magazine *Americana*, and the other was the ongoing publication of the six-volume *History of the Church the Church of Jesus Christ of Latter-day Saints, Period I,* consisting largely of redacted (by the 1850s Utah clerks and historians) documents from the JS era with Roberts's annotation.[112] Originally planned for volume five in the publication project of the ms history, RC was moved to volume six—the volume finally published in 1912—and the last volume Roberts would produce in the series until 1932, when he added a volume covering 1844 to 1848.[113] Charles W. Penrose, since returned from England, would shortly become a member of the First Presidency; by the time Roberts approached his summary of JS's theology in the *Americana* articles and the publication of volume six of the *History*, Penrose and Lund

"Reconstruction," 33n23; Harrell, "Development of the Doctrine of Preexistence," 82–84.

111. Benjamin E. Park, "(Re)Interpreting Early Mormon Thought: Synthesizing Joseph Smith's Theology and the Process of Religious Formation," 62–64.

112. The base text for much of the history was the serial printing of history in *Latter-day Saints' Millennial Star* in the 1850s–60s. *History* volumes appeared over a ten-year period beginning in 1902, with volume 6 in 1912. The 1932 seventh volume covered 1844–48 apostolic succession to JS.

113. T. Edgar Lyon, "Church Historians I Have Known," 15.

of the Presidency were functioning as Roberts's advisors and consultants for his two history projects.[114]

Penrose and Roberts first crossed paths over Follett when First Presidency counselor and church historian Anthon H. Lund invited then-apostle Penrose to help him review Roberts's history work. Eventually Roberts's interpretations of the Follett sermon came up in review sessions. Lund left a record of the meetings:

> Today [August 25, 1911] we had Bro. Roberts read his article [for *Americana*] on the Philosophy of the Prophet Joseph Smith. Bro. Penrose made a splendid speech on eternalism[115] opposing the view of Bro. B. Roberts who holds that intelligences were self-existent entities before they entered into the organization of the spirit.
>
> [August 29] I spent the forenoon in the H[istorians] O[ffice] where Bro. C. W. Penrose and I listened to Bro. Roberts read his concluding chapter on the prophet Joseph Smith. We got him to eliminate his theories in regard to intelligences as conscious self-existing beings or entities before being organized into Spirits. His doctrine has raised much discussion and the infer-

114. The *Americana* articles were later coalesced and expanded to form Roberts's six volume centennial history of the church, *A Comprehensive History of the Church of Jesus Christ of Latter-day Saints, Century I*. Roberts restored some of the language Penrose and Lund had modified in the serialized magazine printing between July 1909 and July 1915. On the *Comprehensive History*, see Kenneth W. Godfrey, "A Comprehensive History of the Church." Leonard J. Arrington, "The Writing of Latter-day Saint History: Problems, Accomplishments and Admonitions," 123–24. On First Presidency supervision, see also White, *Church, State, and Politics*, 681.

115. *Eternalism*: the word was not invented in 1911. Its historical use referred to the position that various theologians (Augustine) and philosophers (Spinoza) took with regard to time. Time is not reality; it is only appearance. The notion is connected on the more mundane level with the "block universe" of modern cosmology. One senses that Penrose would be repelled by that, though it is present in Mormon scripture: Moses 1:6. See Holt, *When Einstein Walked With Gödel*, 17. Orlando J. Smith, *Eternalism: A Theory of Infinite Justice*, 185–90.

> ence on which he builds his theory is very vague. *The Prophets speech delivered as a funeral sermon over King Follett*, is the basis of Bro. Roberts doctrine: namely where he speaks of mans eternity claim. Roberts wants to prove that man then is co-eval with God. He no doubt felt bad to have us eliminate his pet theory.[116]

Neither the 1907 response to MacDermott, the 1905 manual, nor *Prophet-Teacher* played into this discussion—at least partly because Penrose had not signed off in 1907 (and almost certainly would not have done so had he been in Salt Lake City at the time), and he could safely ignore *Prophet-Teacher*, in status similar to the 1905 manual.

While Penrose worked to correct and then oppose Roberts's religious ontology/cosmology and the Follett sermon, he continued a similar debate and opposition with Brigham Young University teacher and writer Nels Lars Nelson. Nelson's work deployed the Follett sermon in much the same way Roberts did. In 1907 Nelson wrote to Penrose in England for his opinion on his 1904 book, *The Scientific Aspects of Mormonism*, and within his 1884 framework, Penrose called out and firmly objected to Nelson's Follett-inspired ontic claims over human souls.[117]

Roberts's support of the Follett sermon fit, in some sense, his political stance. Democrats of the day were the party of individualism, state rights, and the rural mindset of the west, with Republicans the party of social community and reform, business, and the devel-

116. Emphasis added. Anthon H. Lund Journal, August 29, 1911, see Hatch, *Danish Apostle*, 465. Lund was otherwise very complimentary of Roberts's work in both the *Americana* articles and the *History*. For Roberts's "Penrosed" version of "Joseph Smith's Philosophy," see B. H. Roberts, "History of the Mormon Church," 993. Three principals in the discussion, Roberts, Penrose and Talmage, had previously formed a committee to consider the ongoing testimony given at the Reed Smoot senate hearings in 1904, an onerous task for Roberts. Moyer, "Dancing with the Devil," 396, 480.

117. Charles Penrose diary, April 18, 1907, Utah State Historical Society, Salt Lake City, Utah. Nelson, *Scientific Aspects*, 79n1.

oping American middle class. Paradoxically perhaps—given that Republicans had (historically) been the force behind government repression of polygamy—the latter was in some ways more coherent with nostalgic pre-manifesto Utah, and they had helped Utah in the quest for statehood after Woodruff's 1890 Manifesto ending polygamy. Democrats opposed congressional post-civil war Reconstruction, arguing that its social reforms restricted individual freedom and threatened social orders around the specter of interracial marriage—both deeply important Mormon issues in the environment of polygamy, Utah politics, and restrictions on Black persons, thought to be cursed descendants of Cain and not allowed to participate in many Mormon rituals or be ordained to the priesthood.[118] Continuing the antinomy, Roberts's political ally (Penrose) took an opposing theological position while his political opponent (Lyman) had become an interpretive ally.

§3.6 The First Presidency and RC—Personalities in Debate

Widtsoe's Manual Fallout: A First Presidency Statement in Reaction to Science and Official Church Belief. Follett Ends the History of the Church Project—The 1912 Turn

Joseph F. Smith had a complicated and changing relationship with the Follett sermon. While he had early difficulties with its child resurrec-

118. On the internal logic of Mormon leaders in support of the Republican party, see Flake, *The Politics of American Religious Identity*. Bowman, *The Mormon People*, ch. 6. Moyer, "Dancing with the Devil." On Reconstruction, see Eric Foner, *A Short History of Reconstruction*. On Black persons and Mormonism, see Armand L. Mauss, *All Abraham's Children*. Reeve, *Religion of a Different Color*; Roberts, "What is Man," 387; Roberts, *Seventy's Course in Theology*, 5 vols., 1:163–66.

tion ideas, he still accepted the human protology of the sermon, at least for a time. In 1884, during a funeral sermon for a young girl, he quoted Follett, announcing that the girl's spirit had no beginning and therefore can have no end.[119] In an 1878 funeral sermon for Emma Wells, the daughter of Daniel and Emmeline Wells, Smith quoted from the Follett sermon as authority for the importance of proxy ordinances.[120] But by 1911, Smith's First Presidency (now Smith, Lund, and Penrose) felt that RC was fatally unreliable as a source of doctrine and said as much in a special priesthood meeting of April 8, 1912.

> there are parts of what is known as the King Follett sermon that bear out Bro. Robert's [sic] conclusions but that sermon was imperfectly reported . . . it has not been accepted as authority by the Church the imperfections . . . were emphasized by President Joseph F. Smith at a special Priesthood Meeting held in Salt Lake City, Monday, April 8, 1912[121]

Members of Roberts's quorum generally spoke at the general conferences of the church for many years. But for the April 1912 conference, Joseph F. Smith excluded them—the explanation Smith gave was lack of time. Roberts had ignored Lund and Penrose and their lecture against referring to Follett when they reviewed the *Americana*

---

119. See Seymour B. Young journal, August 1884, page 38.

120. Joseph F. Smith, *The Deseret News* (May 1, 1878): 3.

121. James Duckworth, Letter to Francis T. Pomeroy, February 9, 1928. "Special priesthood meetings" for gathered local church officials were typically held in conjunction with a general conference of the period. They had been held since early Utah. The April 8, 1912 meeting was partly devoted to Joseph F. Smith's and Charles Penrose's suspicions regarding RC and the "Adam-God" teachings of Brigham Young. On Adam-God and the April meeting see the journal of Thomas Clawson, April 12, 1912. Smith and Lund felt comfortable with Penrose's arguments—which reflected the acceptable portions of Middle Mormonism's theology. Compare Penrose's 1917 "Why I am a Mormon." That Lycurgus Wilson's little book was approved by the presidency in 1904 further suggests a developing position for Penrose as critic-in-chief of Follett.

articles. Moreover, the 1911 volume of his First Council of Seventy study manual, *The Seventy's Course in Theology: Fourth Year,* set up the 1909 *Era* text of Follett and the 1907 article as fundamental, even standard, theological texts. Roberts counted on the appearance of RC in the forthcoming publication of volume 6 of the *History of the Church of Jesus Christ of Latter-day Saints, Period I.*[122]

The anathematizing of Follett marked the ultimate in theological strain; in essence, the rejection of the Follett sermon was a kind of rejection of the historical past in the persona of Early Mormonism. *All of JS's reported statements might be suspect.* Only those with continuing approval constituted the true founding narrative, the real history, and that approval might intervene at any time in the future, less in terms of outright rejection, more in terms of emphasis, with Joseph F. Smith's examples of strain marking the path.[123]

A key factor in this dynamic was Joseph F. Smith's apparent wish to distance public Mormonism from nineteenth-century controversies and his developing methodology of ignoring the corpus of Mormon extracanonical texts.[124] Joseph F. Smith's theological and ecclesial

---

122. B. H. Roberts, *The Seventy's Course in Theology. Fourth Year: The Atonement*, 1–23.

123. The church's public relations arm published the relevant piece in 2007: Approaching Mormon Doctrine (https://newsroom.churchofjesuschrist.org/article/approaching-mormon-doctrine).

124. On extracanonical literature like the speeches of Brigham Young, see Smith's letters to his missionary sons in Britain in 1899. They show some ignorance of, and mild disdain for, such literature. See, for example, Joseph F. Smith, Letter to Elder Joseph R. Smith, Bradford England, October 23, 1899. See also his 1897 reply to questions on Young's Adam-God ideas: "Even if there is truth in it, the bare mention of it by Brigham Young without indubitable evidence and authority being given of its truth, was unfortunate to say the least." Joseph F. Smith Letterpress Copybooks, MS 1325, CHL. His claims of scripture cohesion and scripture authority in the face of the historical critical method telegraphed the Mormon twentieth century. For some period, Smith's first circle of literature apparently included

vision was increasingly centered in canon scripture, particularly the revelation texts of the Doctrine and Covenants. In an 1880 speech at the Salt Lake Stake's conference, Smith's remarks served up a critique of Brigham Young's priesthood ordering, appealing to the Doctrine and Covenants as final authority. His fellow apostles were disturbed by this, but Smith never gave in. In his eyes, he was going back to an authentic beginning, following his theological mentor, Orson Pratt, and his systematics.[125] As for the other member of Smith's First Presidency, Anthon H. Lund's view of early Mormonism was filtered through Utah, and he began to see Roberts's interpretation of Follett as a kind of minor heresy.[126]

The April 1912 special priesthood meeting content implicitly argued for the deletion of the Follett sermon from volume six of the published history. The volume was first advertised in the March 1912 issue of the *Improvement Era*. In the same issue, the First Presidency published their January 31, 1912, statement responding to more letters to headquarters over Roberts's interpretations of Follett ("preexistent states") and continuing questions about Brigham Young's Adam-God teaching, still a hot enough topic that it deserved mention. Four years later, church leaders issued a joint statement on God in hopes of further damping the effects of the nineteenth century's wide-ranging preaching (see below).[127]

Franklin D. Richards's *Compendium* and he alluded to its references to JS in those same letters to his missionary sons. For more on Joseph F. Smith's evolution, see Smith, "Early Mormon Priesthood Revelations," 39–46, and Taysom, *Like a Firey Meteor*.

125. See George Q. Cannon journal, January 6, 1880. On Smith and Pratt, see Taysom, *Like a Firey Meteor*, ch. 5.

126. Hatch, *Danish Apostle*, 465.

127. See "Editors' Table–The Father and the Son," *Improvement Era* 19, no. 10 (August 1916): 934–42. On the move from Middle Mormonism, see Philip Barlow, "Shifting Ground and the Third Transformation of Mormonism."

While Lund felt Roberts founded his ideas on Follett, Roberts's correspondence suggests that he also saw links to JS's Book of Abraham.[128] Roberts was likely aware that in December 1911, *Liahona The Elders' Journal* reprinted R1 (this is R2) since he was a long-time subscriber, though Central States mission president Samuel Bennion made no mention of Roberts in the efforts to publish Follett. Indeed, Latter-day Saints at large were interested in the sermon. Many had written to the *Liahona* requesting a separate imprint of the sermon. The magazine often chose past *Improvement Era* articles for reprinting. This was partly a reflection on the relatively small circulation of the *Era*. The demand was enough that Bennion felt the Independence printing establishment could gain useful revenue with a 12,000 copy reprint of R1. Smith and Penrose somehow became aware of the *Liahona* printing and telegraphed the magazine editor, Joseph McRae, to stop printing the sermon and to stop distributing it.[129]

The magazine had already tried to solicit funds to distribute the sermon (see George Albert Smith to Samuel O. Bennion above). The First Presidency's response to the *Liahona* imprint of Follett was a clear signal of their intent in regard to RC and volume 6 of the *History*. Bennion wrote a frustrated reply to the First Presidency's request to stop the presses.

> We have had a large number of calls for the "King Follett" sermon and a number of letters from members of the church stat-

128. See also Wilson's *Philosophy* and Nelson's 1896 *Contributor* article. Some church leaders of a later generation saw Follett in much the same light as Penrose. Bruce R. McConkie, one of the First Council of Seventy after Roberts's generation, even saw Roberts as engaging in subterfuge. Donald B. Horne, *Determining Doctrine: A Reference Guide for Evaluating Doctrinal Truth*, 48–49. Roberts's view was that the Book of Abraham had to be maintained against critics since its contents are "mighty essential to the Mormon System of philosophical thought and . . . must be maintained." B. H. Roberts, Letter to Isaac Russell, April 25, 1913.

129. First Presidency Letterpress Copybooks, December 28, 1911, January 6, 1912.

> ing that they were very glad to get it, however, I don't see anything in it but what I have heard preached and read from time to time in our manuals and in other books, but it proved to be a drawing card for the Liahona, so we were feeling quite jubilant over the returns from it . . . Knowing it had been printed in the Era, I never questioned it. Here we are now with seven thousand copies left on our hands with orders and money accompanying for two or three thousand. What are we to do?[130]

Bennion's frustration stemmed first from finances. He observed that making the *Liahona* self-sustaining was a constant challenge. The Follett reprint had significantly expanded the subscriber base. Second, Bennion felt he and his printing team were more than justified by demand and Follett's appearance in church imprints like the recent *Seventy's Course in Theology*. Apparently, the *Liahona* kept filling orders for the sermon imprint. In the January 23, 1912, issue, the editor inserted a short notice on page 489: "The edition of the King Follett Discourse is exhausted. No more orders can be filled after this date." Eleven years later, Bennion, who was *still* mission president, rejected some of the prevailing suspicion of Follett in his sermon at the October general conference for 1923.[131]

However, by 1912, Joseph F. Smith was thoroughly disenchanted with RC and seemed at least partly persuaded by Penrose—the latter saw Roberts's work with Follett as a misguided enterprise.

When Joseph F. Smith delivered his inaugural address as the new church president in 1901, he made it clear that his presidency would be marked as a true partnership between himself and his counselors. Smith was breaking new ground in his experience. Brigham Young had often dictated by fiat, while John Taylor in reaction resorted

---

130. Samuel O. Bennion, Letter to President Joseph F. Smith & Counselors, January 5, 1912.

131. Samuel O. Bennion, October 1923, *Conference Report*, 80.

to volunteerism, yet he often refused to be counseled.[132] During Woodruff's administration, Joseph F. Smith had often been marginalized by Cannon, and even his own cousin, apostle John Henry Smith, thought of Smith as lacking presence. Joseph F. was determined to do things differently.[133] Hence, it is quite likely that Smith would have been sympathetic to Penrose's particular peeve with Follett; in return, Penrose deployed the skeleton of Smith's arguments about child resurrection that Follett was badly reported and JS corrected his claims in it. In doing so, Penrose was over-generous with his president's chronology (see Penrose's remarks noted below).

Neither Anthon Lund nor Joseph F. Smith commented publicly on Roberts in terms of the Follett sermon. Instead, Penrose became the spokesman in dampening support for RC and Roberts's reading of it.[134] The First Presidency wrote to McRae again on January 6, 1912:

> On receiving notification that a large number of copies of the Liahona were being printed and circulated containing what is

132. On Taylor's stiffness, see Ronald W. Walker, *Qualities that Count: Heber J. Grant as Businessman, Missionary, and Apostle*, 201. See Heber J. Grant's humorous account of Francis Lyman trying to get Taylor to change his mind. *Conference Report*, April 1942, 9. Taysom, *Like a Firey Meteor*.

133. On Joseph F. Smith's address, see Joseph F. Smith, "Duties and Responsibilities of the First Presidency," November 11, 1901, *Conference Report*, 82. On Joseph F.'s, Orson Pratt's, Moses Thatcher's, and John Smith's view of Young, see George Q. Cannon journal, October 6, 1880. On others marginalizing Smith, see Journal of Heber J. Grant, July 7, 1887, September 8, 1887, October 5, 1887, January 4, 1898, CHL.

134. The following incident illustrates some of the differences between the two men. Once when the head of the church bookstore (Deseret Book) asked Roberts about having a certain anti-Mormon book in the store, Roberts said to leave it there if it was selling, they were in the business of selling books. When Joseph F. was then consulted, he replied, "Do not keep the nasty thing in stock." Horace Whitney to Joseph F. Smith, 3 July 1903, First Presidency General Authority correspondence, CR 1 176, Box 5, Deseret News, CHL.

> known as the King Follett Sermon, as it has since been corrected and interpolated, with notes added, we sent the following telegram (text of above telegram repeated). When the sermon was first published it did not receive the revision or sanction by the Prophet Joseph, who preached it, and it was reported from the impressions obtained by four different persons who heard it, neither of whom was a shorthand writer.
>
> There are some points in the sermon which appear to be in direct conflict with revelations accepted by the Church as Divine. Some portions of the original report have been expunged from the version which appears in the Liahona; there are some interpolations also which have been made without authorization. Then there are footnotes added introducing ideas not warranted by the text, which state plainly that the original report is evidently incorrect in some particulars. Such a doubtful production we think is not proper to publish as authentic. For these reasons we sent you the dispatch referred to.[135]

Roberts had removed some text from the sermon in R1, namely the part about the resurrection of infants, which was so repugnant to Joseph F. Smith. The presidency's charge of *interpolation* is curious. The text follows MS2 quite closely. The question of footnotes hints that the writer of the telegram was Charles Penrose, though the others were surely convinced of the point.[136] Penrose wanted Follett to simply go away—in his mind there was plenty of support for developing a twentieth-century Mormon system of teaching without it—much like the disappearance of polygamy as a central belief. Two years later, that is what happened when the joint First Presidency and Quorum

---

135. "Interpolations" referred to Roberts's notes that appeared first in R1. First Presidency Letterpress Copybooks, January 6, 1912. On the fidelity of the text of R2 to RC, see the imprint variorums in Appendices E accessible in http://boap.org/LDS/KFS-Appendices.

136. On the influence of Penrose on Joseph F. Smith, see B. H. Roberts, Letter to Elder Rudger Clawson, November 20, 1914.

of Twelve Apostles issued a Talmage-produced statement over their collective signatures called, "The Father and the Son, A Doctrinal Exposition" (see §3.7).[137]

The fecund heavenly family offered another reason for Penrose and Smith to counter Roberts's interpretation of the Follett sermon. The heavenly reproductive scheme drawn from Middle Mormonism's theology of polygamy argued against what seemed an inevitable consequence of "Darwinism": man has no singularly exalted position in the cosmos. Joseph F. Smith felt that promoting the literal fatherhood of God with the human spirit-self as a special creation (or birth) was a bulwark against the encroachment of science into the exclusive domain of the divine. Indeed, Whitney's final 1909 statement (endorsed by the First Presidency) used this as a reason why biological evolution should be, if not rejected outright, at least modified in its interpretation of the status of man as more than just one current endpoint in natural selection.[138]

Not all Latter-day Saints of the era saw Darwin as a threat. John Henry Evans's 1905 book *One Hundred Years of Mormonism* took a remarkably positive view of Darwin: "As Darwin, the great scientist, spent the best part of his manhood in collecting and arranging data about plants and animals, which obstinately refused to be classified and explained by systems then approved, but which fell at once into harmony and order when the single luminous idea of 'natural selection' was brought to bear on them." The claim is more remarkable for the book being reissued three times.[139]

---

137. See the 1916 Talmage-authored "A Doctrinal Exposition by the First Presidency and the Quorum of the Twelve."

138. See Joseph F. Smith, et al., "The Origin of Man." Duane E. Jeffery, "Seers, Savants and Evolution: The Uncomfortable Interface;" Richard Sherlock, "A Turbulent Spectrum: Mormon Reactions to the Darwinist Legacy;" Alexander, "Reconstruction," 29.

139. Evans, *One Hundred Years of Mormonism*, 307. A number of prominent LDS scientists of the era saw evolution as an aspect of the idea of "eternal progression."

Ominously perhaps, it was 1909 when the word *ectogenesis* came into use. The idea of ectogenesis was one of the more—at the time—culturally odious speculations that made Aldous Huxley's 1932 book *Brave New World* so repugnant to many conservative religious leaders. Huxley wrote of a genesis room (the "hatchery") where humans were conceived and incubated in test tubes, a prophetic image that became largely factual in biology over the following century.[140] For the Saints, perhaps the idea was doubly troubling: if humans could do it, couldn't God? The sacredness, the divinity, and the power of sex—part of the mystique of polygamy and its imprint on the Mormon concept of the afterlife—were now in jeopardy.

Some Latter-day Saint church leaders were, at some level, considering the religious implications of Darwin and modern biology. The November 1909 message marked a thread that became more widespread in church leadership and in Mormon literature, leading, by the 1940s, to a more fundamentalist approach to the Bible and science, one that presided over vigorous schisms among Evangelicals of the day. Those schisms were partly mirrored among Mormon academics.[141] Joseph F. Smith's younger apostle son and namesake became a principal public voice a decade later. A 1920 *Era* issue showcased a Joseph Fielding

---

140. The process of *in vitro* fertilization is now a common procedure. On artificial wombs, see for example, M. Sakata, K. Hisano, M. Okada, and M. Yasufuku, "A New Artificial Placenta with Centrifugal Pump: Long-Term Total Extrauterine Support of Goat Fetuses." Emily A. Partridge, et al., "An Extra-Uterine System to Physiologically Support the Extreme Premature Lamb." Alejandro Aguilera-Castrejon, Bernardo Oldak, Tom Shani, et al., "Ex Utero Mouse Embryogenesis from Pre-gastrultion to Late Organogenesis."

141. In 1910, more questions from church members drew a response in the *Era*. See "Priesthood Quorums' Table–Origin of Man." On the Protestant fractures of the time, see Bradley Longfield, *The Presbyternian Controversy: Fundamentalists, Modernists, and Moderates*; George Marsden, *Fundamentalism and American Culture*; Molly Worthen, *Apostles of Reason: The Crisis of Authority in American Evangelicalism*; Bowman, "The Evangelical Countercult Movement."

Smith article with this caption on his photo, "'The Origin and Destiny of Man' with a sidelight on evolution, and telling arguments showing its inadequacies and inconsistencies, is worth careful study and double reading." The appointment of several conservative apostles near mid-century would make Fielding Smith's views into church standard.[142]

The *Liahona* incident and the April 1912 meeting were heralds. Joseph F. Smith ordered the printer of *History of the Church* vol. 6 (possibly Chicago printers Henry Etten & Co.) to alter the table of contents and excise the King Follett sermon. The printer avoided a problem in the volume's table of contents by some skillful manipulation of the printing master.[143] These sentences on Follett were all that appeared in the newly published volume of the *History*:

> At a quarter-past three p. m., President Smith having arrived, the choir sang a hymn. Elder Amasa Lyman offered prayer. President Joseph Smith delivered a discourse before twenty-thousand Saints, being the funeral sermon of Elder King Follett.

When Roberts found that RC (R1 in fact) had been removed from the *History*, he felt deeply insulted. Roberts discovered the change by

142. Joseph Fielding Smith, "The Origin and Destiny of Man." Smith was apparently taken with another amateur approach to creation, that of Seventh Day Adventist and self-taught geologist George McCready Price, the creationist guru of the 1920s anti-evolution crusade. See Jeffrey E. Keller, "Discussion Continued: The Sequel to the Roberts/Smith/Talmage Affair," 83. Smith's expansion of the article in his 1954 book, *Man: His Origin and Destiny,* had a remarkable and continuing effect on rank and file teaching and it also functioned as a church manual—this time for instructors in the church's religion teachers at seminaries and institutes of religion in the summer of 1954 at Brigham Young University. Once, near the close of the twentieth century, I sat through a sermon by a Brigham Young University computer scientist who eagerly made the astonishing assertion that Fielding Smith's book was the final answer to Darwin.

143. On church printing for the period, see Richard L. Saunders, *The 1920 Edition of the Book of Mormon: A Centennial Adventure in Latter-day Saint Book History*, ch. 1.

accident. Not only were he and his fellow Presidents of the Seventy not invited as speakers in the April 1912 general conference, they were also excluded from the special priesthood meeting of April 8, 1912, and Roberts was not part of the *Liahona* conversation. The church presidency never notified him or explained their move in editing the *History*. He held his peace until two years later, when he privately expressed his frustration over the cut.

> a whole chapter in the sixth volume [of *History of the Church*] was surreptitiously, but by the order of the President [Joseph F. Smith], as I am informed, removed. It was the King Follett sermon with annotations by myself, which had previously appeared in the Improvement Era . . . Why I say this chapter was surreptitiously removed is because it was removed just as the volume was going to be bound, which without any consultation had with me, the printer was called and directed to remove that chapter, and another chapter was divided into two in order that there might be no break in the number of chapters and the removal of this chapter would thus be concealed. The Presidency have never said a word to me about this mutilation of my work, nor have I spoken to them about it. I have suffered the indignity in silence.[144]

Roberts later had the full text of R1 reprinted, paying for it out of his own funds, so he could distribute it himself (R3 in fig. 1) but the cut had important effects. One was Edwin F. Parry's (1860–1935) popular little 1912 book, *Joseph Smith's Teachings*. It had no reference to the King Follett sermon since Parry extracted all his sources from Roberts's *History of the Church* volumes. Parry's book went through five English editions and several in Europe.[145] Other church leaders, even those who had appealed to the sermon in various sidelong ways

144. B. H. Roberts, Letter to Elder Rudger Clawson, November 20, 1914.

145. On Roberts's reprint order for his 1909 text of the sermon, see Lyon, "Church Historians I Have Known," 14–15.

during the period, avoided mentioning it directly in replies to inquiring correspondence.[146]

Neither Roberts nor Penrose softened their positions over the years. By the time of the 1911 interviews with Roberts, Penrose was already circulating a typed, carbon-copy document among the apostles, critical of both Roberts's interpretations of RC and his arguments from scripture. Penrose had read Roberts's 1907 and 1909 (R1) articles and responded to them. Even so, Roberts's scriptural interpretations survived, though they bypassed his name and ultimately became attached to JS or various passages of scripture (see chapter 4).[147]

§3.7 Follett and the Evolution of Regularity in Church Teaching

Jesus the Christ and a Doctrinal Exposition

Charles Penrose spoke with some frequency against the reliability of RC. In 1918, he repeated his critique of Roberts's 1909 annotation at a church gathering in Salt Lake City:

> Now, understand, the elements composing [the] individual spirit are eternal, and the elements of the body eternal and exist for all eternity, but had their beginning in an organized capacity in the birth, through the laws of generation established for that

146. "we must not take too mechanically the statement, 'that as we are now, God once was, as God now is we may become.'" John A. Widtsoe, Letter to Daniel Rawlings, April 13, 1932.

147. Several copies of Penrose's document survive, and it quite likely influenced George Albert Smith's opinion as noted above. George Albert's copy is found in his papers at the Marriott Library, University of Utah, Salt Lake City, Utah. Joseph F. Smith's copy is found as "Immortality of the Spirit and Soul," Joseph F. Smith Papers, 1854–1918, MS 1325 Box 47, fd. 7, CHL. The popularity of Parry's book was a part of the motivation for Joseph Fielding Smith's production of *Teachings of the Prophet Joseph Smith* in 1938.

> purpose. So in the eternal worlds the spirit of man was born of God and when he came into that state of being as a personality, as an individual intelligence, he was a son of God and was an organized being. . . . their essence, the material so to speak, the spiritual substance of which they were organized, never had a beginning, but the being, the personality, had [a] beginning[148]. . . . Now don't confound, as some of our brethren have done, the expression "intelligences," referring to individual spirits, and that intelligence that is an attribute of those spirits, that "never was created, neither indeed can be". . . . It always existed and always will persist, and it is the life and light of all things that have life; but intelligences are individual spirits born of God. . . . as the offspring of Deity.[149]

In 1924, Penrose added the idea that JS had responded to a text of Follett:

> that King Follett sermon was very badly put together to begin with, and was never fully corrected; *so the Prophet Joseph, as we have ample evidence, corrected some things that appear in that sermon that he preached, and he did not say just exactly what they reported he said.*[150]

Penrose's claim that JS corrected ideas in the Follett sermon simply expands on Joseph F. Smith's story of his search for Nauvoo witnesses that could counter the sermon's point on the resurrection of children. The problem for Follett, however, is that the reminiscences of Joseph F. Smith's witnesses claimed memory of an event *prior* to the Follett sermon. Joseph F. failed to find any corporate church record

---

148. Ironically, this interpretation is suggested by changes made by the original RC editors (noted above).

149. Charles W. Penrose, "Religious Problems Solved by 'Mormonism'," 1029–30. Penrose repeated his remarks on the sermon in later issues of the same magazine (*Liahona The Elders' Journal*). Penrose may have been under the impression that RC was the original imprint text of Follett rather than TS.

150. Emphasis added. Penrose, "Earth Life a Definite Part of the Divine Plan," 42.

showing that JS recanted any point of the sermon in public or private (§3.2). There is no record that JS interacted with the initial written texts of the sermon, either the manuscripts or Bullock's fusion text (TS). In fact, JS's teaching about static resurrected children bracketed the testimony of Smith's witnesses.[151]

Roberts's response was characterized by his reply to one correspondent:

> Certainly my convictions as to the eternity of intelligent entities has undergone no change in late years, except to be intensified... Joseph Smith's discourse known as "King Follett's Sermon" was published in every administration of the Church, and is one of the noblest and most certain documents that we have reporting the doctrines of the Prophet.... I get impatient sometimes at the tenacity with which men hold to partial truths and seek to demonstrate them to no good purpose on earth.[152]

Roberts's estimate of the relative robustness of RC compared to other available JS sermon texts was not hyperbole.

Joseph F. Smith revealed some of his expanding discomfort with the Follett sermon after John A. Widtsoe finished another priesthood quorum study manual for 1915, *Rational Theology*, essentially a rewrite of his 1909 manual.[153] The new manual contained passages on eternal "intelligences" (souls) with no beginning that were inspired by Roberts's work and on Gods, from Orson Pratt's idea that once upon a time, there was no God. God had to pull himself up by his own bootstraps in a kind of (anonymous) homage to Pratt and Leibniz.

---

151. On Joseph F. Smith's search and his witnesses, see his summary in *Improvement Era* 21, no. 7 (May 1918): 571–73. On JS's preaching, see, for example, his sermons of March 20, 1842 and of course, Follett (April 7, 1844), *Parallel Joseph*.

152. B. H. Roberts, Letter to F. T. Pomeroy, February 28, 1928. Compare JS's remarks to William Clayton, May 18, 1843, Smith, *An Intimate Chronicle*, 104.

153. John A. Widtsoe, *Rational Theology: As Taught by the Church of Jesus Christ of Latter-day Saints*.

Roberts was part of the church reading committee for *Rational Theology*, and though he approved of the manual himself, he warned the rest of the committee that the church presidency would likely object and should be consulted before printing to avoid embarrassing Widtsoe after the fact. The passages on God's beginning and the eternity of souls were modified by the Smith presidency so as to appear within the Penrose universe, but as can happen with spot editing, some orphan passages remained in logical limbo. Smith felt that Widtsoe's ideas made man less dependent on God and Lund had anxiety about speaking of a time when there was no God, just intelligences, one of whom would eventually rise up to be God, or a first God (again, Orson Pratt-like). Smith, Penrose, and Lund met with Widtsoe just prior to printing to see that the ideas were removed. Follett was proving hard to kill.[154]

Utah Mormonism in its early twentieth-century elaboration had few ways to create a significant ontological gulf between God and man. Indeed, the Follett sermon audits announced that God "is a man."[155] The creation of individual pre-mortal human *personhood*[156] "out of nothing" was one way to preserve the distance of benevolent contingency in a somewhat lesser but important way.[157] The Follett

154. See, for example, Widtsoe, *Rational Theology*, 23. On the draft manuscript, see Alexander, "Reconstruction," 31. Journal of Anthon H. Lund, December 7, 11, 1914; see also, Hatch, *Danish Apostle*, 558–59. B. H. Roberts, Letter to Rudger Clawson, November 20, 1914.

155. Both aural audits and several content audits of the sermon use these words. The same words appear in an audit of one of JS's sermons delivered July 9, 1843. See Parallel Joseph. *JSP*, D12:453–56.

156. "Person," as illustrated in arguments between Locke and his early critics, is much more than just consciousness or intact memory in this scheme, given Mormon teaching about a memory "veil" between preexistence and mortality. For a summary of Locke, see *Stanford Encyclopedia of Philosophy*, sv. "Locke on Personal Identity."

157. See, for example, Stewart Goetz and Charles Taliaferro, *A Brief History of the Soul*, ch. 4.

sermon's apparent removal of that gulf (as Nelson, Roberts, and eventually Widtsoe and others interpreted it) contributed to Joseph F. Smith's discomfort about the text. It seems unlikely that British Idealism, in the person of Cambridge philosopher John McTaggart, was known among Utah church leaders of the early twentieth century. But one senses that church president Joseph F. Smith's discomfort with Roberts's sempiternal souls—"intelligences"— may have intuitively echoed McTaggart's logic that uncreated souls made God unnecessary, even impossible, reifying some subtle danger, no matter how Roberts worked to stir the ontologies of Utah and Nauvoo together. Smith expressed exactly such fears over the *Rational Theology* manuscript.[158]

JS, in Follett and other connected sermons, had created a deep philosophical tension in twentieth-century church thought that hoped for a non-miraculous Deity: that is, a God who worked through law, not from a position outside the cosmos (as Widtsoe, Talmage, and others saw it). What humans saw as God's miracles were merely God acting through physical laws that were as yet to be discovered by man. God was a scientist, a rational, a *natural* builder of worlds on the one hand, with a system for creating his own successor gods. The problem for this picture of the Divine was JS's completely *super*-natural claim of originless, sempiternal souls. The latter was a violation of Leibniz's rule of the rational world and a fundamental rule of science—Sufficient Reason (see §1.4)—and by Kant's logic, made Follett's theology a strange suturing of mystery and analogy.

Outside this largely unseen logical conflict, banishing Follett achieved a different kind of reconciliation for Joseph F. Smith, a

---

158. McTaggart's work on souls appeared in his 1901 *Studies of Hegelian Cosmology* and more fully in his 1906 *Some Dogmas of Religion* (chps. 3, 4), and finally in his masterwork, *The Nature of Existence*. McTaggart extracted the relevant chapters from *Dogmas* and had them printed as *Human Immortality and Pre-Existence* in 1915.

deeply emotional one. The banishing strategy failed in three fundamental ways: it did not (probably could not) confront JS's frequent insistence on those uncreated souls, well before he delivered the King Follett sermon; it could not account for the permanence of print; and it could not prevent his own son's reconsideration of the "imperfect clerks" hypothesis twenty years after his death.

Widtsoe took Roberts's interpretations and put a nineteenth-century scientific sheen on them. Chapter 3 of *Rational Theology* was titled "Eternalism," a word both Penrose and Roberts had used for their respective interpretations of JS. Widtsoe had moved from his observation of several possible ontologies laid out in *Science* to Roberts's in *Rational Theology*. Widtsoe never used the name Follett when he quoted JS's sermon in either book. Whether he deployed the title in the unredacted version of *Theology* is unknown, and he may have been unaware of the ongoing sparring between Penrose and Roberts.[159] *Rational Theology* eliminated or avoided any reference to Young, the Pratts, as well as Penrose and Roberts.[160] However, there was a nod to the November 1909 First Presidency statement: "we must also have a mother who possesses the attributes of Godhood. . . . sex is eternal." While Widtsoe modified his manuscript, he continued his belief that Roberts's interpretation of Follett was the correct one.[161]

---

159. In one 1909 letter Widtsoe admitted that he believed souls were uncreate, apparently in the fashion outlined in Roberts's 1907 report. John A. Widtsoe, Letter to Mr. S. J. Rawlinson, March 30, 1909.

160. Widtsoe had digested Roberts by this time as evidenced by his penultimate manuscript of *Theology*. See, for example, Widtsoe, *A Rational Theology*, 25. Also pages 13, 14, 16, 17, which survived the editorial cutting floor to some extent.

161. "sex is eternal" was not a reference to sexual intercourse but to gender as the word is now deployed in church leader discourse. Widtsoe, *A Rational Theology*, 69, 155, 157. Compare *Science and the Gospel*. Also, compare, *The Family: A Proclamation to the World*. On Widtsoe's ongoing belief, see John A. Widtsoe, Letter to N. B. Lundwall, May 12, 1943.

In September 1915, the First Presidency announced the publication of James E. Talmage's *Jesus the Christ: A Study of the Messiah and His Mission, According to the Holy Scriptures both Ancient and Modern*. Purposefully excluding modern approaches to the New Testament and the Bible in general (usually referred to under the rubric "higher criticism"), the book helped to solidify a movement to normalize Mormon references to God and quiet many nineteenth-century teachings, including Follett. At the same time, the *Era* ran a series of articles marking a fundamentalist and a rather anti-science outlook, claiming the fallacy of evolutionary biology along with higher criticism. University of Utah professor and Latter-day Saint Frederick Pack had a low opinion of these, telling Anthon Lund that they hurt Mormon students even though Joseph F. Smith agreed with their positions.[162] An important source for Talmage's book was British churchman Frederic William Farrar's book *The Life of Christ*. Farrar became a popular advocate of higher criticism later

162. Several articles appeared under the byline, "Dr. Robert C. Webb, PhD." For example, "Criticism of the 'Higher Critics,'" *Improvement Era* 19, no. 8 (June 1916): 706. Webb was a pseudonym for James Edward Homans, a Harvard graduate and former student at Harvard Divinity School (though never a PhD). An Episcopalian, he disliked the trend he observed toward scholarship invading devotional teaching. In many ways he was in sympathy with developing fundamentalism. Homans published widely on various topics from the care of automobiles to the telephone industry. Homans probably used the pseudonym to disguise his Episcopal roots that might lead to the perception of an affiliation with Episcopal scholars critical of Mormon claims. Homans's continuing contributions on evolution gradually fell out of favor when Talmage and Pack began to take issue with the logic of the pieces. On Homans, see Kevin Barney, "Robert C. Webb," By Common Consent website, October 18, 2006, https://bycommonconsent.com/2006/10/18/robert-c-webb/ accessed August 15, 2018. On Talmage's and Pack's complaints, see Anthon H. Lund journal, January 27, 1914, September 22, 1914, September 28, 1914, January 16, 1915; also, Hatch, *Danish Apostle*, 531, 550, 551, 590, 596. For Joseph F. Smith's agreement with Webb, see his "Theory and Divine Revelation," 549.

in his career. Talmage mostly drew a hard line between scholarship's debate and his relatively naïve approach to the New Testament and generally treated the Gospels as something on the order of a mixture of aural audits and content audits of Jesus and struggled with their frequent dissonance. Talmage did approach some topics of Follett, but he carefully avoided citing the sermon itself. Instead he used a secondary source, *A Compendium of the Doctrines of the Gospel* and also quoted from a version of JS's June 11, 1843, sermon as edited in *History of the Church* vol. 5.[163] The most enduring text of twentieth-century Mormonism was cut off from what was arguably the most essential text of JS's preaching.

The church was facing what Catholics and Protestants were facing: modernism, at least in the sense of biblical historical criticism and evolution. The church, in its relative isolation, could control the narrative for a time. Its stand in the first decade of the twentieth century helped to insulate it from the these more objectionable aspects of the modernist wave for almost six decades.[164] The church's power to control the impact of these trends would begin to fade in the 1970s and continue to do so into the next century. The Internet, the increasing expectation of a college education, and the increasing sophistication of secular and American Protestant religious critics of Mormon beliefs—and in a way these are the same thing—have manifested in

---

163. B. H. Roberts, ed., *History of the Church of Jesus Christ of Latter-day Saints,* 5:426. Franklin D. Richards and James A. Little, *A Compendium of the Doctrines of the Gospel,* 190. The latter is a quotation from the TS text of Follett. See the timeline in chapter 1. Roberts held a point of view about higher criticism rather different from many of his church leader associates. See Barlow, *Mormons and the Bible,* 121–32.

164. J. Reuben Clark's position in the church's First Presidency from 1933 to 1961 allowed him to set a highly conservative policy for church education and his book *Why the King James Version* was influential in stopping biblical scholarship from penetrating LDS curricula.

a strengthened impulse to historicize Latter-day Saint policies, doctrine, and even scripture. These are strains that represent profound concerns among church leaders.[165]

A year after the release of *Jesus the Christ*, the First Presidency and Quorum of the Twelve issued (after joint redaction) another work by Talmage over their collective signatures, "The Father and the Son: A Doctrinal Exposition by The First Presidency and The Twelve."[166] Appearing as an *Improvement Era* article, Talmage and his brethren generally derived their claims from Bible passages, but in the final paragraph, they included the Utah theology of spirits without reference, at the same time making reference to Follett in its most common form—*eternal progression*:

> So far as the stages of eternal progression and attainment have been made known through divine revelation, we are to understand that only resurrected and glorified beings can become parents of spirit offspring. Only such exalted souls have reached maturity in the appointed course of eternal life; and the spirits born to them in the eternal worlds will pass in due sequence through the several stages or estates by which the glorified parents have attained exaltation.

Of course, there was no JS revelation that did this, and none was referenced. The statement was a summary of tradition, a clear reflection of an amended Brigham Young—souls aren't eternal, but the process of their production is. Talmage's edited essay regularized Mother in Heaven, sex in heaven, and souls originating in heaven. Perhaps the certainty of the document on those points went beyond

165. By "in a way," I mean that it is the democratization of Christianity and the subsequent talk of "World Religions" defined against the triumphal world colonization by European Christian powers that set the talking points of the *acceptable* in a secular world. See Coviello, *Make Yourselves Gods*, 44.

166. James E. Talmage journal, June 23, 1916.

Talmage's own thinking, as illustrated by his later correspondence with Mary Parker.

The censure of Follett meant it would not appear in official teaching for more than two decades, and even then its text was refracted through the lens of 1912–1915. By mid-century, theological writing among church leaders fell largely to Joseph Fielding Smith, who had much of his father's drive to make the face of the Utah church consistent.

§3.8 As Man is, God Once Was; As God is, Man May Become

An Advocate for TS

While the Follett sermon was only anonymously referenced in LDS church manuals like *Rational Theology*, the LDS young women's summer instruction outline for 1919 alluded directly to it.[167] The late church president Lorenzo Snow's son by his youngest wife Sarah Minnie Ephramina Jensen Snow, LeRoi (or Le Roi) Snow (1876–1962), wrote an article for the *Young Woman's Journal* on his father's history and the famous statement, "As man now is, God once was: As God now is, man may be."[168] The ultimate source of this sentence is somewhat murky. Brigham Young claimed it on several occasions.[169] "While on a mission to England, the following came forcibly to my

---

167. The First Presidency had already declared that the existence of church manuals didn't constitute any official approval of their content. See the message noted above for January 1912.

168. LeRoi C. Snow, "Devotion to a Divine Inspiration," 303–9.The succinct summary of Snow's cosmology appeared in numerous Mormon imprints. The one quoted above was found in a crossword puzzle in the LDS children's magazine, *The Friend* (March 2002): 23.

169. That cross-claims existed, see Thomas C. Romney, *The Life of Lorenzo Snow: Fifth President of the Church*, 46–47.

mind—'As God was, so are we now; as he now is, so we shall be.' Our Father was once born of parents, having a father and mother, the same as we have," and seven years later he repeated the assertion,

> President Young said while conversing upon Eternal improvement that He knew by revelation while in England that there would be an Eternal increase in knowledge & as we now are God once was & as he now is we shall be if we continue faithful. I told this to Br Lorenzo Snow.[170]

Snow claimed ownership out of a reminiscent 1840 experience, which his sister, Eliza R. Snow, said he told to Young.[171] Both men probably saw the phrase, common on grave monuments in the typical fatalism of the time, "As you are, I once was. As I am, you will be." The words as used by Young/Snow depend on Follett, in the sense that both men claimed they never would have dared public originality without Smith's public teaching.[172] Whatever the source, LeRoi Snow was well aware of its link to Follett, and in his *Young Woman's* supplement, he gave a remarkably good discussion of Follett's textual evolution. LeRoi noted that several versions of the sermon were in print, and crucially, he noted R1. Just how much of the controversy and suppression LeRoi was aware of is not explicit, but he clearly wished to rehabilitate Follett as a support for his father's saying. LeRoi Snow carefully registered his father's love of the Follett sermon as it appeared in the 1844 *Times and Seasons*.[173] Prominent Latter-day Saint leader Bathsheba W. Smith solidly linked the Snow/Young state-

170. See "History of Brigham Young," February 16, 1849, for the first quote. See Wilford Woodruff journal, August 23, 1856, Kenney, *Wilford Woodruff's Journal*, 4:439 for the second.

171. See Eliza R. Snow Smith, *Biography and Family Record of Lorenzo Snow* (1884), 46. Brigham Young Jr, diary, September 13, 1898, CHL. Journal History, September 13, 1898, April 5, 1900, CHL.

172. Snow, "Devotion," 305–6.

173. Snow, "Devotion," 306.

ment with the Follett sermon. Lorenzo Snow didn't broadly mention his summary of God's history until after Brigham Young's death. Indeed, Lorenzo may have given a different take on the famous phrase in an 1886 sermon. "As man now is, God once was—even the babe of Bethlehem, advancing to childhood—thence to boyhood, manhood, then to the Godhead. This, then, is the 'mark of the prize of man's high calling in Christ Jesus.' "[174]

Charles Penrose died in 1925. The following year, R1 was reprinted by David Lyon's *Magazine Printing* in Salt Lake City.[175] In the years after the sermon was deleted from *History of the Church*, Roberts handed out copies of the sermon to local church leaders in his ministerial assignments. Lyon found a continuing market for the work, and his company reprinted Roberts's pamphlet a number of times over the next seventy years. These reprints made their way into American libraries and then surfaced in some secular academic work.[176]

---

174. LeRoi Snow speaks of ownership of the phrase in "Devotion," 305–6. Bathsheba W. Smith, "We Have Still a Greater Mission" (1906), in *At the Pulpit: 185 Years of Discourses by Latter-day Saint Women*, 100. Lorenzo Snow penned a poem about the idea written in a letter from the Utah State Penitentiary in 1886. See Andrew H. Hedges and Richard Neitzel Holzapfel, *Within These Prison Walls: Lorenzo Snow's Record Book 1886–1897*, 32. On the sermon quotation, see Lorenzo Snow, 1886, *Journal of Discourses* 26:368.

175. Chad J. Flake and Larry W. Draper, eds., *A Mormon Bibliography 1830–1930*, 2:284. Flake and Draper wrote that this is a reprint of the August 1, 1844, *Times and Seasons* text. This is incorrect on two counts. It was an edition of R1 and thus a descendant of RC.

176. Copies of R2 had already made their way outside the United States, for example, to the church's Auckland, New Zealand mission. See M230 S653k 1912?b, CHL. In addition to the first printing of R3, I have discovered imprints from 1926, 1945, 1962, 1963, 1973, and 1981. There were perhaps others. The 1963 reprint was the source of Follett used by New York psychologist Francis H. Touchet in a 1976 article in *The Journal of Psychology and Theology*, "Perfection in Religion and Psychotherapy or: On Discerning the Spirits."

§3.9 The Era in Summation

The decades surrounding 1900 saw the rise of some division over JS's preaching. That division was based in the nature of sermon culture within early Mormonism, the methodology of preservation of the sermon experience, the struggle to reconcile Mormon ideologies of various epochs, and the ways in which JS's successors created strain in those ideologies to address the practicalities of preservation of a new religion. The Follett sermon was often near the center of many of those issues, either philosophically or explicitly.

The Utah branch of Mormonism, with its embrace of polygamy and a tradition based on the Nauvoo temple liturgy, evolved a presentation of Mormon ontic claims that conflicted with Follett in various ways. Out of that disagreement came theological strain, exhibited in the 1856 sermon text and with competing theological positions. Joseph F. Smith's discomfort with static eternal children in heaven, Charles W. Penrose's insistence that the individual human soul/consciousness was contingent, and B. H. Roberts's reading of the Follett sermon as authentically Mormon—these all helped create a permanent theological rift. Their cosmological assertions were refracted by Follett, and the resultant ideological strain was revealed in their studied explanations of that sermon.

Penrose found a way out of the conundrum of arguing with JS by arguing with his clerks. Roberts made use of other sources from JS to support his points drawn from RC. Smith found support in the memories of the elderly and the logic of his sorrows. Each man's devotion to their respective positions reflected their separate conflations of what the Mormon gospel meant: ultimate independence from external will (popularly expressed as "free agency") or ultimate dependence on divine origin. Follett was—acknowledged or otherwise—the nexus of what became fundamental variants of thought in twentieth-century Mormonism on some key religious questions: What is the nature of God? What is the nature of the human soul? What is the nature of Christian resurrection? What is Hell? What is Heaven?

CHAPTER 4

The Heritage of the 1909 Edition, 1926–1996 and the 1938 Turn

A Sermon of the Ages. An Epilogue of Mixed Meaning.

God has wrought out a salvation for all men, unless they have committed a certain sin.

—TB

§4.1 Looking Ahead: A Transformation of Purpose

The death of Charles Penrose signaled the beginning of the end of public hierarchical arguments over Mormon cosmology. Mormonism was moving away from its metaphysical work (by leadership at least) to a world where tools of the Progressive Era[1] ("where performance is measured, performance improves") and business school analytics would absorb much more of the behind the scenes work of church

1. Lepore, *The Mansion of Happiness*, ch. 6.

leadership and its attendant burgeoning bureaucracy. As religion scholar Philip Barlow has written,

> This new absence [of broad, adventurous, tomes by individual church leaders] does not signify a decline in intellectual capacity among leaders, though the church's modern general authorities do tend to be drawn from those experienced in the practical worlds of business, law, and educational administration[2] . . . perhaps the absence results from a hierarchy recoiling at the controversies and perceived distractions spawned [by such earlier efforts]. A . . . more likely cause is the long-term effects of the church's Correlation Program. . . . [which] has blanched the color from individual public voices and may account for the paucity of great synthetic treatises from recent Mormon leaders.[3]

The movement toward systematization tamed the internal Mormon thought-world through a "correlation" program that made the Church of Jesus Christ of Latter-day Saints an isotropic phenomenon—it was (in principle at least) the same no matter where you looked: the global church would use the same structure and lessons for the faithful, while missions began to use highly structured and uniform proselytizing lessons for the prospective convert.[4]

In a powerful way, the church's xeroxing of a simplified Utah gospel for everyone was the opposite of the "church growth movement" of evangelical conservatives who saw only one immovable principle to preserve: some version of biblical inerrancy. The rest should be fluid, customized via cultural geography. The latter's idea proved itself in converts, at least until recent years. For the Saints, perhaps there was another force at work as well. Following the horrible wars of the nineteenth and twentieth centuries, there was a distinct trend toward a

---

2. For a survey of recent church leader backgrounds, see "General Authority Stats," https://bycommonconsent.com/2011/06/20/general-authority-stats/

3. Barlow, *Mormons and the Bible*, xxxix.

4. Bowman, *The Mormon People*, ch. 7.

more thoughtful and less elaborated version of religion, that is, one more accessible to reason. Such a trend seems evident in the simpler message of Latter-day Saint missionaries, among many others.[5]

Bits and pieces of Follett and the outflow of early twentieth-century thought had worked their way firmly into Mormon language with ideas of deification: "eternal progression,"[6] "becoming like God,"[7] "I'm trying to be like Jesus,"[8] and other expressions. As a whole, however, Follett, as a theological foundation stone (or perhaps stumbling block), lost much of its public significance in the Gospel According to the Twentieth-Century Church.[9]

The impact of forced interface with American and international pluralism made the isolationist othering of Middle Mormonism a thing of the past in many ways. If my non-Mormon neighbor showed the highest of Christian-like charity, should she still be seen as a threat to the fate and faith of my offspring? The old ways of thinking about this were complicated by practical observation. Englobement of the faithful in the formerly dreaded Gentile world made many of the Follett sermon's key points seem less vital, even less relevant to a faith that was now one among many *good* ways.[10]

---

5. On growth, see Worthen, *Apostles of Reason*, ch. 6. On the wars, Taylor, *A Secular Age*, 168.

6. One of the most common phrases in twentieth-century Mormon literature. For a few of the early references, see Brigham Young, "The Gifts of Prophecy and Tongues, etc.," *Journal of Discourses*, 3:375; Anthon H. Lund, *Conference Report*, October 1902, 81.

7. See "Becoming Like God," https://www.churchofjesuschrist.org/study/manual/gospel-topics-essays/becoming-like-god.

8. The title of a popular LDS children's hymn.

9. LaGrand Richards's, 1950 mission manual, *A Marvelous Work and A Wonder*, had elements of Follett but the far more brief and structured *A Uniform System for Teaching Investigators* of the next decade had none.

10. Matthew Bowman, "Eternal Progression: Mormonism and American Progressivism."

The church's *Improvement Era* seemed to shift in its content with this perceived new world. Emphasis on manners, fashion, book reviews, and recommendations of non-Mormon literature, with far less emphasis on the heavy theology and "circle the wagons" defence of the faith of previous decades saw a change in view that reflected and enhanced a positive outlook on society at large, and this was remarkably true of the magazine's content as the Great Depression engulfed the modern world.[11] That said, the twentieth-century church certainly did not renounce long-held theological positions still reflected in teachings like deification (exaltation) and metaphysical explanations supported by teachings like preexistence (Black people and the temple) or abandoned theological pessimism ("through your faithfulness" clauses) at least in forms that developed after 1912.[12]

---

11. Part of this shift was due to the *Era*'s incorporation of the YWMIA mission with the dissolution of the *Young Woman's Journal*. It is difficult to do more than simply require the reader to browse issues of the magazine over the years to completely prove my point. Two example issues may suffice. Compare the contents of the *Era* for, say, January 1909 (a signature year for our purposes) and January 1936.

12. This kind of transition and assimilation was occurring in many ways and places during the same period. I'll offer one brief example. The trend away from nineteenth-century explorations of Mormon uniqueness in theological foundations was quite analogous to what was happening in Vienna, Austria, at nearly the same time. There, the "Vienna Circle," a gathering of thinkers were working to move philosophy out of the shadow of Platonism (where ideas have an independent existence and only wait to be "discovered" by thinkers—there is something of JS and thinkers of Middle Mormonism like Orson Pratt in this) by jettisoning such metaphysics and making over philosophy in the image of science. It can still be argued whether the notion was really a good idea or even possible. Yet there is a kind of time sync between the end of hierarchical arguments over Mormonism's various pictures of the background "world," and the Vienna Circle's goal to move from swimming in a sea of "real" abstractions to a kind of experimentally driven search for "truth." JS might have appreciated one of the hopes of the Circle: construct a precise language that would make expressions of true statements reducible without ambiguity to founding experience. See Rudolph Carnap, "The Elimination

§4.2 The 1938 Turn

The Conversion of Joseph Fielding Smith and the Resurrection of the King Follett Sermon.

Church leaders gradually fell into different camps over the positions of Penrose and Roberts and their respective interpretations of RC. Along with Widtsoe, the Columbia-educated attorney and First Presidency member J. Reuben Clark absorbed Roberts's interpretive structure, probably from R1 or in the case of Clark, one of its reprints.[13] Penrose attempted to quench R1 in the pages of the widely-circulated *Millennial Star* in November 1909 with a critique of the sermon; this probably had a significant effect on the perception of Follett in the minds of some European Saints (and perhaps more importantly the Utah missionaries working there), though it was likely hard to avoid Roberts's widely adopted pamphlets and articles like *Joseph Smith, The Prophet-Teacher* or his church study manuals like *New Witnesses for God* or *Seventy's Course in Theology*, the First Presidency's January and April 1912 statements notwithstanding.

---

of Metaphysics Through Logical Analysis of Language." For a brief account of the Circle, see Solomon Feferman, *In the Light of Logic*, 130–31. See also Rebecca Goldstein, *Incompleteness: The Proof and Paradox of Kurt Gödel*, 44, 78–79.

13. For example, J. Reuben Clark, *On the Way to Immortality and Eternal Life*, 34. Clark, a Republican, had more reservations about Roberts as a church leader than he did as a thinker. See Heath, *In the World*, 501. Clark ran into Roberts in 1919 when Roberts delivered a rebuttal to Clark's criticism of the League of Nations. The cut never healed. Clark (1871–1961) went on to despise FDR while Roberts's political doppelganger, James Moyle, loved the New Deal. Clark's experience entailed a sharp suspicion of higher education (something that had led to a personal period of faith declension) and its products like modern biology (evolution), sociology (government social welfare efforts in particular), biblical criticism, and what he saw as the secular invasion of church educational institutions.

The death of the members of the Joseph F. Smith First Presidency led to one of the most important events for Follett—its restoration as a church-published and at least nominally approved text. Its interpretation was still another matter, one that came to be filtered through the priorities of the *correlation* movement and the adoption of broader American culture by Latter-day Saints.

In 1921, a committee of editors including Joseph F. Smith's son, namesake, and apostle, Joseph Fielding Smith, recommended changes to the faith's book of *Doctrine and Covenants.* Historically, the book's title referred to its double nature. *Covenants* was an 1830s era name for JS's revelations. *Doctrine* referred to an 1835 series of lessons that later became known as the *Lectures on Faith*. The committee decided that the lectures had some problematic text and failed to represent the doctrines of the church. The committee proposed that they be dropped from the book. The title of the book remained unchanged, though the page count was considerably reduced. In 1917, Fielding Smith had noted to his fellow apostles that the *Lectures* differed markedly from the text of Follett.[14] However, Smith took the side of his father and the First Presidency that RC was a suspect text. Sometime between 1932 and 1938, Fielding Smith changed his assessment of the Follett sermon. In 1938, Joseph Fielding Smith published *Teachings of the Prophet Joseph Smith*, and somewhat miraculously, Smith selected Follett as part of the book (R4) *as an edition of R1* along with significant parts of Roberts's annotation from 1909.

The popularity of *Teachings of the Prophet Joseph Smith* and its immediate incorporation in the church curriculum helped to diminish the controversy over the reliability of R1. Books like church writer John Henry Evans's 1933 biography of JS, *Joseph Smith, An American Prophet* (not published by a church press), exploited the ideas of the Follett sermon as friendly to Progressives (i.e., mankind was far less

14. Heath, *In the World*, 374.

hampered by Calvinist anthropology than the Old Time Religion once required). Evans continued the project of painting the Saints as ideal Americans.[15] Then in 1952, under the direction of Fielding Smith again (the official Church Historian since Anthon Lund's death in 1921) a revised version of volume six of *History of the Church* was printed, again as a church course of study, incorporating RC (more precisely, *it again incorporated an edition of* R1) as originally planned by Roberts, creating R5. In some sense, Roberts's 1907 article then became perhaps the most widely accepted articulation of preexistence among Latter-day Saints (perhaps because of his 1909 notes found in both R4 and R5) and put the Follett sermon—in its 1856 RC form—back in the position of normative belief—though not for everyone, and not permanently.[16]

Joseph Fielding Smith was aware of the First Presidency's critique of Follett during his father's tenure as church president, and he supported it for many years. Yet he eventually came to champion the Follett sermon. Fielding Smith's overruling of the 1912 ban on Follett,

---

15. The MIAs made *Teachings* a part of its reading course in 1938. Evans's volume was one of those adopted by church president Heber J. Grant for his ubiquitous Christmas giving. On Grant's book giving hobby, see Walker, *Qualities that Count*, 278. On *Teachings*, see "M.I.A. Reading Course Books." On the complicated path to parallel the mainstream, see W. Paul Reeve, *Religion of a Different Color: Race and the Mormon Struggle for Whiteness*. J. B. Haws, *The Mormon Image in the American Mind: Fifty Years of Public Perception*. Thomas W. Simpson, *American Universities and the Birth of Modern Mormonism, 1867–1940*. Shipps, *Mormonism*. Bowman, *The Mormon People*, ch. 6. Alexander, *Mormonism in Transition*. Armand Mauss, *The Angel and the Beehive: The Mormon Struggle with Assimilation*. Flake, "Re-placing Memory." Taysom, "A Uniform and Common Recollection."

16. As an example, see Bowman, *The Mormon People*, 166. Roberts's interpretation found its way *sub rosa* into a wildly popular Mormon work, which quoted from Follett without attribution. See LeGrand Richards, *A Marvelous Work and a Wonder*, 238–39. Unlike the first edition of the *History*, this one was printed locally in the modern offset facility of Deseret Press.

as represented by his 1938 *Teachings of the Prophet Joseph Smith*, suggests that he embraced Roberts's arguments as confirmed by his correspondence over the issue. His transition is clearly illustrated in two letters written by him, one in 1932 and one in 1952. Church members who had difficulties with historical and doctrinal issues frequently wrote to Smith as a court of last resort. Smith was one of the last group of apostles in the mid-twentieth century who achieved high church office outside the common modern trajectory of church leadership. He was never a congregation official like bishop or stake president. He found his role not as a model of administration but as the main doctrinal technician in the post Talmage-Roberts era (both men had died in 1933).[17]

In March 1932, Joseph Fielding Smith received a letter that laid out an incident that had confused the writer, who sought Smith's clarification.

> While discussing lesson seven in this year's outline for the [Sunday School] Gospel Doctrine Classes, the question arose as to whether or not the spirit of man was created or made or was eternal with God, or whether the Father is the creator of the spirit of man. The first position was taken by one of the members of the class who quoted from the sermon of the Prophet at the funeral services of King Follett. I would like to know for my own information as to whether or not this sermon on this particular part is authentic or whether it has been and is considered to be a misrepresentation of the Prophet's view on this subject. I will appreciate an answer if it is not asking too much of you.[18]

17. Smith's son-inlaw, Bruce R. McConkie (1915–1985), followed a similar path and assumed the same self-defined theological role after Smith's death in 1972. See, for example, http://www.eugeneengland.org/wp-content/uploads/2012/07/BRM-to-EE-Feb-80-Combined.pdf

18. U. G. Miller, Letter to Mr. Joseph F. Smith, Jr, March 7, 1932.

Smith's response is important for several reasons. Italicized phrases are my emphasis and are not in the original.

> The doctrine of the Church, *as I have been taught it*, and as it has been *taught from the beginning of this dispensation*, is as follows.
>
> The spirits of men were begotten sons and daughters of God. Jesus Christ is the first begotten in the spirit and the Only Begotten in the flesh. *This is the teaching which has come down from the Prophet Joseph Smith.* The Savior has said: "And now, verily I say unto you, I was in the beginning with the Father, and am the Firstborn; and all those who are begotten through me are partakers of the glory of the same, and are the church of the Firstborn. Ye were also in the beginning with the Father; that which is Spirit, even the Spirit of truth."—D. and C. 93:21–23.
>
> In this same section the Lord says: "Man was also in the beginning with God. Intelligence, or the light of truth, was not created or made, neither indeed can be."
>
> *This is interpreted to mean* that the intelligence in man was never created, but that man is a begotten spirit, the son of God, and Jesus Christ is the first-born among the spirits.
>
> The King Follett sermon was reported in longhand *and partly from memory*. The Prophet never had the opportunity to revise or correct it. It contains errors without question. It [is] apparent that *the Prophet taught just what is given in the revelations, but has not been fully and correctly quoted. It was for this reason that that discourse was not published in the History of the church.*[19]

Smith's *as I have been taught it* is reminiscent of Talmage's closing paragraph from his manuscript for the "Doctrinal Exposition" quoted in the last chapter. The idea of a divine domesticity with "spirit" children resulting from sexual congress in heaven was a Utah interpretive doctrine, linked strongly to plural marriage theology (as noted in the preceding chapters). Smith's final paragraph draws a vector parallel-

19. Emphasis added. Joseph Fielding Smith, Letter to Uriah G. Miller, Murray, Utah, March 9, 1932.

ing the 1912 turn: Follett was badly recorded, parts were even (faulty) memories and JS never went beyond his canonical revelations in his cosmology, etc., not an unusual position—even polygamy became assigned to the earliest revelation corpus (1831) in its Utah exposition.[20]

Fielding Smith's eventual about-face from the 1912 critique is illustrated through another letter twenty years later. He answered an inquiry similar to the 1932 question in a very different way. Smith wrote,

> The King Follett discourse was preached in April 1844. It has been published several times in the early publications of the Church and is found in Chapter Fourteen, Documentary History of the Church, Vol. 6. This discourse *has been accepted by the Church*... You will find some excellent comments in Elder B. H. Roberts' "Mormon Doctrine of Deity."

Four years prior to this correspondence, Smith had also defended Follett in a 1948 letter to his cousin Israel A. Smith, head of the Reorganized Church of Jesus Christ of Latter Day Saints..[21]

Fielding Smith's statement that the Follett discourse was "accepted by the Church" is remarkable in the face of its disavowal by his father's 1912 First Presidency.[22] Smith also observed that,

---

20. Twentieth-century introductory headings to the polygamy revelation (Doctrine and Covenants 132) made this clear, assigning its essential origin to the year 1831. That claim seems problematic for several reasons. See Smith, *Plural Marriage Revelation*.

21. Emphasis added. See Smith's correspondence with Frank N. Jonas. In particular, Joseph Fielding Smith, Letter to Dr. Frank N. Jonas, January 25, 1952. Unfortunately, Roberts's little book was rather rare by 1952. See Joseph Fielding Smith, Letter to Israel A. Smith, March 8, 1948.

22. *Mormon Doctrine of Deity* was a rather glowing reference to B. H. Roberts, *The Mormon Doctrine of Deity, The Roberts–Van Der Donckt Discussion, to Which is Added a Discourse, Jesus Christ: The Revelation of God. Also a Collection of Authoritative Mormon Utterances on the Being and Nature of God* (Salt Lake City: Deseret News, 1903). The book owed its genesis to a 1901 sermon by Roberts and a subsequent critique of that sermon by the Catholic pastor of Pocatello, Idaho,

> the King Follett Discourse in which the Prophet Joseph Smith sets for[th] his views, *by revelation*, regarding God. *I have always felt that this doctrine was too far advanced for general circulation even among members of the Church, and surely a disturbing thing to the outside religious world.*[23]

Fielding Smith's change of course was likely connected to his work on *Teachings of the Prophet Joseph Smith*. Again, not only did Smith publish RC, he in essence reprinted R1. It is worth noting that Smith was not a church apostle when Roberts and Lyman produced their 1907 report (see chapter 3), but his argument that Follett had been published in earlier church administrative eras quotes Roberts. Smith's worry that the now-rehabilitated Follett was just too "advanced" for a post-war audience was prescient. After Smith's death, Follett would once again become the focus of Protestant criticism within a new industry: the counter-cult movement.

§4.2 The Hidden Influence of Follett in Academic and Popular Teaching in a Post-War Church

Were Latter-day Saints generally aware of the Penrose–Roberts arguments and the reaction to the published version of their mutual critiques? Certainly some were, but the breadth of that awareness is hard to judge. Surviving correspondence suggests that at least some knew of the differing ideas, and they took sides in the debate. Moreover, the 1912 ban made the sermon disappear to some degree for a whole generation. Meanwhile, the discussion of the first decades of the century generated various ideological strains with dialogues and claims

---

Father C. Van der Donckt, which was published by the church's own *Improvement Era* in 1902. Van der Donckt had emigrated to Idaho in 1887. For Van der Donckt's critique, see Rev. C. Van Der Donckt, "Reply to Roberts' View of Deity."

23. Emphasis added. Smith, Letter to Jonas.

that often centered on the colorful Roberts as much as they did on JS and his scribes. Penrose's repeated critiques in public and private had an effect. For example, influential Idaho stake president and friend of James Talmage, James Duckworth (1865–1947), kept up with the controversy and in 1928 still saw Penrose as the authoritative voice.[24]

Arguments on both sides worked through local church venues, sometimes with vigor, and have surfaced occasionally in recent years, sometimes with ad hominems attached. The author witnessed such an incident (not without irony) during a funeral sermon and its aftermath at a Latter-day Saint service in 1996. One of the antagonists called Roberts a drunkard (Penrose was a moderate wine drinker; Roberts was a recovering alcoholic who became an early [1910] campaigner for Prohibition in Utah).[25]

Remnants of the fraught speech over Follett during 1896–1925 may be seen in later years, but the issues had lost at least some of their energy. For example, compare Truman G. Madsen's 1966 book *Eternal Man* (chapter 1) with Bruce R. McConkie's 1966 edition of *Mormon Doctrine* (page 442). Madsen's work alluded to Roberts's

---

24. See Duckworth, Letter to Pomeroy, February 9, 1928.

25. All presumably reflected in the 1919 Volstead Act (Prohibition). On Roberts's alcohol problems in 1898, 1901, 1906, and 1908, see Quinn, *Extensions of Power*, 145–46, 483. On Roberts not drinking in 1900, see journal of John Henry Smith, January 28, 1900, White, *Church, State, and Politics*, 445. On Roberts's and Prohibition, see B. H. Roberts, Letter to Mr. Moyle, October 29, 1910. See also Gene A. Sessions, *Mormon Democrat: The Religious and Political Memoirs of James Henry Moyle*, 191. Mikkelsen, "The Politics of B. H. Roberts," 31. Roberts's political opponents circulated stories of Roberts's drinking, decades after he had gone permanently on the wagon. See B. H. Roberts, Letter to George E. Hill, November 19, 1928. As for Penrose, the same might be said of some of his apostolic contemporaries. Up until 1906, the apostles used red wine with the meal-like Lord's Supper they celebrated at their extended quarterly meetings. See Thomas G. Alexander, "The Word of Wisdom: From Principle to Requirement." Abraham H. Cannon journal, April 9, 1890, LTPSC, see also, Lyman, *Candid Insights*, 85.

1907 paper and the Follett sermon. McConkie's entries on the nature of man in his encyclopedic work carried on the train of thought running from Parley and Orson Pratt, Brigham Young, Charles Penrose (forms of panpsychism), Lorenzo Snow and James Talmage (effectively, a genetic mechanism), and the 1909 presidency statement in the wake of Widtsoe's *Science and the Gospel* (see §4.3).[26]

A discussion of the Follett sermon and Roberts's exegesis occurred in the church's apostolic review meetings vetting the manuscript of Roberts's controversial magnum opus, *The Truth, The Way, The Life*, but by that time (1929–1932), the argument over RC had deflated and was largely replaced by Roberts's ideas about possible explanations of Darwinian evolution and the idea of pre-Adamic humans or "pre-Adamites." One of the controversial issues, framed by Darwin's ideas, was whether death existed on earth prior to the fall of Adam and Eve from paradise.[27] RC was not a focus of concern.[28] The reasons for that change of focus are complex but may involve, as noted in the previous chapter, an outward rather than an inward facing church, a change that

26. In correspondence over the issue, McConkie revealed some misapprehension regarding Roberts's writing as well as the evolution of ideas it represented. McConkie's correspondence shows him complaining of Roberts inventing the word *intelligences*. Roberts noted the word as a misprint, not an invention. In fact, the word appeared in the first edition of JS's Book of Abraham, edited by JS himself. McConkie, Letter to Walter F. Horne, October 2, 1974, copy in possession of the author. Godfrey, "Intelligence in Latter-day Saint Thought." See also Bruce R. McConkie, "Pre-existence," ms of address given at the University of Utah LDS Institute of Religion, October 9, 1967 (copy in possession of the author). In the latter speech, McConkie calls out Roberts's ideas as an invention, telling the faculty that at least they ought to know *that*. See also Leonard Arrington's statement below.

27. See James B. Allen, "The Story of The Truth, The Way, The Life," *BYU Studies* 33, no. 4 (1993): 1–36.

28. George Albert Smith, then a member of the review committee, brought up some issues that seem to be drawn from Penrose's privately circulated critique of Roberts and the Follett sermon.

began with the public cessation of church officer officiated/approved/winked-at polygamy emerging in 1890, which was cemented by 1913.[29] A halting, limited reconvergence between Mormon thought and Protestantism began on the heels of Brigham Young's death in 1877. Young's successor, John Taylor, the staunchest of polygamists himself, nevertheless saw the excesses of theology and free form divergence from biblical texts as a drift from the central message of Christianity. Taylor's 1882 work on Jesus and his mission, *The Mediation and Atonement of Jesus Christ,* formed a proto-foundation for the message of 1980s Mormonism.[30] Then there was the at first artificial and then vigorous division of Latter-day Saints along Republican, Democrat, and sometimes other smaller political loyalties.[31]

The mission of the church to spread rather than gather moved to the forefront with the administration of Heber J. Grant. Joseph F. Smith presided over the end of polygamy, and his desire to create thematic consistency put an end to much of theological distinctiveness. Grant and his successors saw the need for a uniform focus on fundamental principles, which flowered in post-war mission work literature such as *A Uniform System for Teaching Investigators.* JS and his immediate apostolic successors had shaped many of the teachings of Mormonism, but for an expanding organization with a mission to convert every continent and culture, only the basic and clearly agreed-upon tenets were needed to define a twentieth-century Mormon missiology. That meant a focus on founding elements like JS's 1838–1839 memories of his early life and the Book of Mormon and only surreptitiously, JS's 1843 revela-

29. B. H. Roberts, Letter to Isaac Russell, September 4, 1909.

30. See Bowman, "The Crisis of Mormon Christology." Bowman, *Mormon People*, 161–64, 170. Turner, *Mormon Jesus*, ch. 10. Taylor critiqued his predecessor's moves at times by pointing out Young's crossing of scriptural passages. Young's hierarchy of value placed himself above the written word while Taylor took the opposite view.

31. Bowman, *Mormon People*, ch. 6.

tion on polygamy along with Follett (*exaltation*) and its Utah interpretations within the catchphrase, "families are forever." Symmetrically, those basic "articles of faith" dictated a more organized, uniform, and focused church curriculum for the rising generation.[32]

RC did not completely disappear. Its ideas, their subsequent interpretations, and the history of Utah teachings could not be erased from the consciousness of a people still headquartered in the pioneer west, a people still led largely by men and women whose traditions and parentage linked them to those who contended for the faith in the nineteenth century. The interface of Mormonism with the science and humanism of university education encouraged a different revival of Follett via a now mostly anonymous B. H. Roberts. It was Roberts's compromise interpretation of Follett, preserving a Mother-in-Heaven imagery in the face of JS's more sterile adoptive theology, that allowed for the sermon to find a home in "families are forever," at least for a time.

In the middle of the twentieth century, Follett began to edge into the position of a liberal theological hallmark for many teachers in the church's Institutes of Religion. These were brick and mortar facilities

---

32. For a narrative of this movement and the transition of church-mediated polygamy to dissenter-mediated polygamy, see Daymon Smith, "The Last Shall be First and the First Shall be Last: Discourse and Mormon History;" also Mauss, *The Angel and the Beehive*. On Mormon missiology, see David Golding, "The Foundations and Early Development of Mormon Mission Theory" (Masters thesis, Claremont Graduate University, 2010), http://scholarship.claremont.edu/cgu_etd/4. doi: 10.5642/cguetd/4. Also Bowman, *Mormon People*, 197–200, 216–29. One of the more important examples of twentieth-century systemization was LeGrand Richard's mission handbook, "The Message of Mormonism," (Np. 1937). Later (1950) revised and enlarged, it appeared in print as *A Marvelous Work and a Wonder*. Another was Richard L. Anderson's "Anderson Plan," ca. 1948.

Anderson's work was much more concise than "Message" and pointed the way to a different philosophy of teaching: let the Spirit convince and place the test of faith less on the missionary, more on the potential believer.

that were being established near major college campuses as spiritual refuges for Latter-day Saint students. These Institutes were staffed by faculty who held advanced degrees and were thus better able to relate to student populations subject to university faculties and modern ideas. The printing of R1 in the official *History of the Church* in 1952 and its 1938 appearance in *Teachings of the Prophet Joseph Smith* had rejuvenated it as a source.

A representative example of the revival appears in the work of George T. Boyd (1909–2004). Boyd established the church's Institute of Religion in Berkeley, California. and then joined the Institute faculty for the University of Utah in Salt Lake City and later moved to the University of Southern California.[33] Boyd's writing echoed an optimistic Christianity, a positive anthropology/anti-determinism that students found encouraging especially as Boyd selectively drew on some of JS's preaching (the Follett sermon in particular) and revelations somewhat in the fashion of the less-sophisticated John Henry Evans.[34] Many of Roberts's ideas filtered back into this teaching of collegiate Latter-day Saints from teachers like Boyd and other Mormon educators like Sterling McMurrin.[35] Boyd wrote:

> The knowledge Mormons claim to have of man in the pre-existence is limited and is based principally upon what is found in Mormon scripture. Yet, these scriptures tell considerable, and imply a great deal more, relative to the status and nature of

33. Boyd's departure from Utah was in part perhaps because the Institute at the University of Utah had become a nexus for the sort of thinking Boyd championed. See Mary Lythgoe Bradford, *Lowell L. Bennion: Teacher, Counselor, Humanitarian*, ch. 7.

34. For example, see Boyd, *The Moral Nature of Man*. See also James B. Allen, Dale C. LeCheminant, and David J. Whittaker, eds., *Views on Man and Religion: Collected Essays of George T. Boyd*.

35. On Boyd, see Bradford, *Lowell L. Bennion*, 106–7. On McMurrin, see Sterling M. McMurrin, *The Theological Foundations of the Mormon Religion*.

> man in his pre-earth life. Among other things, all men are said to have been in the beginning with God as uncreated, self-existing egos, or "intelligences" as the Prophet Joseph Smith referred to these ultimate, individuated, conscious entities. The ground of man's being, therefore, is in himself, giving him permanent ontological status in the universe. The use of the term "intelligence" may seem awkward, but if one thinks of the term as it is most commonly applied to man, as capacity or potentiality, then man defined as "intelligence" is an insatiable capacity to know, to will, and to feel in a universe which offers inexhaustible opportunities for knowing, willing, and feeling. The term "intelligence," therefore, is well adapted to the expression of Mormon thought at this point.[36]

Boyd's thought alludes to Roberts's interpretation of Follett. Boyd quoted Roberts on the issue of God eternally progressing but never noted him while deploying much of the terminology of Roberts's 1907 article.[37] This represents the depth that Roberts's work on Follett had entered the thinking of many Latter-day Saints at the time and their simultaneous hiatus in Widtsoe-physics. No one would make JS into a twentieth-century scientist. Boyd made no mention of Follett in his article.

Boyd continued,

> These primordial selves, or "intelligences," are defined in terms of the same psychic activities or functions, i.e., thinking, willing, feeling, oughting, and desiring, which define the person for us today, however embryonic these functions may have been; otherwise there seems to be no basis for the continuity of the person throughout eternity. It was the presence of these functions, either actually or potentially, which made it possible for God to enlarge the experience of "intelligences" by bringing them into a "spiritual estate" where the original "intelligences," or centers of consciousness, were clothed with spiritual bodies—allow-

36. George T. Boyd, "A Mormon Concept of Man," 57.
37. For example, Boyd, "A Mormon Concept of Man," 57–58.

> ing a greater range of psychic activity. Living as a community of spirits, they had increased opportunities for mental, moral, and emotional development. Spirits were free agents, capable of making moral commitments and capable of breaking them. As free agents they had the power to distinguish the good from the bad and were responsible for their choices.

Here Boyd represents a common theme that drew on Follett, via Roberts, and continued for some time as a kind of axiomatic thinking about the human race and God among many Latter-day Saint teachers and thinkers. The evident enthusiastic assumptions were questioned in succeeding decades. Penrose's critique of Roberts still echoed within Mormon discourse, and the optimism connected to JS's Cartesian-like instrumental salvation was questioned through a more pessimistic outlook and a resurgence in discussions of Pauline grace—rather in the way the Reformers disentangled grace from hierarchy and, to a large extent, ritual.[38]

The 1938 turn brought Follett (often in anonymous fashion) into a growing market of lay church publishing. An interesting example was the printing of a series of lectures by LDS actor and radio personality Lynn McKinlay. An engaging speaker, McKinlay published a volume of some of his 1949 speeches titled *Life Eternal*. It brought Roberts's interpretation of Follett to a popular church audience much like Boyd did for university students. McKinlay wrote,

> As we go into classes, many times this question arises, "Alright, so we were born of a Father in Heaven and a Mother in Heaven, and have a spirit body; what were we before that?" . . . What precisely is the situation before He became our Father we do not

38. See, for example, George Boyd, Rodney Turner, and Kent Robson, "Roundtable: The Nature of Man." On grace, efforts like Stephen E. Robinson's *Believing Christ* served as a counterpoint to the instrumental view (essentially) that holy rites are the repositories of grace. On Cartesian salvation as struggle to work out one's own salvation, see Taylor, *A Secular Age*, 100.

> know . . . Hereafter, after we will learn all there is to know about the principles and powers that govern pristine intelligences, for such we once were, existing as distinct identities co-eternal with God[39]

Well-known Latter-day Saint essayist and BYU professor Eugene England reacted to Follett's claims about the brute fact of the soul with anxiety. England wrote in a 1982 essay that "there is finally no answer to the question of how I exist . . . I just always have, and that is where my mind balks in horror." Orson Pratt, James Talmage, and Anthon Lund might have sympathized.[40]

Roberts's 1909 version of Follett, R1, was reflected in Latter-day Saint thinker Francine Bennion's 1995 address on theodicy, where Bennion traced thoughts like Boyd's back to Follett. Bennion's address offered a profound applied theological reflection on the complex of ideas coming out of the era of R1.

> It is not enough that theology be *either* rational *or* faith promoting. It must be both . . . Theology does not prevent all hurt and anguish. No knowledge of theology can remove all pain . . . Nor can it fill an empty stomach. What sound theology *can* do is to help those who believe it to make some sense of the suffering, of themselves, and of God . . . There is no single theology of suffering in our church, one framework uniform in all respects in the minds of all leaders and all other members . . . If it were God who originally created our personal capabilities and quiddities, or if they originally came about by any kind of "chance," then any differences among us, and results of them must ultimately be attributed to God or to chance. We could not be responsible for what we are or what we do.[41]

39. Lynn A. McKinlay, *Life Eternal*, 27–28.

40. Eugene England, *Dialogues with Myself*, 196.

41. Francine R. Bennion, "A Latter-day Saint Theology of Suffering," in *At the Pulpit*, 217, 223, 223n35 (421).

The inaugural year of the LDS Church's new *Ensign* magazine (1971) sported an edited version of R5 (creating R6), its publication split between the April and May issues. R6 was stripped of Roberts's notes as well as the passage on child resurrection, reflecting some of its controversial past and perhaps a developing stance of church correlation (see below). In 1978, Brigham Young University's *BYU Studies* produced a special issue of the journal with several articles devoted to the Follett sermon. Manuscript audits of the sermon appeared in a 1980 book edited by Andrew Ehat and Lyndon Cook with the optimistic title *The Words of Joseph Smith*.[42] Since then, various audits of the sermon have appeared, though none in official imprints.[43]

If public church criticism of Follett was long dead, the interpretive discussion did not rest—it just became less visible. The open political conflicts among Mormon leaders in the last decades of the long nineteenth century seemed to allow public exchanges over church teachings, but the retrenchment movement in the latter half of the twentieth century transformed insider public criticism of the teachings of an ecclesiastical authority into an offense against the church at large.[44]

42. Donald Q. Cannon, "The King Follett Discourse: Joseph Smith's Greatest Sermon in Historical Perspective." Stan Larson, "The King Follett Discourse: A Newly Amalgamated Text." Van Hale, "The Doctrinal Impact of the King Follett Discourse." Andrew F. Ehat and Lyndon W. Cook, *The Words of Joseph Smith*.

43. The Willard Richards text appears in *JSP*, J3:217–22. The Joseph Smith Papers published three other source manuscripts for RC online at the same time. See the enumerated bibliography in chapter 1 above.

44. Mauss, *The Angel and the Beehive*, 179. Roberts's continuing political adventures probably helped solidify such an ethic. In 1912, half the Salt Lake Stake walked out of their conference when Roberts was asked to speak. Anderson, *Cowboy Apostle*, 511. See, also, for example, James E. Talmage, Letter to John A. Widtsoe, October 29, 1928, James E. Talmage collection, MS 1232, Box 4, fd. 18, CHL.

§4.3 Church Manuals Once Again and a Revival of the Critique from the Protestant Right

In 1969, Brigham Young University philosophy professor Truman Madsen was asked to write a Sunday School manual for a teen-level audience initially titled *My Relationship to My Heavenly Father*.[45] The correlating committee asked for three rewrites, largely over Madsen's use of Follett. The process was so drawn out that the manual first arrived to church teachers in unbound, pre-review format, contained clear references to the Follett-Roberts cosmology, and followed Madsen's own work in his 1966 book *Eternal Man* mentioned above. After the third requested rewrite, Madsen bowed out of the process. When the final form of the manual arrived a few months later, references to Follett had been largely removed in favor of church general authority Bruce R. McConkie's writings, the manual was retitled *My Religion and Me*, and rewritten by another hand. When the manual arrived in print, its original themes of freedom and eternalism were exchanged for obedience and penance.[46] The diverging Roberts and Penrose pictures of the Follett sermon were still alive—if less publicly discussed—and some of its essentials live on in the entries of the officially sanctioned 1992 *Encyclopedia of Mormonism*.[47] Correlation, among other things, the church's literature vetting arm,

45. Early manuscript copy in possession of the author.

46. To see some of the editing process, see "Publication Files." On Madsen asking to be excused from further work on the manual, see Publication Files, fd. 14, cover letter.

47. Daniel H. Ludlow, ed., *Encyclopedia of Mormonism* 4 vols. See articles like "Teachings about Premortality" written in a Penrose-McConkie style, "Premortal Life" (written in the Roberts ideology), "Intelligences" (an attempt at showing different ideas about the Follett sermon), "Mankind," along with other related articles suggesting one side or the other. It seems clear that the encyclopedia was purposeful in ambiguity and unfortunately less careful historically than it might have been.

gave McConkie's work increasing influence on the church's public teachings from the 1970s toward the end of the twentieth century.[48]

In December 1980, Leonard Arrington, then the Church Historian of the Church of Jesus Christ of Latter-day Saints, made some important comments in his diary that reflected the current state of thought as it related to the early twentieth-century dialogue over Follett. Arrington wrote:

> There are two schools of LDS theology or philosophy . . . One of them begins with Joseph Smith's statements of his later years, particularly the King Follett discourse, proceeds through Brigham Young to B. H. Roberts, and best expressed in our day by Sterling McMurrin and Lowell L. Bennion. This school emphasizes man's potential, the law of eternal progression, the importance of learning and knowledge, tolerance of different points of view, and so on. This is the view I was brought up on—it was commonly expressed by LDS intellectuals and teachers during the 1930s and 1940s. We may call it the progress or liberal school of thought.
>
> The other school derives from the Book of Mormon, early revelations, and early statements of Joseph Smith, proceeds through some statements of Brigham Young to Orson Pratt, Joseph Fielding Smith, and best expressed today by Bruce R. McConkie. This school emphasizes the dependent and depraved status of man, the absolute power and perfection of God, the importance of "works," such as temple work, ordinances, following church regulations, discipline, obedience, "narrow is the way," and so on. This philosophy is emphasized in the New Orthodoxy which emerged at BYU in the 1950s and has continued among some people there, particularly in the College of Religion. A sort of Mormon Fundamentalism like

---

48. On McConkie, see Mauss, *Angel and the Beehive*, 162–76; Barlow, *Mormons and the Bible*, 185–87, 190, 214; Turner, *Mormon Jesus*, 283–94. Bowman, *Mormon People*, ch. 7. Gary James Bergera, "The 1911 Evolution Controversy at Brigham Young University." An example of that influence qua Follett may be Marion G. Romney, "The Worth of Souls," *Conference Report*, October 1978.

> Protestant Fundamentalism. Emphasized Biblical literalism, rejects Higher Criticism, the law of evolution, the New History, cultural approaches to an understanding of Mormonism.[49]

The status of the Follett sermon and other JS addresses in present Mormon teaching is not uniform, certainly not that of Franklin D. Richards's *Compendium*. One may see church president Gordon B. Hinckley's remarks to reporters, when asked if Mormons believed that God the Father was once a man, "I don't know that we teach it. I don't know that we emphasize it . . . I don't know a lot about it and I don't think others know a lot about it,"[50] as a frank and insightful statement more than an attempt to avoid embarrassing questions. Compare Hinckley's brief reference to these interviews at the October 1997 opening session of the church's general conference meetings. It is possible that Hinckley was in some way taken by surprise by the question, but that seems a naïve assessment. Perhaps no other Latter-day Saint leader in modern times has been more poised in public forums than Hinckley. Eager to engage the world of journalism, at least on his own terms, the church may not see his like again for some time.[51] A search of the church's recent official publications and correlated teaching manuals verifies Hinckley's statement to the reporters. Nevertheless, Hinckley offered the Follett sermon a place among church teachings.

---

49. Gary James Bergera, ed., *Confessions of a Mormon Historian: The Diaries of Leonard J. Arrington, 1971–1997, vol. 3: Exile, 1980–97*, 132. Arrington names others in his second category and tellingly, they were all, save the last, general authorities of the LDS Church who had expressed doubts about Arrington's work: Ezra Taft Benson, Mark E, Petersen, Boyd K. Packer, and Bruce R. McConkie. The pericope represents Arrington's picture, and things were certainly more complex.

50. David Van Biema, *Time Magazine* (August 4, 1997): 56; Don Lattin, "Musings of the Main Mormon," *San Francisco Chronicle*, April 13, 1997.

51. Bowman, *The Mormon People*, 229.

> the soul is immortal and keeps on growing... the year [JS] died—1844—the Prophet had amplified this doctrine in a monumental address which he delivered in the grove which was just below the temple site. The text of that address has become an important doctrinal document in the theology of the Church. It is known as the King Follett Sermon.[52]

The Follett sermon and JS's follow-up response to its critics (a sermon delivered June 16, 1844) have been consistently published by the church on various levels of officially sponsored literature, but there is little discussion and comment on them beyond occasional minor quotation in twenty-first-century church devotional publications and addresses.[53]

It was JS's ideas about the human soul and the resurrection of the human body that made church leaders in the early twentieth century want to discard the Follett sermon. The sermon's teachings on Christ would make it a centerpiece of Protestant evangelical critique in the twentieth century.[54]

As 1983 began, a counter-cult movement among conservative evangelicals, aided by former Latter-day Saints, opened a publicity

52. See Gordon B. Hinckley, "Nauvoo's Holy Temple," 59–62; see also his emphasis during the October 1994 church general conference. Others among the church's apostolic leaders have mentioned the sermon or at least Roberts's interpretation. See these church conference settings: Spencer W. Kimball (April 1977), Richard G. Scott (April 2010), D. Todd Christofferson (April 2015), Dallin H. Oaks (October 2019, April 2020).

53. On the June 16 sermon, see Smith, *Every Word Seasoned With Grace*, ch. 10. In the last few decades such publication has been limited to reprints of historical materials, though short excerpts of RC appeared in the JS entry of the LDS church manual series *Teachings of the Presidents of the Church* (Salt Lake City, 2007). Remarkably, the manual writers still deployed Roberts's then-obsolete *History of the Church* as a source text despite having primary sources from the Joseph Smith Papers Project.

54. Turner, *Mormon Jesus*, 288–94. Matthew Bowman, "The Evangelical Countercult Movement and Mormon Conservatism."

war against the Church of Jesus Christ of Latter-day Saints, a war at least partly founded on the Follett sermon. The anti-Mormon film *The God Makers* (a reference to JS's "learn to be gods yourselves" ideas that flowered in the Utah church through polygamy, Adam-is-God preaching, and temple rites) began showing to large audiences in Southern California, a historic Latter-day Saint stronghold. Its presentation and a following book would have a negative effect on Latter-day Saint growth there and eventually around the United States.[55] One character in the film states that the whole of Mormonism flows from the idea of becoming gods with many goddess wives who, in the words of one woman on screen, will be "eternally pregnant." The film had a cartoon sequence depicting God the Father living on the planet Kolob with many blonde wives nurturing spirit children conceived by sexual unions with God. In general, the film portrays a Mormonism that barely recognizes the Jesus of the New Testament.

The film made various claims about devil worship among Mormons, that they have two carefully cultivated faces, one that shows the ideal of familial love and togetherness, another that shows demonic possession and Satan worship. Such extreme claims eventually brought criticisms from various religious leaders and commentators. As was the case in earlier times, few critiqued Follett's view of the soul. The film, along with the extreme Mormon views of the Equal Rights Amendment, the Mark Hofmann murders, and ensuing circulating claims that the church was holding back embarrassing historical data, served to energize continuing uncomfortable publicity about the church.[56]

55. J. B. Haws, *The Mormon Image in the American Mind*, 115–19.

56. The film *The God Makers* was produced by J. Edward Decker and written by Decker, David Hunt, and T. A. McMahon. The film was followed up by a book *The God Makers: A Shocking Exposé of What Mormons Really Believe* in 1984, written by Decker and Hunt. On the film and its subsequent controversy, see Massimo Introvigne, "The Devil Makers: Contemporary Evangelical Fundamentalist Anti-

As Latter-day Saint temples rose in the Deep South, in particular in Atlanta, Georgia, and Dallas, Texas, evangelical organizations like the Southern Baptist Convention began a campaign to target LDS beliefs as other than Christian.[57] The Church of Jesus Christ of Latter-day Saints had been labeled a cult by conservative Christian elements for decades, but conservative evangelical thought leaders like Franklin Graham, Jerry Falwell, James Dobson, and others cringed at the conversions Latter-day Saints were making in their backyards. It was not that Mormons were simply Christians with a few odd beliefs. As Latter-day Saints built new temples in America, protests sprouted on the sidewalks with placards announcing that Mormons were destroying souls with their counterfeit Jesus.[58]

Mormons were, by self-description, excluded from the denominational fold via their narrative of a Great Apostasy of Catholic and Reformed Christianity.[59] At the same time, LDS conferences in Salt Lake City, saw an influx of "street preachers"—evangelicals who were often local Utahns, though others traveled from distant cities to stand on street corners near church conference venues with megaphones and placards declaring that the Mormon God was not the God of

---

Mormonism." On the relative effectiveness of the film and other new critics through the internet in particular, see Haws, *The Mormon Image*, chs. 5, 7. Bowman, *The Mormon People*, ch. 8. Max Perry Mueller, "The Pageantry of Protest in Temple Square," 260–62.

57. Haws, *Mormon Image*, 129–30. "Mormons Spotlighted," *Sunstone Review*, 2, no. 1 "Dallas Baptists Arm for Mormon Onslaught," *Sunstone Review* 2, no. 5 (April 1982): 9–10.

58. Haws, Ibid. "Temple Open House Boycotted in Denver," *Sunstone* 6, no. 10 (1986): 40. On fears of growth, see Carl Mosser, "And the Saints Go Marching On: The New Mormon Challenge for World Missions, Apologetics, and Theology." Bowman, *Christian*, 210–26.

59. Based on an interpretation (common among Latter-day Saints) of Joseph Smith's 1839 narration of his First Vision, a standard reference during the first half of the twentieth century was James E. Talmage's 1909 volume, *The Great Apostasy*.

the Bible while ridiculing LDS temple rites and Joseph Smith.[60] At the heart of such conservative Christian fears was the Follett sermon and its summary statement (see §3.8) attributed to Lorenzo Snow, "As man now is, God once was: As God now is, man may be."[61]

Some Latter-day Saints followed Hinckley's lead in trying to create space for theological normalization, but both sides found unity difficult.[62] At the same time, the church was moving to rejuvenate its image as a Christian faith with a number of public changes. Conference addresses made more frequent mention of Jesus Christ and the centrality of Christ's atonement in church teachings, quoting an 1838 statement usually attributed to JS as saying that the faith was centered in the teachings of the ancient apostles about Jesus Christ.[63]

In 1982, the Book of Mormon was renamed, *The Book of Mormon: Another Testament of Jesus Christ*. Church President Ezra Taft Benson (1985–1994) fervently declared that this scripture was the foundation of the church, the "keystone of our religion" as a Christ-centered faith

---

60. The Associated Press reported on clashes between a few Mormons and preachers at the October 2003 conference. AP Archives for October 7, 2003. Compare https://www.heraldextra.com/news/local/3-arrested-or-cited-as-lds-conference-attendees-clash-with-street-preachers/article_20dc86c2-16d7-590e-a2f6-65886b9347e3.html (accessed March 10, 2021). Mueller, "The Pageantry of Protest in Temple Square."

61. Quoted from a crossword puzzle in the LDS children's magazine, *The Friend* (March 2002): 23.

62. See, for example, Ronald V. Huggins, "Lorenzo Snow's Couplet: 'As Man Now is, God once was; as God Now is, Man May Be': 'No Functioning Place in Present-Day Mormon Doctrine?' A Response to Richard Mouw."

63. The statement appears as an unsigned piece from the Far West, Missouri church periodical, *Elders' Journal* (July 1838): 44. See https://bycommonconsent.com/2018/03/13/joseph-smiths-statement-on-the-fundamental-principles-of-our-religion-part-i-authorship-attribution-revision-and-publication/. https://bycommonconsent.com/2018/03/16/joseph-smiths-statement-on-the-fundamental-principles-of-our-religion-part-ii-the-significance-of-willard-richards-1853-revisions/

and should be studied by all in order to remove a historic curse upon the church because of a 200-year neglect of the text.[64] Benson was noted for requesting a favorite hymn in church meetings, the Billy Graham standard, "How Great Thou Art," rather than a more typical Latter-day Saint product. In 1996, church meeting houses began placing new signage, where the name of the church had "Jesus Christ" in larger, all capital letters.[65]

In the years since the beginning of that portion of the evangelical counter-cult movement directed against the Church of Jesus Christ of Latter-day Saints, other forces have replaced doctrinal otherness as

---

64. Turner, *Mormon Jesus*, 44–47. Ezra Taft Benson, "Cleansing the Inner Vessel," *Conference Reports* (April 1986), https://www.churchofjesuschrist.org/study/general-conference/1986/04/cleansing-the-inner-vessel. Barlow, *Mormons and the Bible* preface to the 2013 edition. Patrick Q. Mason, "Ezra Taft Benson and Modern (Book of) Mormon Conservatism," 67–78, 80. The "keystone" phrase came from a November 28, 1841 Wilford Woodruff journal audit of JS, apparently in response to missionaries just returned from England, where they had encountered challenges about the origin and content of the Book of Mormon, often derived from American newsprint republished in pamphlet form. In any case, Woodruff reported in his journal some days after the incident that he "Spent the day at B. Young in company with Joseph & the Twelve in conversing upon a variety of subjects it was an interesting day Elder Joseph Fielding was present he had been in England four years we also saw a number of English Brethren Joseph said the Book of Mormon was the most correct of any Book on earth & the key stone of our religion & a man would get nearer to God by abiding by its precepts than any other Book." Wilford Woodruff journal, Sunday, November 28, 1841. On mission challenges, see, for example, Joseph Fielding, 1838 journal, August 1, 1838, p. 35. Joseph Fielding 1841 journal, pp. 57, 62–63, 73–78, MS 1567, CHL. On criticisms of the Book of Mormon at the time that these missionaries had to answer, see, for example, Richard Davis, *The Imposture Unmasked; or, A Complete Exposure of the Mormon Fraud* 2nd ed.

65. Benson may have first heard the hymn in an LDS setting in Sweden about 1965 while he was president of the European mission (private communication). The hymn subsequently appeared in the 1985 LDS hymnal. Karen Lynn Davidson, *Our Latter-day Hymns: The Stories and the Messages*, 88. Michael Hicks, *Mormonism and Music: A History*, 144–45.

a reason for regional decreases in active LDS membership. Prominent in surveys of disaffected or troubled members is a loss of community feeling. There is a sharp decrease in the retention of LDS college students who see the church's stand on various social issues as antiquated, irrelevant, or harmful. Falling birth rates and later marriage among Mormon women contribute to flattening growth rates of membership in industrialized regions. Follett and its theological cousins like temple rites seem to be becoming less important, deliberately so in the case of Follett, but also by cultural disinterest for the beliefs of the American past. The cosmos of Nauvoo and Middle Mormonism may seem like a hard fit, even irrelevant, to the questions of twenty-first-century life.[66]

§4.4 Follett and the New Science— The Sermon Gets a Mathematical Proof

> *God had materials to organize from—chaos—chaotic matter.—element had an existence from the time he had. The pure pure principles of element are principles that never can be destroyed—they may be organized and re organized—but not destroyed.*
>
> —*WC*

> *The Holy Ghost intended to teach us how to go to heaven, not how the heavens go.*
>
> —*Galileo*

> *It has always been my province to dig up hidden mysteries, new things, for my hearers*
>
> —JS[67]

66. See Jana Riess, *The Next Mormons*. See also Emma Penrod, "Growth in the LDS Church is Slowing—But not for Reasons You Might Expect," https://religionunplugged.com/news/2020/4/15/growth-in-the-lds-church-is-slowingbut-not-for-reasons-you-might-suspect (April 20, 2020).

67. May 12, 1844, sermon.

The calculations of Copernicus, Galileo, and Newton that reigned in the science of JS's world were a shocking correction to the Ptolemaic, geocentric cosmos where earth was the center of creation. That geocentric cosmos seemed to be confirmed by the book of Genesis. The heliocentric universe of Copernicus went against a doctrinal superstructure largely constructed in opposition to it. Religious opposition was mild at first but gradually became fierce decades after his death. It was Galileo who took the brunt of the insult for the Copernican contradiction of Scripture. In JS's era, the common conception of creation was biblical but had incorporated Copernicus. The earth, sun, moon, and stars and seven of the eight known planets of the solar system had been discovered. The science of Newton and Galileo had been a part of commonplace knowledge, and a sun-centered system had been in place among common folk for more than 300 years.

JS believed in what is called the argument from design and that God "holds the world in its sphere or orbit."[68] In addition, JS held to a world that was created, formed by God (or the Gods) just as the Genesis story outlined, and considered a worldwide flood more or less a thousand years later—in Archbishop James Ussher's (1581–1656) chronology—as a given fact.[69] Ussher's famous calculation that the world began on October 22, 4004 BC at 6:00 pm was not so ludicrous as it seems now, and it reflected a framework that required historical necessity for landmarks of Christian belief extracted from an Old Testament literalism—something still evident in a number of strong voices in early-twentieth-century Mormonism.[70]

68. Alma 30:44. See L. Rex Sears, "Philosophical Christian Apology Meets 'Rational' Mormon Theology."

69. Duane E. Jeffery, "Noah's Flood: Modern Scholarship and Mormon Traditions."

70. On this framework, see Taylor, *A Secular Age*, 242. A Latter-day Saint version is seen in chapter 3. On the continuing discussion, see Barlow, *Mormons and the Bible*, ch 4.

For JS, the Cosmos was found in a more or less literal interpretation of Genesis 1, one that did not bound the Einsteinian Universe as that was articulated in 1905–1919. *Cosmos* was too narrow for what happened in the twentieth century. There was a *universe* that cut through, severed at the heart, the early semi-enchanted Cosmos into which JS was born. This inconceivably vast "Universe" became the term and idea of choice. In a sense, JS's cosmos had been built by Christian history, and that history was enshrined within it largely by definition. Latter-day Saint worldviews mostly inhabited that cosmos and were partly framed by it. The Utah Mormon definition of the engine of salvation was more material than that of historical Christian belief, but it fit within that world as a branch of the Christian background. As the notion of "Universe" took center stage in the first half of the twentieth century, the structure of Latter-day Saint institutions made it difficult to adapt the nineteenth-century picture. In fact, prominent church figures placed belief in opposition to science.[71] This was not inevitable. As was seen in chapter 3, a number of thinkers made attempts to situate at least parts of Latter-day Saint beliefs in the universe, but those attempts did not find their way into the institutionally correlated core of the second half of the twentieth century. That core became smaller rather than more expansive, following a trend from the 1940s onward.

The scientific work of the first half of the twentieth century saw a revolution in conceptions of space and time. Einstein's work in 1905 (diffusion, proof that atoms exist, special relativity, the photoelectric effect, $E = mc^2$) opened new vistas in science and foreshadowed a drastically new picture of the universe. Scientists had long held a picture of the material universe as consisting of what we call the Milky Way, a single galaxy existing forever, an unchanging eternal creation. Much

71. For the broader world, see Taylor, *A Secular Age*, 70–71. The discussion in chapter 3 and the 1909 First Presidency message suggests the LDS trajectory.

to Einstein's discomfort, astronomer Edwin Hubble (1889–1953), using powerful new instruments, determined that there were many galaxies beyond our own and that they were all receding from each other: the further away they were, the faster they were running away. The stars themselves were all on a path of eventual destruction, their internal engines (nuclear fusion was established as the energy source of stars by the 1930s)[72] would run out of fuel, ending in dead ash or explosions leaving behind strange objects like neutron stars and black holes. The expansion implied several things. First, it meant that the part of the universe we can observe must have once been much closer together. Eventually, it was shown that in the deep past (about 13.5 billion years ago) the *observable* universe occupied a space smaller than the size of a proton, much smaller. Second, the work of Einstein and Hubble added further complications. Because this expansion is faster the further out we look, eventually we can no longer see more distant objects. They are invisible because the light they emit is going too slow to overcome the recession speed between the earth and those distant objects. We cannot see their light and never will. And recent observations seem to assure us that the distance between us and those most distant objects is infinite in this sense: no matter how far out we choose to consider some object, there is something more distant yet, all forever beyond the boundary of perception.

This broader universe is not part of the observable universe—what we can observe with the naked eye or with enhancing instruments. An infinite universe has some interesting features. For example, since there are only finitely many chemical elements, they can only be combined in a (perhaps very large but) finite number of ways. This sug-

72. The breakthrough began with the understanding of stellar composition. Cecilia H. Payne, "A Contribution to the Observational Study of High Temperature in the Reversing Layers of Stars," PhD diss, Radcliffe College, 1925. Prior to Payne, it was assumed that stars consisted of the same composition of elements found on earth.

gests that our present earth and its flora and fauna are repeated many times beyond the observable universe. How might JS have seen such identical multiples of himself? MIT physicist Max Tegmark calculates that the closest identical copy of yourself is very far away. The number is hard to imagine: in miles, 1 followed by more than a million billion billion billion zeros.[73]

Consequences of the expansion of the observable universe include an eventual, in the far, far, distant future, dissolution of all worlds, including atoms themselves. Only space, virtually devoid of matter in its familiar forms, will be left. This cannot be dismissed as theoretical wanderings of mad scientists. It will come to pass. Moreover, not only will matter, even atoms and their component parts disperse out of sight, important parts of those structures (protons!) will decay. Death is the ultimate end of everything in this world. JS's world rebels against that end, though he never approaches the mental entanglements of immortality of an already infinite lifespan. As Eugene England observed, there is a kind of horror at such infinities, perhaps this horror is an embedded realization that the flow of time is in fact just the long march, in the present universe, from order to, on the average, ever-encroaching disorder.[74]

JS never faced facts like these. How would his teaching report such things? JS saw the ideas surrounding him as free for the taking, modifying, adapting, or rejecting. He was always looking to broaden the horizons of the Latter-day Saints. His ideas about matter would be different today, certainly more sophisticated in terms of what "flesh and bones" bodies might be in a resurrection. His teaching about the permanence of souls could be rationalized by following it to its

---

73. For a readable account, see Robert Kuhn, "Confronting the Multiverse: What 'Infinite Universes' Would Mean." Also Max Tegmark, *Our Mathematical Universe: My Quest for the Ultimate Nature of Reality*.

74. Brian Greene, *Until the End of Time: Mind, Matter, and Our Search for Meaning in an Evolving Universe*.

inevitable conclusions: souls are not made of physical materials subject to dissolution and decay. They are some more stable substance, and in resurrection, bodies would not be the same particles making up earthly counterparts. Paul's words of First Corinthians 15:39–44 might come into focus: the resurrected are not the material of *this* world. Since JS's souls are already miraculous because they have no beginning or end, JS might characterize them as somehow more distant from the baryonic (ordinary) matter of the present universe. One might say he had already taken a step in that direction.

If physics might have altered the presentation of the Follett sermon in the twentieth century, biology may have done more yet. How would JS's vision of the beings of eternity account for evolutionary biology? How might JS have considered the idea that human bodies are quantum simulations of Newtonian mechanics?[75] In the abstract, JS's theology was already infused with the idea of lesser evolving into greater. Eternal progression could subsume biological change over the eons. The specifics of what JS might have preached in the modern setting of a Follett sermon are not clear, but given his philosophy of seeking truth wherever it may be found, it seems doubtful he would follow a path like that of Christian fundamentalists of the modern era.[76]

In late scientific literature, mathematics has something to say about JS's philosophical claims, in particular his oft-repeated phrase about the human soul: anything that has a beginning must have an end. Or equivalently, anything that has no end must have had no beginning—and JS uses the converse in his encouragement of Louisa Follett: do not fear—because King's soul has no beginning, it can

---

75. This may be thought of as a consequence of Bell's Theorem. See George S. Greenstein, *Quantum Strangeness: Wrestling with Bell's Theorem and the Ultimate Nature of Reality*.

76. For one Latter-day Saint biologist's take on such issues, see Steven L. Peck, "Crawling Out of the Primordial Soup."

have no end. He waits in another place, "the world of spirits," to greet you when the time comes.

Chapter 1 mentioned the Copernican Principle. Repurposed and abstracted from its astronomical reading (the original context) to a statement about duration, the Principle reads that the present state of something is nothing immediately special. It follows that the probable continuance of that state can be calculated. Some simple probability arguments turn this into an assertion about existence, that is, things that have been around for a long time will tend, on average, to be around for at least a while longer and one can predict their probable ending. For example, Homo sapiens has been around for about 200,000 years. With 95% probability, the species will exist for at least another 5,128 years and will die out within about 7.8 million years. The principle is oddly invariant with circumstance, and it has been verified in a large number of examples. The proof follows from J. Richard Gott III, "Implications of the Copernican Principle for Our Future Prospects."

The arithmetical argument leads to the 95% estimates from either dividing current duration by 39 (95% probability as to how far that duration will extend) or multiplying by 39 to get, with 95% probability, an upper bound of that duration. The number 39 is approximate and changes if the level of certainty (95% in Gott's work) is adjusted higher or lower (for 99% the factor is 199). The percentage may be adjusted as close to 100% as desired and this creates a kind of proof of JS's ontological assertions. Thus, if souls have no beginning, their certain continuation recedes into infinity (a very simple Calculus argument), a statement equivalent to the one JS directed to Louisa Follett: the only things that last forever are the things without beginning. Gott's theorem gives a somewhat troubling probabilistic view of "anything that has a beginning must have an end." One can predict the end of things that begin, such as the observable universe.[77] Of course, one must assume there is some background space where souls (or whatever else) get to exist forever—and that place is not the present universe mortals inhabit. Some sort of *transcendence* seems to be a corollary to any modern theological anthropology in this space. Now there are other questions too, ones that plagued classical theism, such as how do souls interact with the baryonic world of the here and now? Some thinkers, like LDS philosopher Truman Madsen, thought JS's materialism could blunt such questions. But it probably cannot.[78]

As pointed out at various places in this work, JS frequently drew on opinions and assertions from various figures before and during his own time and made them his own. JS held common beliefs such as that the moon and the planets of our solar system were inhabited. JS seemed to have had fewer philosophical and practical prejudices than many of his contemporaries. This suggests that he may have approached the deeper, modern insights of the physical world with some freedom, seeking his own inspired spiritual vision of the relationships between the modern world, interpretation of scripture, the spiritual realm of the Divine, and the light he found to reconcile

---

77. Gott's argument is *not* specific. For example, the earth has been around as a planet for about 4.5 billion years. Gott's calculation predicts that it will likely come to an end before another 176 billion years. Astrophysical arguments show it will be consumed by the expansion of the sun as it expands into a red giant in less than another 4 billion years. Gott's calculation suggests that the earth will be around for *at least* another 115 million years. But does it account for horrendous accidents, like a collision with another celestial object, say? The answer is embedded in probabilities.

78. There are important critiques of Gott's argument, but those critiques are of somewhat lesser importance to the "limiting" logic here—though they don't rule out other possibilities (perhaps souls are contingent or questions involving things like "Strong AI"). Often called the "Doomsday Argument," Gott's paper has generated much cross-talk. For a non-specialist approach, see William Poundstone, *The Doomsday Calculation: How an Equation that Predicts the Future is Transforming Everything We Know About Life and the Universe.*

them. JS was never a scientist (apologies to John Widtsoe), but he did not shrink from the struggle to understand the world he perceived alongside the "world of spirits."[79]

§4.5 Summary: A Brief Look Back

While the Follett sermon may have formed part of Latter-day Saint teaching at various times, its expansions, contractions, and other textual struggles over the years distanced it from any authentic archetype and not just in terms of some verbatim ideal. Early redaction was less concerned with fidelity to expression and context than with a tidy, readable, reasonably lengthy, and "currently" relevant text. That redaction continued and has determined for the most part the present form of RC in church usage. That form is in a sense canonical, though not historical, much like some reports of JS's speeches that Orson Pratt inserted in the Latter-day Saint canon in 1876.[80]

In light of the Presbyterian Teachers' Association's 1903 reprint of VOT in a pamphlet (see chapter 3) claiming was it the *real* view of the Mormon church, one may ask: was the Follett sermon a success? As

79. On beliefs about human life on planets in the solar system, see Michael Crowe and Matthew F. Dowd, "The Extraterrestrial Life Debate from Antiquity to 1900." Dick, *Philosophy of a Future State.* Several early Saints believed the solar system planets were inhabited by humans. Hyrum Smith, Joseph Smith's brother, spoke of it, Geroge Laub journal, April 27, 1843. See Brigham Young, "The Gospel–The One-Man Power," July 24, 1870. Van Hale, "Mormons and Moonmen."

80. For example, Doctrine and Covenants 130:22–23, whose source document reads rather differently: "The appearing of the Father and the Son in Jn 14:23 is a personal appearance; and the idea that the Father and the Son dwell in a man's heart is an old sectarian notion, and is false. The Father has a body of flesh and bones as tangible as man's; the Son also; but the Holy Ghost is a personage of spirit. *A person cannot have the personage of the Holy Ghost in his heart. He may receive the gift of the holy Ghost. it may descend upon him but not to tarry with him.*" Emphasis added, see *JSP*, J2:403–6.

a statement of belief for all time, the answer must be no. Of the five major points of the sermon, the nature of man, the nature of God, the resurrection, the nature of Hell, and baptism as the pivotal rite (and here I include the sermon's famous call to perform proxy rites like baptism for the dead), all but two have largely disappeared from sponsored Latter-day Saint discourse; the surviving two principles, baptism and resurrection, generally do not rely on the Follett text. The sermon's discussion of Hell, along with that of Doctrine and Covenants 132, may linguistically derive from Alma 39 in the Book of Mormon. However, Follett and Doctrine and Covenants 132 both complicate meanings considerably. The Book of Mormon is largely silent on the protology and eschatology that appear in the later documents, whatever B. H. Roberts may have claimed in 1905. Joseph Fielding Smith's turn on the subject of Follett, while it meant that he trusted the text, also made him feel that the text was not useful in the public space where it might foster dual challenges: confusion among the Saints (as his own correspondence files suggest) and fodder for church critics. Smith's placement of scripture (as he interpreted it) as the judgment of all other Latter-day Saint teaching made the sermon a secondary text, though he came to see it as revelation. This meant that Follett's radical assertions about God, the path of salvation, and the souls of mankind weren't pulpit material in a correlated, televised age.

JS's radical beliefs about mankind turned preacher Dow's words on their collective heads, wrecked Christian anthropology as a bulwark of divine separatism, befuddled his own most loyal followers, erected—by broad Christian standards—a truly heretical theogony (God has a genealogy), and largely failed to be completely owned by any of the churches that exploded from his prophetic legacy. In fact, in every case, it was (hermeneutically and/or editorially) reconstructed/discarded/ignored in various ways over fears that it failed to match (or sometimes, matched too closely) the prevailing theology that came to prominence in Utah less than a decade after JS's death.

JS's claim of a progressive God, one who came to be God in some distant past, was sharply criticized by Protestants and important Mormon insiders. But that vista survived through Middle Mormonism and helped to rationalize a heaven built around polygamy: the Saints were treading the paths of the gods. Follett was freighted with JS's more stunning but less public claims characterized by his teaching observed by Wilford Woodruff in 1842, as noted in chapter 1. The twentieth century brought some adaptation of Mormonism to the broader culture of America. People like Thomas Dick and later, the thought of the Progressive Era might have cottoned to the notion that Man could become more like God, but the idea that God came from a Mankind that populated the cosmos/qua universe—a major point of Follett—was allowed to fade away in silence. Doctrinal technicians like Penrose and Roberts, who argued over the reliability of Follett, might have had another argument with that. But they died and left the church landscape to a somewhat more normative Christian—even fundamentalist—thread, as Arrington noted. Within the world of the sermon itself, this seems odd; JS argued (via Jn 17) that true salvation depends on a certain complete and right knowledge of God which only exists when the correct understanding of human beings exists.

Follett's emphasis on a class of persons who would be damned without hope gradually morphed from quotidian Nauvoo (recall that it was preached early and often there) to an object of mystery and quixotic definitional limbo. JS's preaching on the subject of permanent damnation, what he called "eternal judgment" (Heb. 6), was frequent after the Missouri debacle.[81] It served a purpose in JS's life as a warning to and about apostates. Designated a first principle of the Gospel by JS, the idea quickly became tangential and partly submerged and then virtually disappeared in the twentieth century.

81. See sermons of July 9, 1839; May 16, 1841; October 15, 1843; May 12, 1844 (Parallel Joseph), *JSP*.

Recent surveys among Americans on the characteristics of Latter-day Saints mention things like strong nuclear families, deep religious commitment, a world-wide mission force, the Book of Mormon, or a sober lifestyle. Though few of the specifics of the Follett sermon remain in contemporary church discourse, the sermon made a crucial public point all the same. The 1843 revelation on polygamy (Doctrine and Covenants 132) made the practice of a man with more than one wife an integral part of church male and female identity. The revelation's "they shall be Gods" (Doctrine and Covenants 132:20) phrase was a silent (at the time) pre-endorsement of Follett, and Follett served as a fungible voice for polygamy, though the sermon texts do not theologize marriage. There was a paradox though. In Follett, God was the *adoptive* Father of uncreated necessarily forever-existing indivisible minds/souls/spirits. In the post-JS heaven, spirits were born to Mothers in Heaven. Few spoke of the paradox until the post-Manifesto era, when the paradox would contribute to the sermon's 1912 ban by Joseph F. Smith.[82] The sermon's lack of female presence serves a common narrative that women were silent partners in the domestic heaven that was fleshed out in Utah preaching, after the 1843 polygamy revelation became public in 1852. Follett evoked some promise, some explanation, some answer, to the question of what it meant to be a (male) God, but it added little to the discussion of what it meant to be female and going to heaven. The modern church consists of more single adults than married adults. How do the metaphysical mechanics of earlier centuries apply there without trivializing the present? Such hard questions will only increase as social realities evolve over the next century.

---

82. As already noted in chapter 3, even outsiders noticed the problem. Another example is Harold Bloom, *The American Religion: The Emergence of the Post-Christian Nation,* 124. For a troubled insider, see Joseph Lee Robinson's reminiscence in his autobiography/journal.

The eventual interpretive superstructure of the 1843 revelation and the King Follett Sermon shed joint light on God and humankind. God was a Man, and He was most certainly then, a numerically superior (that is, a polygamous) family Man. That logic remains, though among Latter-day Saints overt polygamy does not.[83]

Internally, the 1843 revelation's sealing subtext took the place of polygamy in the twentieth–century church, while Follett did not need to be moved from its support position as it became brokenly but ably summarized by Lorenzo Snow/ Brigham Young: "As God is, man may become."

Young also made it clear that in his mind and for many other Saints, God was white—Black people played an even lesser role in the God-making machinery of Heaven than they did in the American social hierarchy. It was not until the 1978 deracialization of the Mormon temple that Follett could be read without racial rankings. But by then, it was rarely read institutionally, surfacing only occasionally within terminology and hermeneutics often silently inherited from Follett through the lens of the Roberts era in later thinkers like George Boyd, Francine Bennion, Truman Madsen, and Bruce R. McConkie. Still, Follett in many ways is an important—if rather invisible—anchor of belief in the Church of Jesus Christ of Latter-day Saints. And perhaps in answer to the opening of the Introduction, it is a fractured *hidden* Standard Work for Latter-day Saints.

Louisa Tanner Follett, thank you, and may you rest in peace.

83. Alma 30:44. See Sears, "Philosophical Christian Apology Meets 'Rational' Mormon Theology."

APPENDIX A

A New Critical Text of the King Follett Sermon

Our past is sedimented in our present, and we are doomed to misidentify ourselves, as long as we can't do justice to where we come from.

—Charles Taylor, *A Secular Age*

§A.1 Introduction and Explanation of Notation

In this appendix I present a version of the text of the Follett sermon set around the various independent witness texts, privileging the two first order aural audits of Bullock and Clayton (TB, WC), then the second order text of Woodruff (WW) and the text of Willard Richards (WR), with notes based on the more distant witnesses like Samuel Richards, George Laub and others, as well as the final Grimshaw-generated pivot text that reflects the "common tradition" of RC, for example in R1 (Roberts's 1909 text) and R4 (Joseph Fielding Smith's *Teachings of the Prophet Joseph Smith*). I will not discuss liminal texts of the sermon in the annotation. I have done that elsewhere.[1] In constructing an apparatus for the text, I wished to avoid a "clear" text format (one that hides the dependence on source texts) but also avoid the highly technical (and expensive) typesetting difficulties of a classical apparatus. I settled on the following procedure.

Text that is witnessed (word for word) by at least two of the privileged witnesses (TB = Bullock, WC = Clayton, WR = Richards, WW = Woodruff) is generally, though not always, left un-annotated in normal typeface. Usually this un-annotated text represents agreement between TB and WC (and possibly other witness texts). Text that has only one witness among the privileged texts is enclosed by brackets followed immediately by the identity of the witness, such as

[that sits in the heavens for us to take up]WC

(that is, the bracketed text comes from the Clayton audit). Where the two aural audits differ, perhaps from on-the-fly content auditing, compression, or perceptive difference, etc., the two differing texts are displayed successively with a slash, as in

[hardly possible]TB/[impossible]WC

This level of reveal may seem unimportant, or at times awkward, but it coincides with my general intent to provide as transparent and economical a version as possible in an inline reading format. (For more graphical version, see Appendix F.)

Standard footnotes rather than more elegant line number based notes are used to simplify typesetting. For example, text that was essentially invented (constructed after JS's death) appearing in RC,

1. By liminal text I mean notations like divisional headings and footnotes as in R1 and R4 for example. The text of the sermon in this appendix is largely based on the material appearing in Appendices C and F. Typographical facsimiles of sources are found in Appendices D and E and a source criticism is found in Appendix C.

whether through dependence on VOT or later redaction is found in footnotes rather than the main text. The reader is warned that despite attempts to simplify the presentation, some persistence is required to follow the text, and questions of meaning often go unanswered and sentences may appear incomplete. The text became more complicated as auditors got tired, and as JS delved into speaking about non-English translations of the Bible, about halfway through the sermon text. However, as B. H. Roberts once noted, Follett is JS's most robustly audited extemporaneous sermon.

I have tried to keep intrusions in the text to a minimum beyond the apparatus itself, but I have supplied paragraphs in the text to ease reading. These paragraphs do not generally appear in any source text. I have standardized spelling to some extent but not wholly, to give the reader some flavor of the original without belaboring annotation or the patience of the reader. Moves like this may introduce further distance from the archetype. Where audits are the same in all respects except in spelling or punctuation, I have not noted this and counted those sources as identical. At times, and for similar reasons as above, I have completed what appears to be a partially written word with braces, as in mater{ially} for example.

§A.2 A King Follett Sermon Critical Text

[I now]WW call[2] the attention of the congregation while I address you [on]TB the subject contemplated in the fore part of the conference. As the wind blows [very]TB hard, it will be [hardly possible] TB/[impossible]WC to make [you all]TB hear [unless profound attention]WC

2. RC follows VOT by inserting the greeting, "Beloved Saints:" to open the text. This was an invention by the VOT editors, W. W. Phelps and John Taylor.

[It is]TB of the greatest importance and the most solemn [of any] TB that could occupy our attention [and that is]TB the subject of the dead on the decease of our brother Follett who was crushed to death in a well.[3] [I have been requested to speak by his friends and relatives] WC and inasmuch as [there are a]TB great many in this congregation who live in this city as well as [elsewhere]WC who have lost friends I shall speak on this subject in general and offer my ideas as far as I [have] TB ability and as far as [I shall be]TB inspired by the Holy [Spirit] TB/[Ghost]WC to [dwell on this]TB subject I want your prayers and faith the [inspiration]WC/[instruction]TB of Almighty God [the gift of the Holy Ghost]WC [that I may set forth truth]WC/[to say] TB things that [are true]TB/[can easily be comprehended]WC and [will]WC/[shall]TB carry the testimony to your hearts;[4] pray that [he]TB/[the L{ord}]WC may strengthen my lungs [stay]TB/[control]WC the wind [and let the pray of the saints to heaven appear]TB [that it may enter into the ear of the L{or}d of Sabaoth for]WC the [fervent effectual]WC prayer of [the]TB righteous [man]WC avail much– [and I verily believe that]TB your prayers [will]WW/[shall] TB be heard [I will speak in order to hold out]WC[5]

---

3. WR adds "by the falling of a tub of rock." RC then adds the un-sourced redundant text, "has more immediately led me to that subject."

4. RC restructures and shifts the text somewhat here. The main difference has "and which can be easily comprehended by you; and."

5. "to hold out" probably refers to JS's lung capacity and suggests in speaking less forcefully many would be unable to hear the sermon distinctly. JS held a considered opinion on the effectiveness of prayer based on this passage in James 5:16 Jesus's story of prayers by the sinner and the Pharisee. In reply to the question. Do you want a wicked man to pray for you? Willard Richards reported that JS answered, "Yes, if the fervent effectual prayer of the righteous availeth much. a wicked man may avail a little when p[r]aying for a Righteous man. There is none good but one. the better a man is the more his prayer will prevail. like the publican & pharasee one was justified rather than the other showing that both were justified in a degree. the

Before [I]TB enter fully into [this]TB/[the]WC investigation of [the]TB/[this]WC subject [that is lying before us]TB[6] I wish to pave the way – make a few preliminaries – bring up the subject from the beginning in order that you may understand [the subject]WC[7] when I come to it I do not calculate to please your ears with [superfluity of words]WC oratory [with]TB much learning but [I calculate to]TB edify you [by the]WC/[with]TB simple truths of heaven

[First place]WC [I]TB wish to go back to the beginning of creation[8] [then {or there} the starting point in order to fully aquainted with purposes]WC/[it is necessary to know the mind purposes] TB decrees [and ordination]TB of the great Elohim[9] [that sits in the h{eavens} for us to take up]WC beginning at the creation it is necessary for us to have an understanding of God [himself]WC in the beginning. If we start right [it is very]TB easy [for us]TB to go right all the time but if [we]TB start wrong [it is]TB hard [matter] WC to get right.[10] [There are very]TB few [beings in the world]WC who understand [rightly]TB the character of God [and do not comprehend their own character]WC[11] They [do not]TB/[cannot]WC

---

prayer of the wicked man may do a Righteous man good when it does the one who prays no good" JS diary December 24, 1842 (*JSP*, J2:193).

6. RC has "which is laying before me".

7. RC has "understand *it. I will*".

8. WW has "*to the morn of creation*". RC includes this.

9. TB has Eloi or Eloe. WW has Eloheem, WC has Elohem.

10. RC has a number of small changes, largely based on minor inclusions of WW and some invented text. For examples of the latter, (RC adds text in italics) "starting point *for us to look to*" and "Elohim *who* sits in *yonder* heavens *as he did* at the creation *of this world*."

11. Taken together, the text is equivalent to "if you comprehend the character of God you probably comprehend your own character {nature}. WR has "if men do not comprehend the character of God, they do not comprehend themselves." These are not equivalent statements. Later in the sermon JS offered that mankind and God have much in common metaphysically.

comprehend [the beginning nor the end]WC/[any thing that is past or that which is to come]TB [neither their own relation to God]WC and [com{prehend}]TB but little more [than]TB the brute beast [it does]WC/[comp{rehends?}]TB the same thing eat drink sleep [arise and not any more and what the designs of Jehova what better than the beast it does the same thing–eat drink–sleep and comprehends present]WC and knows [nothing more and how are we to do it]TB/[as much as we unless we are able to com{prehend}]WC by [no other way than]TB the inspiration of Almighty God. [I want to]TB go back to the beginning [and so]TB [lift]WC/[get]TB your minds into a more [lofty sphere]TB/[a more exalted standing]WC than the human [being]TB/[mind]WC [generally understands I]TB want to ask this congregation every man woman and child [to answer the question in their own heart]TB what kind of being is God [ask yourselves]WC.[12]

I [ag{ain}]TB repeat the question what kind of a being is God. [does]TB Any man or woman know have any of you seen him? heard him? communed with him?[13] Here [is the]TB question that will peradventure [from this time henceforth]TB/[while you live]WC occupy your attention.

The apostle says this is eternal life to know God and Jesus Christ whom he has sent. If any man enquire what kind of a being is God [if he will search diligently his own heart]TB/[cast his mind to know if the declaration of the apostle be true he will realize]WC [that unless he knows God]TB he has not eternal life [there can be eternal life

---

12. RC incorporates WW and unwitnessed (in italics) text : "*The great majority of mankind* do not comprehend *anything either* that *which* is past, or that which is to come, *as it respects* their relationship to God; they do not know, neither *do they understand the nature of that relationship* and *consequently, they know* but little."

13. RC reads "[turn your thoughts in*to* your hearts, and say if any of you have seen, heard or communed with him: this a question that may occupy your attention]WW *for a long time.*

on no other principle]WC[14] [My]TB first object [to]TB comprehend [and explain]WR God [and I comprehend them to]TB your hearts [so that the spirit seal it upon you hearts]WC let every man and woman [henceforth]TB [put his hand on his]WC/[shut their] TB mouth sit in silence and never say anything against the man of God [and]TB/[again but]WC[15] if I [do not do it]TB/[fail]WC [it becomes my duty to renounce all my]WC/[I have no right to]TB pretentions to revelation inspiration if [all are]TB/[I should do so] WC[16] [pretensions to God]TB [they will all]TB/[should I not]WC be as bad [off as I am]TB/[as all]WC the rest of the world. [they will all say I ought to be damned there is]TB not a man or woman would not breath [out an]TB anathema [on my head]TB if [they knew]WC I was [a]WC false [prophet.]WC [and]TB Some would [feel authorized to]TB take away my life.

If any man is authorized to take [away]TB my life [who say{s}] TB/[because]WC I am a false teacher [so I should have the same right to all]TB/[then upon the same principle am I authorized to take the life of every]WC false teacher [and where would be the end of blood] TB [and who would not be the sufferer]WC [and there is no law in the heart of God that would allow anyone to interfere with the rights of man]TB[17] every man has the right to be a false prophet as well as

14. SR: "Must know the only living and true God and Jesus Christ. to have eternal life". WW: "I would say If you dont know God you have not eternal life, go back & find out what kind of a being God is."

15. WR alters the sense somewhat with "never lift your voice against the servants of God again."

16. RC has redundant text from WW here and then inserts this unwitnessed text: "{I should} be hailed as a friend, and no man would seek my life; but if all religious teachers were honest enough to renounce their pretensions to Godliness when their ignorance of the knowledge of God is made manifest, they will all be as badly off as I am."

17. This phrase was not added to either TS or RC, though it suggests JS's position on federal protection of rights. It alludes to a quotation from James Madison's

a true prophet [but no man is authorized to take away life in consequence of their religion all laws and]WC government ought to [tolerate {religion?}[18] whether right or wrong]WC If I show [verily]TB that I have the truth of God and [show that]TB ninety-nine of one hundred are false [prophets]TB/[teachers]WC [while they pretend to hold the keys of God[19] and go to killing them because &c]WC[20] it would deluge the [whole]TB world [with]TB/[in]WC blood.[21]

I want you all [to]TB know God[22] [to]TB be familiar [with him and]TB if I can [get you to know {him} I can]WC bring [you]TB to him[23] [all]TB persecution [against]TB me will cease [and let you know that I am his servant for]TB I speak [as one having]TB/[in]WC authority [and not as a s{cribe?}]TB[24] What kind of a being was God

---

inaugural address, which William W. Phelps wrote into JS's presidential campaign "position paper" *General Smith's Views of the Powers and Policy of the Government* (which also appears in the *Voice of Truth*). In TS, Bullock chose the less colorful language from WC. WW suggests TB is more representative of Follett.

18. RC adds, "and protect". A number of additions in RC show its composition after the 1852 public avowal of polygamy and consequent arguments with federal authorities over the meaning of the first amendment of the US constitution.

19. RC: "keys of God*'s kingdom on Earth*".

20. TS (and VOT, RC) expands &c as "they are false teachers."

21. RC added the following italicized text, emphasizing the importance of "legal" divine authority: "and show that ninety-nine *out* of *every* hundred *professing religious ministers* are false teachers, *having no authority*."

22. RC adds, modifying WW, "I will *prove that* the world is wrong, by showing what God is. I am going to inquire after God."

23. Bullock added the following italicized text to the phrase "bring you to *a knowledge of* him" while editing GM1 and it subsequently appeared in RC.

24. JS may have alluded to Mk 1:22/Mt 7:29. Bullock left out "and not as a s{enr or crb}" from TS. What I have inserted as "scribe" may also be rendered as "senr" —an abbreviation of senator? Possibly a jab at some political figure? Calhoun? Benton? Perhaps Bullock was confused by his own ms while producing TS and so left out the phrase from it and simply followed WC.

in the beginning.[25] [Open your ears and eyes]TB all ye ends of the earth and hear [and]TB I am going to prove it [to you]TB [with]TB/[by]WC the Bible [and]TB I am going [to tell you the designs of God to the human race]TB/[and the relation the human family sustains with God]WC [and why he interferes with the affairs of man]TB

[1st]WC God himself who sits enthroned in yonder heavens is a man like [unto]TB one of yourselves[26] [This is the great secret]WC If [the veil was rent today and [that]WW/[the great]WC who holds this world in its orbit [its sphere or the planets]WC[27] [and upholds all things by his power]TB[28] if you were to see him to day you would see him [in all the person image, very form of]WC[29] a man for Adam was [created in the very fashion of God]WC/[formed in fashion and image like unto him]TB[30] Adam [received instruction]WC walked talked an [conversed]TB as one man [talks and communes]TB with another. In order to [speak for]TB/[understand the subject of the de{a}d]WC the consolation of those who mourn for the loss of their friend [it is]TB necessary [they should]WC/[to]TB understand [the character and being of]TB God [for I am]TB going to tell you [what sort of a being of God]TB [how God came to be God]WC.

We [suppose]WW/[have imagined]WC that God was God from all eternity I will refute [the]WR/[that]WW idea[31] [truth is the

25. WW has "I go back to the beginning to show what kind of a being God was, I will tell you & hear it O Earth!" WR uses "in the beginning before the world was" to summarize the whole paragraph as given here.

26. GM2/RC rewrites this as "God himself *was once as we are now, and* is *an exalted* man, *and* sits enthroned in yonder heavens!"

27. WC a reference to pre-Copernican geocentric astronomy.

28. An alternate premodern image.

29. WR and WW attest to "form".

30. SR attests to "fashion", WW attests to "image".

31. TB reports this as "for he was God from the begin{ning} of all Eternity & if I do not refute it". WR renders this as "refute the Idea that God was God from all eternity." WW adds "or I will do away or take away the veil so you may see."

touchstone]TB[32] [these are incomprehensible {things?} to some] WC [they]TB are the [simple and]TB first principles of [the gospel] WC/[truth]TB to know [for a certainty the character of God]TB that we may converse with him {the} [same]TB as [a]TB/[one]WC man [with another]WC and God himself the father [of us all]TB was once [as one of]WC/[like]TB us [was]WC/[dwelt]TB on an [earth] TBWW/[planet]WC [as Jesus was in the flesh]WC/[same as Jesus Christ himself]TB.[33]

I wish [I had the trump of an Archangel]TB/[I was in a suitable place to tell it]WW/[If I have the privilege]WC I could tell the story in such a manner [as]WC/[that pers{ecution} should]TB cease forever said Jesus mark it [Br.[34] Rigdon What did]WC Jesus [say]WC/[said] TB[35] as the Father hath power in himself [~~to do~~]TB even so hath the Son power to do what{?} [why]WC what the Father did [that answer is obvious in a manner]TB to lay down his body and take it up again. [Jesus what are you going to do– to lay down my life as my father did that I might take it up again]WC If you don't believe it you don't believe the Bible.[36] [the scripture says and]TB I defy all hell [all learning and wisdom and records of hell together]TB/[all the records and wisdom and all the combined powers of earth and hell]WC to refute it. [here then is Eternal life to know the only wise and true God]TB

---

32. JS's use of *touchstone* means something similar to "canon."

33. WW has "he [God] was once a man like us and the Father was once on an earth like us".

34. TS and RC have Elder. WC may read Er. instead of Br.

35. WR, TB, WW have "Jesus said. . . ."

36. Jn 5:19. WC has "If you deny it you deny the bible". GL1 gives a specific interpretation of John 5 that is quite close to JS's teaching in 1842. "we choose tabernacles for ourselves that we might be exalted equal with God himself and therefore, Jesus Christ spoke in this manner; I do as my Father before me did. Well what did the Father do? Why he went and took a body and went to redeem a world in the flesh and had power to lay down his life and to take it up again and this is the way we become heirs with God and joint heirs with Jesus Christ."

you have got to learn how to be a God yourself [in order to save yourself]WC [and]TB/[to]WC be [a K{ing} and ~~God~~ Priest to God]TB/[priests and kings]WC[37] as all [Gods]WC have done by going from a small [capacity]TBWW/[degree]WC to another from [grace to grace]TB/[exaltation to ex{altation}]WC [until the resurrection of]TB [of the dead]WW till they are able to dwell in everlasting burnings in everlasting power[38] [till they are able to sit in glory as doth those who sit enthroned]WC [as they who have gone before]TB [and]TB/[I want you to know while]WC [in the last days while certain individuals are]TB proclaim{ing}[39] [his name]TB [that he]WC is not trifling with [us]TB/[you or me]WC[40]

[I want you to know the]WW first principles [of this law]WW/[of consolation]WC how consoling to the mourner when they [are]TB called to part with a wife, father [mother, father, dear relative]TB [husband, child]WC friend to know that although [earthly tabernacles shall be dissolved]TB [their very being will rise]WR [to]WR/[and]WW dwell in everlasting burnings [in immortal glory to sorrow die nor suffer any more and not only that to contemplate the say-

37. Bullock originally wrote, "learn how to be a God yourself & be a K. & God" then canceled "God" and wrote "Priest to God." WW attests to something like this however: "learn to make yourselves God, king and priest." WR: "learn how to make yourselves Gods Kings. Prie{s}ts."

38. WR has "dwell in everlasting burning". WW has "dwelling in everlasting burnings". These readings are in a slightly different order from TB. WC has "sit in glory" but no mention of *everlasting burnings* (from Isa 33:14–17, see also Rev. 15:1–4; Rev. 4:6; D&C 137:2; Hel. 5:23; Ezk. 1:4).

39. WC used "ing", TB has "ed" to terminate proclaim.

40. "certain individuals" is likely a reference to a new group of Nauvoo dissenters who would shortly establish the True Church of Jesus Christ of Latter Day Saints and, on June 7, 1844, publish the *Nauvoo Expositor* exposing JS's polygamy and repeating a number of shocking passages from Follett among other critiques. Lyndon W. Cook, "William Law, Nauvoo Dissenter," 47–72. *Nauvoo Expositor*, 1, 2.

ing]WC they shall be heirs of God and joint heirs with Jesus Christ[41] [what is it{?}]WC to inherit the same glory powers [and]WC exaltation as those who are gone before. What did Jesus do{?} [Why]WC I do the things I saw the Father do [before]TB/[when]WC worlds came [rolling]TB into existence

I saw the Father work out his kingdom with fear and trembling and I [must]TB/[can]WC do the same [and]WC when I [get my kingdom]WC I will give/[present]WC [my kingdom]TB to the Father [and it will exalt his glory]WC [so that he obtains Kingdom rolling upon Kingdom so that]TB Jesus treads/[steps]WC in his tracks [as he had gone]TB/[to inherit what God did]WC before.[42] [It is plain beyond comprehension[43] and you thus learn]TB [this is some of]WC of the first principles of the gospel [about which so much hath been {said?}]WC[44] [You have got to find the beginning of this history and go on till you have learned the last]WC/[when you climb a ladder you must begin at the bottom run{g} until you learn the last principle of the gospel]TB[45] [will be a great while before you learn the last]WC/

41. Rom. 8:17.

42. WW reports the expansion of Jn 5 as, "he will take a higher exhaltation and I will take his place and am also exhalted". WR has "god is {glorified/gratified?} in salvation Exaltation – of his creations &c".

43. In TS, Bullock wrote "disputation" for "comprehension."

44. "about which so much hath been said"[TS] may reference previous sermons of the conference by Sidney Rigdon (a very long sermon) and Hyrum Smith. First principles is found in Rigdon in the context of his own history in the new religion, and in Smith's instructions for missionaries during earlier parts of the conference. JS himself had spent considerable energy since 1839 preaching on Hebrews 6:1–3, expanding a more commonly known list to faith, repentance, baptism by immersion, laying on of hands for the gift of the Holy Ghost, resurrection, and "eternal judgement." The latter largely referred to terrible sins like murder or "denial of the Holy Ghost" both discussed or mentioned in the Book of Mormon and the Bible.

45. GM1 (and hence RC) alters the source material to read, "When you climb a ladder you must begin at the bottom and *ascend step by step until you arrive at the*

[for it is a great thing to learn salvation]TB [after]WW/[beyond]TB the grave it is not all to be comprehended in this world.[46]

I suppose [that]WC I am not allowed to go into [an]WC investigation [but what is contained]TB/[of any thing that is not]WC in the Bible [and I think is]TB so many [learned and]WC wise men [who would put me to death for]TB treason [I shall turn commentator today]TB.[47]

I will go to the [first Hebrew word in]TB the Bible [make a comment on the very]WC first sentence [of the history of creation]WC. in the beginning Barosheit.[48] want to analyze the word—Be—in, by through, and everything else. Rosh—the head. when the inspired man wrote [it]TB he did not put [the Ba there but]WC [the first part to it a man]TB a Jew [without any authority thought it too bad to begin to talk about the head of any man]TB It read [in the first]WC—The head on of the Gods brought forth the Gods is the true meaning [of the word]TB[49] —[rosheet signifies to bring forth the Elohim]WC [if you do not believe it you do not believe the learned man of God—no man can tell you any more than I do thus]TB the Hed God brought

---

top, and so it is with the principles of the Gospel. you must begin with the first and go on until you learn all the last principle*s of exaltation but it* will be a great while *after you have passed through the tomb vail* before you *will have* learned *them*."

46. WW has "take a long time after the grave to understand the whole."

47. GL1 is a ripe example of a higher order content audit for this paragraph. It reads "For we are to go from glory to glory and as one is raised to a higher, so the next under him may take his degree and so to take the exaltation through the regular channel. When we get to where Jesus is, he will be just as far ahead of us again in exaltation." The phrases on treason and wise men are inverted in WC compared to TB.

48. TB, WW, and WC all give different spellings for this word. TB: Berosheat; WW: Barasheet; WC: Berosheit. Bullock selected WC's spelling for TS.

49. TS/GM1/RC add the word, Baurau (baw-raw) here. This does not reflect the sources at this point, however the word does appear later in multiple sources. See below.

forth the Gods in the grand council[50] [will simplify it in]WC/[I want to bring it to]TB the English language [Oh ye]TB lawyers [ye]TB Doctors[51] [who]WC/[that]WR have persecuted me I want you know that the Holy Ghost knows something [as well as you do—the Head God called together the Gods and set]TB in Grand Council. The Grand Counsellors set [in yonder heavens]WC and contemplated the creation of the world's [that was created at that time]WC.[52]

When I say [Doctor and]WC lawyer I mean [the Doctors and] WC lawyers of the scriptures. [I have done so hither to let the lawyers flutter and let everybody laugh at them.]TB Some learned doctor might [take a notion to]TB say thus and so [and we must believe the scriptures]WC/[and are not to be altered]TB [{I am} going to show you an error I have]TB an old book in the Latin Greek Hebrew and German [I have been reading the German: I]TB find it to be the most correct [that I have found and]TB it corresponds [the nearest to]TB/ [with]WC the revelations [that I have given]TB/[I have received]WC [the last 14 years]TB[53] It [tells]TB/[talks]WC about [Jachabod]TB/

50. TB has "head council."

51. GM1/RC adds, *and ye Priests!* "Priests" was a common term in Mormon discourse of the day for Protestant ministers—used in a generally derisive way. "Methodist priest" was a typical usage. Church missiology rarely singled out Catholics at the time. They seem relatively rare among Mormon contacts at the period of the sermon.

52. For some discussion of JS's Hebrew readings, see Lance S. Owens, "Joseph Smith and the Kabbalah: The Occult Connection," 180–81. Barney, "Joseph Smith's Emendation of Hebrew Genesis 1:1." Louis C. Zucker, "Joseph Smith as a Student of Hebrew." Huggins, "Joseph Smith and the First Verse of the Bible."

53. The book JS was referring to was a four column parallel (polyglot) of the New Testament printed in 1602. Elias Hutter, *Novum Testamentum harmonicum ebraice, graece, latine et germanice* (Nuremberg, 1602–1603), 2 vols. JS was reading from volume 1. JS likely borrowed it from his German/Hebrew tutor in Nauvoo, Alexander Neibaur. Owens, "Joseph Smith and the Kabbalah," 174, 177. An 1845 hand-colored lithograph by George Lloyd depicting JS with his arm raised in emphasis preaching

[Yachaubon the son of Zebedee]WC {it}means Jacob [in English]TB/ [The New Testament says]WC James [now if Jacob had the keys]WC you [may]TB/[might]WC talk about James [through all Eternity]TB [and never get the keys]WC [in the]TB 21 verse of the 4th chapter of Matthew [where it]TB gives [the word]WC/[the testimony that it is to]TB Jacob [instead of James]WC How can we escape the damnation of hell [without]TB/[unless]WC God [reveal to]TB/[be with] WC us. [Men bind us with chains]WC[54] [Latin says that Iachobus means Jacob]TV/[Latin Yacobus—Jacob too—]WC [(Read from the Hebrew)]WC/[Hebrew says]TB [Yingcacoub]WC [means]TB

---

with the polyglot is found on the dust cover of Glen M. Leonard, *Nauvoo: A Place of Peace, A People of Promise*. The Hutter polyglot is in evidence in JS's April 8, 1844 sermon and it is referenced again in JS's May 12, 1844 sermon. The image of Hutter's work in association with JS was strong enough that on August 19, 1844, Wilford Woodruff reported a dream about JS and the polyglot. (Kenney, *Wilford Woodruff's Journal*, 2:449. The German translation in Hutter was Martin Luther's, first published in 1522).

54. The charges circulating in Nauvoo that JS was a "fallen prophet" had their foundation largely in the secret practice of polygamy. Critics also found leverage in several of the ideas JS had been teaching in public, like the nature of God as it appears in the present sermon. JS's point in demonstrating a difference in the English and Latin, etc. was that a rigid adherence to the KJV text may bind people with false ideas. The Latin text for Mt 4:21 reads "et procedens inde vidit alios duos fratres Iacobum Zebedaei et Iohannem fratrem eius in nave cum Zebedaeo patre eorum-reficientes retia sua et vocavit eos." "Iacobum" translated as James. The Greek text reads Ἰάκωβος (Iakōbos). The descent of the name James from Jacob is somewhat parallel to Jesus from Joshua. The KJV translators appear to have used the Geneva bible here. Yacob (Hebrew Jacob)—the Greek has no 'y' and Yacob became Iakobos. In Latin this was rendered Iacobus. Centuries later this name had become vulgarized as Jacomus (Iacomus), which in French gave rise to James, a name transmitted by the Norman conquerors into English. Hence, James and Jacob are linked by a long passage from Hebrew through the Romance languages. JS would be correct in claiming that the equivalence of the names was not understood by common readers of the Bible. JS saw the opaqueness of the text to this equivalence as an error and one that seemed to deprive it of some power as a kind of charged object.

Jacob [Greek says ~~Jachem~~ Jacob German says Jacob]TB [thank God I have got this book and I thank him for the gift of the Holy Ghost] TB/[He has got the oldest book in the world—but he has got the oldest book in his heart]WC[55] [I have all 4 Testimonies come here ye learned men and read if you can. I]TB should not have [brought it up this word only to shew that I am right]TB/[introduced this testimony were it not to back up the word rosh—the head father of the Gods.] WC[56]

When we begin [to learn]TB/[in]WC this way we begin to [learn the only true]TB/[find out]WC God[57] [what kind a being we have got to worship]WC When we begin to know how to come to him he begins to [unfold the heavens]TB/[come]WC to us [and tell us all about it before our prayers get to his ears]TB [When we are ready to come to him he is ready to receive us.]WC[58]

[Now I ask all the]TB learned doctors [who hear me whether the learned men who are preaching salvation say that]TB God created the heavens and the earth out of nothing. [They account it blasphemy to contradict the idea]WC They [will call]WC/[think]TB you a fool—[You ask them why they say 'don't the Bible say he created the world' and they infer that it must be out of nothing.]WC[59] [and the reason is that they are unlearned and I]TB know more than the world [and

---

55. WC shifts to the third person for this phrase. GM1 adds, "even the gift of the Holy Ghost."

56. GM1/RC add text from WR and WW together with some unwitnessed text: [In the beginning the head of the Gods called a council of the Gods and]WR *they* [came together and concocted a plan]WW [to create the world]WR *and people it*.

57. Jn 17:1.

58. The attempts to discuss translation of biblical passages were the most difficult for the auditors. The divergence of the audits suggests that the auditors were becoming fatigued and possible ambient noise made accuracy more challenging.

59. GM1/RC expands this portion of the sermon: "You ask *the learned doctors* why they say *the world was made out of nothing? and they will answer* 'don't the bible say he created it the world? and they infer *from the word create that* it must *have been*

if the Holy Ghost in me comprehends more than all the world]TB I will associate [myself]WW with it. [The word create came from the word Barau—]WC it means to organize, same as [you]TB/[man]WC would [organize]TB/[use to build]WC a ship—[hence we infer that] WC God himself had materials to organize the world out of chaos—chaotic matter [which is]TB element[60] [and in which dwells all the glory]TB [—element had an existence from the time he had. The pure pure principles of element are principles]WC that [nothing can destroy they never have an ending they coexist eternally]TB/[never can be destroyed—they may be organized—and reorganized—but not destroyed.]WC[61]

---

made out of nothing. *Now* the word create came from the baurau, *which does not mean to create out of nothing*."

60. JS likely means the smallest unit of any given material thing: we might think, an atom, though the notion of atom was not scientifically accepted until Einstein—the smallest part of something that still preserved its identity. The word element was also used to describe "air." "Chaotic matter" was defined at the time as a "confused mass, in which matter is supposed to have existed, before it was separated into its different kinds and reduced to order by the creating power of God," Noah Webster, 1828. Plato, in the *Timaeus*, set the primordial state of the world as uncreated matter in a state of chaos. Platonism may have entered JS's thought through literature of the time, see Stephen Joseph Fleming, "The Fulness of the Gospel: Christian Platonism and the Origins of Mormonism." The Book of Mormon, 2 Ne. 2:11–13 appears to rely on both the idea that the creative act leads out of chaos and that passing from existence to nothingness is paradoxical. Charles Buck's *A Theological Dictionary*, a work JS used with some frequency, has several relevant entries. Buck (page 126) wrote, "CHAOS, the mass of matter supposed to be in confusion before it was divided by the Almighty into its proper classes and elements. It does not appear who first asserted the notion of a chaos. Moses, the earliest of all writers, derives the origin of this world from a confusion of matter . . . Moses goes no farther than the chaos, nor tells us whence its confused state; and where Moses stops, there precisely do all the rest." Under the entry for "Creation" (page 190) Buck notes the controversy over creation and frames the discussion in a way that suggests JS's argument.

61. John Corrill, an important figure in pre-Nauvoo Mormonism, wrote a short history of the movement after his departure from it. He noted that, "They believe

[I have]TB another subject[62] [to dwell on and it is impossible for me to say much but to touch upon them—for time will not permit me to say all]TB [so I must come to]TB/[It is associated with the subject in question.]WC the resurrection of the dead. The soul—the mind of man [the immortal spirit]TB [Doctors of Divinity]WW/[all men] WC say God created [it]WC in the beginning. The [very]TB idea lessens man in my [idea]TB/[estimation]WC. [I]TB don't believe the doctrine [hear it all ye ends of the world for]TB [I]WW know better God has told me so [I am going to tell of things more noble]TB [If you don't believe it, it won't make the truth without effect]WW/[Make a man appear a fool before he gets through, if he don't believe it.]WC We say that God himself was [a]TB self-existent [God]TB, who told you so? [It's]WC correct enough [but]WC how did it get into your heads—who told you that man did not exists [in like manner]TB/[upon the same principle]WC [(refers to the bible)]WC [how doest it read in the]TB/[Don't say so in the old]WC Hebrew—God made

that matter is eternal, and that nothing of all God's works will ever be destroyed or lost; but in the end all things will be restored to their proper place, and the sons of perdition alone will endure the lowest hell, or lake of fire and brimstone." John Corrill, *History of the Church of Christ*, 47. A facsimile of Corrill's work is found in *JSP*, H2:120–201.

62. The thought order here may be that the comment about a subject being associated with the resurrection of the dead applied to the idea of element being eternal, rather than the next subject of the speech. WC suggests this, although TB and WW do not. However, WC's ordering appears more appealing. TS follows TB but seems even more disjointed. TS: "I have another subject to dwell upon and it is impossible for me to say much, but I shall just touch upon them; for time will not permit me to say all; so I must come to the resurrection of the dead, the soul, the mind of man". WC: "organized and reorganized–but not destroyed. It is associated with the subject in question the resurrection of the dead[.] Another subject–the soul–the mind of man–they say God created it in the beginning".

man [out of the earth]WC and put into [it Adam's]TB/[him his]WC spirit and [so]TB became a living [spirit]TB/[body]WC[63]

The mind of man—the mind of man [the intelligent part]WC [is as immortal as]TB coequal with, God himself [I know that my testimony is true]WC hence [while]TB/[when]WC I talk to these mourners [what have they lost—]WC They are only separated from their bodies for a short [period]TB/[season]WC [but]WC their spirits existed coequal with God [and they now exist in a place where they]WC converse [as much]WC/[same]TB as we do on the earth. [does not this give you satisfaction I want to reason more on the Spirit of Man for]TB I am dwelling [on the body of man on the subject of the dead]TB/[on the immutability of the spirit of man]WW.

Is it logic to say [that a spirit is immortal and yet have a beginning{?} because if a spirit have a beginning it will have an end—good logic—illustrated by his ring]WC [if man had a beginning he must have an end]WR [It does not have a beginning or end,]WW[64]

[I take]TB my ring [from my finger and]TB liken [it unto the mind]TB of man, [the immortal spirit because]TB it has no beginning [or end]WW.[65] [Suppose you]TB cut it into [but as the Lord

---

63. WW reads, "Human soul." A distinction between human and animal souls seems to exist in the text.

64. William Patterson McIntire journal, March 28, 1841: "[JS] says the spirit or the intelligence of men are self Existent principles he before the foundation this Earth–& quotes the Lords question to Job 'where wast thou when I laid the foundation of the Earth' Evidence that Job was in Existing somewhere at that time he says God is Good & all his acts is for the benifit of infereir [inferior] intelligences– God saw that those inteligences had Not power to Defend themselves against those that had a tabernicle therefore the Lord Calls them togather in Counsel & agrees to form them tabernicles so that he might Gender the Spirit & the tabernicle togather so as to create sympathy for their fellowman—".

65. Mormon collector Buddy Youngreen suggested that the ring used in the sermon was one handed down by Emma Smith to her son Alexander Hale Smith and thence to Glaud Leslie Smith, a great-grandson of JS. Youngreen, also a JS descen-

lives]TB there would be an end all the fools [learned]WC and wise men [from the beginning of creation]TB [who say]TB/[that comes and tells]WC that man had a beginning [proves that he]WC must have an end [and if that doctrine is true]WC then the doctrine of annihilation [would be]TB/[is]WC true.

But if I am right I might [with]TB boldness proclaim [from the house top]TB that God never had power to create the spirit of man at all. God himself could not create himself. Intelligence exists upon a self-existent principle [it]TB is a spirit from age to age and [there is]TB no creation about it—[the first principles of man are self exist{ent} with God]TB—All minds and spirits God ever sent into [the]WR/[this]WC world are susceptible of enlargement.

That God himself finds himself in the midst of spirit{s}[66] and [glory]WC because he [was greater]WC saw proper to institute laws [for those who were in less intelligence]TB/[to instruct the weaker intelligences]WW[67] [that they might have one glory upon another

dant, purchased the ring from Glaud Smith prior to his death in 1986. (*Ensign* 13, no. 1 (1984): 32.)

66. For the plural, see TB and WW.

67. Compare the McIntire journal entry in the note above. For JS, the nature of divine grace in human life is modeled in this scheme of adoption/instruction. It is one aspect of a mechanical anti-Calvinist scheme. God makes laws for progress, humankind must conform to the procedures (ordinances) to be "saved"—that is, to experience deification. At least part of that theme is still present in church teachings. See below. The previous two topics of the sermon, the nature of God and the nature of man, come together in these statements from TB/WW. It is attested in the Clayton audit as well. This may be thought of as an interpretation of the Book of Abraham 3:21b, 22, 23. The organization referred to in Abraham 3:21 is the political/family one explained here and in Abraham 3:22–23. In an earlier sermon, JS is reported as saying, "The Father called all spirits before him at the creation of Man and organized them" (Willard Richards, "Pocket Companion," July 1839.) "At the first organization in heaven we were all present and saw the Savior chosen and appointed and the plan of salvation made and we sanctioned it." (William Clayton's Private Book, January 5, 1841.) "He who rules in the heavens when he has a certain

in all that knowledge power and glory and so took in hand to save the world of spirits]TB/[whereby the rest could have a privilege to advance like himself]WC [you say honey is sweet and so do I]TB I can [also]TB taste the [principle]WW/[spirit]TB of eternal life [I know it is good and]TB/[This is good doctrine, it tastes good]WW[68] when I tell you these words of eternal life that were given to me by [inspiration of the Holy Spirit]TB/[the revelations of Jesus Christ]WW and I know you believe it [you are bound to receive it as sweet and I rejoice more and more.]TB

[Wants to talk more about]WC Man's relation to God [I will open your eyes]TB in relation to your dead. All things [whatsoever]WC/[which]TB God [of his infinite reason]TB has seen fit and proper to reveal to us while dwelling in mortality [in regard to our mortal bodies]TB are revealed to us [in the abstract and independent of affinity of this mortal tabernacle but they]WC are revealed to us as though we had no bodies [at all]WC Hence the responsibility, the awful responsibility that rests upon us [for]TB/[in relation to]WC our dead.[69] For all [the]TB spirits [who have not obeyed the gospel in the flesh]WC must [either]TB obey the gospel or be damned. [Solemn thought, dreadful thought]TB Is there [nothing to be done for those]TB/[no preparation—no salvation for our fathers and friends]WC who have [gone before us without obeying]TB/[died and not obeyed]WC the decrees of [God]TB/[the son of man{?}]WC Would to God I had 40 days and nights [to tell you all to]TB/[I would]WC let you know that I am not a fallen prophet. What kind of [characters are those who]

---

work to do calls the Spirits before him to organize them. they present themselves and offer their Services—" (Martha Coray notebook, May 21, 1843.) The idea that God invites souls to follow him is the New Testament paradigm.

68. One of the more commonly quoted phrases of RC. Whether JS used the words here is of course unknown but they do seem to allude to Ps. 119:103.

69. This is JS's justification for proxy rituals for the dead. The rules apply to all, embodied or not.

TB/[beings]WC can be saved although their bodies are [decaying in the grave]TB/[moldering in the dust]WC[70]

The greatest responsibility [that God has]TB laid upon us in this [life]WW/[world]WC is to seek after our dead. [the apostle says]TB/[Paul said]WW they without us cannot be made perfect [now I am speaking of them I say to you Paul you cannot be perfect without us—those that are gone before and]TB[71] those who come after [must be made perfect and God has made it obligatory to man—and]TB/[should have salvation in common with us—and thus had God laid this upon the men of the world]WC Hence the saying of Elijah.[72] [God said he shall send Elijah &c]TB[73]

---

70. WR: all things God has seen fit proper to reveal while dwelling in mortality, are revealed. precisely the same as though we were destitute of bodies.—what will save our spirits will save our bodies.

71. WW inserts, "cannot be made perfect without us. for it is necessary that the seals are in our hands to seal our children & our dead for the fullness of the dispensation of times. A dispensation to meet the promises made by Jesus Christ befor the foundation of the world for the salvation of man." Compare audits of JS's sermons of June 11, 1843, August 13, 1843, October 5, 1840.

72. Clearly a reference to the saying of Malachi 4.

73. The idea that Elijah would return informed much of JS's later thinking and a number of his sermons were linked to it. He notes in his 1839 history that in a vision the angel Moroni quoted the Malachi passage to him in the visions of the night in September 1823. The Moroni version differs from the KJV Bible:

Authorized Version Malichi chapter 4

Moroni (From Ms History Book A-1 p. 5–6.)

4:5 Behold, I will send you Elijah the prophet before the coming of the great and dreadful day of the LORD: 4:6 And he shall turn the heart of the fathers to the children, and the heart of the children to their fathers, lest I come and smite the earth with a curse.

And again he quoted the fifth verse thus, "Behold I will reveal unto you the Priesthood by the hand of Elijah the prophet before the coming of the great and dreadful day of the Lord." He also quoted the next verse differently, "And he shall plant in the hearts of the Children the promises made to the fathers, and the hearts

[I have a declaration to make as]TB to the provisions [which]TB God [hath]WC made [from]TB before the [foundation of]TB the world What has Jesus said. All sins and all blasphemies every transgression [that man may be guilty of]TB [except one]WC there is a provision [either in this world]WC or in the world to come. [Hence God hath made a provision that]WC every spirit in the eternal world

---

of the children shall turn to their fathers, if it were not so the whole earth would be utterly wasted at his coming."

The differences may have seemed enigmatic to a young JS (assuming that he recalled them accurately fifteen years later). Modern Latter-day Saints point to the vision of April 3, 1836 as a fulfillment of this promise as in Doctrine and Covenants Section 110. JS and Oliver Cowdery, who were designated as receiving this visit of Elijah (and other figures), apparently never discussed it in public. One or both dictated the experience to Warren A. Cowdery (brother to Oliver) who wrote it in the third person as the final entry in JS's journal for that year. There is little contemporary evidence that anyone including the two Cowderys, and JS thought of the vision as any sort of "sealing" text. In 1836, William W. Phelps mentioned the vision very briefly in a letter to his wife, then living in Missouri. Phelps apparently saw the vision as one of many warnings that the Second Coming of Christ was "near, even at the doors." Whether Phelps was privy to the diary entry at the time Warren Cowdery penned it is unclear. Much later (1851), Phelps told Brigham Young and others that "I was there when Joseph received the keys" in reference to the 1836 vision. At the time (1836) however, it seems clear that no one understood the vision in terms that heralded the notion of marriage or generational parent-child sealings. Whatever the case, the vision was not shared widely among the Latter-day Saints after it was penned. Oliver Cowdery does not mention it in his final testimony regarding restored ancient authority, and JS omits Elijah from his list of heavenly messengers in his 1842 letter found in D&C 128. Willard Richards knew of the JS diary report of the vision since he copied the journal entry into the ms history of the church. The first mention in the press does not occur until the ground-breaking August 1852 polygamy discourse of Orson Pratt (*Journal of Discourses* 1:58, *Deseret News Extra*, September 14, 1852). The revelation was first published in full in the November 6, 1852 issue of the Deseret News as part of the history of JS. (On Phelps' letter to his wife in April 1836 see Papers of William Wines Phelps, LTPSC; On the vision, see Bushman, *Rough Stone Rolling*, 320. On Phelps claiming to be "there" at the vision, see Thomas Bullock, booklet #10, February 2, 1851.)

can be ferreted out [and saved unless he has committed that sin which can't be remitted to him—that God has wrought out]TB salvation for all men [unless they have]TB committed a certain sin [a friend who]TB/[Every man who]WC has a friend in the [eternal]WC world can save him [unless he]TB has committed the unpardonable sin [and so you see how far you can be a Savior]TB. A man cannot commit the unpardonable sin after the dissolution of the body and there is a way possible for escape. [not particularly d–d{damned?} those that are without wisdom until they get exalted to wisdom]TB Knowledge saves a man [and in the world of spirits a man can't be exalted but by knowledge]WC So long as a man will not [give heed to the commandments he must abide without salvation]WC [If he has been guilty of great sins, he is punished for it[WW] [when he consents to obey the gospel whether Alive or dead, he is saved]WW/[No way for a man to come to understanding but give his consent to the commandment] WR

[a sinner has]TB his own mind [and is in his own condemner] TB/[A man is his own torment]WC [Damned by mortification]WR/ [his own mind damns him]WW [hence the saying they shall go into the]WC lake [that burns with]WC fire and brimstone as exquisite as a lake burning with fire and brimstone [so is the torment of a man]WC [I have no fear of hell fire that dont exhist]WW [I know the scriptures I understand them]TB [I said]WC no man can commit the unpardonable sin after the dissolution of the body Hence the salvation [of Jesus Christ]TB/[that the saviour]WC[74] wrought out for [all men to triumph over the devil for he stood up for a Savior]TB/[the salvation of a man]WC [if it did not catch him in one place it would another]

74. WW adds a slight twist on this passage. "No man can commit the unpardonable sin untill he receives the Holy Ghost."

WC[75] [The contention in heaven was]WC/[Jesus contended that] TB there [were]WC/[would be]TB certain [souls that]TB/[man] WC [would be condemned]TB/[would not be saved]WC the devil said he could save them [all. As the grand council gave in for Jesus Christ]TB [so the devil fell and all who put up their hands for him] TB/[he rebelled against God and was thrust down]WC [all sin shall be forgiven except the sin against the Holy Ghost]TB [After a man has sinned the sin against the Holy Spirit there is no repentance for him]WC [What must a man do to commit the unpardonable sin they must receive the Holy Ghost have the heavens opened unto them, and know God, and then sin against him]WW [from that time they begin to be enemies like many of the apostates of the Church of J. C. of L.D.S.—when a man begins to be an enemy he hunts him—for he has got the same Spirit that they had who crucified the Lord of life—the same Spirit that Sin against the Holy Ghost]TB/[Hence like many of the apostates of the C of J. C. L.D.S. they go to far the spirit leaves them hence they seek to kill me they thirst for my blood—they never cease—he has got the same spirit that crucified Jesus. You can't renew them to repentance—awful is the consequence]WC[76]

---

75. WR's audit evokes ideas from JS's July 12, 1843 revelation on plural marriage. "Must commit the unpardonable sin in this world. {otherwise he} will suffer in the eternal world until he will be exalted.– work of the devil. the plans the devil laid to save the world. - Devil said he could save them all - Lot fell on Jesus. = - - - All sin &c forgiven except the sin against the Holy Ghost. - Got to deny the plan of salvation . &c. with his eyes open. - Like many of the apostates of Christ of the Church of Jesus Christ of lat Days."

76. WW: "they make open war like the Devil." GL1 reports this section as, "But those who die without the obedience of the gospel here will have to obey it in the world of spirits for so long as they do not obey they will be miserable and as if they were in torment of fire and brimstone. Thus is the signification of torment . . . But Satan, or Lucifer, being the next heir and had allotted to him great power and authority even prince of power of the air. He spake immediately and boasted of himself saying send me I can save all and [he] sinned against the Holy Ghost because

I advise all to be careful what [you do]TB Stay [do not give way] TB/[all that hear]WW you may find [that some one has laid a snare for you]TB/[by and by find out that you have been deceived]WC [be cautious—await—]TB/[dont make any hasty moves you may be saved]WW [when you find a Spirit wants bloodshed murder same is not of God but is of the devil]TB [if a spirit of Bitterness is in you, dont be in haste, say you that man is a sinner, well, if he repents he shall be forgiven.]WW [out of the abundance of the heart man speaks]TB [the man that tells you words of life is the man that can save you—]TB/[Best man brings forth best works]WR. [I warn you against all evil characters, who sin against the Holy Ghost for there is no redemption for them in this world nor in the world nor in the world to come]TB

[I can enter into the mysteries. I can enter largely into the eternal worlds]TB/[I could go back and trace every subject of interest concerning the relationship of man to God]WW [if I had time for Jesus said In my Fars. mansion there are many mansions &c]WW [There is one glory of the moon Sun and Stars &c.]TB [their is many mansions in my father's kingdom what have we to console us in relation to our dead.]WW we have the [reason to have the greatest hope and consoln. for our dead—]TB/[greatest hope in relation to our dead of any people on earth]WW [for we have aided them to the 1st princ for] TB we have seen them walk [in the the midst and sink asleep[77] in the arms of J]TB/[worthy on the earth and]WW [those who have died in the faith are now in the selestial kingdom of God]WW/[and hence is

he accused his brethren and was hurled from the counsel for striving to break the law immediately. There was a warfare with Satan and the gods and they hurled Satan out of his place and all them that would not keep the sayings of the council. But he himself being one of the councilors would not keep the first estate for he was one of the sons of perdition and consequently all the sons of perdition become devils."

77. See Willard Richards' audit of JS's sermon delivered April 16, 1843.

the glory of the Sun]TB [—you mourners have occn. to rejoice[78] for your husband]TB [has gone to wait unto the res{urrection} and your expn. {expectation} and hope are far above what man can conceive] TB/[they have gone to await the resurrection of the dead, to go to celestial glory]WW [God has revealed to us]TB while [worlds must wait myriads of]WR/[there is many who die who will have to wait many]WW years [before they can receive the like blessings]WR

[But]WW I am authorized to say [and by the authority of the Holy Ghost]TB/[to you my friends in the name of the Lord]WW [that you have no occasn. to fear]TB [for he is gone to the home of the just—]TB/[that you may wait for your friends to come forth to meet you in eternity in the morn of the celestial world]WW [don't mourn don't weep I know it by the test{imony} of the H. G. that is within me—rejoice O Israel—]TB [your friends]TB/[those saints who have been murdered in the persecution]WW shall triumph gloriously while their murderers shall [welter for years—]TB/[dwell in torment untill they pay the utmost farthing[79]]WW [I say for the benefit of strangers]TB I have a Father, Brothers, [Friends]TB [children] WW that are gone [they are absent]TB for a moment— [the time will soon be gone, the trump will soon be blown]WW [they are in the Spirit {world?} then shall we hail our Mothers, Fathers, Friends and all no fear of mobs—&c but all one]TB Eternity of felicity—[80]

78. RC adds "(speaking of the death of Elder King Follett)".

79. Mt 5:26.

80. RC adds some additional text, "They are *only* absent for a moment; they are in the spirit, *and we shall* soon meet *again;* the time will soon *arrive when* the trump*et shall sound. When we depart* we shall hail our mothers, fathers, friends, and all *whom we love who have fallen asleep in Jesus. There will be* no fear of mobs, *persecutions, or malicious law-suits and arrests;* but *it will be an* eternity of felicity."

[A question.][81]WW Shall mothers have [their]WR children Yes. [they shall have it without price.]WR [for their]TB [debt]TB/[redemption]WR is paid [there is no damnation awaits them for they are in the Spirits]TB [as the Child dies]TB/[But as it falls so]WW so shall it rise [from the dead]TB [It will never grow]WW [and be living in the burning of God]TB [—it shall be as it was before]TB/[It will be in its precise form as]WW it died out of your arms [Children dwell and exercise power in the same form as they laid them down]TB/[Eternity is full of thrones upon which dwell thousands of children]WW [reigning on thrones of glory not one cubit added to their stature.]WW [thrones upon thrones. Dominion upon dominion just as you]WR

[I will]TB Leave this subject [here and make a few remarks upon Baptism]TB [Bless those who have lost friends.]WR [The]TB Baptism of Water [without the]TB Baptism of Fire and [the]TB Holy Ghost [attending it are necessary]TB/[are inseparably connected]WR [he must be born of water and spirit to get into the Kingdom of God]TB [and in the German text bears me out]TB/[found in the German Bible to prove]WR [same as the revelations which I have given for the 14 years—]TB/[what I have taught for 14 years about baptism.]WR [I have the test{imony} to put in their teeth—that my test{imony} has been true all the time. You will find it in the declaration of John the Baptist (reads from the German) John says]TB I baptize you with Water but when Jesus comes who [has the power]TB/[having the keys]WR he shall administer the baptism of Fire and the Holy Ghost. [Great God, now where is all the Sectarian world.]TB [and if this testimony is true they are all damned]TB/[Many talk of any baptism not being essential to salvation, but this would lay the foundation of their damnation]WW [as clearly as any Anathema ever

81. WC ends the sermon here with the notice, "He continued his discourse—& told of parents receiving their children—concluded his remarks by Baptism"

was—I know the text is true—I call upon all {Germans?} to say I {aye} —(shouts of I {aye}) Alex Campbell[82]—how are you going to save them with water—for]TB John said his baptism was nothing without the baptism of Jesus Christ. [One God, Father, Jesus, hope of our calling, one baptism—all three baptisms make one]TB/[Leaving the principles of doctrine of baptism &c[83]—one god, one baptism, & one baptism—I.E. all three]WR[84] [I have the truth and I am at the defiance of the world to contradict. I have preached Latin Hebrew Greek German and I have fulfilled all I am not so big a fool as many have taken me for—the Germans know that I read the German correct—Hear it all ye Ends of the Earth—[all ye sinners Repent Repent—turn to God for your religion won't save you and]TB/[called upon all

---

82. Long-time critic of JS and well known restorationist Alexander Campbell, argued for water baptism only. For example, see Campbell's debate with John Thomas, *Millennial Harbinger* (Feb. 1836).

83. GM1/RC alters this text and adds more. "Therefore *not* leaving the principles of *the* doctrine *of Christ, let us got on unto perfection; not laying again the foundation of repentance from dead works, and of faith toward God, of the doctrine of baptisms, and of laying on of hands, and of resurrection of the dead, and of eternal judgment. And this will we do, if God permit. (Heb 6 chap 1st. to 3r. v.).*" The insertion of *not* follows JS's revison of the Bible.

84. The GL1 content audit has a long summary of the sermon to this point, "Jesus Christ being the greater light or of more intelligence, for he loved righteousness and hated iniquity, he being the Elder Brother presented himself for to come and redeem this world as it was his right by inheritance. He stated he could save all those who did not sin against the Holy Ghost and they would obey the code of laws that were given. But their circumstances were that all who would sin against the Holy Ghost should have no forgiveness neither in this world or in the world to come, for they strove against light and knowledge after they tasted of the good things of the world to come. They should not have any forgiveness in the world to come because they had a knowledge of the things of the world to come and were not willing to abide of the laws of the world to come. Therefore they can have no forgiveness there, but must be most miserable of all and never can be renewed again (referred to Hebrews Ch. 6)."

men Priests and all to repent and obey the gospel—]WR [ye will be damned but I do not say how along {long?}]TB/[if they do not, they will be damned.—]WR

[There has also been remarks made concerning all men being redeemed from Hell]WW[85] [but]TB those who [Sin against the Holy Ghost cannot be forgiven in this world or in the world to come but they shall die the 2nd death—[86]]TB/[commit the unpardonable sin are doomed to Gnaolom[87] {Eternity?} with out end]WR [but as they concoct scenes of bloodshed in this world so they shall rise to that resurrection which is as the lake of fire and brimstone—some shall rise to the]TB [everlasting burning of God]TB/[God dwells in everlasting burnings]WR [and some shall rise to the damnation of their own filthiness—same as the lake of fire and brimstone—I have intended my remarks to all—to all rich and poor bond and free great and small I have no enmity against any man. I love you all[88]—I am their best friend and if persons miss their mark it is their own fault—if I reprove a man and he hate me he is a fool—for I love all men especially these

85. It is not clear whether JS is referring to earlier conference addresses or to belief systems like Universalism which claimed that even Satan would be redeemed, finally.

86. WW has, "But I say any man who commits the unpardonable sin must dwell in hell worlds without end."

87. WR inserts a Hebrew word JS used in his initial publication of the Book of Abraham. Richards was scribe for the printer's manuscript of the Book of Abraham as it appeared in the *Times and Seasons* of March 1, March 15, and May 1, 1842. Whether JS used the word or Richards inserted the word in his audit as a summary term is difficult to know. The spelling is like that used in JS's Hebrew instruction materials from his early 1836 work in studying biblical Hebrew.

88. WR has, "Love all men but hate your deeds." GM1/RC expanded this as "I love you all, but I hate some of your deeds".

my brethren and sisters—I rejoice in hearing the test{imony} of my aged friend—]TB[89]

[You never knew my heart. No man knows my history[90]—I can not do it. I shall never undertake—]TB/[You don't know me—you never will I don't blame you for not believing my history.]WR [if I had not experienced what I have I should not have known it myself—] TB/[Had I not experienced it, I could not believe it myself]WR [I

89. This is a reference to Sidney Rigdon's long speeches over the previous two days. Rigdon was 52 at the time, so calling him "aged" may have been overdoing it. Rigdon was in ill health, and could not speak for an extended period without rest; he had basically been silent in the public outdoor services since 1839. Rigdon's remarks may have been directed toward the practice of plural marriage to some degree, since he emphasized living well within the laws of the country. He went on to rehearse "the vision" and the tar and feathering incident in Hiram, Ohio in the early years (1832). Rigdon spent some time in his conference remarks excusing the practice of "secret meetings." He probably meant the nascent kingdom of God/Council of Fifty organization then in the making as well as some of the endowment instruction, the latter tradition he partially continued in his own church in later years. When Follett was first published, however, JS was dead, and there was a struggle over leadership in the church. Rigdon was claiming the "guardianship" of the church, the apostles led by Brigham Young claimed the keys for temple ordinances—and the First Presidency—while other individuals claimed revelation appointing them as succeeding prophet. In the midst of this turmoil, any reference by the church press to JS's goodwill toward Rigdon may have seemed dangerous to the editors who were in favor of the twelve apostles as successors. Perhaps this is why Bullock or John Taylor edited TS to read, "I rejoice in hearing the testimony of my aged *friends*." By the time of Follett, Rigdon had largely become a figurehead; records show him to have shrinking involvement in internal church affairs. Second Counselor William Law was out of the church; apostle Amasa Lyman, who had replaced Orson Pratt during his temporary disaffection over polygamy and his wife's seduction, was suggested by JS as an extra counselor in the presidency to make room for the returning Pratt though Lyman never actually functioned as JS's counselor. For Rigdon's April 1844 speeches, see General Church Minutes, April 5, 6, 1844.

90. The phrase the late Fawn M. Brodie used to title her widely known biography of JS, *No Man Knows My History*. See the end of §1.1.

never did harm any man since I have been born in the world—my voice is always for peace—I cannot lie down until my work is finished—I never think evil nor think any thing to the harm of my fellow man—and when I am called at the trump and weighed in the balance you will know me then—I add no more God bless you. {A}men—The choir sung an hymn at ½ p 5.]TB

APPENDIX B

Reference Material for Chapter 3

§B.1 Arthur MacDermott, Letter to Dr. James E. Talmage

Spelling and punctuation preserved from the original.

[This letter was found in the files of B. H. Roberts, CHL, and was labeled, COPY. The letter was labeled with the date of November 1906.]

Dr. James E. Talmage
Salt Lake City,
Utah

Dear Brother:

You will probably remember our interesting conversation of last August in St. Thomas, on the subject of my letter to you of about one year ago—The eternal existence of the individual intelligences or spirits of men—and which you at the time of receiving, on account of press of S. S. work, turned over to the YMMIA Board for consideration and reply.

In our conversation you told me that if I did not get a reply from Brother B. H. Roberts (who you expected would be asked to reply) or from the Board, to communicate with you again on the subject.

I have been waiting now for more than 13 months for a reply to the letter I wrote to Pres. Jos. F. Smith inquiring about this subject, and I have no reply. Also the same doctrine is reiterated in this year's manual, and questions are made from the 3rd volume of the "History of the Church" (I have only seen Vol. I, and am unable to purchase the work at present, or "Roberts Mormon Doctrine of Deity" which is also quoted freely in the same connection) which are strained into props for the doctrine. Also it is asserted in a quotation from Roberts "Mormon Doctrine of Deity" that this doctrine is the accepted doctrine of the Church.

If you will examine the new Manual, Lesson VI-B the Godhead, and C, the Father hood of God (pages 57 and 58 and No. 10 of the review questions you will see that the pre-existence of the spirits of man is now extended back beyond the "beginning" that is so often spoken of in the revelation of God, and the doctrine that we are co-eternal with the Father is specifically taught.

If this is indeed the truth, then some such explanation as Prof. Nelson gives in his work <u>Scientific Aspects of Mormonism</u> will be necessary to satisfy any inquiring mind. For it will surely voice the question in the mind of any thinking person "How is it we are so far behind in the order of eternal progression if we have had all eternity in which to make progress? If we have had as long as God the Father and started from the same place of intelligence as He did?

Prof. Nelson redicules the Hindoo idea that for 15,000,000 years the supreme God is awake. . . . [ellipsis in original]

Our God was with them and in the same state and condition of inert knowledge and power to change conditions and each was (relatively) omnipotent, and so continued until each, of its own free will, concluded to progress by obeying law, and so becoming born of the

Heavenly Parents and starting on the road of progression—seems to me just as hard to accept.

I think it must lead to the idea that the number of intelligences that could eventually become (by the exercise of their dormant free agency) human beings, must be limited—That is—all that can ever come into existence as human beings, already exist and have always existed, and when they have all concluded (if they have not already done so) to progress by obeying law, then there will be an end to "creation" to the works (New works) of God.

It may lead to the idea that only one person from each world could ever attain to Godhood; as the idea that the Father has passed through just such actual experiences as we have to pass through, and that a large number of the inhabitants of the world in which He gained his experience attained to a similar exaltation, would seem difficult of conception, in connection with the idea that a few hundred million had, after an eternity of inaction, concluded to commence a life of progression all about the same period, or near enough the same period to all the present in their first estate of progression at a council in heaven for providing ways and means for their further progress.

I remember that one writer in the ERA of about a year ago said that he considered the fact that we were eternal—co-eternal with the Father—the most glorious thing connected with the Gospel! It seems to me we should be ashamed, if indeed it is a fact, to think that we had wasted an eternity before making any effort to start upward in the scale of intelligence—for if we had not, we might be nearer to what God is now.

The doctrine of Eternal progress must be modified to a parallel of what most of us have heretofore been believing of man—viz. that progress commenced some time in the past and will continue without end—for those at least who attain to the high order of salvation, if not to all who attain to any degree of salvation. But this will refute the principle axiom that Brother Roberts and Prof. Nelson rely on for the very foundation of their theory—That anything that will have no end, could have had no beginning.

I don't know how the fact that our mortal bodies which most certainly had a beginning as bodies, will be made immortal and have (no) end as bodies, can be made to harmonize with this axiom. (I believe this was said by the Prophet Joseph Smith all illustrated by a ring, but I doubt if the application is correct.)

If the solution of this question of the eternity of the lives or intelligences of the human family is as we reasoned it out in our discussion (in St. Thomas), that the life of the parent is imparted to the offspring, and that while it is still a part of the same life or spirit of the parent, and as such did not have a beginning at the time of birth, yet as a separate individual it did have a beginning at the time of birth or conception, is the correct one, we have a solution both reasonable and more in accordance with the apparent plain meaning of many passages of both ancient and modern scriptures.

In order to verify the claim that the hymn "O My Father" was inspired (and I have often this statement made by those in responsible positions in the Chruch we must understand that, as in the formation of the human body, two individuals of (in certain respects) opposite, or complementary qualifications (sex) is absolutely necessary. If we believe in the eternal increase that the faithful are promised, we can hardly accept the theory that the spiritual children promised are already existent, and independent of our salvation as they would in justice have to be.

I should like to hear something from the one who has a right to receive revelation for the Church on this. I think it would be right for us to receive this knowledge from him in place of either Elder Roberts or Prof. Nelson, or anyone else.

We have utterances by the Prophet John Taylor that would be conclusive if it were not for the interpretation of the "no end—no

Beginning" axiom, of these two elders, Though I suppose the same question would have arisen some time.

But an explanation of this subject since it has arisen it seems to me should come from the only one who has the right to receive and disseminate doctrine for the Church.

I understand from Brother Ellis Turnbaugh, our School teacher in Overton, that Orson Pratt's work "The Seer" treats of the subject but that it was suppressed, not as being incorrect, but as being before the time when the doctrine or information it contained was necessary or advisable for the body of the Church. Can you tell me where I can borrow or procure this work? I am informed there are a few copies extant.

I wish that the new year may bring you and yours all the blessings that you can contain, and remain,

Your Brother in the Gospel,
L. MacDermott

§B2. James E. Talmage,
Letter to President Joseph F. Smith

Spelling and punctuation preserved from the original

Salt Lake City, Utah
January 5, 1907

President Joseph F. Smith,
City.

Dear Brother:-

Over a year ago I had the privilege and pleasure of a brief interview with you, during which I brought to your notice a communication in my hand signed by A. L. F. MacDermott dated Dec. 20th, 1905, and mailed from St. Thomas, Lincoln county, Nevada. You informed me that a letter had been delivered at your office similar to if not identical with the communication addressed to me.

I inferred from your remarks to me that the letter from Brother MacDermott had been referred to Elder B. H. Roberts with the request that he reply to same. Such reference seemed to me to be eminently proper, inasmuch as the question raised by the enquirer was based on the "manual" of that period as published by the Y.M.M.I.A. of which "Manuel" Elder Roberts was generally understood to be the author.

In accordance with your suggestion I referred Bro. MacDermott's letter to the Y.M.M.I.A. Board, through Elder Edward H. Anderson, of the editorial staff of the "ERA". A prompt and courteous replay from Bro. Anderson informed me that an early answer would be sent to Bro. MacDermott or published, that a copy of same would be sent to me, and that Brother MacDermott's letter to me, which had been forwarded to the "ERA" office, would be returned to me. THus far I have seen no published answer, nor has the letter been returned.

Permit me to add that in August last I was at St. Thomas, and that while there I was visited by Brother MacDermott. He presented to me the question embodied in his letters to yourself and to me, saying that he had received no reply to his earlier communication.

I have this day received the enclosed letter from Brother MacDermott. May I explain that he feels somewhat <u>sore</u> over the seeming ignoring of his inquiries.

Please return the enclosed letter to me when you have no further use for same,—after having a copy made should you desire such.

I venture to say that among our young people many discussions have arisen on the point raised by Bro. MacDermott. He quoted to me, as indeed many others have cited, the statements made in the little book issued by L. A. Wilson, which book, by the way, is accepted by many as authoritative because it bears the inscription "Salt Lake Temple" at the close of the preface, and as it sets forth a virtual endorsement by Church Authorities. This book proclaims an absolute limitation as to the children of our Heavenly Father, and denies the possibility of eternal increase and development, both as to God and man. I know that much discussion, not only profitless but greatly injurious, has arisen from the promulgation of the opinions referred to. The troublesome statements about which Bro. MacDermott inquires are specified as to source and authorship in his letter enclosed, as also in his letters to yourself and to me, now over a year old.

Allow me to suggest that there appears to be a danger both real and great in the seeming certainty of profitless debate on questions such as that brought forward by Bro. MacDermott. Would it be agreeable to you, President Smith, to publish something in the form of a short article on the subject referred to? If so, please command me for any assistance I can render.

Believe me, in this suggestion I am actuated by no other motive than the hope of suppressing injurious debate and that of setting forth the principles of truth in plain and acceptable form.

My excuse in thus addressing you lies partly in the circumstance of my privileged interview a year ago, in which you kindly discussed the substance of Brother MacDermott's letters, one addressed to yourself and one to me, and partly in the hope expressed in the enclosed letter that some answer may appear from an authoritative source.

Truly your brother,
James E. Talmage
970 First Street.

§B3. James E. Talmage, Letter to President Joseph F. Smith

Spelling and punctuation preserved from the original

Salt Lake City, Utah
February 13, 1907

President Joseph F. Smith,
City.

Dear Brother:-

In view of the fact that I have already been privileged to converse with you regarding the questions submitted by Brother A. L. M.[sic] MacDermott, from whom one letter, practically a duplicate of the communication received by me, was sent to yourself as you informed me, I beg to say that once again our inquiring brother has honored me with an epistle.

Earlier communications from this correspondent have been sent to your office, in accordance with your request and instructions given to me on the occasion of a personal interview with yourself shortly after the arrival of Brother MacDermott's first letter to me on the matter as to which he inquires.

Enclosed is the latest of Brother MacDermott's communications thus far received by me. Permit me to say that in no way am I corresponding with the writer of the enclosed except so far as to acknowledge receipt of his letters and notify him of my having forwarded same.

From my brief personal meetings with Brother MacDermott I have come to regard him as an earnest though somewhat eccentric brother, not insistent on discussion or debate as to uncertain questions: yet very desirous of securing reliable instructions on Church doctrines.

The questions he presents have been brought to me by a number of our people. I confess that I shrink from writing and publishing anything in the nature of an attack or a contradiction in relation to utterance by our own people, in view of the fact that we have to meet sufficient opposition from the outside. In the interest of brevity I beg to refer to my personal letter dated January 5 last. If I can be of any assistance in replying to inquiries referred to, please so direct.

Truly and most heartily, your brother,
James E. Talmage

[in longhand on the reverse: "This subject is now being treated by Bro. B. H. Roberts, and will be published."]

§B4. "The Immortality of Man"

B. H. Roberts, *Improvement Era* 10, no. 6 (April 1907): 401–423.

This was Roberts's reply to MacDermott's November 1906 letter (§B1, above) and it is evident that Roberts had MacDermott's letter §B1 in front of him as he wrote. Spelling and usage preserved from the original. Where Roberts interprets passages of scripture as he quotes them, he encloses those interpretations in [brackets].

The Immortality of Man

By Elder B.H. Roberts

[Elder Roberts submitted the following paper to the First Presidency and a number of the Twelve Apostles, none of whom found anything objectionable in it, or contrary to the revealed word of God, and therefore favor its publication.—ERA EDITORS.]

INTRODUCTION.

In the May number of the IMPROVEMENT ERA, 1906, the editors promised their readers an article by me, in the then near future, on the

Immortality of the Soul, as taught in the Book of Mormon; and having special reference to some questions that had been asked respecting the doctrine as set forth in the Young Men's Manual of that year. The neglect on my part to enable the editors to fulfil their promise to their readers surely calls for explanation, and perhaps apology. The fulfiling of the promise given to the editors to write such an article seemed perfectly easy when it was given; but about the time it should have been fulfiled one call and duty after another so pressed me—one trod upon another's heels, so fast they followed—that it was impossible to write the article. Then, towards the close of the volume within which at least I determined to publish the article, I was called to visit the Eastern and Southern States Missions in company with Elder George Albert Smith, of the council of the Twelve Apostles, which again postponed the writing of the article until now; and even now it is undertaken in the midst of many other duties that urgently demand attention and frequently interrupt the work. Such is my apology to the editors and readers of the ERA for the delay of this article; and which I trust will be accepted as an evidence, at least, that I have not been wilfully neglectful of my promise.

Meantime, judging from the number and urgency of letters written on the subject to the editors of the ERA, I am happy to see there has been no abatement of interest in relation to the subject itself. If anything, one is tempted to believe the interest has been increased rather than diminished by the delay, and some, whose anxiety is particularly great, have expressed a desire to hear something upon the subject "from the one who has a right to receive revelations for the Church." "I think," he says, "it would be right for us to receive this knowledge from him in place of either Elder Roberts, or Prof. Nelson, or anyone else." Undoubtedly, if the Lord has anything further just now to reveal to the Church upon that or any other subject, it will, of course, be revealed through the person referred to in the above quotation, the President of the Church. My purpose in mentioning the foregoing remark at this point is that I may correct any idea that may be entertained by anyone, and in howsoever slight degree, that what I have written, or what I shall now write, on this or any other subject, is given out as the doctrine of the Church. I am in no way deluded with the idea that my writings are setting forth in any authoritative way the doctrines of the Church. What I have written, what I shall write, are my views of the doctrine of the Church; and it is of value as instruction in, and exposition of, the truth, only in so far as it is in harmony with what God has deemed wise to reveal on the various subjects treated. In this respect, what I have written or shall write is on exactly the same plane with what other elders have written or spoken respecting the gospel, and associated subjects.

THE SUBJECT AND OBJECTIONS STATED.

In the article on immortality promised the editors, it was proposed to limit inquiry on the subject to what the Book of Mormon taught; but owing to the wide range of objections that have been urged to the conclusions set forth in the Manual, I think it proper to enlarge the scope of evidence for this article, so as to include a consideration of all that has been revealed, at least in modern days, upon the subject. And here let the reader be reminded that all that is known by man upon the nature and immortality of the soul is what God has been pleased to reveal upon it. The writer, at least, pretends to no knowledge beyond what has been revealed, and when this is collected and reviewed, he freely confesses that much remains to be revealed before our information can be entirely satisfactory respecting the nature of the intelligence in man and the mode of its existence.

What the writer conceives to be the sum of the teaching of the Book of Mormon on the subject, was stated in the following paragraph, and it was this paragraph that elicited the questions, objections, and correspondence referred to in the foregoing:

Here, then, stands the truth so far as it may be gathered from God's word and the nature of things: There is in man an eternal, uncreated, self existing entity, call it "intelligence," "mind," "spirit," "soul"—what you will, so long as you recognize it, and regard its nature as eternal. There came a time when in the progress of things, (which is only another way of saying in the "nature of things") an earth-career, or earth existence, because of the things it has to teach, was necessary to the enlargement, to the advancement of these "intelligences," these "spirits," "souls." Hence an earth is prepared; and one sufficiently advanced and able, by the nature of him, is chosen, through whom this earth-existence may be brought to pass.

This passage is preceded by another which it is necessary to quote:

By the immortality of the spirit of man, I mean not only a never-ending existence for the "soul" of man in the future, through the resurrection, but a proper immortality that means the eternal existence of the "ego"—interchangeably called "mind," "spirit," "soul," "intelligence"— mean existence before birth as well as existence after death; for I believe, with some of our modern writers, that the theory that immortality refers to existence after death only is evidently but half a truth. A real immortality is forever immortal, and is existence before life on earth as surely as an existence after death.

To this statement of the immortality of the intelligent part of man, it is objected, first, that

"The pre-existence of the spirit of man is now extended back beyond the 'beginning' that is so often spoken of in the revelations of God, and the doctrine that we are co-eternal with the Father is specifically taught."

Second, that it raises the question, "How is it that we are so far behind in the order of eternal progression, if we have had all eternity in which to make progress?—if we have had as long as God the Father, and started from the same plane of intelligence as he did?"(1)

Third, the Manual doctrine of immortality must lead to the idea that the number of intelligences that could eventually become * * * * human beings, must be limited, that is, all that can ever come into existence as human beings already exist, and have always existed, and when they have all concluded (if they have not already done so) to progress by obeying law, then there will be an end to creation; to the works (new works) of God.

Fourth, the "true doctrine of eternal progress must be modified to a parallel of what most of us have heretofore been believing of man, viz., that progress commenced some time in the past and will continue without end for those, at least, who attain to a high order of salvation, if not to all who attain to any degree of salvation. But this will refute the principal axiom that Brother Roberts and Prof. Nelson rely on for the very foundation of their theory--that anything that will have no end, could have had no beginning." "I don't know," says the objector, "how the fact that our mortal bodies, which most certainly had a beginning as bodies, will be made immortal and have no end as bodies, can be made to harmonize with this axiom."

Fifth, "in order to verify the claim that the hymn, 'O My Father' was inspired (and I have often heard this statement made by those in responsible positions in the Church), we must understand that, as in the formation of the human body, in the creation of the spirit, the union of the life of two individuals of (in certain respects) opposite or complementary qualifications (sex) is absolutely necessary. If an individual cannot be produced without the union of two other separate individuals, I do not see how we can deny the beginning of the begotten individual. If we believe in the eternal increase that the faithful are promised, we can hardly accept the theory that the spiritual children promised are already existent, and independent of our salvation as they would, in justice, have to be."

Sixth, it is tentatively suggested as a counter theory to the Manual theory, by the objectors quoted above, "that the life of the parent is imparted to the offspring, and that while it is still a part of the same life or spirit of the parent, and as such did not have a beginning at the time of birth, yet as a separate individual it did have a beginning at the time of birth or conception." This is thought to be a solution of spirit existence "both reasonable, and more in accordance with the apparent, plain meaning of many passages both of ancient and modern scripture."

WORDS USED INTERCHANGEABLY.

It is often the case that misconceptions arise through a careless use of words, and through using words interchangeably, without regard to shades of differences that attach to them; and this in the scriptures as in other writings. Indeed, this fault is more frequent in the scriptures perhaps than in any other writings, for the reason that, for the most part, they are composed by men who did not aim at scientific exactness in the use of words. They were not equal to such precision in the use of language, in the first place; and in the second, they depended more upon the general tenor of what they wrote for making truth apparent than upon technical precision in a choice of words; ideas, not niceness of expression, was the burden of their souls; thought, not its dress. Hence, in scripture, and I might say especially in modern scripture, a lack of a careful or precise choice of words, a large dependence upon the general tenor of what is written to convey the truth, a wide range in using words interchangeably that are not always exact equivalents, are characteristics. Thus the expressions, "Kingdom of God," "Kingdom of Heaven," "the Whole Family in Heaven," "the Church," "the Church of Christ," "the Church of God," are often used interchangeably for the visible Church of Christ when they are not always equivalents; so, too, are used the terms "Spirit of God," and "Holy Ghost;" "Spirit of Christ," and "the Holy Ghost;" "Spirit," and "Soul;" "intelligence," and "spirits;" "spirits," and "angels." I mention this in passing, because I believe many of the differences of opinion that exist arise out of our not recognizing, or our not remembering these facts; and I hope that some of the difficulties that are supposed to exist, in relation to what, for brevity, I shall call the "Manual Theory of the Soul's Immortality," may disappear.

THE MANUAL THEORY RE-STATED.

Let us first re-state more explicitly, and, if possible, more clearly, the Manual Theory; and then see, not if what has been revealed favors such a conception of things as are set forth in the Manual; but if what has been revealed does not absolutely demand such conclusions; for I hold that, in the main, it is not a matter of choice between two theories, both of which have more or less of reason or scripture to support them, but if credence is to be given at all to what is revealed upon the subject, the Manual Theory of the eternity of the intelligent entity in man must be accepted as true. Now to the restatement of that theory.

1.—There is in that complex thing we call man an intelligent entity, uncreated, self existent, indestructible. He--for that entity is a person, because, as we shall see, he is possessed of powers that go with personality only, hence that entity is "he," not "it,"–he is eternal as God is; co-existent, in fact, with God; of the same kind of substance or essence with deity, though confessedly inferior in degree of intelligence and power to God. One must needs think that the name of this eternal entity–what God calls him–conveys to the mind some idea of his nature. He is called an "intelligence;" and this I believe is descriptive of him. That is, intelligence is the entity's chief characteristic. If this be a true deduction, then the entity must be self-conscious. He must have the power to distinguish himself from other things–the "me" from the "not me." He must have power of deliberation, by which he sets over one thing against another; with power also to form a judgment that this or that is a better thing or state than this or that. Also there goes with this idea of intelligence a power of choosing one thing instead of another, one state rather than another. These powers are inseparably connected with any idea that may be formed of an intelligence. One cannot conceive of intelligence existing without these qualities any more than he can conceive of an object existing in space without dimensions. The phrase, "the light of truth" is given in one of the revelations as the equivalent for an "intelligence" here discussed; by which it is meant to be understood, as I think, that intelligent entities perceive the truth, are conscious of the truth, they know that which is, hence "the light of truth," "intelligence." Let it be observed that I say nothing as to the mode of the existence of these intelligences, beyond the fact of their eternity. But of their form, or the manner of their subsistence nothing, so far as I know, has been revealed, and hence we are without means of knowing anything about the modes of their existence beyond the fact of it, and the essential qualities they possess, which already have been pointed out.

2.—These intelligences in the many kingdoms of God, and before the "beginning" of that earth-order of things, with which we are now connected, were begotten spirits. That is to say, a spirit body was provided for them, of which God is the Father; for he is called in the scriptures "the father of the spirits of men," hence our "Father in heaven." I use the term "begotten" above instead of "created," advisedly; and because I believe we are warranted in believing that the "begetting" of spirit-bodies for "intelligences" is an act of generation rather than of creation. The distinction is well stated by one of the early Christian fathers, Athanasius, as follows: "Let it be repeated that a created thing is external to the nature of the being who creates; but a generation (a begetting, as a father begets a son,) is the proper offspring of the nature." That is to say, through generation the father imparts of his own nature to his offspring; so that intelligences when begotten spirits have added to their own native, underived, inherent qualities somewhat of the father's nature also, and are veritably sons of God. More has been revealed upon this spirit-state of existence than upon the one that precedes it. We know for instance that the form of the spirit in outline, at least, is like the form of the human body of flesh and bone, which subsequently the spirit inhabits in the earth life, that he meets in the assemblies of spirits; that he exercises agency, that he is obedient to law, or rebels against it, as he chooses; that he is righteous or unrighteous as he wills; that he is capable of receiving or imparting intelligence. In a word, he is capable of participating in a very wide range of activities. And so far as the Savior was concerned, even in spirit-life he was capable of exercising creative powers, "for by him were all things created, that are in heaven, and that are in earth, visible and invisible, whether they be thrones, or dominions, or principalities, or powers; all things are created by him and for him."

3.—Spirits are begotten men through generation, and the spirit-body inhabits one of flesh and bone, which the spirit moulds and fashions after its own likeness, which shines out of, and expresses itself through, the earth-body. The spirit in this earth-life united to himself certain elements of this world-matter which he makes peculiarly his own. These elements are as eternal as the substance of his spirit-body, or the intelligent entity inhabiting it. No one of these was ever created in the sense of being brought forth of nothing, they always existed; they are eternal things brought into the relationship in which we see them—relationship essential to their highest good. The union of spirit and element we are told, is in some way essential to "a fulness of joy; and when separated, man cannot have a fulness of joy."

4.—The spirit and body of man are separated by death, but only for a time; the revelations of God assure us that there shall be a resurrection as universal as death has been; and that man after the resurrection, and through it, becomes inseparably connected with his body—he becomes a "soul;" for "the spirit and the body is the soul of man; and the resurrection from the dead is the redemption of the soul." What such a redeemed soul may become, by accepting the truth and living it, with God and good men as friends and guides, and also an eternity in which to work out the problems of existence, opens a field for thought that is very inviting, but foreign to our immediate purpose.

IS THE ABOVE ORDER DEMANDED BY REVELATION?

The task now before us is to ascertain if the above order of things respecting man's existence is demanded by what has been revealed upon the subject.

Our system of eschatology teaches that Jesus Christ and men are of the same order of beings; that men are of the same race with Jesus, of the same nature and essence; that he is indeed our elder brother; and while very far removed from us in that he is more perfect in righteousness, and more highly developed in intellectual and spiritual powers, yet these differences are of degree, not of kind; so that what is revealed concerning Jesus, the Christ, may be of infinite helpfulness in throwing light upon the nature of man and the several estates he has occupied and will occupy hereafter.

The co-eternity of Jesus Christ with God, the Father, is quite universally held to be set forth in the preface of John's gospel, which is so familiar that it need not be quoted here. Moreover, to us who accept the new dispensation of the gospel, through the revelations of God to the Prophet Joseph Smith, the doctrine of John's preface comes with increased emphasis by reason of the proclaimed extension of the principle of the co-eternity of God, the Father, and Jesus Christ, to other beings, namely, to men; and by asserting also the fact that the intelligent entity in man, the mind, was "not created or made, neither indeed can be." The following is from the revelation:

John saw and bore record of the fulness of my glory * * * * and he bore record saying, I saw his glory that he was in the beginning before the world was; therefore in the beginning the Word was, for he was the Word, even the messenger of salvation, the Light and the Redeemer of the world, the Spirit of Truth who came into the world because the world was made by him, and in him was the life of men and the light of men.

Such is the account which Jesus gives of John's testimony; and now Jesus himself:

And now, verily, I say unto you, I was in the beginning with the Father, and am the first born * * * * Ye [referring to the brethren who were present when the revelation was given] were also in the beginning with the Father, that which is spirit, even the spirit of truth. * * * * Man [meaning the race] was also in the beginning with God. Intelligence, or the light of truth, was not created or made, neither indeed can be. All truth is independent in that sphere in which God has placed it, to act for itself, as all intelligence also; otherwise there is no existence. Behold here is the agency of man, and here is the condemnation of man, because that which was from the beginning is plainly manifest unto them and they receive not the light. And every man whose spirit receiveth not the light is under condemnation, for man is spirit.

Here we have the co-eternity of Jesus and of all men most emphatically stated: "I was in the beginning with the Father. * * * * Ye were also in the beginning with the Father, that which is spirit;" that is, that part of you that is spirit. "Man," that is all men, the term is generic—"man was in the beginning with God." And then mark what follows: "Intelligence"—the part that was with God in the beginning, the entity of man which cognizes the truth, that perceives that which is, mind, say,—"intelligence, or the light of truth, was not created or made, neither indeed can be."

Again, in the Book of Abraham, this true eternity of the "intelligence" or "mind" of man, is affirmed; though the term "spirit" is used when it would have been clearer if "intelligence" had been the word used. Reference to the context quoted will show that "spirits" and "intelligences" are used interchangeably.

If there be two spirits [intelligences], and one shall be more intelligent than the other, yet these two spirits [intelligences], notwithstanding one is more intelligent than the other, have no beginning; they existed before, they shall have no end, they shall exist after, for they are gnolaum, or eternal.

The foregoing it should be remembered is the word of God. It is revelation. I know not how more emphatically what some of the critics of the Manual Theory call the "no-beginning, and no-end axiom," could be more strongly stated. Then again the Lord said to Abraham: "I rule in the heavens above, and in the earth beneath, in all wisdom and prudence, over all the intelligences thine eyes have seen from the beginning; I came down in the beginning in the midst of all the intelligences thou hast seen. Now the Lord had shown unto me, Abraham, the intelligences that were organized [intelligences who had been begotten spirits] before the world was; and among them were many of the noble and great ones; and God saw these souls(2) that they were great, and he stood in the midst of them, and he said: These I will make my rulers; for he stood among them that were spirits(3) [the above "organized intelligences," or intelligences that had been begotten spirits], and he saw that they were good." What is said in these scriptures warrant what the Prophet Joseph taught at the April conference of the Church, in 1844; and what the Prophet then said emphasizes and makes very clear the meaning of these revelations by which he had been instructed:

The soul—the mind of man—the immortal spirit—where did it come from? All learned men and doctors of divinity say that God created it in the beginning; but it is not so: the very idea lessens man in my estimation. I do not believe the doctrine. I know better. Hear it, all ye ends of the world, for God has told me so, if you don't believe me, it will not make the truth without effect * * * * We say that God himself is a self-existent being. Who told you so? It is correct enough, but how did it get into your head? Who told you that man did not exist in like manner, upon the same principles? * * * * Is it logical to say that the intelligence of spirits is immortal, and yet that it had a beginning?

The intelligence of spirits had no beginning, neither will it have an end. That is good logic. That which has a beginning may have an end. There never was a time when there were not spirits(4), for they are co-eternal with our Father in heaven. * * * * The spirit of man is not a created being; it existed from eternity, and will exist to eternity.

Here, then, is our proof from God's word that there is a part of man, the intelligent entity in him, that is not a "created" or even a "begotten" thing. It not only was not created, but is declared to be uncreatable. Then it must be self-existent, uncreated. It always existed. It follows, therefore, that it is co-eternal with God and Jesus Christ. It existed before all "beginnings" that relate to the earth-order of things; it has been present in all "beginnings," and will be in many more, since it is truly immortal, truly eternal, without beginning and without end; as indestructible as it is uncreatable. The evidence for what is here presented, I think must be conclusive to those who accept the revelations of God to men in our dispensation, and the testimony of the Prophet Joseph Smith.

THE FATHER OF SPIRITS.—SPIRIT BODIES.

And now as to the second statement in the Manual Theory; viz., These intelligences are begotten spirits, and live as spirit bodies before they tabernacle in the flesh.

Sure it is that God, the Father, is the Father of the spirits of men. "We," says Paul, "have had fathers of our flesh which corrected us, and we gave them reverence: shall we not much rather be in subjection unto the Father of spirits and live?"

According to this, then, there is a "Father of spirits." It follows, of course, that "spirits" have a father—they are begotten. It should be remarked that the term, "spirits" in the above passage cannot refer to the self-existent, unbegotten intelligences of the revelations, considered in the foregoing pages; and certainly this relationship of fatherhood to spirits is not one brought about in connection with generation of human life in this world. Paul makes a very sharp distinction between "Fathers of our flesh" and the "Father of spirits," in the above. Fatherhood to spirits is manifestly a relationship established independent of man's earth-existence; and, of course, in an existence which preceded earth-life, where the uncreated intelligences are begotten spirits. Hence, the phrase "shall we not be subject to the Father of spirits and live?"

Christ is referred to, by the writer of the epistle to the Colossians, as the "first born of every creature;" and the Revelator speaks of him as "the beginning of the creation of God;" and in the revelation already quoted so often in this article(5), Jesus represents himself as being in the "beginning with the Father;" and as "the first born."

The reference to Jesus as the "first born of every creature" cannot refer to his birth into earth-life, for he was not the first-born into this world; therefore, his birth here referred to must have reference to the birth of his spirit before his earth life.

The reference to Jesus as the "beginning of the creation of God," cannot refer to his creation or generation in earth-life; for manifestly he was not the beginning of the creations of God in this world; therefore, he must have been the "beginning" of God's creation elsewhere, viz. in the spirit world, where he was begotten a spiritual personage; a son of God.

The reference to Jesus as the "first born"—and hence the justification for our calling him "our Elder Brother"—cannot refer to any relationship that he established in his earth-life, since as to the flesh he is not our "elder brother," any more than he is the "first born" in the flesh; there were many born as to the flesh before he was, and older brothers to us, in the flesh, than he was. The relationship of "elder brother" cannot have reference to that estate where all were self-existent, uncreated and unbegotten, eternal intelligencies; for that estate admits of no such relation as "elder," or "younger;" for as to succession in time, the fact on which "younger" or "elder" depend, the intelligences are equal—equal as to their eternity. Therefore, since the relationship of "elder brother" was not established by any circumstance in the earth-life of Jesus, and could not be established by any possible fact in that estate where all were self-existing intelligences, it must have been established in the spirit life, where Jesus, with reference to the hosts of intelligences designed to our earth, was the "first born spirit," and by that fact became our "Elder Brother," the "first born of every creature," "the beginning of the creations of God," as pertaining to our order of existence(6).

Now take these several circumstances together, count them as cumulative evidence and cumulative argument, and the truth here sought in them becomes very apparent.

But it is in the Book of Mormon that we have the revelation which gives most light upon this spirit-existence of Jesus, and, through his spirit-existence, light upon the spirit-existence of all men. The light is given in that complete revelation of the pre-existent, personal spirit of Jesus Christ, made to the brother of Jared, ages before the spirit of Jesus tabernacled in the flesh. The essential part of the passage follows:

Behold, I am he who was prepared from the foundation of the world to redeem my people. Behold, I am Jesus Christ; * * * * and never have I showed myself unto man whom I have created, for never has man believed in me as thou hast. Seest thou that ye are created after mine own image? Yea, even all men were created in the beginning after mine own image. Behold this body which ye now behold, is the body of my spirit; and man have I created after the body of my spirit; and even as I appear unto thee to be in the spirit, will I appear unto my people in the flesh.

What do we learn from all this?

First, let it be re-called that according to the express word of God "intelligences" are not created, neither indeed can they be. Now, with the above revelation before us, we are face to face with a something that was begotten, and in that sense a creation, a spirit, the "first born of many brethren;" the "beginning of the creations of God." The spirit is in human form—for we are told that as Christ's spirit body looked to Jared's brother, so would the Christ look to men when he came among them in the flesh; the body of flesh conforming to the appearance of the spirit, the earthly to the heavenly. "This body which ye now behold is the body of my spirit"—the house, the tenement of that uncreated intelligence which had been begotten of the Father a spirit, as later that spirit-body with the intelligent, uncreated entity inhabiting it, will be begotten a man. "This body which you now behold is the body of my spirit." There can be no doubt but what here "spirit," as in the Book of Abraham, is used interchangeably with "intelligence," and refers to the uncreated entity; as if the passage stood; "This is the body inhabited by my intelligence." The intelligent entity inhabiting a spirit-body make up the spiritual personage. It is this spirit life we have so often thought about, and sang about. In this state of existence occurred the spirit's "primeval childhood;" here spirits were "nurtured" near the side of the heavenly Father, in his "high and glorious place;" thence spirits were sent to earth to unite spirit-elements with earth-elements—in some way essential to a fulness of glory and happiness—and to learn the lessons earth-life has to teach. The half awakened recollections of the human mind may be chiefly engaged with scenes, incidents and impressions of that spirit life(7); but that does not argue the non-existence of the uncreated intelligences who precede the begotten spiritual personages as so plainly set forth in the revelations of God.

Relative to the earth-life of spirits, as men and women, we have no occasion to speak further in this writing; nor are we called upon to consider man's future life, since it is conceded that the future life of man will be the life of a resurrected, immortal—that is, never-ending being, with immense possibilities. The questions that have arisen in respect of what we have called the "Manual Theory" of the immortality of the intelligence of man, related to the past rather than to the future; and, therefore, with the past we have more especially dealt; that the doctrine of the Manual is in harmony with what God has revealed, and what the Prophet Joseph taught upon the subject, admits of no doubt.

DIFFICULTIES OF THE THEORY.

That there are difficulties involved in the theory of self-existing, uncreated intelligences, is freely conceded. Such, for instance, as the difficulty of understanding how the first transition took place from self-existent, intelligent entity to spiritual personage, such as the Book of Mormon reveals the Christ to have been. Is the answer to this "there was no 'first;' these things, this process, has always been going on; 'beginnings,' 'first transitions' from self-existing intelligences to spirit personages are terms that deal with relative conditions, not absolute ones"—is this the answer? If so, it must be conceded that such an answer is as difficult to understand as the doctrine that would require a "beginning" or a "first transition."

Relative to the idea that the human body, as a body, had a beginning, and that in its resurrected state will continue always to exist, and this necessary admission being destructive of the axiom that holds that that which has no end could have had no beginning; the objectors themselves meet the objection thus raised by recognizing the fact that it is only as an organization that man's body has a beginning; the matter of which it is composed confessedly had no beginning, the elements composing it existed before, under other forms; but the elements of which the body is composed are eternal according to the express word of God. Eternal elements are begotten bodies, of definite form: but there is no particle of the body that did not have an existence from eternity, so that in the larger and truer sense of things even the body of man had no beginning, even as it will have no end.

I appreciate the difficulty suggested by one who questions the correctness of the Manual Theory—"How is it we are so far behind in the order of eternal progression if we have had all eternity in which to make progress?" On every hand, we feel the pressure of our own intellectual limitations, when dealing with these questions; and, therefore, for one, I feel the more need of relying upon what God has revealed upon these subjects, and trusting to time and more enlightenment from the Lord through revelation to make clear what now seems obscure; to make easy to understand what now seems incomprehensible. It is because I believe what God has revealed upon the subject that I presented the views set forth in the Manual, and which I have amplified in this paper. I trust one thing is made clear, for I have had but that one object in view in this writing, and that is, that whatever difficulty in the way of apprehension may exist, or however unexplainable some features of the Manual doctrine may be in our present state of knowledge and limited development of intellectual powers, I trust it is clear that this Manual theory is now seen to be in harmony with what God has revealed upon the subject; if that appears, my task is completed. I shall trust the rest to a further development of knowledge, and to further enlargement of intellectual powers in man, for the explanations and removing of difficulties that seem to exist.

It might be suggested, however, that we are not in such state of knowledge respecting man's status or relationship to "eternal progression," as to form any adequate judgment upon it. To what extent his splendid powers may be veiled, who can say? It is said of Jesus, "in his humiliation his judgment was taken away." "It pleased the Father that in him should all fulness dwell;" yet "he received not a fulness at the first, but received grace for grace." From which I gather that the awakening of the Son of God in his earth-life to the consciousness of the really great powers he possessed was a gradual awakening. It was not until after his resurrection, that he seems able to come to his disciples and say: "All power is given unto me in heaven and in earth, go ye therefore and teach all nations." And what latent powers may be in like manner hidden in man, until after his resurrection, or what station in the line of "eternal progression" he now holds, we may not say. In his humiliation, in this earth-life, his judgment, too, may be taken away, his station in the line of eternal progression concealed, and his shining qualities veiled.

VALUE OF THE DOCTRINE OF ETERNAL EXISTENCE.

But what is the value of this doctrine of the eternal existence of uncreated intelligences? In what way does it contribute to the better apprehension of that which is, the truth? These considerations, of course, should not be and are not our first concern. Our first consideration should be and has been the truth of the thing. But since that is now settled by what God has revealed about it, we may well, if possible, ascertain what helpfulness there is in the doctrine, for the right apprehension of the general scheme of things. This apprehension, I believe, it affects in a very vital way. As matters now stand, the usually accepted Christian doctrine on the matter of man's origin is that God of his free-will created of nothing the spirits and bodies of men. That they are as he would have them, since in his act of creation he could have had them different if he had so minded. Then why should he—being infinitely wise and powerful and good, for so the creeds represent him—why should he create by mere act of volition beings such as men are, not only capable of, but prone to, moral evil? Which, in the last analysis of things, in spite of all special pleadings to the contrary, leaves responsibility for moral evil with God? God's creative acts culminating thus, the next pertinent questions are: Then what of the decreed purpose of God to punish moral evil? and what of the much vaunted justice of God in that punishment? Wherein lies the just responsibility of man if he was so created as to love evil and to follow it? It is revolting to reason, as it is shocking to piety to think, that God of his own free will created some men, not only inclined to wickedness, but desperately so inclined; while others, he of his own volition created with dispositions naturally inclined toward goodness. In like manner stands it with man in relation to his inclination to faith, and to disbelief: and yet, under the orthodox belief all are included under one law for judgment!

THE PARENT-DERIVED THEORY OF EXISTENCE.

I shall be told, however, that this is not the case of those objectors to the Manual Theory to whom this article is an answer; since they hold "that the life of the parent is imparted to the offspring, and that while it is still a part of the same life or spirit of the parent, and as such did not have a beginning at the time of birth, yet, as a separate individual it did have a beginning at the time of birth or conception." But even this theory is not free from its difficulties. First in the way of it is the very positive statements in the revelations of God, and the teaching of the Prophet Joseph Smith, that hold to the independent, self-existent intelligences, as already set forth. Second, under this parent-derived theory there is an accounting to be made for the fact of perfect beings, celestial, resurrected beings, bringing forth by act of generation spirit-offspring so widely different from one another, as spirits are known to be, some inherently pious, holy by nature, others vicious, and of all varieties of disposition and intelligence; which facts, while not involving those who hold to this theory in all the difficulties of the generally accepted orthodox, or Christian theory of spirit origin, still in lessened degree it involves them in those difficulties.

On the other hand, under the conception of the existence of independent, uncreated, self-existent intelligences, who by the inherent nature of them are of various degrees of intelligence, doubtless differing from each other in many ways, yet alike in their eternity and their freedom; with God standing in the midst of them, "more intelligent than them all," and proposing the betterment of their condition—progress to higher levels of being, and power(8) through change—

under this conception of things how stand matters? There is the begetting of these intelligences, spirits; the spirits, men; the men, resurrected personages of infinite possibilities; at each change increased powers for development are added to intelligences, yet ever present through all the processes of betterment is the self-existent entity of the "intelligence" with the tremendous fact of his consciousness and his moral freedom, and his indestructibility;—he has his choice of moving upward or downward in every estate he occupies; often defeating, for a time, at least, the benevolent purposes of God respecting him, through his own perverseness; he passes through dire experiences, suffers terribly, yet learns by what he suffers, so that his very suffering becomes a means to his improvement; he learns swiftly or slowly, according to the inherent nature of him, obedience to law; he learns that "that which is governed by law, is also preserved by law, and perfected and sanctified by the same; and that which breaketh law abideth not by law, but seeketh to become a law unto itself and willeth to abide in sin, cannot be sanctified by law, neither by mercy, justice nor judgment. Therefore they must remain filthy still."(9) This conception of things relieves God of the responsibility for the nature and status of intelligences in all stages of their development; their inherent nature and their volition makes them primarily what they are, and this nature they may change, slowly, perhaps, yet change it they may. God has put them in the way of changing it by enlarging their intelligence through change of environment, through experiences; the only way God effects these self-existent beings is favorably; he creates not their inherent nature; he is not responsible for the use they make of their freedom; nor is he the author of their sufferings when they fall into sin: that arises out of the violations of law to which the "intelligence" subscribed, and must be endured until its lessons are learned.

This conception of the order of things, as to the existence of "intelligences" and in the moral government of the world, discovers a harmony in that government which at once challenges our admiration, and bears evidence of its truth, that attaches not to other conceptions of spirit existence or of that government, notwithstanding some existing difficulties that our limited comprehension of such high things leave unexplained.

REFLECTIONS.

Meantime, I rejoice in so much of knowledge as is vouchsafed to us in the revelations of God about the existence of man, past and future. By the light thus given, we may see further than by any other light whatsoever. We can see further, and know more than the philosophers have taught or can teach. I think we may know more about those things in this dispensation of the fulness of times than men have known even in the previous dispensations of the gospel. Not because there is any way of excellence in us over and above men in times past; that we are otherwise endowed with intellectual or spiritual power than they were; but simply that God has been pleased to reveal more upon these matters in our dispensation than in former ones. And in his revelations upon these subjects in our day, how marvelously has man been exalted! God has introduced him unto the very midst of his eternities, and there given him the opportunity to contemplate things as they have been, as they are, as they shall be—to contemplate truth! To stand in the temple of the universe and be instructed of God! Then, again, the things which God has revealed concerning the eternity of the intelligent entity in man but matches with other great truths he has revealed that might be called the Great Correspondences. Let me state a few of them:

1. "There are many kingdoms, * * * and there is no space in the which there is no kingdom; and there is no kingdom in the which there is no space." By "kingdoms," here, the prophet does not have reference to a body of people ruled by a monarch; but to existences or substances under the dominion of law. This affirmation of the correl-

ative existence and infinite extension of space and substance (matter) anticipated the best thought of modern scientists upon the subject.

2. "Unto every kingdom," (again existences, substances under the dominion of law)—"unto every kingdom is given a law, and to every law there are certain bounds also and conditions." In other words, "even laws have their laws," which latter statement of the same truth Henry Drummond, sixty-one years after the prophet, characterized as "one of the most striking generalizations of recent science."

3. The existence of uncreated intelligences; and the corollary, eternal elements. "The elements (meaning matter in the last analysis of it)—the elements are eternal." The elements, then, have no beginning, and have no end, any more than intelligences have; both are eternal. "The elements are the tabernacle of God," says the prophet, "yea, man is the tabernacle of God, even temples."

4. There is a necessary opposition in all things: good, evil; joy, sorrow; pain, pleasure; light, darkness; freedom of intelligences, but responsibility for the use of that freedom. All which is essential to the harmony, to the progress, of things, to working out the highest glory, and happiness of eternal intelligences.

These are a few parallel truths in the "Mormon" system of eschatology. As they are combined and worked out in "Mormon" thought, you shall not find the like of them for excellence elsewhere among the conceptions or doctrines of men.

There is the correlative existence, and the necessary existence, of space and matter.

There is the reign of law co-extensive with space and substance.

There is the doctrine of opposite existences, the thing alone which makes the agency of intelligences possible.

There are uncreated intelligences, and uncreated elements.

Something with power to know, something to be known.

Something to act, something to be acted upon. Truth, and "the light of truth."

"Uncreated intelligences, and elements that are their tabernacle."

And last of all, but not least, this as a working principle of the universe:

The work and glory of God is "to bring to pass the immortality and eternal life of man," as man.

And this as the result:

"Men are that they might have joy."

"Beloved, now are we the sons of God, and it doth not yet appear what we shall be; but we know that, when he [Christ] shall appear, we shall be like him; for we shall see him as he is. And every man that hath this hope in him, purifieth himself, even as he, [the Christ] is pure." (I John 3:2, 3.)

* * * * * *

In the presence of these great principles revealed of God, I say—Father from my lowly station in this world, where limitations, intellectual and spiritual, press heavily upon us from every side, and where human weakness humbles the spirit and hinders its attainment of that knowledge which but for this it might attain: where temptations are constant and power of resistance is intermittent; where, at best, we see things but in part, and therefore imperfectly—as through a glass darkly—from the midst of these conditions, I venture to uplift a thought to thee, and thank thee for the revelation of these truths to thy children. I thank thee for making us to know that we are so near akin to thine own self; that in very essence we are akin to thee, and that by the keeping of thy law—to which, of our own volition, acting on that agency which is an inherent quality of intelligences, we did subscribe—we may dwell with thee eternally in the heavens. For all this, I thank thee, and humbly pray for grace, that in my day, and with such strength as thou canst supply, I may be constant in these great truths, and teach them to others, until they feel their full power and uplifting strength.

Salt Lake City, Utah.

Notes

1. Respecting this last question, involving the statement that man started from the same plane of intelligence as God did, I desire to say that in nothing I have written, neither in the Manual, nor in Mormon Doctrine of Deity, nor in the History of the Church, all of which, as also the present year's Young Men's Manual, are criticised for setting forth the above doctrine of the immortality of the "intelligence" of man by the objector quoted—nowhere, I repeat, have I taught that man started on the same plane with God, because I am aware, and have been now a long time, that the word of God in the Pearl of Great Price is directly to the contrary. It is there affirmed that there are differences in the "intelligences" that exist, that God is "more intelligent than them all," but that notwithstanding one spirit may be more intelligent than another, they may be equal in their eternity: "If there be two spirits, and one shall be more intelligent than the other, yet those two spirits, notwithstanding one is more intelligent than the other, have no beginning; they existed before, they shall have no end, they shall exist after, for they are gnolaum, or eternal;" "I am the Lord thy God, I am more intelligent than them all."—Abraham 3:18–19 (1902, edition always quoted); and that is doubtless why he is God, because he is more intelligent than the other intelligences or all of them collectively.

2. Observe how in this passage "souls," "organized intelligences," "spirits," are used interchangeably.—Abraham 3:21–23.

3. Here the prophet doubtless uses the word "spirit" interchangeably with "intelligence," and means the latter.

4. Doctrine and Covenants 43.

5. "As pertaining to our order of existence." I call attention to this qualifying clause in a foot note because I do not wish to delay the conclusion of the argument in the text at this point by inserting a discussion of it there; and yet I believe the principle indicated in the clause is very important, not only in the discussion in hand, but it has an important bearing upon the whole phraseology and meaning of our scripture. The fact is that the revelations from God in the Bible and all other scriptures are, in the main, local; that is, they pertain to our earth and that order of worlds with which it is connected, and that order of existence to which we belong. Hence, when God's word says, "In the beginning God created the heaven and the earth," etc.; and "thus the heavens and the earth were finished and all the hosts of them," he has reference not to any absolute "beginning," or absolute "finishing," but only the "beginning" and "finishing" as pertaining to our earth and the order of creation with which it is connected; and the "hosts" that pertain to our order of existence, not absolutely to all existences. The revelations we have received of God, let it be said again, are local, they relate to us and our order of existence; they may

not at all, except in the most casual and general way, refer to that order of worlds connected with and governed by the Pleiades, or of Orion, much less to the further removed constellations and their systems of worlds.

We learn from the Pearl of Great Price that when the Lord gave those revelations to Moses by which the prophet was enabled to write the creation history of our earth, the local character of those revelations was expressly stated: "Worlds without number," said the Lord to Moses, "have I created—but only an account of this earth and the inhabitants thereof give I unto you—Behold, I reveal unto you concerning this heaven, and this earth; write the words which I speak * * * * * In the beginning I created the heaven and the earth on which thou standest." The subject is too important for treatment in a footnote, but in passing I merely desired to call attention to the important bearing it has upon the subject in hand, as also upon our whole system of thought and exposition of the scriptures.

6. It is interesting to note that this truth, at least in part, seemed to impress itself upon the great minds of the antique world. Cicero says, in speaking of the spirit of man: "I might add that the facility with which youth are taught to acquire numberless very difficult arts, is a strong presumption that the soul (spirit) possessed a considerable portion of knowledge before it entered into the human form, and what seems to be received from instruction is, in fact, no other than a reminiscence or recollection of its ideas." "This at least," he adds, "is the opinion of Plato."

7. Abraham 3: 19.

8. Abraham 3.

9. Doctrine and Covenants 88:34, 35.

Acknowledgements

I am indebted to many people for the production of this work. Steve Evans offered the services of BCC Press to publish it and gave insightful editorial advice. Jonathan Stapley read an early draft and drew my attention to source material I had overlooked. Max H. Parkin facilitated my first archival work on early Mormon preaching decades ago. Historian Ardis E. Parshall was deeply generous in sharing her own resources and time. Reviewers who read the manuscript gave crucial information and advice. My excellent fellow bloggers at By Common Consent have put up with and encouraged my interest in antebellum American sermon culture over the years. The staffs of the Church History Library of The Church of Jesus Christ of Latter-day Saints, Salt Lake City, Utah, the Marriott Library at the University of Utah, Salt Lake City, Utah, the Harold B. Lee Library at Brigham Young University, Provo, Utah, the Merrill-Cazier Library at Utah State University, Logan, Utah, and The Huntington Library, San Morino, California have all been key figures with their very kind assistance in making available many rare and important sources. Mark Ashurst-McGee, Robin Scott Jensen, and Sharlyn D. Howcroft very kindly solicited my thoughts on JS's preaching record for their volume, *Foundational Texts of Mormonism* from Oxford University Press. This made me believe that the present volume might have an audience. Finally, to my wife, Gailan, to whom this volume is dedicated, who put up with the many hours I was locked away in my office, tapping away on my keyboard, leafing through books, overflowing bookcases, and files piled on the floor and furniture, I give my deepest gratitude.

Bibliography

A Uniform System for Teaching Investigators (Salt Lake City: The Church of Jesus Christ of Latter-day Saints, 1965–).

Aquinas, St. Thomas, *Summa contra Gentiles, Book Two: Creation*, trans. J. F. Anderson (Notre Dame, I.N.: University of Notre Dame Press, 1975).

Anderson, Edward H., "Age of the Earth," *Improvement Era* 12, no. 6 (April 1909): 489–490.

"Adventures of a Mormon Settler," *The Times* (London) 8, no. 4 (Jan. 9, 1857): 8.

Aguilera-Castrejon, Alejandro, Bernardo Oldak, Tom Shani, et al., "Ex Utero Mouse Embryogenesis from Pre-gastrultion to Late Organogenesis," *Nature* (17 March 2021).

Alexander, Thomas G., *Mormonism in Transition: A History of the Latter-day Saints, 1890–1930*, (Urbana and Chicago: University of Illinois Press, 1986).

Alexander, Thomas G., "The Reconstruction of Mormon Doctrine: From Joseph Smith to Progressive Theology," *Sunstone Magazine* (July–August 1980): 24–33.

Alexander, Thomas G. "The Word of Wisdom: From Principle to Requirement," *Dialogue: A Journal of Mormon Thought* 14, no. 3 (Autumn 1981): 78–88.

Allen, James B., "Editing William Clayton," *Dialogue: A Journal of Mormon Thought* 30, no. 2 (Summer 1997):129–38.

Allen, James B., Dale C. LeCheminant, and David J. Whittaker, eds., *Views on Man and Religion: Collected Essays of George T. Boyd* (Provo, U.T.: Friends of George T. Boyd, 1979).

Ariès, Philippe, *The Hour of Our Death: The Classic History of Western Attitudes Toward Death over the Last One Thousand Years*, trans. Helen Weaver (New York: Alfred A. Knopf, Inc., 1981).

Aristotle, *Generation of Animals*, trans. by A. Platt in *The Complete Works of Aristotle*, ed. Jonathan Barnes (Princeton, N.J.: Princeton University Press, 1984).

Arrington, Leonard J., Feramorz Y. Fox, and Dean L. May, *Building the City of God: Community and Cooperation Among the Mormons* (Salt Lake City: Deseret Book, 1976).

Arrington, Leonard J., *Great Basin Kingdom: An Economic History of the Latter-day Saints, 1830–1900* (Cambridge: Harvard University Press, 1958).

Arrington, Leonard J., papers, 1839–1999, Special Collections and Archives Division, Merrill-Cazier Library, Utah State University, Logan, Utah.

Arrington, Leonard J., "The Writing of Latter-day Saint History: Problems, Accomplishments and Admonitions," *Dialogue: A Journal of Mormon Thought* 14, no. 3 (Autumn 1981): 119–129.

Bagley, Will, "Perilous Journey: The Grimshaw Family's Narrow Escape, 1856," *Overland Journal* 7, no. 5 (Winter 2015–2016): 157–164.

Baker, Joseph O., Dalton Rogers, and Timothy Moser, "Acceptance of Evolution among American Mormons," *Journal of Contemporary Religion* 33, no. 1 (2018): 123–134.

Barlow, Philip, "Shifting Ground and the Third Transformation of Mormonism" in *Perspectives on American Religion and Culture*, ed. Peter W. Williams (Malden, MA: Blackwell Publishers, 1999), 140–153.

Barlow, Philip, *Mormons and the Bible: The Place of the Latter-day Saints in American Religion*, 2nd ed. (New York: Oxford University Press, 2013)

Barney, Kevin L. "Joseph Smith's Emendation of Hebrew Genesis 1:1," *Dialogue: A Journal of Mormon Thought*, 30, no. 4 (Winter 1997): 103–135.

Barney, Kevin L., "'Faith Alone,' in Romans 3:28 JST," in *Bountiful Harvest: Essays in Honor of S. Kent Brown* eds., Andrew C. Skinner, D. Morgan Davis, and Carl Griffin (Provo, UT: Brigham Young University Press, 2012), 1–30.

Barney, Ronald O., "Joseph Smith and the Conspicuous Scarcity of Early Mormon Documentation," in *Foundational Texts of Mormonism: Examining Major Early Sources* edited by Mark Ashurst-McGee, Robin Scott Jensen, and Sharalyn D. Howcroft (New York: Oxford University Press, 2018), 373–401.

Beecher, Edward, *The Conflict of Ages; or the Great Debate on the Moral Relations of God and Man* (Boston: Phillips, Sampson and Company, 1853).

Beecher, Edward , *History of Opinions on the Scriptural Doctrine of Future Retribution*, (New York: D. Appleton and Company, 1878).

Benes, Peter, *Meetinghouses of Early New England* (Amherst, M.A.: University of Massachusetts Press, 2012).

Bennion, Samuel O., Letter to President Joseph F. Smith & Counselors, January 5, 1912, First Presidency mission administration correspondence, Box 45, Central, CR 1 174, CHL.

Bennion, Samuel O., October 6, 1923, *Conference Report*, 80.

Benson, Ezra Taft, "Trust Not the Arm of Flesh," *Improvement Era* 70 (December 1967): 55–58.

Berger, Jacob, "A Dilemma for the Soul Theory of Personal Identity," *International Journal for Philosophy of Religion* 83 (2018): 41–45.

Bergera, Gary James, "The 1911 Evolution Controversy at Brigham Young University," in *The Search for Harmony: Essays on Science and Mormonism* edited by Gene A. Sessions and Craig J. Oberg (Salt Lake City: Signature Books, 1993), 23–41.

Bergera, Gary James, "The Orson Pratt-Brigham Young Controversies: Conflict Within the Quorums, 1853–1868," *Dialogue: A Journal of Mormon Thought* 13, no. 2 (Summer 1980): 7–49.

Bergera, Gary James, and Ronald Priddis, *Brigham Young University: A House of Faith* (Salt Lake City: Signature Books, 1985).

Blair, Alma R., "Reorganized Church of Jesus Christ of Latter Day Saints: Moderate Mormonism," in *The Restoration Movement: Essays in Mormon History* eds., F. Mark McKlernan, Alma R. Blair, and Paul M. Edwards (Independence, MO: Herald House, 1979), 207–230.

Blair, Ann M., "Textbooks and Methods of Note-Taking in Early Modern Europe," in *Scholarly Knowledge: Textbooks in Early Modern Europe*, edited by Simone De Angelis, Anja-Silvia Goeing, and Anthony Grafton (Paris, France: Librairie Droz, 2008), 39–73.

Blair, Ann M., *Too Much to Know: Managing Scholarly Information Before the Modern Age* (New Haven, C.T.: Yale University Press, 2010).

Bloom, Harold, *The American Religion: The Emergence of the Post-Christian Nation* (New York: Simon & Schuster, 1993).

Blythe, Christopher James, "Recreating Religion: The Response to Joseph Smith's Innovations in the Second Prophetic Generation of Mormonism," masters thesis, Utah State University, Logan, Utah, 2010.

Blythe, Christopher James, "'Would to God, Brethren, I Could Tell You Who I Am!': Nineteenth-Century Mormonisms and the Apotheosis of Joseph Smith." *Nova Religio: The Journal of Alternative and Emergent Religions* 18, no. 2 (2014): 5–27.

Bouwsma, William, *John Calvin* (New York: Oxford University Press, 1988).

Bowman, Matthew, *Christian: The Politics of a Work in America* (Boston: Harvard University Press, 2018).

Bowman, Matthew , "The Crisis of Mormon Christology: History, Progress, and Protestantism, 1880–1930," *Fides et Historia* 40, no. 2 (Summer/Fall 2008): 1–26.

Bowman, Matthew, " Matthew Philip Gill and Joseph Smith: the Dynamics of Mormon Schism," *Nova Religio* 14, no. 3 (February 2011): 42–63.

Bowman, Matthew, *The Mormon People: The Making of an American Faith* (New York: Random House, 2012).

Bowman, Matthew, "The Evangelical Countercult Movement and Mormon Conservatism," in *Out of Obscurity: Mormonism Since 1945* eds., Patrick Q. Mason and John G. Turner (New York: Oxford University Press, 2016), 259–277.

Bowman, Matthew, "Eternal Progression: Mormonism and American Progressivism," in *Mormonism and American Politics*, eds., Randall Balmer and Jana Riess (New York: Columbia University Press, 2015), 53–70.

Bowman, Matthew and Samuel Brown, "The Reverend Buck's Theological Dictionary and the Struggle to Define American Evangelicalism, 1802–1851," *Journal of the Early Republic* 29, no. 3 (Fall 2009): 441–73.

Boyd, George T., *The Moral Nature of Man* (Provo: U.T.: Brigham Young University, 1962).

Boyd, George T., "A Mormon Concept of Man," *Dialogue: A Journal of Mormon Thought* 3, no.1 (Spring 1968): 57–73.

Boyd, George, Rodney Turner, and Kent Robson, "Roundtable: The Nature of Man," *Dialogue: A Journal of Mormon Thought* 3, no. 1 (Spring 1968): 55–97.

Bradford, Mary Lythgoe, *Lowell L. Bennion: Teacher, Counselor, Humanitarian* (Salt Lake City: Dialogue Foundation, 1995).

Bradley, Martha Sonntag and Mary Brown Firmage Woodward, "Plurality, Patriarchy, and the Priestess: Zina D. H. Young's Nauvoo Marriages," *Journal of Mormon History* 20, no. 1 (Spring 1994): 84–118.

Braude, Benjamin, "The Sons of Noah and the Construction of Ethnic and Geographical Identities in Medieval and Early Modern Periods," *William and Mary Quarterly* 54 (January 1997): 103–142.

Brackenridge, R. Douglas, "Hostile Mormons and Persecuted Presbyterians in Utah, 1870–1900: A Reappraisal," *Journal of Mormon History* 37, no. 3 (Summer 2011):162–228.

Brooks, Joanna, "From Edwards to Baldwin: Heterodoxy, Discontinuity, and New Narratives of American Religious-Literary History," *Early American Literature* 45, no. 2 (2010): 425–40.

Brown, Alexandra R., "*Kairos* Gathered: Time, Tempo, and Typology in 1 Corinthians," *Interpretation: A Journal of Bible and Theology* 72, no. 1 (2018): 43–55.

Brown, Thomas D., "I gave notice . . . ," *Latter-day Saints' Millennial Star* 11, no. 6 (March 15, 1849): 96.

Brown, Samuel, "William W. Phelps's Paracletes: An Early Witness to Joseph Smith's Divine Anthropology," *International Journal of Mormon Studies* 2 (2009): 62–82.

Brown, Samuel M., "Believing Adoption," *BYU Studies Quarterly* 52, no. 2 (2013): 45–65.

Brown, Samuel M., and Jonathan A. Stapley, "Mormonism's Adoption Theology: An Introductory Statement," *Journal of Mormon History* 37, no. 3 (Summer 2011): 1–2.

Brown, Samuel, "Early Mormon Adoption Theology and the Mechanics of Salvation," *Journal of Mormon History* 37, no. 3 (Summer 2011): 3–52

Brown, Samuel Morris, *In Heaven as it is on Earth: Joseph Smith and the Early Mormon Conquest of Death* (New York: Oxford University Press, 2012).

Buerger, David John, "The Adam-God Doctrine," *Dialogue: A Journal of Mormon Thought* 15, no. 1 (Spring 1982): 14–58.

Buck, Charles, *A Theological Dictionary* (Philadelphia: Whitehall, 1807).

Bullock, Thomas, booklet (#10) 1850 December 29–1851 March 9, CR 100 318, CHL.

Bushman, Richard Lyman, *Joseph Smith: Rough Stone Rolling* (New York: Alfred A. Knopf, 2005).

Call, Robert M., "Anatomy of a Rupture: Identity Maintenance in the 1844 Latter-day Saint Reform Sect," masters thesis, 2017, Utah State University, Logan, Utah.

Cannon, Donald Q., "The King Follett Discourse: Joseph Smith's Greatest Sermon in Historical Perspective," *BYU Studies* 18, no. 2 (Winter 1978): 179–92.

Cannon, George Q., journal, October 6, 1880, (Salt Lake City: Church Historian's Press, 2017 issue).

"Church Historian's Office. History of the Church, 1839-circa 1882," CR 100 102, CHL.

Clark, J. Reuben, *On the Way to Immortality and Eternal Life* (Salt Lake City: Deseret Book, 1950).

Clawson, Thomas Alfred, diary, April 12, 1912, Box 2, fd. 4, pp. 69–70, MMS B 106, Utah State Historical Society, Salt Lake City, Utah.

Clayton, William, *Revelations* (Salt Lake City: published by the author, ca. 1857). Also known as "William Clayton's Private Book."

Clift, Dean, and Melina Schuh, "Restarting Life: Fertilization and the Transition from Meiosis to Mitosis," *Nature Reviews Molecular Cell Biology* 14 (2013): 549–62.

Collier, Fred, ed., *The Teachings of President Brigham Young*, 3 vols. (Salt Lake City: Collier's Publishing Company, 1987).

Combs, Isaiah M., collection 1835–1938, diary, Monday September 27, 1875, MS 1198, CHL.

Compton, Todd, *In Sacred Loneliness: The Plural Wives of Joseph Smith* (Salt Lake City: Signature Books, 1997).

"Conference Minutes," *Times and Seasons* 5, no. 9 (May 1, 1844): 522.

"Conference Minutes," *Times and Seasons* 4, no. 15 (August 15, 1844): 612–17 (613).

Conforti, Joseph, *Samuel Hopkins and the New Divinity Movement* (Grand Rapids, M.I.: Eerdmans, 1981).

Cook, Lyndon W., "William Law, Nauvoo Dissenter," *BYU Studies* 22, no. 1 (Winter 1982): 47–72.

Coviello, Peter, *Make Yourselves Gods: Mormons and the Unfinished Business of American Secularism* (Chicago: The University of Chicago Press, 2019).

Cracroft, Richard H., ed., *Believing People: Literature of the Latter-day Saints* (Salt Lake City: Bookcraft, 1974).

Crawley, Peter L., *A Descriptive Bibliography of the Mormon Church*, 3 Vols. (Provo, U.T.: Religious Studies Center, 1997–2012).

Crowe, Michael and Matthew F. Dowd, "The Extraterrestrial Life Debate from Antiquity to 1900," in *Astrobiology, History, and Society: Life Beyond Earth and the Impact of Discovery* ed. Douglas A. Vakoch (New York: Springer, 2013), 3–56.

Corrill, John, *A Brief History of the Church of Christ of Latter Day Saints* (St. Louis, M.O.: Corrill, 1839).

"Crossword Puzzle," *The Friend* (March 2002): 23.

Davis, Richard, *The Imposture Unmasked; or, A Complete Exposure of the Mormon Fraud* 2nd ed. (Douglas: Robert Fargher, 1841).

Davis, Matthew L., Letter, Washington D.C. to Mrs. Matthew L. Davis, New York City, New York, February 6, 1840, MS 522, CHL.

Davis, Rodney O. and Douglas L. Wilson, eds., *The Lincoln–Douglas Debates* (Galesburg, Illinois: Knox College Lincoln Studies Center, 2008).

Deer, Jill Mulvay and Karen Lynn Davidson, eds., *Eliza R. Snow: The Complete Poetry* (Provo, U.T.: Brigham Young University Press and University of Utah Press, 2009).

Derr, Jill Mulvay, Carol Cornwall Madsen, Kate Holbrook, and Matthew J. Grow, eds., *The First Fifty Years of Relief Society: Key Documents in Latter-day Saint Women's History* (Salt Lake City: Church Historian's Press, 2016).

The Deseret Evening News (January 16, 1909): 5

Dick, Thomas, *Philosophy of a Future State* (New York: G. & C. & H. Carvill, 1829).

Dick, Thomas, *Latter Day Saints' Messenger and Advocate* 3 (December 1836): 423–425.

Dow, Lorenzo, *History of a Cosmopolite or the Four Volumes of Lorenzo's Journal, Concentrated in One: Containing His Experience & Travels, From Childhood to 1814, Being Upwards of Thirty-Six Years* (New York: John C. Totten, 1814).

Dow, Lorenzo, *Hint to the Public: Thoughts on the Fulfillment of Prophecy in 1811*, in, *The Dealings of God, Man, and the Devil* 2 vols., eds., Lorenzo Dow and Peggy Dow (New York: Nafis & Cornish, 1849).

"Draft Notes, History of the Church" *JSP*.

Drummond, Lewis, *Spurgeon: Prince of Preachers* (Grand Rapids, M.I.: Kregel Publications, 1992).

Duckworth, James, Letter to Francis T. Pomeroy, February 9, 1928, B. H. Roberts collection, MS 1278, CHL.

Editors' Table (Edward H. Anderson), "William Jennings Bryan," *Improvement Era* 28, no. 11 (September 1925): 1092–93.

Ehat, Andrew F., and Lyndon W. Cook, *The Words of Joseph Smith* (Provo, U.T.: Religious Studies Center, BYU, 1980). Later editions appeared in 1990 and electronically ca. 1996.

Ellison, Robert, "The Tractarians' Sermons and other Speeches," in *A New History of the Sermon: Nineteenth Century* edited by Robert H. Ellison (New York: Brill, 2010), 15–58.

England, Eugene, *Dialogues with Myself* (Salt Lake City: Signature Books, 1984).

Ertman, Martha, "Race Treason: The Untold Story of America's Ban on Polygamy," *Columbia Journal of Gender and Law* 19, no. 2 (2010): 287–366.

Evans, John Henry, *One Hundred Years of Mormonism: A History of the Church of Jesus Christ of Latter-day Saints from 1805 to 1905* (Salt Lake City: Deseret Sunday School Union, 1905).

Evans, John Henry, *Joseph Smith, An American Prophet* (New York: Macmillan, 1933).

Feferman, Solomon, *In the Light of Logic* (New York: Oxford University Press, 1998).

Finch, Martha L., *Dissenting Bodies: Corporealities in Early New England* (New York: Columbia University Press, 2010).

First Presidency Letterpress Copybooks, December 28, 1911, January 6, 1912, transcript in Scott Glen Kenney papers, Special Collections, Marriott Library, University of Utah, Salt Lake City.

First Presidency office journal in, Historical Department journal history of the Church, 1830–2008, CR 100 137, CHL.

First Presidency and the Quorum of the Twelve Apostles, "A Doctrinal Exposition by the First Presidency and the Quorum of the Twelve," *Improvement Era* 19, no. 6 (August 1916): 934–42.

Flake, Chad J. and Larry W. Draper, eds., *A Mormon Bibliography 1830–1930* 2nd ed. 2 Vols. (Provo, U.T.: Religious Studies Center, 2004).

Flake, Kathleen, "Re-placing Memory: Latter-day Saint Use of Historical Monuments and Narrative in the Early Twentieth Century," *Religion and American Culture: A Journal of Interpretation* 13, no. 1 (Winter 2003): 69–109.

Flake, Kathleen, *The Politics of American Religious Identity: The Seating of Senator Reed Smoot, Mormon Apostle* (Chapel Hill, N.C.: The University of North Carolina Press, 2004).

Fleming, Stephen Joseph, "The Fulness of the Gospel: Christian Platonism and the Origins of Mormonism," (PhD diss., University of California, Santa Barbara, CA, 2014).

Foner, Eric, *A Short History of Reconstruction 1863–1877* (updated edition) (New York: Harper Perennial Modern Classics, 2015).

Foster, Lawrence, *Women, Family, and Utopia: Communal Experiments of the Shakers, the Oneida Community, and the Mormons* (Syracuse, N.Y.: Syracuse University Press, 1991).

Gasparov, Boris, *Speech, Memory, and Meaning: Intertextuality in Everyday Language* (Berlin/New York: Walter de Gruyter GmbH & Co., 2010).

Geertz, Clifford, "Ideology as a Cultural System," in *Ideology and Discontent* edited by David Apter (New York: Free Press, 1964), 47–76.

General Board of the YMMIA, Letter to Lorenzo Snow, January 17, 1901, First Presidency administrative files, 1878–1918, CR 1 169, CHL.

General Board of the YMMIA, Letter to President Wilford Woodruff and Counselors, February 5, 1896, First Presidency administrative files, 1878–1918, CR 1 169, CHL.

General Church Minutes, 1839–1877, Thomas Bullock, April 7, 1844, Box 1, fd. 19, page 7, CR 100 318, CHL.

General Church Minutes, 1839–1877, April 4, 1844, William Clayton, page 1, Box 1, fd. 19, CR 100 318, CHL.

General Church Minutes, 1839–1877, Thomas Bullock, December 6, 1847, Box 1, fd. 59, CR 100 318, CHL

Givens, Terryl L. and Matthew J. Grow, *Parley P. Pratt: The Apostle Paul of Mormonism* (New York: Oxford University Press, 2012).

Givens, Terryl L., *When Souls Had Wings: Pre-Mortal Existence in Western Thought* (New York: Oxford University Press, 2012).

Givens, Terryl L., *Wrestling the Angel: The Foundations of Mormon Thought: Cosmos, God, Humanity* (New York: Oxford University Press, 2014).

Goetz, Stewart and Charles Taliaferro, *A Brief History of the Soul* (Oxford: John Wiley & Sons, 2011).

Godfrey, Kenneth W., "The History of Intelligence in Latter-day Saint Thought," in *The Pearl of Great Price: Revelations from God*, edited by H. Donl Peterson and Charles D. Tate Jr. (Provo, UT: Religious Studies Center, Brigham Young University, 1989), 213–36.

Godfrey, Kenneth W., "A Comprehensive History of the Church," in *Encyclopedia of Latter-day Saint History* edited by Donald Q. Cannon, Richard O. Cowan, Arnold K. Garr, and Richard Neitzel Holzapfel (Salt Lake City: Deseret Book, 2000).

Goldstein, Rebecca, *Incompleteness: The Proof and Paradox of Kurt Gödel* (New York: W. W. Norton & Co., 2005).

Gordon, Melton, J., "When Prophets Die: The Succession Crisis in New Religions," in *When Prophets Die: The Postcharismatic Fate of New Religious Movements*, edited by Timothy Miller (Albany, N.Y.: State University of New York Press, 1991).

Gott III, J. Richard, "Implications of the Copernican Principle for Our Future Prospects," *Nature* 363, no. 6427 (May 1993): 315–319.

Grabiner, Judith V. and Peter D. Miller, "Effects of the Scopes Trial," *Science*, New Series 185, no. 4154 (Sept. 6, 1974): 832–837.

Grant, Heber J., journal, March 13, 1896, MS 1233, CHL.

Grant, Heber J., journal, July 7, 1887, September 8, 1887, October 5, 1887, January 4, 1898, MS 1233, CHL.

Greene, Brian, *Until the End of Time: Mind, Matter, and Our Search for Meaning in an Evolving Universe* (New York: Alfred A. Knopf, 2020).

Greenstein, George S., *Quantum Strangeness: Wrestling with Bell's Theorem and the Ultimate Nature of Reality* (Boston, The MIT Press, 2019).

Grey, Matthew J., "Approaching Egyptian Papyri through Biblical Language: Joseph Smith's Use of Hebrew in His Translation of the Book of Abraham," in *Producing Ancient Scripture: Joseph Smith's Translation Projects in the Development of Mormon Christianity*, eds., Michael Hubbard MacKay, Mark Ashurst-McGee, and Brian M. Hauglid (Salt Lake City: University of Utah Press, 2020), 390–451.

Grimshaw, Jonathan, Journal, 1850–December 1851, MS 7289, CHL.

Grimshaw, Jonathan, Journal, June 1853–April 1854, CR 100 416, CHL.

Grimshaw, Jonathan, Letter to Brigham Young, September 6, 1852, Brigham Young incoming correspondence, 1839–1877, Box 22, fd. 15, CR 1234 1, CHL.

Haglund, Kristine, "Leapfrogging the Waves: A Nakedly Unacademic Response to 'Rethinking Mormonism's Heavenly Mother,'" ByCommonConsent.com, September 7, 2016.

Hale, Van, "The Doctrinal Impact of the King Follett Discourse," *BYU Studies* 18, no. 2 (Winter 1978): 209–25.

Hale, Van, "Mormons and Moonmen, *Sunstone* (September-October 1982): 12–17.

Hambrick-Stowe, Charles, *Charles G. Finney and the Spirit of American Evangelicalism* (Grand Rapids, M.I.: Eerdmans, 1996).

Hanks, Walter E., notebook, 1888–1926, MS 3870, CHL.

Harper, Steven C., *First Vision: Memory and Mormon Origins* (New York: Oxford University Press, 2019).

Harrell, Charles R., "The Development of the Doctrine of Preexistence, 1830–1844," *BYU Studies* 28, no. 2 (Spring 1988): 75–96.

Hatch, John P., ed., *Danish Apostle: The Diaries of Anthon H. Lund, 1890–1921* (Salt Lake City: Signature Books, 2006).

Haws, J. B., *The Mormon Image in the American Mind: Fifty Years of Public Perception* (New York: Oxford University Press, 2013).

Heath, Harvard S., ed., *In the World: The Diaries of Reed Smoot* (Salt Lake City: Signature Books, 1997).

Hedges, Andrew H., Alex D. Smith, and Brent M. Rogers, *Journals, Vol. 3: May 1843–June 1844*. Vol. 3 in The Joseph Smith Papers series, edited by Dean C. Jessee, Mark Ashurst-McGee, and Richard L. Jensen (Salt Lake City: Church Historian's Press, 2015).

Hedges, Andrew H., Alex D. Smith, and Richard Lloyd Anderson, *Journals, Vol. 2: December 1841-April 1843*. Vol. 2 in The Joseph Smith Papers series, edited by Dean C. Jessee, Ronald K. Esplin, and Richard Lyman Bushman (Salt Lake City: Church Historian's Press, 2011).

Hedges, Andrew H. and Richard Neitzel Holzapfel, *Within These Walls: Lorenzo Snow's Record Book 1886–1897* (Salt Lake City: Deseret Book, 2010).

Heeren, John, Donald Lindsey, Marylee Mason, "The Mormon Concept of Mother in Heaven: A Sociological Account of Its Origins and Development," *Journal for the Scientific Study of Religion*, 23, no. 4 (December 1984): 396–411.

Hedrick, Granville, *Truth Teller* 1, nol 4 (1864): 53.

Hicks, Michael, *The Mormon Tabernacle Choir: A Biography* (Chicago: University of Illinois Press, 2016).

Hicks, Michael, *Mormonism and Music: A History* (Chicago: University of Illinois Press, 1989).

Hicks, Michael, "'O My Father': The Musical Settings," *BYU Studies* 36, no. 1 (1996–97): 32–57.

Hicks, Michael, "Poetic Borrowing in Early Mormonism," *Dialogue: A Journal of Mormon Thought*, 18, no. 1 (Spring 1985): 132–142.

Hill, Marvin S., "The First Vision Controversy: A Critique and Reconciliation," *Dialogue: A Journal of Mormon Thought* 15, no. 2 (Summer 1982): 31–46.

Hinckley, Gordon B., "Nauvoo's Holy Temple," *Ensign* (September 1994): 59–62

Hirrel, Leo P., *Children of Wrath: New School Calvinism and Antebellum Reform* (Lexington, K.Y.: University Press of Kentucky, 1998).

Historical Department office journal 1844–2012, CR 100 1, CHL.

Historian's Office History of the Church (draft) 1845–1867, CR 100 92, CHL.

Historian's Office Reports of Speeches, 1845–1885, CR 100 317, CHL.

History of Brigham Young, February 16, 1849, CR 100 102 vol. 19, p. 16, CHL.

Hodges, Blair Dee, "'My Principality on Earth Began': Millennialism and the Celestial Kingdom in the Development of Mormon Doctrine," *Dialogue: A Journal of Mormon Thought* 46, no. 2 (Summer 2013): 40–54.

Holland, David F., "Anne Hutchinson to Horace Bushnell: A New Take on the New England Sequence," *New England Quarterly* 78, no. 2 (June 2005): 163–201.

Hollinger, David A., "Christianity and Its American Fate: Where History Interrogates Secularization Theory," in Joel Isaac, et al., *The Worlds of American Intellectual History* (New York: Oxford University Press, 2016), 280–306.

Holmes, David L., *The Faiths of the Founding Fathers* (New York: Oxford University Press, 2006).

Holt, Jim, *When Einstein Walked With Gödel: Excursions to the Edge of Thought* (New York: Farrar, Straus and Giroux, 2018).

Horne, Donald B., *Determining Doctrine: A Reference Guide for Evaluating Doctrinal Truth* (Salt Lake City: Eborn Books, 2005).

Howe, Daniel Walker, *What Hath God Wrought: The Transformation of America, 1815–1848* (New York: Oxford University Press, 2007).

Hubler, J. Noel, "*Creatio ex nihilo*: Matter, Creation, and the Body in Classical Philosophy through Aquinas," (PhD diss. University of Pennsylvania, 1995).

Huggins, Ronald V., "Lorenzo Snow's Couplet: 'As Man Now is, God once was; as God Now is, Man May Be': 'No Functioning Place in Present-Day Mormon Doctrine?' A Response to Richard Mouw," *Journal of the Evangelical Theological Society* 49, no. 3 (September 2006): 549–68.

Huggins, Ronald V., "Joseph Smith and the First Verse of the Bible," *Journal of the Evangelical Theological Society* 46, no. 1 (March 2003): 29–52.

Hughes, Richard A., "A Civic Theology for the South: The Case of Benjamin M. Palmer," *The Journal of Church and State* 25 (1983): 447–467.

Hyde, Orson, "The Marriage Relations," October 6, 1854, *Journal of Discourses* 2:75–87.

Improvement Era 12, no. 3 (January 1909): 169.

Improvement Era 12, no. 2 (December 1908): 157–58.
Improvement Era 11, no. 12 (1908): vii (unnumbered front matter in the issue).
Introvigne, Massimo, "The Devil Makers: Contemporary Evangelical Fundamentalist Anti-Mormonism." *Dialogue: A Journal of Mormon Thought* 27, no. 1 (Spring 1994): 153–169.
Jensen, Robin Scott, Richard E. Turley, and Riley P. Lorimer, *Revelations and Translations. Volume 2: Published Revelations*. Vol. 2 in The Joseph Smith Papers series, edited by Dean C. Jessee, Ronald K. Esplin, and Richard L. Bushman (Salt Lake City: Church Historian's Press, 2011).
Jeffery, Duane E., "Seers, Savants and Evolution: The Uncomfortable Interface," *Dialogue: A Journal of Mormon Thought* 34, no. 1 (1973): 183–224.
Jeffery, Duane E., "Noah's Flood: Modern Scholarship and Mormon Traditions,"
Sunstone Issue 134 (October 2004):27–45.
Kant, Immanuel, *Critique of Practical Reason* (Berlin: de Gruyter, 1968).
Kazin, Michael, *A Godly Hero: The Life of William Jennings Bryan* (New York: Anchor Books, 2007).
Keller, Jeffrey E., "Discussion Continued: The Sequel to the Roberts/Smith/Talmage Affair," *Dialogue: A Journal of Mormon Thought* 15, no. 1 (): 79–98.
Kenney, Scott G., ed. First Presidency Letterpress Copybooks, Scott G. Kenney papers, MSS 2022, LTPSC.
Kenney, Scott G., ed., *Wilford Woodruff's Journal, 1834–1898, Typescript, 9 Vols.* (Salt Lake City: Signature Books, 1983).
Kesler, Frederick, Journal 3, page 210, December 11, 1869, MS 49, Utah State Historical Society, Salt Lake City, Utah.
Kesler, Frederick, diary, April 11, 1878, Special Collections, University of Utah, Salt Lake City, Utah.
Kesler, Frederick, diary, April 23, 1874, Special Collections, University of Utah, Salt Lake City, Utah.
Kimball, Heber C., "Condition of the People," etc., *Journal of Discourses,* 1:356.
Kimball, Heber C., "Journey to the North," etc., *Journal of Discourses*, 4:329.
Kimball, Heber C., September 27, 1857, "Spiritual Dissolution—Ignorance of the World," *Journal of Discourses* 5:271.
King, Hannah T., "Meditations on the Passing Year—1884," *Woman's Exponent* 13, no. 14 (December 1, 1884): 97.
Kimball, Stanley B., ed., *On the Potter's Wheel: The Diaries of Heber C. Kimball* (Salt Lake City: Signature Books, 1987).
Kochiras, Hylarie, "Gravity and Newton's Substance Counting Problem," *Studies in History and Philosophy of Science* 40 (2009): 267–280.

Kuhn, Robert Lawrence, "Confronting the Multiverse: What 'Infinite Universes' Would Mean," December 23, 2015, Space.com.

Lambert, Malcolm D., *Franciscan Poverty* (London: Allenson, 1961).

Landau, Iddo, "The Meaning of Life *Sub Specie Aeternitatis*," *Australian Journal of Philosophy* 89, no. 4 (2011): 727–734.

Lapore, Jill, *The Mansion of Happiness: A History of Life and Death* (New York: Alfred A. Knopf, 2012).

Larson, A. Karl, and Katherine Miles Larson, eds., *Diary of Charles Lowell Walker*, 2 vols. (Logan, Utah: Utah State University Press, 1980).

Larson, Stan, ed., *A Ministry of Meetings: The Apostolic Diaries of Rudger Clawson* (Salt Lake City: Signature Books, 1993).

Larson, Stan, "The King Follett Discourse: A Newly Amalgamated Text," *BYU Studies* 18, no. 2 (Winter 1978): 193–208.

Lattin, Don, "Musings of the Main Mormon," *San Francisco Chronicle*, April 13, 1997.

Laub, George, (first) journal, MS 9628, CHL.

Laub, George, (copy) journal, MS 1983, CHL.

Lauinus, Roger D., "An Ambivalent Rejection: Baptism for the Dead and the Reorganized Church Experience," *Dialogue: A Journal of Mormon Thought* 23, no. 2 (Summer 1990): 61–83.

Lewis, Robert Q., "Petitionary Prayer—Caught in the Chaos of Strange Attractors: A Study of Divine Action in the Writings of John Polkinghorne," *Theology and Science* 19, no. 3 (2021): 245–260.

Liahona The Elders' Journal 6, no. 2 (June 27, 1908): 33.

Liahona The Elders' Journal 6, no. 35 (1909): 848.

Linforth, J., in "Foreign Correspondence," *Latter-day Saints' Millennial Star* 19, no. 2 (Jan. 10, 1857), 27–8.

Longfield, Bradley, *The Presbyterian Controversy: Fundamentalists, Modernists, and Moderates* (New York: Oxford University Press, 1991).

Ludlow, Daniel H., ed., *Encyclopedia of Mormonism* 4 vols. (New York: Macmmillan, 1992).

Lund, Anthon H., diary, March 23, 1893, MS 1256, CHL.

Lyman, Edward Leo, ed., *Candid Insights of a Mormon Apostle: The Diaries of Abraham H. Cannon, 1889–1895* (Salt Lake City: Signature Books, 2010).

Lyman, Francis M., Letter to Charles W. Penrose, January 18, 1909, Francis M. Lyman papers, Binder 1, item 160, MS 14514, CHL.

Lyman, Francis M., Letter to George Teasdale, July 8, 1904, Box 1, fd. 3, MS 14514, CHL.

Lyon, T. Edgar, "Church Historians I Have Known," *Dialogue: A Journal of Mormon Thought* 11, no. 4 (Winter 1978): 14–22.

MacDermott, A. L. F., copy of a Letter to Dr. James E. Talmage, November 1906, B. H. Roberts collection, MS 1278, CHL.

McIntire, William Patterson, "Journal by Wm P McIntire," January 5, 1841, MS 1014, page 6, CHL. A digital image of the McIntire journal is available at https://dcms.lds.org/delivery/DeliveryManagerServlet?dps_pid=IE1091060.

MacKay, Michael Hubbard, Gerrit J. Dirkmaat, Grant Underwood, Robert J. Woodford, and William G. Hartley, *Documents: Vol. 1: July 1828–June 1831*. Vol. 1 in The Joseph Smith Papers series, edited by Dean C. Jessee, Ronald K. Esplin, and Richard Lyman Bushman (Salt Lake City: Church Historian's Press, 2013.

McKay, David O., diaries, Special Collections, MS 688, J. Willard Marriott Library, University of Utah, Salt Lake City, Utah.

McKinlay, Lynn A., *Life Eternal* (Salt Lake City: Deseret Book Co., 1954).Oxford University Press, 2006).

M'Clintock, John, and James Strong, *Cyclopedia of Biblical, Theological, and Ecclesiastical Literature* (New York: Harper & Brothers, 1894).

McMurrin, Sterling M., *The Theological Foundations of the Mormon Religion* (Salt Lake City: University of Utah Press, 1965).

McTaggart, J. M. E., *Some Dogmas of Religion* (London: Arnold, 1906).

McTaggart, J. M. E., *The Nature of Existence* 2 vols. (Cambridge: Cambridge University Press, 1921–27).

McTaggart, J. M. E., *Human Immortality and Pre-Existence* (New York: Longmans, Green & co., 1915).

McTaggart, J. M. E., *Studies of Hegelian Cosmology* (Cambridge: Cambridge University Press, 1901).

Marsden, George, *Fundamentalism and American Culture, 2nd ed.* (New York:

Martens, Peter W., *Origen and Scripture: The Contours of the Exegetical Life* (New York: Oxford University Press, 2012).

Martin, Raymond and John Barresi, *The Rise and Fall of Soul and Self* (New York: Columbia University Press, 2006).

Mauss, Armand L., *The Angel and the Beehive: The Mormon Struggle with Assimilation* (Urbana and Chicago: University of Illinois Press, 1994).

Mauss, Armand L., *All Abraham's Children: Changing Mormon Conceptions of Race and Lineage* (Chicago and Urbana: University of Illinois Press, 2003).

Merrill, Philemon C., journal, August 12, 1856 (typescript) at https://familysearch.org/photos/artifacts/1276686.

"M.I.A. Reading Course Books," *Improvement Era* 41, no. 9 (September 1938): 542.

Melamed, Yitzhak and Martin Lin, "Principle of Sufficient Reason," in *Stanford Encyclopedia of Philosophy*, plato.stanford.edu.

Mikkelsen, D. Craig, "The Politics of B. H. Roberts," *Dialogue: A Journal of Mormon Thought* 9, no. 2 (1974): 25–43.

Missionary Department Missionary Register, 1860–1959, book C, page 127, CR 301 22, CHL.

Morrill, Susanna, *White Roses on the Floor of Heaven: Mormon Women's Popular Theology, 1880–1920* (New York: Routledge, 2006).

Mortensen, Joann Follett, "King Follett: The Man Behind the Discourse," *Journal of Mormon History* 31, no. 2 (2005): 113–133.

Mortensen, Joann Follett, *The Man Behind the Discourse: A Biography of King Follett* (Salt Lake City: Greg Kofford Books, 2011).

Mosser, Carl, "And the Saints Go Marching On: The New Mormon Challenge for World Missions, Apologetics, and Theology," in Francis Beckwith, Carl Mosser, and Paul Owens, eds., *The New Mormon Challenge* (Grand Rapids, MI: Zondervan, 2002), 59–90.

Moyer, Jonathan H., "Dancing with the Devil: The Making of the Mormon-Republican Pact," (PhD diss., University of Utah, 2009).

Mueller, Max Perry, "The Pageantry of Protest in Temple Square," in *Out of Obscurity: Mormonism Since 1945* (New York: Oxford University Press, 2016).

Mueller, Max Perry, *Race and the Making of the Mormon People* (Chapel Hill, NC: The University of North Carolina Press, 2017).

Nagel, Thomas, *Mortal Questions* (New York: Cambridge University Press, 1979).

Nauvoo Female Relief Society Minute Book, July 15, 1843, page 98, CHL.

http://www.josephsmithpapers.org/paper-summary/nauvoo-relief-society-minute-book/95

Nauvoo Expositor, 1, no. 1 (June 7, 1844): 1.

Nauvoo Neighbor 1, no. 47 (March 20, 1844): 2.

Nelson, Nels, "Theosophy and Mormonism," *The Contributor* 16 (1896): 736–38.

Nelson, Nels, *Scientific Aspects of Mormonism or Religion in Terms of Life* (New York: G. P. Putnam's Sons, 1904).

Neuman, Meredith Marie, *Jeremiah's Scribes: Creating Sermon Literature in Puritan New England* (Philadelphia: The University of Pennsylvania Press, 2013).

Nibley, C. W., *Reminiscences of Charles W. Nibley, 1849–1931* (Salt Lake City: Nibley family, 1934).

Numbers, Ronald L,. ed., *Galileo Goes to Jail and Other Myths about Science and Religion* (Boston: Harvard University Press, 2009).

Nuttall, L. John, "Extracts of William Clayton's Private Book," L. John Nuttall Papers, Box 6, fd. 6, MSS 790, LTPSC.

Nuttall, L. John, diary, August 24, 1877, MSS 790, LTPSC.

O'Dea, Thomas F., *The Mormons* (Chicago: University of Chicago Press, 1957).

Orsi, Robert A., *History and Presence* (Boston: Harvard University Press, 2016), 48–71.

Ostler, Blake T., *Exploring Mormon Thought*, 3 vols. (Salt Lake City: Greg Kofford Books, 2001-).

Ostler, Blake T., "The Idea of Pre-existence in the Development of Mormon Thought," *Dialogue: A Journal of Mormon Thought* 15, no. 1 (Spring 1982): 59–78.

Owens, Lance S., "Joseph Smith and the Kabbalah: The Occult Connection," *Dialogue: A Journal of Mormon Thought* 27, no. 3 (1994): 131–208.

Packer, Boyd K., "The Snow-White Birds," August 29, 1995 BYU University Conference, https://speeches.byu.edu/talks/boyd-k-packer/snow-white-birds/.

The Parallel Joseph, http://boap.org/LDS/Parallel/.

Park, Benjamin E., "Early Mormon Patriarchy and the Paradoxes of Democratic Religiosity in Jacksonian America," *American Nineteenth Century History* (2013) [http://dx.doi. org/10.1080/1466458.2013.785194]

Park, Benjamin E., "(Re)Interpreting Early Mormon Thought: Synthesizing Joseph Smith's Theology and the Process of Religion Formation," *Dialogue: A Journal of Mormon Thought* 45, no. 2 (Summer 2012): 59–88.

Park, Benjamin E., "'Reasonings Sufficient': Joseph Smith, Thomas Dick, and the Context(s) of Early Mormonism," *Journal of Mormon History* 38, no. 3 (Summer 2012): 210–224.

Park, Benjamin E., *Kingdom of Nauvoo: The Rise and Fall of a Religious Empire on the American Frontier* (New York: Liveright Publishing Corp., 2020).

Parshall, Ardis E., "Leaving Mormonism: Jonathan Grimshaw Crosses the Plains from West to East, 1856," *Salt Lake Tribune* (October 31, 2013).

Partridge, Emily A., et al., "An Extra-Uterine System to Physiologically Support the Extreme Premature Lamb," *Nature Communications* 8 doi:10.1038/ncomms15112.

Paulsen, David L., and Martin Pulido, "'A Mother There': A Survey of Historical Teachings about Mother in Heaven," *BYU Studies Quarterly* 50, no. 1 (2011): 71–97.

Pearl of Great Price (Salt Lake City: The Church of Jesus Christ of Latter-day Saints, 2013).

Peck, Steven L., "Crawling Out of the Primordial Soup," *Dialogue: A Journal of Mormon Thought* 43, no. 1 (2010): 1–36.

Penrose, Charles W., "Earth Life a Definite Part of the Divine Plan for the Salvation of Mankind. Address Delivered in the Eighteenth Ward Chapel, Salt Lake City, March 2, 1924," *Liahona The Elders' Journal* 22, no. 3 (July 29, 1924): 42.

Penrose, Charles W., "Who and What God is, etc." November 16, 1884, *Journal of Discourses* 26:23–4.

Penrose, Charles W., "Life, Matter, The Creature and The Creator," *Latter-day Saints' Millennial Star* 71, no. 46 (November 18, 1909): 728–31.

Penrose, Charles W., "Why I am a Mormon," *Latter-day Saints' Millennial Star* 79 no. 33 (August 16, 1917): 513–19.

Penrose, Charles, diary, April 18, 1907, Utah State Historical Society, Salt Lake City, Utah.

Penrose, Charles W., "President Penrose on Intelligences," George Albert Smith papers, Special Collection, Marriot Library, University of Utah, Salt Lake City, Utah.

Penrose, Charles W., "Immortality of the Spirit and Soul," Joseph F. Smith papers, 1854–1918, Box 47, fd. 7, MS 1325, CHL.

Penrose, Charles W., "Religious Problems Solved by 'Mormonism'," (Ensign Stake priesthood meeting, June 24, 1918), *Liahona The Elders' Journal* 16, no. 13 (September 24, 1918): 1025–1034.

Penrose, Romania B., papers, circa 1881–1975, MS 4811, CHL.

Petrey, Taylor G., *Tabernacles of Clay: Sexuality and Gender in Modern Mormonism* (Chapel Hill, N.C.: The University of North Carolina Press, 2020).

Phelps, W. W. "A Voice From the Prophet: Come to Me," *Times and Seasons* 6 (January 15, 1845): 783.

Phelps, W. W., "Paracletes," *Times and Seasons* 6, no. 8 (May 1, 1845): 891–2.

Phelps, W. W., "The Paracletes, Continued," *Times and Seasons* 6, no. 10 (June 1, 1845): 917–8.

Portrait and Biographical Record of Johnson and Pettis Counties Missouri (Chicago: Chapman Publishing Co., 1895) (anonymous).

Poundstone, William, *The Doomsday Calculation: How an Equation that Predicts the Future is Transforming Everything We Know About Life and the Universe.* (New York: Little, Brown Spark, 2019).

Pratt, Orson, *Prophetic Almanac for 1845*, (New York: The Prophet Office, 1844).

Pratt, Orson, *The Absurdities of Immaterialism: or, A reply to T.W.P. Taylder's pamphlet, entitled, 'The materialism of the Mormons or Latter-day Saints, examined and exposed* (Liverpool, U.K.: R. James, 1849).

Pratt, Orson, *The Seer* (Washington, D.C.: Orson Pratt, 1853).

Pratt, Orson, "The Pre-Existence of Man," *The Seer* 1, no. 7 (February 1853): 102–103.

Pratt, Orson, "Absurdities of Immaterialism," etc., *Latter-day Saints' Millennial Star* 11, no. 11 (June 1, 1849): 161–166, *Millennial Star* 11, no. 17, (September 1, 1849): 257–260, *Millennial Star* 11, no. 18 (September 15, 1849): 273–274.

Pratt, Orson, "Revelation on the Judgments," etc., December 28, 1873, *Journal of Discourses* 16:335.

Pratt, Parley Parker, *A voice of warning and instruction to all people, containing a declaration of the faith and doctrine of the Church of the Latter Day Saints, commonly called Mormons* (New York: Printed by W. Sandford, 1837).

Pratt, Parley P., "A Treatise on the Regeneration and Eternal Duration of Matter," in *The Millennium and Other Poems: to which is Annexed, a Treatise on the Regeneration and Eternal Duration of Matter* (New York: Molineux, 1840).

Pratt, Parley P., *An Appeal to the Inhabitants of the State of New York, Letter to Queen Victoria, (Reprinted from the tenth European Edition,) The Fountain of Knowledge, Immortality of the Body, and Intelligence and Affection* (Nauvoo, Ill.: John Taylor, 1844).

Pratt, Parley P., "Mormon Proverbs," *Latter-day Saints' Millennial Star* 6 (July 1845): 26.

Pratt, Parley P., "Spiritual Communication," April 6, 1853, *Journal of Discourses,* 1:7–8.

Pratt, Parley P., *Key to the Science of Theology* (Liverpool: F. D. Richards, 1855).

"Priesthood Quorums' Table–Origin of Man," *Improvement Era* 13, no. 6 (April 1910): 570.

"Publication Files," CR 12/32, Box 2, fd. 14 and Box 3, fds. 1–4, CHL.

Pulsipher, John, notebooks, circa 1848–1853, April 9, 1852, MS 1045, Volume 1, 1848–1853, digital images 22, 23, CHL.

Quinn, D. Michael, "Organizational Development and Social Origins of the Mormon Hierarchy, 1832–1932," (MA thesis, University of Utah, 1973).

Quinn, D. Michael, *The Mormon Hierarchy: Origins of Power* (Salt Lake City: Signature Books, 1994).

Quinn, D. Michael, *The Mormon Hierarchy: Extensions of Power* (Salt Lake City: Signature Books, 1997).

Rae, Noel, *The Great Stain: Witnessing American Slavery* (New York: Overlook Press, 2018).

Reichmann, Edward, "The Rabbinic Conception of Conception: An Exercise in Fertility," *Tradition: A Journal of Orthodox Jews Thought* 31, no. 1 (1996): 33–63.

Reeve, W. Paul, *Religion of a Different Color: Race and the Mormon Struggle for Whiteness* (New York: Oxford University Press, 2015)

Richards, Franklin D., "Scriptural Items," MS 4409, CHL.

Richards, Franklin D., "Discourse by Elder Franklin D. Richards," *The Latter-day Saints' Millennial Star* 60, no. 27 (July 3, 1893): 429.

Richards, Franklin D., and James A. Little, *A Compendium of the Doctrines of the Gospel* (Salt Lake City: F. D. Richards and J. A. Little, 1886).

Richards, George F., journal, February 6, 1907, Reel 2, Box 2, fd. 2, MS 1307, CHL.

Richards, LeGrand, "The Message of Mormonism," (Np. 1937?).

Richards, LeGrand, *A Marvelous Work and a Wonder*, (Salt Lake City: Deseret Book, 1950).

Richards, Samuel W., "Joseph's Sayings," in Samuel W. Richards notebook, circa 1844–1845, pages 88–9, MS 1841, CHL.

Roberts, B. H., "Christ a Revelation of God to Man—Pre-Existence and Immortality of Man," April 3, 1904, *Conference Report*, 18–19.

Roberts, B. H., "What is Man," *Deseret News Weekly* 50 (March 16, 1895): 387.

Roberts, B. H., *A New Witness for God* (Salt Lake City: George Q. Cannon & Sons, 1895).

Roberts, B. H., collection, MS 1278, CHL.

Roberts, B. H., *Conference Report*, October 6, 1909, 101–108.

Roberts, B. H., "The Immortality of Man," *Improvement Era* 10, no. 6 (April 1907): 401–423. A digital facsimile is available here: https://archive.org/details/improvementera106unse.

Roberts, B. H., *Joseph Smith, the Prophet-Teacher* (Salt Lake City: Deseret News, 1908).

Roberts, B. H., ed., "The King Follett Discourse," *Improvement Era* 12, no. 3 (January 1909): 169–191.

Roberts, B. H., "Seventies Council Table," *Improvement Era* 12, no. 3 (December 1908): 157–58.

Roberts, B. H., *The Seventy's Course in Theology. Fourth Year: The Atonement* (Salt Lake City: First Council of Seventy, Deseret News Press, 1911). Published also in a set of five volumes based on the years 1907–1912.

B. H. Roberts to George E. Hill, November 19, 1928, B. H. collection, MS 1278, CHL.

Roberts, B. H., *A Comprehensive History of the Church of Jesus Christ of Latter-day Saints, Century I*, 6 vols. (Salt Lake City: The Church of Jesus Christ of Latter-day Saints, 1930).

Roberts, B. H., ed., *History of the Church of Jesus Christ of Latter-day Saints, Period I*, 6 vols. (Salt Lake City: The Church of Jesus Christ of Latter-day Saints, 1902–1912). A seventh volume appeared in 1932.

B. H. Roberts, "Joseph Smith's Doctrines Vindicated, I. Men are the Avatars of God," *Improvement Era* 13, no. 5 (March 1910): 432–440;

B. H. Roberts, "Joseph Smith's Doctrines Vindicated. II. The Existence of a Plurality of Divine Intelligences," *Improvement Era* 13, no. 6 (April 1910): 481–488.

Roberts, B. H., "Joseph Smith's Philosophy," in "History of the Mormon Church," *Americana* 6 pt. 2 (October 1911): 993.

Roberts, B. H., Letter to Isaac Russell, February 10, 1913, B. H. Roberts collection, MS 1278, CHL.

B. H. Roberts, Letter to Isaac Russell, April 25, 1913, B. H. Roberts collection, MS 1278, CHL.

Roberts, B. H., Letter to F. T. Pomeroy, February 28, 1928, B. H. Roberts collection, MS 1278, CHL.

Robinson, Joseph Lee, autobiography and journal, fd. 1, Box 1, MSS 5898, LTPSC.

Robinson, Stephen E., *Believing Christ: The Parable of the Bicycle and Other Good News* (Salt Lake City: Deseret Book, 1992).

Rogers, Brent M., *Unpopular Sovereignty: Mormons and the Federal Management of Early Utah Territory* (Lincoln, N.E.: University of Nebraska Press, 2017).

Romney, Marion G., "Man—A Child of God," *Ensign* (July 1973), online at https://www.lds.org/ensign/1973/07/man-a-child-of-god?lang=eng.

Romney, Thomas C., *The Life of Lorenzo Snow: Fifth President of the Church* (Salt Lake City: Morgan, 1955).

Sakata, M., K. Hisano, M. Okada, and M. Yasufuku, "A New Artificial Placenta with Centrifugal Pump: Long-Term Total Extrauterine Support of Goat Fetuses," *Journal of Thoracic and Cardiovascular Surgery* 115, no. 5 (May 1998): 1023–1031.

Scherer, Mark A., "Answering Questions No Longer Asked: Nauvoo, Its Meaning and Interpretation in the RLDS Church/Community of Christ," *Sunstone* (July 2002): 28–32.

Schmidt, Leigh Eric, *Hearing Things: Religion, Illusion, and the American Enlightenment* (Cambridge, M.A.: Harvard University Press, 2000).

Schweiger, Beth Barton, *The Gospel Working Up: Progress and the Pulpit in Nineteenth-Century Virginia* (New York: Oxford University Press, 2000).

Sessions, Gene A., *Mormon Democrat: The Religious and Political Memoirs of James Henry Moyle* (Salt Lake City: Signature Books, 1998).

Seventies Quorum Records, 1844–1975, reel 91, CR 499, CHL.

Sherlock, Richard, "A Turbulent Spectrum: Mormon Reactions to the Darwinist Legacy," *Journal of Mormon History* 5 (1978): 33–59.

Sherlock, Richard, "Campus in Crisis: BYU's Earliest Conflict Between Secular Knowledge and Religious Belief," *Sunstone* 13 (Jan.-Feb 1979): 10–16.

Sherwood, Salmon, *Sangamo Journal* Springfield, Ill. (April 6, 1833): 2.

Shipps, Jan, *Mormonism: The Story of a New Religious Tradition* (Urbana and Chicago: University of Illinois Press, 1987).

Shoemaker, S., "Immortality and Dualism," in S. C. Brown, ed., *Reason and Religion* (Ithaca, NY: Cornell University Press, 1977).

Simon, John Y., ed., *The Papers of Ulysses S. Grant Volume 19: July 1, 1868–October 31, 1869* (Carbondale, Ill.: Southern Illinois University Press, 1995).

Simpson, Thomas W., *American Universities and the Birth of Modern Mormonism, 1867–1940* (Chapel Hill, N.C.: The University of North Carolina Press, 2016).

Smith, Alex D. and Andrew H. Hedges, "Joseph Smith's Nauvoo Journals," in *Foundational Texts of Mormonism: Examining Major Early Sources*, edited by Mark Ashurst-McGee, Robin S. Jensen, and Sharalyn D. Howcroft (New York: Oxford University Press, 2018), 231–267.

Smith, Daymon, "The Last Shall be First and the First Shall be Last: Discourse and Mormon History" (PhD diss. University of Pennsylvania, 2007);

Smith, George A., "Raising Flax and Wool–Home Manufactures–Church Literature–Folly of Using Tobacco and Liquor," April 7, 1867, *Journal of Discourses*, 11:363.

Smith, George A., Letter to Brigham Young, Nov. 12, 1856, St. Louis, Missouri, Box 42, fd. 5, CR 1234 1, CHL.

Smith, George A., "Home Manufacturers, etc.," *Journal of Discourses* 11:359–366.

Smith, George Albert, Letter to Samuel O. Bennion, George Albert Smith papers, January 30, 1912, Special Collections, Marriott Library, University of Utah, Salt Lake City, Utah.

Smith, George Albert, Letter to John A. Widtsoe, February 26, 1929, John A. Widtsoe papers, CR 712 2, CHL.

Smith, John Henry, journal, February 6, 1907, Special Collections, J. Willard Marriott Library, University of Utah, Salt Lake City, Utah.

Smith, Joseph, Letter to Isaac Galland, March 22, 1839, *Times and Seasons* 1, no. 4 (February 1840): 51–56.

Smith, Joseph, "Book of Abraham," *Times and Seasons* 3 (March 15, 1842): 720;

Smith, Joseph, Book of Abraham, *Pearl of Great Price*.

Smith, Joseph, and John Taylor(?), "Try the Spirits," *Times and Seasons* 3 (April 1, 1842): 743

Smith, Joseph, diary, April 7, 1844, Joseph Smith Collection, MS 155, CHL.

Smith, Joseph III, Letter to Joseph Davis, October 13, 1899, Francis M. Lyman letterpress copybooks, Box 1, MS 2497, CHL.

Smith, Joseph F., *Another Plain Talk: Reasons why the People of Utah should be Republicans* (Salt Lake City: Republican Central Committee, 1892).

Smith, Joseph F., "Our Indestructible, Immortal Identity," *Improvement Era* 12, no. 8 (June 1909): 591–99.

Smith, Joseph F., "Status of Children in the Resurrection," *Improvement Era* 21, no. 7 (May 1918): 571–73.

Smith, Joseph F., *Conference Report*, October 6, 1909, 123–125.

Smith, Joseph F., "Holy Ghost, Holy Spirit, Comforter," *Improvement Era* 12, no. 5 (March 1909): 389–91.

Smith, Joseph F., John R. Winder, Anthon H. Lund, "The Origin of Man," *Improvement Era* 13, no. 1 (November 1909): 75–81.

Smith, Joseph F., April 11, 1878, *The Deseret News* 27, no. 13 (May 1, 1878): 3.

Smith, Joseph F., Letter to Heber J. Grant, October 19, 1906, MS 1325, Box 34, fd. 2, page 506, CHL.

Smith, Joseph F., Letterpress Copybooks, MS 1325, CHL.

Smith, Joseph F., "New 'History of the Mormon Church,'" *Improvement Era* 12, no. 10 (August 1909): 833.

Smith, Joseph F., "Duties and Responsibilities of the First Presidency," November 11, 1901, *Conference Report*, 82.

Smith, Joseph F., "Theory and Divine Revelation," *Improvement Era* 14, no. 6 (March 1912): 548–551.

Smith, Joseph Fielding, "The Origin and Destiny of Man," *Improvement Era* 23, no. 5 (March 1920): 374–393.

Smith, Joseph Fielding, Letter to Israel A. Smith, March 8, 1948, Joseph Fielding Smith papers, 1893–1973, MS 4250, Box 118, fd. 21, CHL.

Smith, Joseph Fielding, Letter to Dr. Frank N. Jonas, January 25, 1952, Joseph Fielding Smith papers, 1893–1973, MS 4250, CHL.

Smith, Joseph Fielding, *Man: His Origin and Destiny* (Salt Lake City: Deseret Book co. 1954).

Smith, Joseph Fielding, *Doctrines of Salvation* (Salt Lake City: Bookcraft, 1954).

Smith, Orlando J., *Eternalism: A Theory of Infinite Justice* (New York: Houghton Mifflin and Company, 1902).

Smith, William V., "Joseph Smith's Sermons and the Early Mormon Documentary Record," in *Foundational Texts of Mormonism: Examining Major Early Sources*, eds., Mark Ashurst-Mcgee and Robin S. Jensen, and Sharalyn D. Howcroft (New York: Oxford University Press, 2018), 190–230.

Smith, William V., "Early Mormon Priesthood Revelations: Text, Impact, and Evolution," *Dialogue: A Journal of Mormon Thought* 46, no. 4 (Winter 2013):1–84.

Smith, William V. (WVS), "Jonathan Grimshaw and Honorable Doubts, parts 1, 2, 3," June-July 2009, BoAP.org's blog. https://boaporg.wordpress.com/2009/06/18/jonathan-grimshaw-and-honorable-doubts-part-1/ (accessed September 22, 2017).

Snow, Eliza R., "Integrity," *Quincy Whig* (March 6, 1841).

Snow, Eliza R., "My Father in Heaven," *Times and Seasons* 6, no. 17 (November 15, 1845): 1039.

Snow, LeRoi C., "Devotion to a Divine Inspiration," 30, no. 6 *Young Woman's Journal* (June 1919): 303–309.

Snow, Lorenzo, Letter to Elder Walker, MS 224, CHL.

Snow, Lorenzo, "Progression—The Fatherhood of God," *Journal of Discourses* 14 (January 14, 1872): 300–309, (302).

Staines, Wm C., report, April 24, 1855, Joseph Smith Collection, Box 4, fd. 5, MS 155, CHL.

Stapley, Jonathan A., "Brigham Young's Garden Cosmology," *Journal of Mormon History* 47, no. 1 (January 2021): 68–86.

Stapley, Jonathan A., *The Power of Godliness: Mormon Liturgy and Cosmology* (New York: Oxford University Press, 2018).

Stapley, Jonathan A., "Adoptive Sealing Ritual in Mormonism," *Journal of Mormon History* 37, no. 3 (Summer 2011): 53–117.

Storm, Jason A. Josephson, *The Myth of Disenchantment: Magic, Modernity, and the Birth of the Human Sciences* (Chicago: University of Chicago Press, 2019).

Strong, Douglass M., "The Eccentric Cosmopolite: Lorenzo Dow and Early Nineteenth-Century Methodism," in *From Aldersgate to Azusa Street: Wesleyan, Holiness, and Pentecostal Visions of the New Creation*, edited by Henry H. Knight III (Eugene, O.R.: Pickwick Publications, 2010).

"Sunday School Lesson for Theological Department," *Latter-day Saints' Millennial Star* 70, no. 39 (September 24, 1908): 623–24.

Sydenham, Floyer and Thomas Taylor, *The Works of Plato,* 5 vols, (London: R. Wilks, Chancery-Lane, 1804).

Talmage, James Edward, Articles of Faith manuscript material, James E. Talmage collection 1879–1933, Box 12, fd. 5, MS 1232, CHL.

Talmage, James E., James E. Talmage, Letters to Joseph F. Smith, January 5, 1907, February 13, 1907, Joseph F. Smith papers 1854–1918, MS 1325, CHL.

Talmage, James E., diary, July 22, 1906, MSS 229, LTPSC.

Talmage, James E., *The Great Apostasy* (Salt Lake City, Deseret News Press, 1909).

Talmage, James E., "Man's Eternal Progression—Infinite Possibilities of His Estate," *Liahona The Elders' Journal* 16 no. 5 (July 30, 1918): 902–903.

Talmage, James E., "Deity as Exalted Humanity—Never Ending Advancement," *Liahona The Elders' Journal* 16, no. 7 (August 13, 1918): 932–934.

Talmage, James E., Letter to Mary B. Parker, June 22, 1932, MS 1232, CHL.

Talmage, James E., Letter to Joseph F. Smith, February 13, 1907, Joseph F. Smith papers 1854–1918, MS 1325, CHL.

Talmage, James E., Letter to John A. Widtsoe, 29 October 1928, James E. Talmage collection, MS 1232, Box 4, fd. 18, CHL.

Talmage, James E., "The Methods and Motives of Science," *Improvement Era* (February 1900): 250–258.

Talmage, James E., journals, James E. Talmage papers, MSS 229, LTPSC.

Tanselle, G. Thomas, "Editing without a Copy-Text," Studies in Bibliography 47 (1994): 1–22.

Taylor, Charles, *A Secular Age* (Cambridge, M.A.: Harvard University Press, 2007).

Taylor, John, "Our Religion is From God," April 7, 1866, *Journal of Discourses,* 11:220.

Taysom, Stephen C., "A Uniform and Common Recollection: Joseph Smith's Legacy, Polygamy, and the Creation of Mormon Public Memory," *Dialogue: A Journal of Mormon Thought* 35, no. 3 (Fall 2002): 121–52.

Taysom, Stephen C., *Shakers, Mormons, and Religious Worlds* (Bloomington, I.N.: The Indiana University Press, 2011).

Taysom, Stephen C., "'There is Always a Way of Escape': Continuty and Reconstitution in Nineteenth-Century Mormon Boundary Maintenance Strategies," *Western Historical Quarterly* 37 (Summer 2006): 183–206.

Taysom, Stephen C., "Abundant Events or Narrative Abundance?: Robert Orsi and the Academic Study of Mormonism." *Dialogue: A Journal of Mormon Thought* 45, 4 (2012): 1–26.

Taysom, Stephen C., *Like a Firey Meteor: The Life of Joseph F. Smith* (forthcoming, University of Utah Press).

Tegmark, Max, *Our Mathematical Universe: My Quest for the Ultimate Nature of Reality* (New York: Knopf, 2014).

Thompson, Charles, "Inspired Enoch," *Zion's Harbinger and Beneemy's Organ* 2, no. 10 (October 1852).

"To the Elders of the Church," *Times and Seasons* 1 (November 1839): 13–14.

Touchet, Francis H., "Perfectionism in Religion and Psychotherapy or: On Discerning the Spirits," *The Journal of Psychology and Theology* 4 (Winter 1976): 25–33.

Trembath, Kern Robert, *Evangelical Theories of Biblical Inspiration: A Review and Proposal* (New York: Oxford University Press, 1987).

"Trial of Rev. Charles Beecher," *New York Times* (July 26, 1863): 5.

Tullidge, Edward William, *The Women of Mormondom* (New York: Tullidge & Crandall, 1877).

Turner, John G., *The Mormon Jesus: A Biography* (Cambridge, M.A.: Belknap Press, 2016).

Turner, J. B., *Mormonism in All Ages: or the Rise, Progress, and Causes of Mormonism with the Biography of its Author and Founder, Joseph Smith* (New York: Platt & Peters, 1842).

Turner, Jonathan H., Leonard Beeghley, and Charles H. Powers, *The Emergence of Sociological Theory* (New York: Wadsworth, 1995).

Turner, Victor, *The Ritual Process: Structure and Anti-Structure* (Chicago: Aldine Publishing Company, 1969).

Tweed, Thomas A., *Crossing and Dwelling: A Theory of Religion* (Boston: Harvard University Press, 2006).

Ulrich, Laurel Thatcher, *A House Full of Females: Plural Marriage and Women's Rights in Early Mormonism, 1835–1870* (New York: Alfred A. Knofp, 2017).

Underwood, Grant, "Baptism for the Dead: Comparing RLDS and LDS Perspectives," *Dialogue: A Journal of Mormon Thought* 23, no. 2 (Summer 1990): 99–104.

United States Census, 1910, National Archives and Records Administration, roll 858. (digital facsimile at https://familysearch.org/ark:/61903/3:1:33S7-9RJ6-6WP?mode=g&i=1&cc=1727033).

Van Biema, David, *Time Magazine* (August 4, 1997): 56.

Van Der Donckt, Rev. C., "Reply to Roberts' View of Deity. I," *Improvement Era* 5, no. 10 (August 1902): 759–767; "Reply to Roberts' View of Deity. II," *Improvement Era* 5, no. 11 (September 1902): 856–867.

Van Nada, M. L., ed., *The Book of Missourians* (St. Louis, M.O.: T. J. Steele & Co., 1906).

Walker, Ronald W., *Qualities that Count: Heber J. Grant as Businessman, Missionary, and Apostle* (Provo, U.T.: BYU Press, 2004).

Watkins, Jordan, "The Great God, the Divine Mind, and the Ideal Absolute: Orson Pratt's Intelligent-Matter Theory and the Gods of Emerson and James," *The Claremont Journal of Mormon Studies* 1, no. 1 (April 2011): 33–52.

Watkins, Jordan and Christopher James Blythe, "Christology and Theosis in the Revelations and Teachings of Joseph Smith," in *How and What You Worship: Christology and Praxis in the Revelations of Joseph Smith*, eds. Rachel Cope, Carter Charles, and Jordan T. Watkins (Provo, UT: BYU Religious Studies Center, 2020),

Watkins, Jordan T., "Early Mormonism and the Re-Enchantment of Antebellum Historical Thought," *Journal of Mormon History* 38, no. 3 (Summer 2012): 187–209.

Weber, Max, *The Sociology of Religion*, transl. Talcott Parsons (Boston: Beacon Press, 1993).

Wayment, Thomas A. and Haley Wilson-Lemmon, "The Use of Adam Clarke's Bible Commentary in Joseph Smith's Bible Translation," in *Producing Ancient Scripture: Joseph Smith's Translation Projects and the Making of Mormon Christianity*, eds., Michael Hubbard MacKay, Mark Ashurst-McGee, and Brian M. Hauglid (Salt Lake City: University of Utah Press, February 2020), ch. 12.

Whittaker, David J., "Mormon Administrative and Organizational History: A Source Essay," in *A Firm Foundation: Church Organization and Administration* eds. David J. Whittaker and Arnold K. Garr (Provo, U.T.: BYU Religious Studies Center, 2011), 611–95.

White, Jean Bickmore, ed., *Church State and Politics: The Diaries of John Henry Smith* (Salt Lake City: Signature Books, 1990).

Widtsoe, John A., "Ether, Holy Spirit, and Holy Ghost," *Improvement Era* 12, no. 5 (March 1909): 391–93.

Widtsoe, Ph.D., John A., "Time Length of Creation," *Improvement Era* 12, no. 6 (April 1909): 491–493.

Widtsoe, John A., *Science and the Gospel: Joseph Smith as Scientist* (Salt Lake City: The General Board of the Y.M.M.I.A., 1908).

Widtsoe, John A., *Rational Theology: As Taught by the Church of Jesus Christ of Latter-day Saints* (Salt Lake City: General Priesthood Committee, 1915).

Widtsoe, John A., Letter to N. B. Lundwall, John A. Widtsoe papers, CR 712 2, CHL.

Wight, Orange L., Reminiscences, 1903 May-December, MS 405, CHL.

Wilcox, Linda, "The Mormon Concept of a Mother in Heaven," in *Sisters in Spirit: Mormon Women in Historical and Cultural Perspective* eds. Maureen Ursenbach Beecher and Lavina Fielding Anderson (Urbana: University of Illinois Press, 1985), 64–77.

Williams, L. Pearce, *Michael Faraday: A Biography* (Chapman & Hall, London, 1965).

Wilson, Lycurgus Arnold, *Outlines of Mormon Philosophy or The Answers Given by the Gospel, as Revealed Through the Prophet Joseph Smith, to the Questions of Life* (Salt Lake City: The Deseret News, 1905)

Woodruff, Wilford, "Book of Revelations," MS 23152, CHL.

Worster, Donald, *Rivers of Empire: Water, Aridity, and the Growth of the American West* (New York: Oxford University Press, 1985).

Worthen, Molly, *Apostles of Reason: The Crisis of Authority in American Evangelicalism* (New York: Oxford University Press, 2013).

Young, Brigham, January 27, 1860, Kenney, *Wilford Woodruff's Journal*, 5:426.

Young, Brigham, sermon, January 31, 1861, Kenney, *Wilford Woodruff's Journal*, 5:544.

Young, Brigham, sermon, June 3, 1855, *The Deseret News* 5 (June 3, 1855): 298–308.

Young, Brigham, sermon, February 19, 1854, Leonard J. Arrington papers, series 12, Box 55, fd. 7, Special Collections, Merrill-Cazier Library, Utah State University, Logan, Utah.

Young, Brigham, July 3, 1859, "Nature of Man, etc.," *Journal of Discourses,* 7:2–3.

Young, Brigham, sermon, January 22, 1854, Leonard J. Arrington papers, series 12, Box 55, fd. 7, Special Collections, Merrill-Cazier Library, Utah State University, Logan, Utah.

Young, Brigham, February 27, 1853, "Duties and Privileges," etc., *Journal of Discourses* 1:112–120.

Young, Brigham, sermon, April 17, 1853, LaJean Carruth transcript, CR 100 912, CHL.

Young, Brigham, June 22, 1856, "The Gifts of Prophecy," etc. *Journal of Discourses* 3:373.

Young, Brigham, June 27, 1858, "Peculiarity of 'Mormons'," etc., *Journal of Discourses,* 7:57.

Young, Brigham, July 31, 1859, "Human and Divine Government," etc., *Journal of Discourses,* 6:343.

Young, Brigham, sermon, October 9, 1859, LaJean Carruth transcript, CR 100 912, CHL.

Young, Brigham, sermon, July 10, 1853, *Journal of Discourses* 1:349–353.

Young, Brigham, sermon, August 14, 1853, *Journal of Discourses* 1:264–276.

Young, Brigham, sermon, June 27, 1858, *Journal of Discourses,* 7:54–58.

Young, Brigham, sermon, January 12, 1862, *Journal of Discourses* 9:147–150.

Young, Brigham, funeral sermon, January 31, 1861, Wilford Woodruff journal.

Young, Brigham, June 3, 1868, "Opposition Essential to Happiness," *Journal of Discourses,* 11:238.

Young, Brigham, February 20, 1870, "The Saints are Strange People Because They Practice What They Profess," *Journal of Discourses,* 13:242.

Young, Brigham, sermon, February 19, 1854, Leonard J. Arrington papers, series 12, Box 55, fd. 7, p. 3, Special Collections and Archives, Utah State University, Logan, Utah.

Young, Brigham, December 6, 1847, Council Minutes, Leonard J. Arrington papers, Special Collections, Merrill-Cazier Library, Utah State University, Logan, Utah, (Referenced as Arrington papers).

Young, Seymour B., journal, August 1884, page 38, Box 2, MS 1345, CHL.

Zucker, Louis C., "Joseph Smith as a Student of Hebrew," *Dialogue: A Journal of Mormon Thought* 3, no. 2 (Summer 1968): 41–55.

William Victor Smith is an emeritus faculty member of Brigham Young University where he taught mathematics for thirty years. Among the books he has written are three online texts, "A First Course in Partial Differential Equations," "The Calculus, a Combined Single and Multivariable Approach," "Scattering and Inverse Scattering on the Line and the Korteweg-De Vries equation," and a book on Joseph Smith's July 12, 1843 revelation on plural marriage, *Textual Studies in the Doctrine and Covenants: The Plural Marriage Revelation*. He has contributed chapters to several publications on Mormonism through various university presses, and articles in Latter-day Saint focused journals like *Dialogue: A Journal of Mormon Thought*. He has published in many mathematics, scientific, and engineering journals. His professional interests have included subjects in partial differential equations, operator theory, functional analysis, mathematical physics, and applied probability in mathematical biology. He has long had interests in antebellum American preaching and related subjects out of which this present volume comes. He and his wife Gailan reside in Orem, Utah and are the parents of six children and have eighteen grandchildren.

Made in the USA
Monee, IL
28 September 2023